Promoting Peace, Inciting Violence

This book explores how media and religion combine to play a role in promoting peace and inciting violence. It analyses a wide range of media – from posters, cartoons and stained glass to websites, radio and film – and draws on diverse examples from around the world, including Iran, Rwanda and South Africa.

- Part One considers how various media forms can contribute to the creation of violent environments: by memorialising past hurts; by instilling fear of the 'other'; by encouraging audiences to fight, to die or to kill neighbours for an apparently greater good.
- Part Two explores how film can bear witness to past acts of violence, how film-makers can reveal the search for truth, justice and reconciliation, and how new media can become sites for non-violent responses to terrorism and government oppression. To what extent can popular media arts contribute to imagining and building peace, transforming weapons into art, swords into ploughshares?

In this interdisciplinary study Jolyon Mitchell combines personal narrative, practical insight and academic analysis to investigate both the incitement of violence and the promotion of peace.

Jolyon Mitchell is Professor of Communications, Arts and Religion, Director of the Centre for Theology and Public Issues (CTPI), and Deputy Director of the Institute for Advanced Study in the Humanities (IASH) at the University of Edinburgh, UK. A former BBC World Service producer and journalist, he has written and lectured widely on issues relating to communications, violence and peacebuilding. His publications include *Media Violence and Christian Ethics* (2007) and *Religion, Media and Culture: A Reader* (2011).

Media, religion and culture
Edited by Stewart M. Hoover, Jolyon Mitchell and David Morgan

Media, Religion and Culture is an exciting series which analyses the role of media in the history of contemporary practice of religious belief. Books in this series explore the importance of a variety of media in religious practice and highlight the significance of the culture, social and religious setting of such media.

Promoting Peace, Inciting Violence

The role of religion and media

Jolyon Mitchell

Routledge
Taylor & Francis Group

LONDON AND NEW YORK

First published 2012
by Routledge
2 Park Square, Milton Park, Abingdon, Oxon OX14 4RN

Simultaneously published in the USA and Canada
by Routledge
711 Third Avenue, New York, NY 10017

Routledge is an imprint of the Taylor & Francis Group, an informa business

British Library Cataloguing in Publication Data
A catalogue record for this book is available from the British Library

Library of Congress Cataloging in Publication Data
Mitchell, Jolyon P.
 Promoting peace, inciting violence : the role of religion and media / Jolyon
Mitchell.
  p. cm. — (Media, religion, and culture)
 Includes bibliographical references (p.) and index.
 1. Mass media and peace. 2. Violence in mass media. 3. Church and mass
media. 4. Mass media—Social aspects. 5. Mass media–Influence. I. Title.
 P96.P33.M58 2012
 303.6'6—dc23
              2012011288

ISBN: 978-0-415-55746-7 (hbk)
ISBN: 978-0-415-55747-4 (pbk)
ISBN: 978-0-203-14808-2 (ebk)

Typeset in Baskerville
by Taylor & Francis Books

MIX
Paper from
responsible sources
FSC® C004839

Printed and bound in Great Britain by
TJ International Ltd, Padstow, Cornwall

To Xanthe, Sebastian and Jasmine

Contents

List of figures

Acknowledgements

Many of those working for peace carry out their craft beyond the glare of publicity. Commonly their work does not make the news headlines, being slow, painstaking and complex. Some are not paid for their efforts, others do not even recognise that they are helping to build peace in their own local situations. This book has evolved with the assistance of many unrecognised peacekeepers, peacemakers and peacebuilders. Without naming themselves as such, many of those who have helped act as local builders of sustainable peace.

I have found conversations with colleagues, friends and students invaluable. I am indebted to my series co-editors, Stewart Hoover and David Morgan, for their encouragement and wise advice. Likewise, thanks to Lesley Riddle, Amy Grant, Katherine Ong and Reanna Young, at Routledge, Brian Fischbacher and Nikky Twyman, for all their help with creating this book. George Conyne, Theodora Hawksley, Becky Artinian-Kaiser and Jenny Wright have provided outstanding assistance and invaluable suggestions on many fronts. I am particularly grateful to colleagues in Edinburgh for their advice, comments and encouragement, including Nick Adams, Afe Adogame, Phil Archer, Andrew Barr, Lizelle Bis-schof, Jay Brown, Cecelia Clegg, Jane Dawson, Alison Elliot, Jo Elliot, David Fergusson, Duncan Fisher, Duncan Forrester, Paul Foster, Susan Hardman-Moore, Hugh Goddard, Liz Grant, Nick Higgins, Hannah Holtschneider, Larry Hurtado, Elizabeth Koepping, Christian Lange, Duncan MacLaren, Karoline McLean, Noe Mendelle, Isabel Mencles, Andrew Newman, Paul Nimmo, Michael Northcott, Oliver O'Donovan, Nigel Ogborne, Nacim Pak-Shiraz, Sara Parvis, Jamie Pitts, Mike Purcell, Milja Radovic, David Reimer, Scott Ross, Adam Shreve, Brian Stanley, Geoffrey Stevenson, Olga Taxidou, Stefanie Van de Peer, Rachel Wood and many other friends.

Since I began working on this project I have learnt much by teaching and talking over *Promoting Peace, Inciting Violence* in Edinburgh and beyond. Listening to friends and colleagues on these and related topics has inspired me to think in new ways about creating peaceful environments. I am particularly grateful to the many different people who have encouraged, assisted and challenged me through offering probing questions, making insightful comments and answering research requests, including Angela Zito, Diane Winston, Murray Watts, Pete Ward,

Graham Ward, Michael Wakelin, Rachel Wagner, Roxanne Varzi, Sham Thomas, David Thomas, Jonathan Terranova, Chris Spring, Amy Richards, Kevin Reinhart, Anna Strhan, Janet Soskice, Paul Soukup, Robert Song, David Smith, Amy Schwartzott, Joshua Rey, Ben Quash, Glen Powell, Philip Plyming, Charles Pickstone, Martyn Percy, George Pattison, Dee Noyes, Brian Nail, Cara Moyer-Duncan, John Milbank, Birgit Meyer, Clive Marsh, Jake Lynch, Gordon Lynch, Sarah Longair, John Lloyd, Christopher Landau, Sebastian Kim, Matthew Kim, Tim Jenkins, Graham Howes, Paul Hobbs, Douglas Hedley, John Harding, Richard Hainebach, Christine Gruber, Owen Gower, Nick Godfrey, Dartmouth College Library in New Hampshire, Tharcisse Gatwa, Gene Garthwaite, Kath Galloway, Dwight Friesen, Charles Foster, David Ford, Elizabeth Everitt, Steve Day, Tom Cooper, Louise Connelly, Piotr Cieplak, Clifford Christians, Yam Chi-Keung, Michael Cazenove, Liz Carmichael, Heidi Campbell, Luke Bretherton, Alina Birzache, Michael Banner, Bertie and Joan Bellis, Diane Apostolos-Cappadona and Scott Appleby.

It was a considerable help to be able to test out some of the ideas contained within this book in different parts of the world through lectures and presentations, including in Iran, Rwanda and South Africa, as well as with colleagues on the International Study Commission in Media, Religion and Culture. In this context the perspectives offered by Kwabena Asamaoh-Gyadu, Lynn Schofield Clark, Roberto Goizueta, Juan Carlos Henríquez, Mary Hess, Stewart Hoover, Peter Horsfield, Adán Medrano, David Morgan, Fabio Pasqualetti, Frances Forde Plude, Germán Rey, Siriwan Santisakultarm and Bob White, as well as the Porticus research fellows, have proved especially enriching. I am very grateful to Porticus for making this cross-cultural research and collaboration possible, and to the Carnegie Trust for helping cover my research costs in the United Kingdom.

I am also grateful for the help that I received from the librarians at New College library and the main University library in Edinburgh, the National Library of Scotland, the University Library in Cambridge, the Bodleian Library in Oxford and the International Institute of Social History in Amsterdam, as well as archivists at the Cambridgeshire Archives, and staff at the British Museum in London, the Aegis Trust in Nottingham, Faye Ginsburg, Robin Gill, the Kigali National Genocide Archive and Library in Rwanda, the Robben Island Museum, South Africa, and the University of Tehran, Iran. Parts of chapters 3 and 6 have been adapted and updated in the light of further research and responses to earlier essays, which are referenced in my endnotes. Thanks to Ashgate, Berg and Equinox publishers, as well as the editors of *The Global Media Journal*.

This book also relates to a couple of research projects housed within the University of Edinburgh's Centre for Theology and Public Issues (CTPI). One is on *Religion and Ethics in the Making of War and Peace*, generously funded by Porticus, and directed by George Wilkes. The conversations and research emerging from this project have underlined for me the significance of understanding the causes of violence and the ways of promoting peace in many different cultural and historical settings. The other is a three-year research project entitled *Peacebuilding Through Media Arts*, generously supported by the Binks Trust. They have been particularly supportive of this publication. As part of this project, we hosted an art exhibition entitled *Shadows of the Divine* (2011), under the leadership of Monique Sliedrecht and Geoffrey Stevenson, which was also supported by Theodora Hawksley, Clare Radford and other members of the CTPI team. Their insights and this process has helped me to think further about the ways in which different media arts can contribute to building peace.

Thanks to Iona Birchall, Rosalind and Julian Birchall, Sarah and John Birchall, Pom and Kit Bowen, Katharine and Matthew Frost, Anna King, F. Ellis Leigh, Fiona and Richard Parsons, Judith and Andrew Matheson, Sorour and Hamish Matheson, Penny and Paul Mitchell, and my mother, Catharine Beck, and my father, Peter Mitchell, for their many generosities that have helped make writing this book possible. I remain immensely grateful to Clare for so much, including her patience, encouragement and creative engagement with the pages that follow. This book is dedicated to our children, Sebastian, Jasmine and Xanthe, who have taught us that creating peace takes time and does not have to be entirely quiet.

The publishers and author have made every effort to trace copyright holders and obtain permission for all the images used in this book. They are very grateful for all the permissions granted and would be delighted to rectify any unintended omissions in future editions.

Introduction

At a distance they look like a conventional chair and normal tree. Move closer and it becomes obvious that the chair would offer little comfort and the tree little shade. They are made not of wood but of weapons. These decommissioned guns are no longer used for their original purpose. Armaments have been turned into art. These creations are composed of a few of the weapons that contributed to the suffering caused by the Mozambican Civil War. The chair known as the *Throne of Weapons*, in particular, has become well known through being housed in the British Museum in London, touring all over the UK and becoming one of the items discussed by the director of the museum, Neil MacGregor, in his BBC radio series *A History of the World in 100 Objects* (2010) (figure 0.1).

Like increasing numbers of radio programmes, this series now has an afterlife, following its original broadcast, no longer in cumbersome cassettes but in easily downloadable podcasts from the BBC's iPlayer. Ephemeral radio broadcasts are increasingly being transformed into artefacts that, like the *Throne of Weapons*, can leave a more permanent legacy. Many months after it was first broadcast it is still possible to hear the programme again, to read the transcript and to learn how, a few years after the end of the Mozambican Civil War in 1992, decommissioned guns were transformed into works of art. Seeing it in the museum, then online and later in the accompanying book to the radio series helps to bring both MacGregor's script for the fourteen-minute radio programme and the *Throne* itself further to life.

The multiple reproductions of this work of art, rather than diminishing, add to its aura.[1] In 2005–6 the *Throne* was exhibited all over the UK, including in nine schools, ten museums and various other settings, each with their own local histories of violence, such as the Ulster Museum in Belfast, Pentonville Prison in London and Coventry Cathedral on Remembrance Sunday. Over 100,000 people saw the *Throne*, many responding through music, poetry and prose. Others participated in discussions, workshops and debates.[2] As audiences interacted with it creatively or critically, the *Throne* took on new layers of meaning.[3]

In the museum, the chair is encased in protective glass, it is possible to see even more clearly than online that the back of the throne is made up of two ageing brown and grey rifles. Linked together, their bullet magazines look like a Gothic archway or 'a door of a church'.[4] They also resemble sentries, their rifle

Figure 0.1 Throne of Weapons, Kester, 2001. © The Artist, courtesy Trustees of the British
Museum

butts like triangular faces. Both have two small screw holes and one also has a
gap for the strap, reminiscent of eyes and a mouth. Kester (Cristóvão Estavão
Canhavato), the Mozambican artist who created the *Throne*, chose guns that had
the 'most expression' and for him 'are smiling at each other as if to say, "Now
we are free"'.[5] By contrast, the Curator of the African Galleries at the British
Museum, Chris Spring, sees them like 'two faces crying in pain'.[6] Kester himself

had relatives who lost limbs during the sixteen years of conflict that claimed over one million lives. While their smiles and tears are not entirely obvious the two 'antiquated' Portuguese G3 rifles at the back of the chair bear witness to the violent legacy of European colonialism in Africa.

These weapons point towards several hundred years of Portuguese rule in Mozambique, which was overturned in 1975 by the Soviet-backed resistance movement FRELIMO.[7] Online it is possible to see from a teachers' resource pack precisely where each weapon came from in the Soviet bloc.[8] The remainder of the chair is made up of weapons created behind the Iron Curtain, from Russia, Poland, Czechoslovakia, and even from North Korea. None were made in Mozambique or Africa. The many different kinds of weapons making up this throne illustrates how it was not only Soviet AK-47s, which were used in the civil war against the South African- and Rhodesian-backed opposition forces of RENAMO, but also guns from all over the world.

The *Throne of Weapons* is by no means unique. Online there are many pictures, not only of the *Throne*, but also of numerous other weapons that have been transformed. Best known is the *Tree of Life* (2005) (figure 0.2 and front cover),[9] which, along with other sculptured animals and an explanatory film, is currently displayed near the *Throne* in the British Museum. The *Tree* contains weapons manufactured in the USA, China and Germany. The international arms trade was one of the few beneficiaries of the civil war (1976–92) in Mozambique, as millions of weapons were imported and then used to kill and to maim. Even after the peace accords were signed in Rome in 1992, countless guns were buried or hidden throughout Mozambique in case they might be needed again in the future.

Both the *Throne of Weapons* and the *Tree of Life* emerged out of the 'Transforming Arms into Tools' project (*Transformacao de Armas em Enxadas* or TAE). 'The project is an attempt to eliminate the threat presented by the hidden weapons. Mozambicans are encouraged to hand them over in exchange for items like ploughs, bicycles and sewing machines. In one case, a whole village gave up its weapons in exchange for a tractor'.[10] Children even exchanged old bullets for pencils. Over 600,000 weapons have been handed over and disabled since the project began in 1995, with many simply being melted down. Some weapons are transformed into objects such as chairs, animals and birds of peace. In a country where one million people lost their lives through the civil war, these silent though eloquent sculptures have contributed to an emerging culture of peace.

'Transforming Arms into Tools' was founded in 1995 by a local Anglican bishop, Dinis Sengulane, who was at first troubled by the huge caches of left-over weaponry in Mozambique from the civil war and then inspired by the words of Isaiah 2:4: 'They shall beat their swords into ploughshares, and their spears into pruning hooks'. He regularly says to people that 'sleeping with a gun in your bedroom is like sleeping with a snake – one day it will turn round and bite you'.[11] Bishop Sengulane was the driving force behind the TAE project that was organised by the Christian Council of Mozambique and supported by Christian Aid. For Sengulane, 'The purpose of the project is to disarm the minds

Figure 0.2 The *Tree of Life*, Kester, Fiel dos Santos, Adelino Mate and Hilario Nhatugueja, 2004. © The Artists, courtesy Trustees of the British Museum. *The Tree of Life* is 3.5 metres high and weighs over half a tonne. It includes parts of decommissioned Russian, German, American and British guns, used during the Mozambican civil war.

of people, and to disarm the hands of people'. He was shocked by the amount of money that 'can be made available, almost instantly, for armament purposes' in contrast to the resources made available for medicines or other kinds of peace-building. Sengulane wanted to be part of 'shaping' peace through his project, which was inspired not only by words from Isaiah but also from similar affirmations from Micah (4.3), where it affirms 'they will turn their swords into ploughshares' and 'people will sit under their trees and nothing will frighten them'. Observing how many artistic monuments glorify war, Sengulane approached local artists and asked: 'What about using your skills to glorify peace? We have got these guns – could you see whether you could convey a message of peace by using the bits and pieces of these guns?'[12]

Emerging out of a religiously inspired vision, the *Throne of Weapons* and the *Tree of Life* represent creative answers to the question of how to transform materials commonly associated with violence into items that point towards peace. Through a range of different media these are not confined to a single physical space, but have a global reach. The different uses to which they are put illustrate how multiple narratives, layers of meaning and religious beliefs can become attached to material objects.[13] It would be possible to transform these pieces into reminders of the killings that have taken place in the name of peace in Southern Africa: names of victims could, for example, be etched onto the *Throne's* guns or fake blood could drip down from the *Tree of Life*. In this way they could become memorials used to incite violence. Instead, they have been used in a range of settings and through a variety of media to promote peace.

They provide a good starting point for this book, which is about the complex and intersecting roles that media and religion play in promoting peace and inciting violence. In the first part of the book, I explore the ways that different media are used to contribute to the creation of communicative environments where violence can be incited. In the second, I analyse how media can be used to promote peacebuilding. In both these contexts, I consider the ambivalent, sometimes repressed, and often hidden, role of religion in these processes. My aim is to tease out the 'ambivalence of the sacred',[14] and also the ambiguities involved in promoting peace and violence, in a number of different communicative contexts. Religious beliefs and practices have a long history of being drawn upon to incite different kinds of violence as well as to promote peace. These ambiguities regarding peace and violence, found in various religious traditions, are expressed, interrogated and reconfigured through different media. While both religion and media are commonly accused of being significant factors behind violent conflicts, it is far less common to hear how media and religion can contribute to building peace.

In the chapters that follow, I examine a range of examples of inciting violence and promoting peace. These reveal the complex interactions that occur when various media and different religious traditions are brought together. In the first half of the book I draw on examples from contrasting cultural and historical contexts such as First World War Europe (chapter 1), Iran during the 1980–8

Iran–Iraq War (chapter 2), Rwanda before, during and after the 1994 genocide (chapter 3). Re-presenting painful memories of violence, injury and loss need not necessarily lead to vengeance, hatred and further conflict. The second half of the book includes an exploration of how documentary and feature films can bear witness to past acts of violence (chapter 4), what films can reveal about the search for truth and reconciliation (chapter 5) and how new media can be used for promoting non-violent responses to terrorism and government oppression (chapter 6). The second half of the book, (chapters 4–6) is not intended to be an answer or direct set of solutions to the issues raised in the first half (chapters 1–3). Rather, they are a set of contrasting examples that will highlight other forms of practice and communication. As will become clear these processes, of inciting violence and promoting peace, are sometimes closely connected. Nevertheless, the book's structure is intended to shed light on the way that different kinds of peacebuilding may not simply follow, but also repair, some of the damage caused through violence.

While I have borne in mind the multiple histories of ethnic or sectarian violence found within Europe, such as in Northern Ireland and in the Balkans, I have intentionally not limited my discussions to the West. Nor have I aimed to provide a comprehensive set of examples from all over the globe. Instead, detailed and in-depth analysis of instances from countries such as Rwanda, South Africa and Iran has proved a rich resource for understanding the processes of inciting violence and promoting peace. While later in the book I do make briefer reference to other examples from countries, such as India, Nigeria and Ireland, I have found my primary areas of focus to be sufficiently representative to illustrate some of the ways in which violence can be escalated and peace promoted.[15]

These detailed studies illustrate how both violence and peace can be celebrated through a range of media, including stained-glass windows, posters, murals and radio broadcasts, as well as new media. Elsewhere, I have discussed in greater detail various uses and meanings of the word 'media'.[16] As will become clear from the examples considered through this book, my working definition of the term 'media' remains intentionally broad, going beyond older forms of media such as radio, newspapers and television. There are many different media, which are converging through the use of digital technologies. Together they contribute to the creation of communicative environments where individuals can connect instantaneously and begin to imagine the lives of others many miles away. As we shall see, media can contribute to the creation and maintenance of the ethnic and 'national imaginaries that do so much to enable violence and envision the resolution of conflict'.[17] Accurate and nuanced descriptions of the role of a range of different media can contribute to understanding, conflict transformation and, in the long term, building peace.

At the outset it is useful to underline that I am moving beyond the notion that powerful media transform the beliefs and actions of passive audiences. I am not suggesting that, through the creative transformation of apparently violent media or the skilful packaging of religious messages, audiences can be turned into more violent or more peaceful citizens. Many scholars correctly highlight the dynamic and productive capacity of different media users who inhabit what Henry Jenkins describes as 'participatory culture'.[18] Building on the work of scholars such as Stewart Hoover in *Religion in the Media Age* (2006), David Morgan in *The Lure of Images* (2007), Heidi Campbell in *When Religion Meets New Media* (2010) and Rachel Wagner in *Godwired* (2011), I examine the dynamic, creative and active role of producers and audiences. I therefore not only analyse the content of specific films, websites and broadcasts, but also investigate the creative roles of the spectator and the media producer, as well as the increasing tendency for these roles to converge in digital and online environments.

My intention is to contribute to existing studies in various fields of research,[19] including those within the areas of media, religion and culture of which this series is a part, film and religion, and peace and conflict studies. Within this later area of research, in particular, a large number of scholars have investigated the role and practices of journalists during war.[20] Less common are studies that investigate the coverage of peace processes, or the ways that journalists can contribute to peacebuilding.[21] Over the last fifteen years, however, this area of research has been enlivened by the publication of books and debates relating to 'peace journalism'.[22] Proponents of this evolving approach aim to encourage journalists to select, to cover and to edit stories in ways that avoid exacerbating violent situations and, instead, through creative, nuanced and critical coverage, provide more opportunities for the analysis and transformation of conflict by non-violent means. While these and other significant texts, such as Scott Appleby's *The Ambivalence of the Sacred: Religion, Violence, and Reconciliation* (2000), James Page's *Peace Education: Exploring Ethical and Philosophical Foundations* (2008)[23] and David Cortright's *Peace: A History of Ideas and Movements* (2008), have provided many valuable insights for my own research, these books do not include any detailed analysis of how media and religion combine to play a role in promoting peace and inciting violence.[24]

This is also largely true of John Paul Lederach's sustained reflection on his own practical work as a mediator. In *The Moral Imagination: The Art and Soul of Building Peace*,[25] he asks: 'How do we transcend the cycles of violence that bewitch our human community while still living in them?'[26] In answer to this question, Lederach, one of the leading scholars in the area of peacebuilding, draws upon his own experience of conflict transformation and mediation in a range of international settings, including Ghana, Colombia and Tajikistan. For Lederach, the development of 'the moral imagination' is one of the ways of transcending apparently never-ending cycles of violence. This requires four moves, each of which is pertinent to the argument of this book: first, 'the capacity to imagine ourselves in a web of relationships that includes our enemies'; second, 'the ability to sustain a paradoxical curiosity that embraces complexity without reliance on dualistic polarity'; third, 'the fundamental belief in and pursuit of the creative act'; and finally 'the acceptance of the inherent risk of stepping into the mystery of the unknown that lies beyond the far too familiar landscape of violence'.[27] There is a daring quality to be found in the curiosity that leads to imagining oneself into an enemy's world. Lederach's emphasis upon artistic and imaginative endeavours, rather than only professional technique, is refreshing as he rightly underlines the significance of creative approaches to building peace.

How far can creating feature, documentary and online films be part of such imaginative and creative processes? Within the rapidly evolving area of study relating to film, religion and theology, while there are many studies about film violence,[28] there are no sustained considerations of the ways that films can represent, challenge and celebrate peacebuilding. This is a surprising omission, which part of this book seeks to address. The area of research investigating the relation between new media and religion has yet to produce an analysis of how new media can be used to promote peace.[29] My hope is that this book will be of interest not only to those working in these lively and rapidly growing areas of teaching, research and publication, but also to practitioners involved in different forms of media production or conflict transformation.

For both scholars and practitioners, it is useful to reflect critically on communicative practices which may incite violence and those which may contribute to the development of sustainable and peaceable communicative environments. Both the *Tree of Life* and the *Throne of Weapons* highlight how violence does not need to be the end of the story, and more peaceful and just futures can be imagined and created. Reflecting upon dynamic practices and diverse settings illustrates the significance of location, cultural contexts and history for building positive peace, as opposed to merely negative peace.[30] Given the number of recent and ongoing actual conflicts, as well as blatant, hidden and structural violence, it is important to understand more clearly the roles that media and religion play when combined in promoting peace and inciting violence.[31] There are plenty of other reasons why this is a vital topic to investigate. These include the need to learn more about, first, how to counter the downward spiral of revenge and the escalation of violence; second, how to contribute to the search for truth and lasting reconciliation; and third, how to reinforce conflict transformation, turning 'swords into ploughshares', and thereby help to imagine and to build sustainable peace.

Part I

Inciting violence

Chapter 1

Visualising holy war

Prologue

At first glance they appear to be a regular set of stained-glass windows. Most of the images are framed by an ornate Gothic canopy, which gives them a three-dimensional quality. From a distance, they look similar to thousands of other windows to be found in churches and cathedrals all over Europe. On closer inspection, they reveal a surprising iconography.

A woman in a bright blue dress holds a golden shell. This is not Mary taking something from the sea, but rather a factory worker packing explosives into metallic casings. Behind her are neatly arranged stacks of shells, reminiscent of stored scrolls (figure 1.1) preserving wisdom. Beneath a text from the Hebrew bible: 'Whatsoever thy hand findeth to do, do it with thy might' (Ecclesiastes 9.10, *KJB*). There is an intensity in her stare, redolent of a saint in prayer clutching a sacred object. The uses of her devotion are made more transparent in the pane above (figure 1.2). A solid silver-coloured object, a howitzer, dwarfs several soldiers. Sleeves rolled up, they prepare their weapon of war. The long brown shells by their feet look like a pile of logs, awaiting use on a winter fire. The heavy gun is directed towards a fort in the distance. Another text from the bible is placed below to underline how the 'blast of the terrible ones is as a storm against the wall' (Isaiah 25.4). The diversity of the soldiers' hats and uniforms, reminiscent of a 1915 Robert Baden-Powell propaganda poster,[1] suggests different nationalities working together to fight a common faceless enemy (figure 1.2).

The smaller stained-glass image above captures a moment in the trenches where British soldiers, in khaki uniform, hunker down for cover. In contrast to the war artist Paul Nash's depiction of no-man's land as a deserted, tree-shattered and broken landscape (*We are Making a New World*, 1918), this window is full of soldiers and action. Out of the shadows German troops charge, spewing red liquid fire as they advance. Two of the defenders return shots with a Lewis machine gun, one more soldier turns his back on the fighting and covers his eyes, while another lies dead with blood oozing from his head. This is by far the most explicitly violent of all the images found in these three windows (figure 1.3).

Figure 1.1 The Shell Factory. 1919 stained-glass window from St Mary's, Swaffham Prior, Cambridgeshire. Photograph courtesy of Steve Day. About 1 million women worked in munitions in Britain during the First World War. They were often called 'Tommy's Sisters' or 'munitionettes'.

Below the scene are the following words: 'And signs in the earth beneath blood & fire & vapour of smoke'. This text is taken from a New Testament scene describing the day of Pentecost, where listeners are surprised to find they can hear their own native languages being spoken by foreigners. Different nationalities are brought together (Acts 2.1–21). In these early twentieth-century windows these prophetic words are taken out of this narrative context and juxtaposed with a graphic depiction of nations violently divided. This snapshot of trench warfare is more evocative of the breakdown of communication between nationalities following the building of the tower at Babel (Genesis 11.1–9) than of the moment at Pentecost when communicative divides are overturned and nationalities are brought back together. More precisely, in the book of Acts, Peter is quoting the prophet Joel and is seeking to persuade a gathered crowd that disciples speaking in many different languages is a sign not of drunkenness but of an outpouring of the spirit where blood, fire and smoke are signs of the 'last days'. At this apocalyptic moment 'young men will see visions' and 'old men will

WHEN ∘ THE ∘ BLAST ∘ OF ∘ THE ∘ TERRIBLE ∘ ONES ∘
IS ∘ AS ∘ A ∘ STORM ∘ AGAINST ∘ THE ∘ WALL ∘ Isaiah xxv. 4.

Figure 1.2 A Howitzer. 1919 stained-glass window from St Mary's, Swaffham Prior, Cambridgeshire. Photograph courtesy of Steve Day.

AND ∘ SIGNS ∘ IN ∘ THE ∘ EARTH ∘ BENEATH ∘ BLOOD ∘ & ∘ FIRE ∘ & ∘ VAPOUR ∘ OF ∘ SMOKE

Figure 1.3 Liquid Fire. British and German soldiers engage in trench warfare. 1919 stained-glass window from St Mary's, Swaffham Prior, Cambridgeshire. Photograph courtesy of Steve Day. Flamethrowers (*Flammenwerfer*) were first used in 1915 by the German army at Verdun and then Hooge.

dream dreams' (Acts 2.17–21). Unlike the apocalyptic visions of Otto Dix (*Der Krieg: War Triptych*, 1929/1932), the visions expressed through these windows provide only glimpses of the suffering caused by trench warfare. The same set of stained-glass panes also includes other tools of war that brought blood and fire, such as an armoured tank, and a biplane marked with a German cross. While not romanticised, the nightmare visions emerging out of the reality of 'the war to end all wars' is largely softened in these pictures, which have a cartoon-like quality.

This style is also to be found in two other nearby windows. Whereas the first window depicts some of the newest military technology, the second portrays some ways in which the effects of these brutal tools of killing were mitigated. In simple colours there is a motor field kitchen and a YMCA hut as places of refreshment, a steel net to keep enemy submarines at bay, a 'French drawing-room converted into a hospital with English Red Cross nurses attending to the wounded', a military chaplain 'blessing a dying man on the field' and the Statue of Liberty, Liberty Island, New York (figure 1.4).[2]

NATION ◦ SHALL ◦ NOT ◦ LIFT ◦ UP ◦ SWORD ◦ AGAINST ◦
NATION ◦ NEITHER ◦ SHALL ◦ THEY ◦ LEARN ◦ WAR ◦ ANY ◦ MORE.

Figure 1.4 The Statue of Liberty in New York Harbour. 1919 stained-glass window from St Mary's, Swaffham Prior, Cambridgeshire. Photograph courtesy of Steve Day. It depicts Frederick Bartholdi's neoclassical sculpture, a gift from the French people to the USA, which was dedicated in 1886.

Beneath the statue is a prophetic text taken from the book of Isaiah: 'Nation shall not lift up sword against nation neither shall they learn war any more' (Isaiah 2.4). While the preceding sentence from Isaiah, which speaks of 'swords being beaten into ploughshares', has been omitted, taken together the windows are clearly intended to point forwards to time when there will be no need for war. Alongside these two war windows is a contrasting third, where images of war are entirely absent. Instead, sheep feed, oxen plough and crops are harvested. Green glass is introduced, evoking more a sense of a 'green and pleasant land' than a country 'fit for heroes'.[3] These images are reminiscent of the frescoes in the *Sala della Pace* in Siena's *Palazzo Pubblico*, which show the effects of good government: the frescoes portray an agricultural idyll, where the benefits of hard work and peace are visually brought to life.[4]

What do these twenty-seven images, encompassed within these three windows in a small parish church in Cambridgeshire, reveal about the violence and peace they depict? On first viewing, these images could easily be interpreted as incitements to join the First World War effort, whether by embracing the tools of war, by resisting the 'diabolical' weapons of the enemy or by caring for the injured. The aim is to lead the viewer through the nightmare vision of the trenches to a new world worth fighting for: a land of fruitful peace. An interpretation that views these windows as direct incitements to violence would be mistaken. They were created not during the war but nearly a year after its end, in 1919. Beneath the window and inscribed on a plaque are the following words:

> War was declared on the 4th August 1914 these windows were inserted to commemorate the Great War and the men of Swaffham Prior who were killed in action or died of wounds or disease fighting nobly for God, King and country against the aggression and barbarities of German militarism.

These windows were therefore not wartime visual propaganda, to be catalogued alongside the Lord Kitchener 'Your Country Needs You' poster,[5] but rather an idiosyncratic war memorial. Here was a visual form of commemoration both of the war itself and to the twenty-three men who died because of the war and who were connected with the small agricultural village of Swaffham Prior in Cambridgeshire.[6] References to the 'aggression and barbarities of German militarism' illustrate how the tone of this plaque is far from conciliatory. This is reinforced not only through the accompanying texts but also through the unusual images.

Introduction

This small local memorial was created in a few months during 1919. Like so many others, it was born of out of the trauma of nearly 1,600 days of conflict. They are part of the graphic 'vocabulary of mourning' which emerged during and after the First World War.[7] This memorial, incorporating the windows, a plaque and a cross at St Mary's in Swaffham Prior is but one example of over

40,000 memorials in the UK and many thousands more local and national memorials scattered across Europe.[8] The UK's *National Inventory of War Memorials* lists over 2,000 stained-glass window memorials.[9] Many of the memorials found in Britain are now overlooked in what the poet Geoffrey Hill describes as 'a nation with so many memorials' yet 'no memory'.[10] Nevertheless, these war and peace windows from an ancient parish church in Cambridgeshire, England, raise questions pertinent to understanding not only other war memorials but also the role of media and religion in promoting peace and inciting violence.

I therefore analyse these pictures, in this chapter, in order to reflect upon the relation between remembering and inciting violence in a religious context. There is already considerable research both on the uses of propaganda during the First World War and the significance of memorials in the shadow of the war.[11] Far less common is an approach that considers the relation of memorials to propaganda. What can be learnt from these memorials about the after-life of wartime propaganda? In other words, how far did incitements to violence produced during the war live on after the end of the war? What evidence does this set of twenty-seven memorial images provide for understanding how violence can be incited? Over the last two decades there has been a turn from examining state-produced propaganda to private sector propaganda, such as art, poems, plays and sermons. This reflects an earlier move by researchers to analyse not only state-funded memorials, but also privately commissioned sites.[12]

These developments in the way propaganda and memorials are analysed provide the backdrop for my own discussion. In this chapter I focus primarily upon this privately funded local memorial that is preserved in a small parish church. In order to answer questions about inciting violence, I begin by briefly considering the mixed responses that these windows have provoked. I then go on to consider five connected processes inextricably connected with these windows: grieving, commemorating, justifying, remembering and vilifying. My aim in this chapter is not to interrogate recent revisionist accounts of the First World War that challenge 'the myth' that the war was a 'disaster';[13] my intention is rather to use this case, which emerged out of the war, to investigate some of the ways in which conflict can be depicted and visualised as something sacred, even after the war is over and most of the dead are buried.

'A Strange Memorial'

Under the headline of 'A Strange Memorial', the London-based daily newspaper the *Morning Post* described how the 'inhabitants' of Swaffham Prior 'elected to place in the parish church painted windows representing various war activities, with explanatory texts beneath'. In this article they are described as a 'curious war memorial' (25 February 1920). An unnamed correspondent, for the Manchester-founded tabloid the *Daily Sketch*, was even more outspoken: 'Many sins against good taste have been committed in the name of war memorials, but few, perhaps are more flagrant than that which has occurred at Swaffham Prior, a village near Cambridge, famed for its two churches in one churchyard'. After describing how the village 'has taken the phrase "war memorial" literally' by producing 'realistic memorials of the war' with depictions of a Zeppelin, a tank or an aeroplane, the article concludes with the (incorrect) claim that 'there is one hope. The windows are of painted, not stained, glass, and here and there already show signs that they will not last for many centuries' (25 February 1920).[14]

These less than favourable reviews have continued to the present day. For example, Simon Jenkins in *England's Thousand Best Churches* does not rate them highly, describing them as 'pictures of comic-book simplicity'.[15] The stained glass usually receives little more than a brief, often critical, reference from contemporary commentators. Historian Jay Winter finds that, while these images of tanks and aircraft add 'to the traditional lexicon of warfare in art', in fact, along with a number of other examples of stained glass, none of 'this iconography is surprising or particularly original'.[16] This point is reinforced by Stefan Goebel in his comparative history *The Great War and Medieval Memory*, where he finds some similarities between Swaffham Prior's pictures with a 'war memorial in Osnabrück, Hanover: a redone façade of a sixteenth-century half-timbered house, owned by a local arms dealer, richly adorned with allegories of war. It featured, among other things, St Michael in the guise of a medieval knight, the sinking of three British cruisers by U-9 in October 1914, and a Zeppelin bombing raid'.[17] While it is not that surprising to find such depictions on the side of an arms trader's house, it is more startling to find these images on the inside of a local parish church.

In spite of such critical comments, one photographer reproduces pictures of many of St Mary's windows on Flickr, describing them as a 'remarkable' set of windows, 'ranging from the horrors of war, through the heroism and self-sacrifice that war brings, to the vision of a world without war'.[18] Another experienced First World War historian calls them a 'jewel', admitting: 'I have never seen anything like them before'.[19] A 1995 BBC radio documentary used the windows as a starting point for a programme on local remembrance, with the presenter describing them as 'awkward, strangely kitsch-looking things, which seem all the more revealing for being in – what even the church leaflet here admits – appalling taste'.[20]

Nevertheless, their strangeness does not appear to put off the programme makers, who include observations about these windows at several points through the programme. Peter Cormack, when curator of the William Morris Gallery in London, asserted that, while there may be 'more sophisticated war memorials with more sophisticated art', this is a 'fascinating' example 'because it is such an explicit tabloid document'.[21] They neither look back towards the Arts and Crafts movement, nor forwards to Art Nouveau. Like many other memorial windows they are framed in neo-gothic arches and are reliant upon daylight to bring them to life. Lawrence Fisher, the vicar of St Mary's Church when they were installed, believed that 'It is doubtful if anything of the sort will be seen elsewhere'.[22] While soldiers are portrayed in other memorial windows around Europe,[23] it is extremely rare to find depictions of actual fighting or the tools of war.[24] They may be idiosyncratic and exceptional in form, but they do reveal traces of earlier violence and recurring aspects of life after conflict. What then are these pictures evidence of? I suggest that at least five related practices were common experiences to be found all over Europe. The first of these is grieving.

Grieving

'The world's first global industrialised conflict' claimed over 15 million lives, casting shadows across many different communities.[25] Numerous sons, brothers, fathers and husbands never returned from the front. Nearly one in seven combatants died, leaving many parents, siblings, lovers and friends grieving.[26] Individuals and communities both experienced and expressed their grief in myriad ways. The windows at St Mary's are a small surviving trace of that sorrow. The word 'grieve' has its roots in Latin, where *gravare* means 'to burden' or 'to oppress' and *gravis* means 'heavy'. Memorials, such as the one at Swaffham Prior, are evidence of the heavy burden of grief that many experienced. In *Sites of Memory, Sites of Mourning*, Jay Winter makes a persuasive case that the 'experience of mass bereavement' was at the 'heart of the experience of the war for millions'.[27] The vast majority of bodies were not brought home. Many were buried at mass war graves near to battlefields on the continent and many others were never recovered. For the vast majority of relatives and friends, there literally was no body to mourn. Out of the twenty-three men named on the Swaffham Prior church memorial, only two were actually buried in the church cemetry. The remains of the other twenty-one appear never to have been brought home. Eleven were buried outside Britain, mostly in cemeteries around France, Belgium or different parts of the Middle East. There are no records of the actual graves of the remaining ten, though their names are to be found on locations such as the Ypres (Menin Gate) Memorial, where missing soldiers with no known graves are commemorated. In the absence of actual remains, memorials became physical reminders. They could be looked at, touched or prayed beside.

At times mourners understandably grieved behind closed doors, while at other moments they expressed their grief more publicly through participating in rituals of remembrance, such as a service of dedication marking the opening of St Mary's memorial. Not surprisingly, there is less written evidence of people making private pilgrimages to the Swaffham Prior memorial than the annual public lamentations on what became Armistice Sunday. Some memorials became, for grievers, magnets. In London 'over a million people made a pilgrimage to the Cenotaph and the grave of the Unknown Warrior in November 1920'.[28] Thousands of individuals and many groups travelled not only to London but also to actual battlefields and cemeteries outside Britain. 'Relatives were allowed to claim the temporary wooden battlefield crosses when they were replaced by permanent headstones, as long as they could collect them. Cost and distance prevented many people from doing so', though a few wooden crosses were 'brought back to Britain'.[29] Various religious groups gave pilgrims certificates with prayers and pictures, with the Church Army providing pilgrims with images depicting a weeping woman in a cemetery with Christ on the cross above them and the phrase 'He was obedient unto death' inscribed beside them.[30] For those grieving, but unable or unwilling to make national or international pilgrimages, the local memorials became places of significance.

Many of the street-shrines that had been set up during the war were transformed into more permanent local memorials.[31] Initially these shrines included 'Rolls of Honour', which comprised the names or even photographs of *all* those who served in the forces. After the War, more permanent locally funded memorials were established at these sites and commonly included lists of 'those who had fallen, rather than all those who [had simply] served'.[32] In Swaffham Prior two rolls of honour were devoted to the fallen: one in brass in the parish church and the other in marble in the nearby Baptist church.[33] In other parts of the country local cinemas also produced cinematic rolls of honour, which were 'compiled from photographs submitted following an invitation to patrons'. Photographs of fallen soldiers were filmed or edited together by the local projectionist. 'Not only did they have a commemorative purpose, but they also had an [sic] commercial function to entice audiences into the cinema … On some of the pictures one can see a message from the man pictured to his loved one, for example – "yours truly"'.[34] Such images are full of pathos. A street corner, a churchyard and even a local cinema became places to remember, to commemorate and to grieve.

Even those who had not lost a close relative would certainly have known someone who had been affected by the War. It was hard to avoid public expressions of memorial and grief. Widows, 'orphans' (fatherless children) and mutilated veterans were commonplace in Britain, Germany and France. Charles Peter Allix (1842–1921),[35] the 'squire' of Swaffham Prior and a major landowner in the parish,[36] was the driving force behind the creation of these windows. He appears not to have lost a close relative, but does note the loss of a cousin in his scrapbooks.[37] It is clear that Allix knew some of the local men, from this small village of around 900 residents, who were maimed or had lost their lives.[38] In his address at the dedication of the Reach memorial (13 June 1920), Allix described meeting a 'young fellow' who had an empty sleeve as 'his right arm' had 'gone, and when he showed me the only arm that was left him half had been blown away'.[39] With the return of 'living memorials', visibly injured or dying soldiers, a small part of the horror of the trenches was brought back home.[40] The verb 'to grieve' also derives from the old French *grever*, which means 'to harm'. After the end of the war, both the visible presence of mutilated servicemen and the absence of loved ones grieved many of those left at home. Vera Brittain, who lost her brother, her best friend and her fiancé, was troubled by nightmares for some ten years from her first involvement with the war as a volunteer nurse. In her autobiography *Testament of Youth*, she reveals: 'try as I would to conceal my memories, the War obstinately refused to be forgotten'.[41] After the war she would go on lengthy 'pilgrimages' to visit the grave of her brother, Edward, in Asiago, northeast Italy, and her fiancé, Roland, in Louvencourt, northeast France. Memories that will not be tamed can be signs of haunting grief.

One way of trying to express, and perhaps also to control, grief was to help finance the building of memorials. Of course there were other motivations for donating to this cause, such as acknowledging communal pressure, admiration and a sense of indebtedness to the dead. Brittain observed a 'post-war frenzy for memorials – as though we could somehow compensate the dead by remembering them regardless of expense'.[42] Members of Swaffham Prior parish funded the second of these windows (£40), along with the mural cross and memorial brass. Altogether this cost the villagers about £96, in 1919, representing a significant amount of money, several thousands of pounds today, for what was primarily an agricultural village.[43] Allix financed the other two windows (£80) and may have contributed more anonymously. In some parts of Cambridgeshire public monuments were scaled down due to the lack of necessary funds, while the colleges in Cambridge financed their own monuments. Nonetheless, large crowds would assemble at their dedications and then at the annual rituals of remembrance.

Another way of overcoming the sense of powerlessness brought on through grief was by commemorating acts of kindness and care. This is reflected in several of the Swaffham Prior images. In the second window, the mitigations of war, there is a pane that depicts a common experience through the First World War (figure 1.5). A wounded soldier is lying on a stretcher. He is reaching towards a mug of some beverage, offered to him by a nurse clad in a blue uniform. Behind her is a motor field kitchen, with doors open, which resembles the back of a modern-day British ambulance. He is surrounded by sympathetic figures, some of whom are clearly also wounded, waiting and watching. Another soldier, possibly an orderly, kneels beside him, while a second nurse with a red cross emblazoned on the front of her dress looks on. Several other memorial windows in Britain celebrate acts of compassion. In the memorial window at St Ebbe's in Oxford a uniformed soldier tenderly holds a wounded compatriot as a medieval knight waits to meet them. Christ looks benevolently down upon them both. Even more daringly, in the memorial window by Douglas Strachan at St Andrews United Reformed Church in Hampstead, London, a British soldier gives a wounded German soldier water to drink. There is an order to each of these scenes, which is some distance from Vera Brittain's description of working as a nurse in a 'kingdom of death'.[44] The text 'Comfort ye, Comfort Ye, My People' (Isaiah 40.1) is placed directly beneath the scene of the field kitchen in Swaffham Prior. One of Allix's daughters was a 'red-cross nurse' in nearby hospitals and in his commentary on the windows Allix describes how 'the call of the text is being taken up and answered by the brave and kind nurses to the best of their power'.[45]

Beneath these depictions of acts of compassion is a phrase taken from the *Book of Revelation*: 'Blessed are the Dead'. As Allix highlights, in his description of the

COMFORT ○ YE ? COMFORT ○ YE ?
MY ○ PEOPLE ○

BLESSED ARE THE DEAD ○

Figure 1.5 Motor Field Kitchen, with Red Cross Workers. 1919 stained-glass window from St Mary's, Swaffham Prior, Cambridgeshire. Photograph courtesy of Steve Day. In 1917 the International Committee of the Red Cross (ICRC) was awarded the only Nobel Peace Prize given between 1914–1918 for their outstanding work during the war.

windows, this text is also to be found in the 'well-known' Book of Common Prayer 'service for the burial of the departed' and runs round the base of the first two windows. If he had had more space he would have added the second half of this text, absent from these windows, which affirms that the departed will 'rest from their labours' (14.13).[46] There is a sense in which the three windows can act as a *memento mori*, a reminder of elements within the burial service and a hopeful affirmation of 'rest' after the troubles of this life. This was a topical message given how many people (over 15 million globally) were actually killed during the War, and then soon afterwards in the wake of the influenza epidemic, which claimed as many as 50 million lives worldwide. In 1919 death had touched this and countless neighbouring villages.

Commemorating

There was a determination to complete this local memorial swiftly. The driving force was the squire Allix, who had already renovated this once derelict church, helping to turn it back into the parish church. 'St Mary's was really the centre of his [C.P. Allix's] life' according to his great-grandson, Michael Cazenove, who also believes that 'he obviously had a very strong faith and that the war windows would have been part of his desire to embellish' the local 'church with his creations and gifts'.[47] The new set of stained-glass windows were a kind of completion of a process of renovation, which had restored a church partly destroyed by lightning in the late eighteenth century.[48] The actual process of creating this visual memorial is illuminating:

> The billiard room table [in Swaffham Prior House] was covered in cuttings from newspapers or magazines or anything he [Allix] thought would fit into his scheme of what he'd got into his mind's eye ... and I think people from the village came up and were asked if they had any ideas on the subject: certainly the family were asked and they had little snippets, and they spent mealtimes with the Bible looking up texts and things that would be suitable for these windows.[49]

So this was a family and communal project, 'a collective creative activity'.[50] There is a creative mixing of texts with easily accessible images. The textual inscriptions are one element that the earliest reviews from the 1920s comment upon. Each image is accompanied by a biblical text. For example, beneath the picture of the tank is a verse from the Hebrew Bible, 'the man that shall touch them must be fenced with iron' (2 Samuel 23.7). The tank became a symbol of hope in early 1918, when the Allied armies were exhausted and on the verge of collapse. Modern technology is celebrated here and points forward to a way which will supposedly create a world of peace. We will return to depictions of peace in a later stage of this book, but by citing a biblical text with each image these windows draw upon earlier interpretative resources. Jay Winter briefly references these windows in Swaffham Prior as one example among many to illustrate how mourners resorted to traditional frames of reference, in this case religious expression, for interpreting the causes of their grief.

Inextricably connected with individual and communal grieving in the face of so much loss are the numerous acts of commemoration that took place soon after the war. On 21 December 1919 at 2.30pm, a special service was held in St Mary's Church, Swaffham Prior, to mark the dedication of the windows, the brass name plaque and the Celtic stone cross. This service provides an example of how war memorials can become a site of ritualised mourning. This kind of service was repeated all over Europe and beyond. The poster advertising the event stated: 'It is hoped that Soldiers and Sailors and demobilised men will be present at the service'. The notice also implies that participation in the ritual was encouraged, with the suggestion that 'Flowers may be placed on the foot of the cross'.[51] The standard Memorial Service for the fallen in the war was used, which also allowed for local acts of memorial.

The parish magazine provides a brief account of what took place towards the end of the service: 'the cross was unveiled by the warden C.C. Ambrose – he was a big local farmer – and a hymn was sung "When I survey The wondrous Cross" and the vicar read the names of the fallen'. For most visitors to the church today, these names are little more than that, names from a distant country called the past, but for many attending the 1919 service, hearing these names read aloud could easily have brought to mind the familiar but now departed faces of close relatives, friends and workmates. For those who had lost a loved one in the War, but had no physical body to grieve over and no funeral to honour their memory, hearing the names of their kin or close friends commemorated must have had added particular poignancy. The reading out of individual names was a common practice across Europe, as was the attempt to etch them permanently into a memorial.[52] 'Memorials in larger towns and cities, because of the number of dead, were normally unable to list the names, which were often recorded elsewhere in Books of Remembrance'. Therefore, as Derek Boorman observes, 'although the scale of the monuments in large towns is normally more impressive, the seemingly disproportionately long lists of the names of the fallen, often with many apparently from the same family, which are common in villages, can be more revealing and moving'.[53]

Other memorials not only commemorated the names of the lost, but also celebrated visions of peace. In what was St Bride's Church and has now become the parish church of West Kilbride, Ayrshire, the First World War memorial window includes both a list of fourteen names and a cherub beating a sword into a curved small scythe-like implement (figure 1.6).

Figure 1.6 Cherub Beating Sword into Scythe. c.1919 war memorial window at St Bride's Church (now the parish church), West Kilbride, Ayrshire, Scotland. Photograph courtesy of George Crawford. The scythe would have been well known as a harvesting tool in this small rural town.

The juxtaposition of the names of the fallen alongside a visual reference to the peaceful vision of Isaiah 2.4, where swords are beaten into ploughshares, is striking and extremely rare. More common are the list of names of the fallen, though there was some controversy in West Kilbride when this Scottish village's memorial was built and the names of the fallen were simply written on a scroll and placed inside, with 'nothing to be seen on the outside'.[54] By contrast putting the names on easily viewed materials, such as a memorial window (as at West Kilbride) or on a plaque (as at Swaffham Prior), was a more public way of commemorating individuals who had lost their lives. The speaking, inscribing or writing of names of those killed in the War represented a simple way of honouring the memory of the dead.

Acts of public worship were common settings for both commemorating the fallen and dedicating memorials. In the dedication service at Swaffham Prior Allix 'explained' the 'two war windows and the peace window'. He does not appear to have gone into great detail about the memorial windows on this occasion.[55] The service ended dramatically: 'the last post was sounded from the Rood loft by the buglers, perhaps the most thrilling part of a very moving service. The church was full – not only with the living, but with the names of the dead'.[56] Through this ritual the church had become a place of both public and private grief, where the dead were remembered and their deaths called to mind.

What did the creation of this local memorial and participating in this ritual of commemoration signify? In *Fallen Soldiers,* George Mosse suggested that such practices reinforced the 'myth of war experience, which looked back upon the war as a meaningful and even sacred event'. There is a sense in which this small memorial is part of an international process of attempting to assert the 'legitimacy of death and sacrifice' of the 'Great War'. As we shall see later, this is by no means unique to the First World War. For Mosse, the memory of this 'mass death' was commonly 'refashioned into a sacred experience which provided the nation with a new depth of religious feeling, putting at its disposal ever-present saints and martyrs, places of worship, and a heritage to emulate'.[57] While Mosse suggests that this took place particularly among the 'defeated nations', it is clear from memorials and rituals such as this one in Swaffham Prior that the local dead were being 'sanctified' in a fashion comparable to the dead in other parts of Europe. Bestowing sacred meaning upon the death of those killed was one way of expressing grief. That is not to paper over the significant variations to be found among British war memorials, French *monuments aux morts* and German *Kriegerdenkmal.* Nonetheless, each one acts as a local or national location for commemorating and thereby remembering the many war deaths.

Justifying

Why did so many men enlist to fight against another supposedly 'Christian' nation?

> Well, I think they went along because all their mates went along ... A kind of mass brainwashing, perhaps. But there was a lot of feeling if you didn't

go. If you didn't volunteer. People like Fisher [the vicar of St Mary's] would imply that it was your duty to volunteer and go and fight ... for your country, and there was a bit of ... , of young men, and there was adventure – and you were ... away from Swaffham, weren't you?[58]

Peer pressure, a sense of duty, an opportunity to escape from a small village, and encouragement from authority figures, such as the vicar and the squire, to serve your country were some of the reasons why young men volunteered to fight. Other locals claim that both Fisher and Allix surreptitiously encouraged young men to join up, sometimes celebrating those who had in the pages of the parish magazine.[59] At the end of the war, how was this process of persuasion to fight remembered? How far was this small agricultural community united by the common enterprise?

Consider first how the story of the war narrated through the glass begins with a page of music, taken from Handel's *Israel in Egypt* (1739) oratory including the words from Exodus 15.3: 'The Lord is a Man of War' (figure 1.7). To one side of the sheet of music is an Italian bugler and on the other a British soldier shouting. Beneath these allies is a verse from one of the prophetic

Figure 1.7 The Call to War. 1919 stained-glass window from St Mary's, Swaffham Prior, Cambridgeshire. Photograph courtesy of Steve Day.

books in the Hebrew bible: 'Proclaim ye this among the Gentiles, prepare war. Wake up the mighty men' (Joel 3.9). The following verse speaks of beating 'ploughshares into swords'. Allix describes this first of twenty-seven panels as 'the call to war'. Beneath the panel is a larger still inscription: 'I heard a voice from heaven' (Revelation 14.3). The 'call' is uncritically represented as divinely sanctioned. This was a common refrain in many churches all over Europe. For example, Vera Brittain, writing to her fiancé in the spring of 1915, observed that in many of the churches in Oxford 'we are always having it impressed on us that "the call of our country is the call of God". Is it? I wish I could feel sure that it was'.[60] There is no evidence in the windows, or in any other part of the memorial, of such questioning. Nor is there a hint of the post-war disillusionment and irony identified in selective post-war literature by Paul Fussell in *The Great War and Modern Memory*.[61] There is instead a celebration of those who answered the call, and, during the 1919 dedication service, a reiteration of the necessity of the war and a justification of why this memorial was placed within the local parish church.

Consider second C.P. Allix's carefully handwritten address delivered at the dedication service, which survives to this day and is entitled 'On the Opening of the War Memorial in St Mary's Church Swaffham Prior'. It merits further attention. Quoting the brass under the first window he speaks of 'our "Glorious Dead"'. The first two pages read partly like a justification for the memorial being placed in the parish church: 'I think it is the most appropriate spot in which a memorial could be placed. It is the best house in the parish, it is God's house and it is our house'.[62] He is careful to reference chapels and churches in his address, suggesting: 'It is high time and more than time, I speak generally of course and with no local reference, that the jars and discords over small matters between various bodies of Christians which we have known so long should be put to an end'.[63] This line of argument is not surprising when local religious traditions and practices are taken into consideration. One local informant confides:

> In those days it was very strict, really, the non-conformists would hardly ever go into the parish church, some wouldn't even go in for a funeral or a wedding. Church people would never go into the chapel … There was a lot of controversy about the war memorial.[64]

Controversy, debates and even conflict surrounded the creation of many other memorials all over the country.

G.K. Chesterton describes the debates soon after the end of the 'Great War' in his hometown of Beaconsfield, Buckinghamshire. In characteristically witty style, Chesterton describes how the community was divided over what kind of memorial should be established: some wanted a 'parish pump', others a 'public fountain' or 'municipal motor bus', or even a 'sports club for ex-servicemen'. These suggestions were used as an alternative to making a 'statue of a soldier' or building a cross. A plebiscite resulted in a narrow win for the club, but to his amusement it was ultimately a crucifix that was erected.[65] Not all discussions were so good-humoured or apparently so amicably settled. The Labour politician Edward Short recalls, in his autobiography, how in his native remote Cumberland village in northern England the 'controversy about the form our memorial should take was long and bitter'.[66] The 'gentry' won the argument because they were meeting the cost. 'In a good may cases, the claim by one denomination to represent all the others proved unacceptable. At Brompton, near Northallerton, Yorkshire, local co-operation broke down over differences of view between Anglicans and Nonconformists about the form and citing of memorials'.[67]

Many memorials were placed not in churches but in public spaces. For example, only a few miles away from Swaffham Prior, Cambridge's most public city memorial to victory was built, after lengthy discussions and over-ambitious fund-raising, at a prominent road junction close to the station in 1921.[68] By contrast, even though it included a stone Celtic cross more commonly found on village greens or roadsides, Swaffham Prior's memorial was confined to the parish church. A church that many Nonconformist villagers would rarely if ever visit, it is not hard to understand why there was controversy surrounding the placement of this memorial in the local Anglican parish church. This must have been exacerbated by the fact that the vicar, the Reverend Lawrence Fisher, was reputed as never entering into a non-conformist chapel. These local divisions stretch back to the English Civil Wars (1642–6 and 1648–9) and the time that this area, along with other parts of East Anglia, produced many of the non-conformist supporters of Cromwell's republican army.

If it was a controversial site of remembering, then C.P. Allix, who was also one of the churchwardens at St Mary's, appears to have tried to build bridges between the two communities through his public addresses. One way he did this was by speaking at the unveiling of the marble memorial tablet at the Zion Baptist chapel, which was across the road from St Mary's in Swaffham Prior. He proclaimed: 'No matter what shades of difference there may be amongst us, which are as inevitable … I see times coming, when all creeds will be melted down'.[69] The unveiling took place on 20 November 1919, a month before the dedication of the windows, and revealed ten names of 'Scholars of the Sunday School who sacrificed their lives in defence of king and country', including four that also appear on the St Mary's memorial. Here is another example of how the First World War encouraged a form of practical ecumenism rooted in sacrifice. Divisions evaporate as men from different denominations came together to fight a common enemy. It may have been ecumenical within nations, but during the war ecumenism rarely crossed national boundaries.[70]

Another way in which Allix attempted to draw his local community together can be found in his December 1919 dedicatory address at St Mary's. He attempts to underline the common task with which they had been engaged:

These windows record the greatest fight in which Britain has ever been engaged, she poured out blood and treasure unstinted to preserve herself and not herself alone but all nations small and great from slavery, for it was nothing less than this that was aimed at. And this would have been their fate if the Germans with all their greed and ferocity had gained victory. That they did not is due, under God, to the gallantry of our soldiers who literally laid down their lives that we might live. No less than 23 men out of this small parish did that great thing.[71]

Notice how the 'gallant' sacrifice of local victims is highlighted. In words reminiscent of the Gospel of John, they are depicted as laying their lives down for those still alive and the freedom of all the nations.[72] Their deaths are justified and sanctified. At least two of them are buried in the churchyard. Loss was close to home. By underlining the sacrificial nature of their deaths, or, to put it more starkly, by 'interpreting slaughter as sacrifice', Allix employs a 'rhetoric of consolation', consoling listeners that these deaths were worthwhile.[73] In the words of Alex King, this was a kind of 'canonisation of common people'.[74] Allix in his public addresses was not afraid of using what Samuel Hynes, echoing Robert Graves, described as 'big words', such as Glory, Courage, Duty and God, to make sense of the countless war deaths.[75] Like many other 'Great War' orators Allix combines the use of euphemisms with 'heroic grandiosity', to underline further how their deaths were both noble and meaningful.[76] By celebrating their sacrifice he is also reaffirming the value of the status quo and those who promoted the war.[77]

There appears to be no evidence of how Allix's listeners responded to his words at these services. There is evidence from other parts of Britain of mixed responses to such events. One veteran, Sergeant Ernest Woodward, represents a recurring sentiment when he describes how 'In the first few years after the war hollow words were used too often at the unveiling of war memorials, glib words about the "great sacrifice". I know that in many cases these words were used with deep feeling by men who had lost their own sons, they became almost a cliché in the oratory of politicians'. As time passed, Woodward, like some other veterans, increasingly grew to dislike Armistice Day, other commemorative ceremonies and 'hollow words', because 'No praise from comfortable men can bring the dead back to the sun they loved'. Both during and after the war, some soldiers were highly critical of what they believed were the 'majority of those at home' who were unable to imagine the actual suffering of the troops.[78] Following the end of the war there is an increasing suspicion of the actions of those who had encouraged young men to enlist: 'It was too easy for the older generation to find a convenient anodyne in the formal politeness of a two-minute silence, in the weaving of wreathes, in the provision of adequate pensions for widows and orphans'.[79] Actions and words intended to honour the dead and care for those left behind were open to multiple interpretations.

Nevertheless, suspicions were rarely publicly expressed in the early days after the war. Allix, like most of his contemporaries, desired peace, but believed that this sometimes needed to be achieved by the use of violent force. In formal ritual settings the justifications of the older and often grieving generations were rarely, if ever, challenged. Relief, exhaustion and war-weariness led many to desire not a change to the social order, but rather a 'speedy return to some kind of normality'.[80] Allix reveals in several of his addresses both admiration at the servicemen's nobility and a sense of indebtedness to those who had died.[81] This celebration of the bravery of 'our soldiers' is sharply juxtaposed with the 'greed and ferocity' of the Germans. Observe the common split between local heroes and foreign evildoers. Such 'splitting' can colour how both the tactics and the weapons of the enemy were remembered.

Remembering

Why, in this small parish church, is there a picture of a large Zeppelin flying in the night sky (figure 1.8)? A clue to help answer this question can be found in an account of what one local resident of Swaffham Prior remembers from her childhood:

> I did see a Zeppelin. It was one night, and we could hear this thing roaring – they made a terrible noise – and of course, everybody went out. We were children, we were in bed, and we were got out of bed and everyone went in the street in their nightclothes. The old grocer next door, he was out; and there was a baker just beyond us and he'd got a boy worked for him, and all of a sudden this boy, he was looking up in the sky, he shouted out 'For God's truth, there the devil be!' And there was this Zeppelin, sailing away over our chimneystacks. Of course, it was up in the sky a good way, but it did make a terrible noise. The little old grocer he kept bending up and down saying, where is it, boy, where is it boy? We says, just above your head! It was a real exciting night. And then there was an old lady farther down the village, they said she came out with a candle in her hand like this, looking for it![82]

Given the repeated negative references about Zeppelins expressed through different media in Britain, it is not surprising that this Swaffham Prior boy cried out 'there the devil be'; though it was a 'devil' that most people wanted to catch a glimpse of, as long as it did not drop its payload upon them as they gawped in amazement. At the start of the war this dramatic spectacle was a rarity across most of Europe. For adults as well as children, the 'Zeppelin provided occasion for aesthetic exhilaration and distraction from what was often a monotonous home front existence. In journal after journal, it appears as a relief from boredom. The Zeppelin allowed a rare opportunity for first-hand experience of the war'.[83] In Shaw's *Heartbreak House* the characters who survive the Zeppelin attack are exhilarated by the experience, comparing the bombing to hearing 'Beethoven'. The last lines of the play capture many of the more romanticised responses to airship raids: 'what a glorious experience! I hope they'll come again tomorrow night'. To which Ellie, 'radiant at the prospect', replies: 'Oh, I hope so'.[84] Seeing a Zeppelin flying overhead was understandably memorable; having them

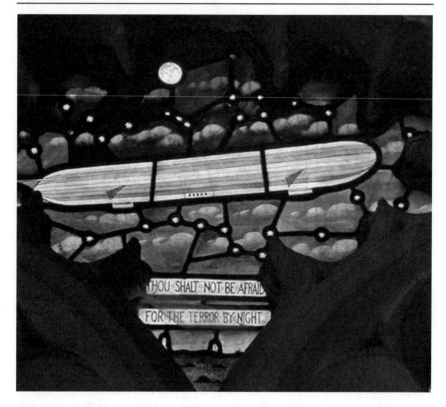

Figure 1.8 A Zeppelin. 1919 stained-glass window from St Mary's, Swaffham Prior,

actually drop bombs nearby was unforgettable. Particularly early in the war, before war-weariness had set in, airships appear to have sparked fascination, awe and excitement.

What other memories and emotions might this depiction of an airship have provoked for viewers in 1919 and soon after? Even though it is the topmost image in the first of the two 'war windows', it is still comparatively easy to make out. The chief designer of the windows, C.P. Allix, chose to place the depiction of the Zeppelin in this highest pane, the rose light. Surrounded by stars and a full moon, it looks to twenty-first-century eyes serene, in sharp contrast to the adjacent image of trench warfare.[85] Given its apparently peaceful appearance it is surprising to read 'Thou shalt not be afraid for the terror by night' beneath this depiction. This comforting verse, taken from the Hebrew Bible (Psalm 91.5), points to another emotion that this new flying weapon of war provoked in the early twentieth century: fear. For Allix and his contemporaries, this would have been a far from serene image. In his hand-written discussion of this image of a Zeppelin Allix remarks that the 'high explosive bombs they drop are very alarming and destructive but the text tells us not to be afraid of them'.[86]

Local experience may explain why they were perceived as so 'alarming and destructive'. In January 1915, two Zeppelins attacked Great Yarmouth and dropped bombs on a number of East Anglian villages. Several civilians were killed and sixteen injured. This attack 'ushered in a feature of twentieth century warfare that was to become all too familiar: strategic air attack'.[87] In St Mary's *Restoration Book*, compiled by the then vicar of the parish, Lawrence Fisher, there are at least two references to Zeppelins. The first was spotted flying back and forth over Swaffham Prior one evening in October 1914. No attacks were noted. More significantly, in the following year, during a raid, 'six Zeppelins dropped about 300 bombs on the East, North East and Midland cities of England, killing 54 people. Several were dropped on Isleham, the explosion shaking the houses in Swaffham Prior'.[88] For those who had felt their own home shudder in the wake of a bombing attack from a Zeppelin, seeing this image in the church could easily have reminded them of those night-time raids.

Isleham is only about eight miles away from Swaffham Prior and feeling the ground shake may well have heightened what some scholars have described as 'Zeppelinitis'.[89] This had its roots in pre-war imaginings, rumours and unfounded press reports. Allix preserved in his scrapbook the 1909 front page of the *Daily Graphic*, which had reproduced an earlier print of a fictional invasion of England by channel tunnel and airship.[90] Other papers probably contributed to fears of invasion by airships. For instance, the *Daily Mail* ran one interview suggesting that 3,500 specially designed airships could land over 350,000 troops onto British soil in 30 minutes.[91] While not exactly 'weapons of mass destruction' (WMDs), these claims resonated with several pre-war novels, such as H.G. Wells' *War in the Air* (1908), which envisaged Germany developing dozens of airships in secret. Zeppelinitis became a European-wide phenomenon, and helped to ensure that the 'airship acquired, very early in the war, a reputation quite disproportionate to its actual effectiveness'.[92] Only 'fifty-seven airship raids hit England, causing almost 2000 casualties'.[93] Compared to the loss of life in the trenches, the actual damage that they caused was minimal.

News and experience of air raids led to what Bernard Shaw described, in the preface to his play *Heartbreak House* (1919), as 'war fever', a kind of 'moral pestilence'. This was heightened by Londoners experiencing what it was like:

> to hide in cellars and underground railway stations, or lie quaking in bed, whilst bombs crashed, houses crumbled, and aircraft guns distributed shrapnel on friend and foe alike until certain shop windows in London, formerly full of fashionable hats, were filled with steel helmets. Slain and mutilated women and children, and burnt and wrecked dwellings, excuse a good deal of violent language, and produce a wrath on which many suns go down before it is appeased.[94]

The 'wrath' that these attacks provoked was both escalated and put to use in a number of ways. In the evolving propaganda war, British and French postcards, posters and cartoons frequently showed Zeppelins attacking or even killing defenceless civilians. Several postcards label them as 'baby-killers'. These were depicted as being flown by 'German pirates or monsters with bestial features', with the evil airship and wicked Kaiser sometimes being merged into one creature. 'Allied depictions painted the airship as a tool of evil accompanying the Teutonic barbarian on his quest for domination'.[95] They represented another reason for fighting the 'hun'. Several recruiting posters played on anxieties provoked by Zeppelin attacks. For example, beneath a picture of an airship caught in the bright beam of a spotlight and floating above a silhouette of St Paul's Cathedral is the following text: 'It is far better to face the bullets than to be killed at home by a bomb: Join the Army at once & help to stop an air raid' (figure 1.9).

In an Australian poster the word 'Enlist' shares the blue sky with two light-brown Zeppelins, beneath an inset where women and children are being blown up.[96] The text below challenges readers who have not yet enlisted: 'By staying at home you are giving your approval to this kind of thing'.[97]

Zeppelins developed different symbolic attachments across Europe. Airship models were used as 'Christmas-tree ornaments in Berlin, board-games in Paris' and as part of '"anti-Zep" candlesticks in London'.[98] In Germany, some saw them as the technology that might be able to break the stalemate of the trenches.[99] Attacks on specific locations such as Great Yarmouth, Brussels and London were commemorated on German postcards. In the same context airships were also celebrated as invincible, with one card depicting two Zeppelins circling Trafalgar Square while Londoners below run in terror for their lives. Ariela Freedman suggests that 'the smooth skin of the Zeppelin became a screen for the projection of fantasies of apocalypse and redemption'.[100] In Britain they were described in both vitriolic and poetic terms, not only as 'baby-killers', but also as 'a universal fish', a 'new moon' or by D.H. Lawrence as a 'bright golden finger'.[101] As these contrasting metaphors underline, fear was not the only response that the Zeppelin provoked.

One way of preserving both emotionally charged memories, as well as insights into new technologies of war, was to collect photographs from magazines and newspapers. Allix's pre-war scrapbooks are full of images of early flying machines, demonstrating a fascination with aeronautical engineering. Beside portrayals of planes and helicopters there is a set of images depicting 'warfare of the future', which included pictures of guns specially designed to bring down airships.[102] These images were produced only a few years after the Wright brothers had flown the first heavier-than-air biplane in 1903. During the war Allix also preserved cuttings from various newspapers relating to the dramatic shooting down of an airship assumed to be a Zeppelin (though in fact was a Schütte-Lanz (SL11)) during the night of 3 September 1916 by William Leefe Robinson.[103] Thousands of Londoners watched, applauded and cheered as it crashed to the ground in flames. Even if not actually seen by the local residents of Swaffham Prior, these preserved paper clippings are evidence of the way the news was disseminated and then retained by some readers. The propaganda

Figure 1.9 Zeppelin Recruiting Poster. © Imperial War Museums (Q 80366). One of several First World War posters that used the menace of the Zeppelin to encourage enlistment in the armed forces.

value of this airborne victory over an airship was, like several others, exploited in graphic detail. Britain might be vulnerable to attack from the air but was no longer defenceless. Like the Psalm's imperative cited earlier, not to be afraid, the message here was clear: the Zeppelin was not invincible and could be countered.

As the war dragged on, feelings of excitement, fascination and patriotism in the face of attacks by Zeppelins were dissipated as people became tired of the conflict and the losses that it brought. In some quarters 'Zeppelin fatigue' set in. For soldiers who had experienced the nightmare of trench warfare, hearing friends at home pontificate about the dangers brought by airships underlined the divide between many combatants and civilians.[104] The Zeppelin window in St Mary's Church is neither triumphalistic nor explicitly inciting violence, but it is an enigmatic rarity.[105] There is a sense in which, by painting this object of fear and fascination onto a small glass window, the Zeppelin has been tamed, brought down to size, almost punctured. Given the contrasting experiences of civilians and soldiers, as well as the cultural history of the Zeppelin, this image would surely have evoked a range of memories and emotions when viewers first looked at it in late 1919. For those exhausted by the war, the Zeppelin may have acted primarily as a reminder of the atrocities carried out by their former enemies. One way of handling and even overcoming traumatic memories is to vilify the enemy.

Vilifying

The apparent barbarity of the Germans is a recurring theme in several of Allix's descriptions of the windows. For example, he describes 'german [sic] liquid fire' as a 'diabolical invention'. For Allix, it 'is difficult even to contemplate the horror of such a death and none but a savage would inflict it upon his worst enemy'.[106] This vitriolic tone continues with his description on the second war window of the *Lusitania* sinking, when she was 'torpedoed off the coast of Ireland' (7 May 1915). Though 'she carried none but civilians she was treacherously sunk and over 1,000 innocent lives were sacrificed by this dastardly exploit'.[107]

The actual image is easy to overlook at St Mary's. The ship is depicted as she is actually sinking, four funnels still steaming as she disappears into the sea. Like all the other biblical verses, this one is taken out of context to provide a gloss for the picture: 'In perils in the sea, in perils among false brethren' (2 Corinthians 11.27). During the war, numerous propaganda postcards and posters were produced commemorating this attack (figure 1.10).

Like the Zeppelin attacks on London and other parts of Britain it was put to use as a way of encouraging men to enlist and fight against the brutal Germans. For example, one card shows the 'three large graves where the bodies of 178 of the "Lusitania" victims rest' in Queenstown, Ireland. The line below explains the depiction within the 'inset'. This 'is the medal which was struck in Germany to celebrate this dastardly crime'. The headline is 'A Memorial to German Savagery'. The attack was also put to use outside Britain. One French postcard shows a child in the ocean crying out, 'Mamam, Mamam, Pourquoi?' Like the Zeppelin

PERILS · IN · THE · SEA · IN · PERILS · AMONG · FALSE · BRETHREN

Figure 1.10 The Sinking of Lusitania, with mines beneath the surface. 1919 stained-glass
  window from St Mary's, Swaffham Prior, Cambridgeshire. Photograph courtesy
  of Steve Day. This image is adjacent to a couple of panes depicting submarines.

attacks discussed earlier, the attack was used as a way of encouraging men to
join up. One American poster, by Fred Spear, depicts a white-robed mother
clutching a baby as they descend to their watery graves.[108] Beneath this ghostly
Madonna-like apparition is one word: 'Enlist' (figure 1.11).

Allix preserved several newspaper cuttings about 'The Lusitania Outrage' and
the ways in which Germans sing and gloat over 'this brilliant achievement by
their navy'.[109] Close to these stories are clippings relating to the execution of the
nurse Edith Cavell, 'Victim of the War's most Damnable Crime', who 'was
brutally done to death by the German murderers of women and children'.[110]
Contrast these images and stories with the 'caring and brave' nurses in the
windows, tending the wounded. Even a dog's paw is bandaged.

Not everyone would drink the propagandistic use of news stories such as
Cavell's execution or the sinking of the *Lusitania* uncritically. For instance,
Bernard Shaw controversially wrote: 'To me, with my mind full of the hideous
cost of Neuve Chapelle, Ypres, and the Gallipoli landing, the fuss about the
Lusitania seemed almost a heartless impertinence'.[111] The 'hideous cost' of
the war is largely left unremarked in the Swaffham Prior windows, with the
exception of the dead soldier considered earlier and the depiction of an army
chaplain in the middle of an empty battlefield giving the blessing to a dying
soldier (figure 1.12).[112]

Figure 1.11 Drowning Mother and Child (1915). Poster by Fred Spear, © Imperial War Museums (Q 79823).

MY ∘ PEACE ∘ I ∘ GIVE ∘ UNTO ∘ YOU ∘ NOT ∘ AS ∘ THE ∘
WORLD ∘ GIVETH ∘ GIVE ∘ I ∘ UNTO ∘ YOU ∘ JOHN XIV. 27.

Figure 1.12 Military Chaplain, blesses dying soldier. 1919 stained-glass window from
St Mary's, Swaffham Prior, Cambridgeshire. Photograph courtesy of Steve Day.
In 1914 there were 117 commissioned military chaplains from three denominations in the British army; by 1918 there were over 5000 temporary chaplains from
11 denominations. Over 100 were killed.

His comrades surround their wounded friend as the sun sets in the distance.
Below, a text from the New Testament: 'My Peace I give unto you, not as the
world giveth, give I unto you' (John 14.27). This depiction at least shows a fragile figure at its centre, but is notable for what it leaves out: neither the lone-
liness, nor the instantaneousness, nor the agony of death is captured. Elsewhere,
some propaganda art muted 'the true horror of war' even further and 'presented
the battlefields merely as picturesque landscapes with no evidence of casualties'.[113]
Some went to the other extreme. One French caricature depicts a skeleton,
identified as the German Crown Prince Wilhelm (1892–1951), ploughing a field
of skulls under a single-word title: 'Verdun' (figure 1.13). This stands in sharp
contrast to one of the images from the third window in Swaffham Prior that
shows a single figure peacefully ploughing the land. Beneath is the text 'He that
ploweth should plow in hope' (1 Corinthians 9.10) (figure 1.14).

Figure 1.13 Verdun, 'the Crown Prince at work', from Hommes du Jour, 1916, by French caricaturist Lucien La Forge (1889–1952). Courtesy of the Art Archive.

In his addresses at the opening of other local memorials, Allix balances talk of the bravery of young men throwing their fragile lives into no-man's land with the recurring barbarity of the Germans. At the public dedication of the Swaffham Bulbeck Memorial (16 June 1921) he claims not to need to detail the crimes of the Germans, only then to mention them. His address is reported in a local paper in the following terms: 'The War was now over, thank God, and so he [Allix] would not draw a harrowing picture of the cruelties, barbarities and fiendish methods against which our soldiers had to fight. Poison gas, bombs, liquid fire and all the other destructive inventions of modern science were already sufficient of an open book to everyone to need no recapitulation'.[114] Compare this with his address over a year earlier at the Reach village memorial (13 June 1920). Allix observes how this war 'has been unlike any of the wars that preceded it, they were wars between armies of one country against the armies of another country, but in this war whole nations have been at war with each other'. In a description which resonates with the picture discussed at the start of this chapter, he speaks of 'women making arms and ammunition'. This reordering of traditional social order also overturned the normal moral constraints: 'Now this war though it produced expressions of every kind of villainy, cruelty, callousness, lust and reeked with atrocities yet did also produce the most brilliant examples of every kind of virtue, gallantry, bravery, endurance and human kindness. All distinctions whether of class or religion were swept away like magic'.[115] Several of his addresses conclude with what reads like an appeal for a return of the status quo, where 'labour and capital' work together harmoniously.

Figure 1.14 Figure Ploughing. 1919 stained-glass window from St Mary's, Swaffham Prior,
    Cambridgeshire. Photograph courtesy of Steve Day.

It is possible to identify propaganda's presence in St Mary's *Restoration Book*, as
there are several examples of propaganda booklets preserved. For example,
Newell Dwight Hillis's *Murder Most Foul* (c.1918), which records a 'thousand
individual atrocities', has been carefully retained. Hillis (1858–1929), Con-
gregationalist minister of the Plymouth church in Brooklyn, spent two months as
'an American observer on the Western Front' investigating the 'crimes of the
Germans'. On his return he spoke at a number of churches in the USA, using
atrocity stories as a way of encouraging the purchase of war bonds. His address
at a church in Baltimore was reprinted as *Murder Most Foul*. It is this sixteen-page
address that had found its way back to Cambridgeshire. Hillis spoke of 'The
murder of Edith Cavell and of hundreds of women and children on the Lusitania,
the rape of Belgium,[116] the assassination of Northern France'.[117] Three times
through this address he refers to the token that every German soldier was purportedly given, which has engraved: 'Smite your enemy dead. The Day of

Judgement will not ask for your reasons'.[118] The barbarities that the Germans supposedly perpetrated leads him to conclude that they are 'controlled by merciless and cruel men, who have given up all faith in God, who practice the Ten Commandments with the "Not" left out, who have stamped out of their soldier every instinct of pity and sympathy'. He goes further, quoting approvingly a letter from a war surgeon: 'This war is of God. Sometimes it is peace that is hell ... I once spoke in ... Plymouth on the blessings of peace; if ever again I have that privilege, I shall speak on the blessings of war'. Hillis later appears to soften these sentiments suggesting that 'this war was not brought by God, but, having come let us believe that His providence can overrule it for the destruction of all war'.[119] Like many popular speakers, his use of atrocity stories led him to a fiercely judgemental approach towards the leader of the central powers: 'When Germany is beaten to her knees, becomes repentant, offers to make restitutions for her crimes, then, and not till then, can this war stop'.[120] The use of atrocity stories by churchmen was by no means restricted to the work of this American pastor.

The popular and bellicose preacher A.F. Winnington-Ingram, the Bishop of London, also made uncritical use of atrocity stories, probably taken from two of Lord Northcliffe's papers *The Times* and the *Daily Mail*,[121] in order to encourage men to enlist and to fight the Germans.[122] In his 1915 Advent Sermon, preached in Westminster Abbey, he justified the war as a necessity 'to save the freedom of the world, to save Liberty's own self, to save the honour of women and the innocence of children', and then infamously claimed:

> [we] are banded in a great crusade – we cannot deny it – to kill Germans: to kill them, not for the sake of killing, but to save the world; to kill the good as well as the bad, to kill the young men as well as the old, to kill those who have shown kindness to our wounded as well as those fiends who crucified the Canadian sergeant, who superintended the Armenian massacres, who sank the *Lusitania,* and who turned the machine-guns on the civilians of Aerschott and Louvain – and to kill them lest the civilisation of the world itself be killed.[123]

Consider here how the atrocity stories are piled together, in order to justify the war and demonise the opponents. In an earlier sermon, *Life for Ever and Ever,* preached at the Canadian Memorial Service at St Paul's Cathedral, he spoke of the 'diabolical act in the sinking of the *Lusitania,* which will stain the name of Germany while time shall last'. Using vivid language he encouraged his listeners to consider: 'The two children clasped in one another's arms found dead in one of the boats of the *Lusitania,* and the hundreds of gallant soldiers gasping for breath as they die in agony from poisonous gases'.[124] In an address to clergy on a quiet day, he uncritically quotes a story from *The Times* which reported how one British soldier found a '"young girl naked in my trench. She has been wronged by a German soldier. I have given her my shirt and all I can. I saw another poor girl last night having her breasts cut off by an Uhlan officer.[125]

I dropped him at seven hundred yards. She is in my trench now, but I am afraid she will die". What a contrast does the conduct of this German present to the splendid chivalry of our knights!'[126] It was not uncommon for both British and German preachers to endorse the knightly and chivalric qualities of their own soldiers. The burning of the medieval library at Louvain, the shelling of Rheims cathedral,[127] and the sinking of the *Lusitania* were common reference points for British and French preachers like Winnington-Ingram who wished to justify this as a 'Holy War'.[128] Allix's addresses were more restrained than the rousing and popular addresses of the Bishop of London.

While Winnington-Ingram was one of the more outspoken and extreme examples of preachers encouraging men to fight, he was by no means a unique voice. Charles L. Warr, a soldier 'badly wounded' at Ypres in 1916 who later became a Church of Scotland minister, observed in spring 1918, soon after he was ordained, that 'too many pulpits had assumed the role of recruiting sergeant'.[129] For those preachers who had initially predicted in 1914 that the war would be a purifying, unifying and holy crusade, it was hard to accept those who later argued that the conflict pointed primarily to the need for national repentance. Even after four long years of struggle, it was not always easy to discard the rhetoric of 'Holy War'.[130] Protestant German pastors also regularly referred to this as a 'Holy War'.[131] Not everyone absorbed this heady mix of religious fervour and national patriotism. The experience of facing the actual horrors of the conflict led poets to leave behind romantic visions of war, and caused writers such as Vera Brittain to reflect:

> I wish those people who write so glibly about this being a Holy War ...
> could see a case – to say nothing of 10 cases – of mustard gas in its early
> stages – could see the poor things burnt and blistered all over with great
> mustard-coloured suppurating blisters, with blind eyes – sometimes tem-
> porarily, sometimes permanently – all sticky and stuck together, and always
> fighting for breath, with voices a mere whisper, saying that their throats are
> closing and they are going to choke ... and yet people persist in saying that
> God made the War, when there are such inventions of the Devil about ... [132]

Brittain's critical reflections, published in 1933, are taken from a letter written to her mother at the end of 1917. They are illustrative of a spreading dissatisfaction with the belief that they were participating in a 'Holy War'. Such sentiments are not to be found at Swaffham Prior and were rarely attached to memorials.[133]

Nevertheless, during the conflict many preachers continued to employ the language of crusade to characterise the war. According to Niall Ferguson the First World War was 'a kind of war of religion ... a crusade without infidels'.[134] This characterisation is open to qualification and criticism, but however it is characterised, the recurring presence and retelling of these commonly embroi-dered atrocity tales helped to turn the Germans into 'vile animals, grotesque and inhuman'.[135] Church leaders played their role in vilifying and demonising the opposition, even if they also publicly encouraged their listeners not to 'hate' their opponents.[136] Put into this wider discursive context, Allix's more public references to German atrocities are by no means uncommon, reflecting the widespread absorption of commonly recycled stories. To include an image of the sinking of the *Lusitania* in this series of stained-glass windows in a church may appear idiosyncratic when placed alongside medieval representations of the life of Christ and Old Testament parallels, but when placed in a symbolic world where pictures and stories of the *Lusitania* 'disaster', Zeppelin attacks and German atrocities are fresh in the memory and still repeated, it is less surprising.

Sowing Seeds for Future Violence?

As we saw in the prologue of this chapter, beneath the picture of the Statue of Liberty is a prophetic text taken from the book of Isaiah: 'Nation shall not lift up sword against nation neither shall they learn war any more' (Isaiah 2.4). In Allix's notes on this panel, he quotes this verse from Isaiah and simply adds: 'Which may God grant!' While the preceding sentence from Isaiah, which speaks of 'swords being beaten into ploughshares' has been omitted, taken together the windows are clearly intended to point forwards to time when there will be no need for war.[137] Allix was no warmonger or propagandist for never-ending war. Like many of his contemporaries he viewed this as a just and necessary war, where many young men had sacrificially given up their lives for a greater good. These series of stained-glass windows shed light on a period of sustained grief, where many communities and individuals were trying to come to terms with both national and personal trauma.

In this chapter I am *not* trying to suggest that these windows, and the related commemorative acts, provide evidence of the effectiveness of wartime propaganda. As I have shown, a range of factors inspired the depictions of 'diabolical' weapons of war such as Zeppelins and liquid fire or the retelling of 'atrocities' such as the sinking of the *Lusitania*. Nevertheless, their inclusion in the windows, the accompanying texts and the designer's commentary point to the fact that memories of the perceived brutality of the enemy lived on after the war. Propaganda does not evaporate as soon as the fighting stops. Once an enemy is demonised it is hard to transform them back into a harmless stranger, let alone a friendly neighbour.

My argument is therefore that incitements to violence are not necessarily buried with the end of the war. They can live on and come back to haunt individuals and communities. Earlier incitements to violence drawing upon experiences of fear, loss and grief can even shape the demands of the victors and damage the possibilities for a lasting peace. Making Germany accept 'sole responsibility' for the war and pay crushing and punitive reparations was one of the platforms upon which several political leaders retained power after the war. Jingoistic sentiments, found among many of the leaders of the victorious nations, contributed to the Treaty of Versailles becoming for some 'an unhappy compromise' and for others a 'vindictive treaty, the like of which was never seen in the modern world before' and ensured that a 'supreme opportunity was thrown away'.[138]

In this context post-war memorials, and the rituals associated with preserving memories of atrocities and loss, can become ways in which memories of past hurts can be kept alive and even amplified. Memories can become weapons used against former opponents, reminders of why conflict should continue. They can also become places where the goodness and sacrifices of the home nation are celebrated, overlooking any of the evils perpetrated in the name of bringing freedom and peace. The sacrifices of soldiers are commonly celebrated and linked with other sacrificial deaths. While Allix spoke of young men 'laying down their lives', the Swaffham windows do not draw upon one of the most commonly used images from the First World War, which juxtapose Christ on the Cross with a prostate, eyes-closed, uniformed figure. This was based upon James Clark's painting *The Great Sacrifice* (1914). It depicts a dead (or possibly dying) soldier whose lifeless hand rests on the actual foot of Jesus. He is still hanging on the Cross, gazing down through bright clouds towards the infantryman's body lying in the mud. By Christmas 1914 it was reproduced in the British newspaper the *Daily Graphic* and then in many other publications.

The image was recycled, adapted and sometimes softened when translated into other media. In the memorial window at St Mary Magdalene, Enfield, the colours are gentler, with shades of purple and pink swirling into the clouds (figure 1.15). In Suffolk, St Mary the Virgin, Mendlesham, the dark, brown, mud is replaced by neat, light, green grass. The image travelled the globe during and after the war. In Canada it appeared in memorial publications, plaques and windows. For example, in Winnipeg, at St John's Cathedral, an angelic figure holding palm fronds and the Crown of Life is added to the original picture.[139] In Australia it was given a local accent. In one stained-glass window, at St George's Church, Malvern, Victoria, 'the non-Australian rifle' was 'removed and a slouch cap' was 'added',[140] along with red poppies and ruined French or Belgian houses in the background. Nevertheless, in each case the central message remains the same, connecting the sacrifice of Christ with the sacrifice of individual soldiers. The lighter clouds point to hope beyond the harsh and dark battlefields. James Clark followed it up with *The Greater Reward* (1917), which portrays a female angelic figure, immersed in light. She holds a bedraggled soldier as they both look up and out of the picture towards heaven. As we shall see in later chapters, these observations relating to the portrayal of sacrifice, glorification and vilification are not confined to what happened in Europe after the conflagration of 1914–18.

Memories can be put to other more irenic uses. For some survivors, keeping memories alive was the way to ensure that this was 'the war to end all wars': 'Memories of the late war must never fade. Let everything about it be known. Teach it to our children. Make it lurid. Emphasise it. Preach it. Glorify it as the biggest and best argument for peace evermore'.[141] These windows, unlike other

Figure 1.15 The Great Sacrifice. c 1919 War memorial window at St Mary Magdalene, Windmill Hill, Enfield, based on the 1914 painting by James Clark. Photograph

more horrific depictions such as Dix's *War Triptych*, are not deliberately lurid, celebrating rather the technologies and practices of war. While they culminate in a series of panes celebrating peace, the cumulative effect of the three windows appears to be a visual argument for using the weapons of war to bring peace, though the final 'peace window' does reveal an absence of the technologies of war and a yearning for a world without violence.

Historians of this period commonly highlight the 'brutalizing effects of war on civilians and soldiers', with war cultures seeping into 'every area of domestic life', which can lead to 'deformations of civility'.[142] Atrocity stories of women raped, civilians shot and children having their hands cut off were commonly recycled during the First World War. Allix is comparatively reticent about these claims, both in the windows and in his public addresses, alluding to rather than depicting such gruesome acts. One 1916 propaganda poster by the Australian artist Norman Lindsay goes much further than Allix, drawing together many of these tales into one picture. A band of fierce-looking German soldiers march angrily forwards. At the centre of the picture is a moustached soldier holding aloft a baby skewered on his bayonet, while stamping on a partly disrobed woman's body.[143] By her head a canister marked 'poison gas' spews out a white smoke, while in the sky an airship appears to be dropping explosives. Nor is this depiction devoid of religious symbolism. A crucified man limply hangs on a T-shaped cross and another soldier holds a flag faintly inscribed with *Gott mit uns* (God with us). This poster therefore combines many of the best-known atrocity stories into one scene. It is emblematic of how the supposed 'barbarism' of the enemy is commonly used for propaganda purposes.

At least one of the British war censors, C.E. Montague, who was involved in the craft of propaganda, became increasingly disenchanted with his role in spreading the 'fog of falsehood' and claims in his 1922 book, aptly titled *Disenchantment*, that 'any weapon you use in war leaves some bill to be settled in peace, and the propaganda arm has its costs like any other'.[144] Books such as *Disenchantment* and Arthur Ponsonby's *Falsehood in War-Time: Propaganda Lies of the First World War* (1928) revealed the widespread use and abuses of propaganda. The invention and uncritical use of atrocity stories during the war ensured that, in the 1920s and 1930s, atrocity tales from the 'Great War' were largely disbelieved. Several scholars suggest that the discrediting of First World War atrocity stories made it harder for many to believe what was happening to Jews during the Second World War as 'fact'. 'In a climate of widespread scepticism about any further atrocity stories, most people refused fully to credit reports of the concentration camps until ocular evidence compelled belief and it was too late'.[145]

Conclusion

As a whole, this set of windows invites the viewer to reflect on both the brutality and the compassion which were brought 'into the centre of social life' through the war.[146] This evoked a wide range of responses and contrasting memories.

Compare the accounts provided by Charles Allix and Vera Brittain for two very different ways of interpreting the war. As Adrian Gregory argues in the *Silence of Memory*, a study of British Armistice Day rituals during the interwar and Second World War period, there was not a single state-controlled account but rather a multiplicity of memories of war, influenced by denomination, local history, competition, region, class and gender. While many other memorials highlighted the 'great sacrifice' of many young men, not all memorials were as supportive of the sacrificial status quo. For example, the Leeds University War Memorial, Eric Gill's controversial sculpture *The Moneychangers* (1923), was also described as a 'curious' and 'strange memorial' in the press. This frieze acts like 'sermon in stone' and provoked outrage among some contemporary viewers for concentrating not on the heroes of the trenches but on the war profiteers, dressed in modern attire, being violently chased out of the temple by Jesus.[147] Few local memorial committees or patrons of memorials dared to support such a critical interpretation of the war. While the memorial windows in Swaffham Prior may be rare in form, the sentiments embedded within them are far from unique.[148]

This chapter began with the description of a woman manufacturing a shell designed to kill. By comparison to *The Hall of the Million Shells*, by Britain's first war artist Muirhead Bone (1876–1953),[149] this is a small-scale production with only a few dozen shells in sight. Like all the other windows, this is a single insight into what was a global and industrialised conflict. In the shadows of the unprecedented deaths through four and half years of war, the practices of grieving, commemorating, justifying, remembering and vilifying are to be found not only in this small village eight miles outside Cambridge, but right across Europe and around the globe. Similar processes are also evident in significantly different historical, cultural and religious contexts. It is to one of those in Iran that we now turn.

Chapter 2

Celebrating martyrdom

Prologue

Driving through Iran it is hard to avoid memorials of those killed during the eight-year Iran–Iraq war (1980–8). These memorials can be found in every province and city of Iran. The common experience of being stuck in a traffic jam in Tehran ensures that there is often time to study in detail the murals, which adorn larger buildings. Smaller Iranian cities also retain visual reminders of wartime martyrdoms. Our taxi driver in the city of Shiraz, for example, pointed out new, brightly coloured posters of Iranian pilots, including pictures of their planes and their names in Farsi (Persian). He himself was a survivor of the conflict, though he had lost several fingers as a prisoner-of-war in Iraq. He spoke in a matter-of-fact fashion about his own traumatic experiences and about those pilots who were now celebrated as martyrs (*shahids* or *shahid*). These posters and murals are representative of the countless visual reminders of people killed in action during the Iran–Iraq war.

In the Iranian capital, one of the best-known martyr depictions was to be found close to the main entrance of the University of Tehran on Enghelab Street. This mural was painted onto the side of a multi-storey building. At its centre was a dark-haired boy staring out towards passing viewers. His eyes and eyebrows match his black hair and, along with his unsmiling countenance, bestow upon him a dignity beyond his years. This was accentuated by the older bearded figure in the background. Depicted in fainter colours than the boy, it was an easily recognisable portrayal of Ayatollah Khomeini. He watches over the boy, but also looks beyond. Beneath Khomeini, several tanks point towards a single large tank in the foreground (figure 2.1).

During and after the war, this 13-year-old child, Hossein Fahmideh, was turned into a national hero. According to one account, this young boy from Qom may have lied about his age in order to join the army, without the knowledge of his parents. This was not unusual in a war that attracted thousands of 'boy soldiers', mesmerised by the exciting prospect of fighting together for their country and for God. What was unusual was how he died. According to another official account, Hossein was fighting in a narrow canal space in the

Figure 2.1 Original mural of the *Boy martyr Hossein Fahmideh*. Photograph courtesy of Christiane Gruber.

besieged southern city of Khorramshahr in November 1980. Seeing that many of his older comrades were killed or injured, he is reputed to have taken several grenades from one of his dead colleagues, held one to his chest and blown himself up under an Iraqi tank, disabling the tank and thereby halting an entire division of advancing tanks. Khomeini regularly praised his actions, saying that this young boy was 'our leader' and the 'value of his little heart is greater than could be described by hundreds of tongues and hundreds of pens'.[1] On the pre-2009 mural itself, Ayatollah Khomeini is recorded as describing this young boy martyr as 'our guide' who 'threw himself under the enemy's tank with a grenade and destroyed it, thus drinking the elixir of martyrdom'".[2]

The picture of Fahmideh's face was reproduced not only on murals, but also on stamps, banknotes and stickers. Plastic rucksacks, portraying his martyrdom, were issued to thousands of Iranian schoolchildren. The story of his martyrdom was retold in school textbooks that were produced to improve literacy among children.[3] His burial place on the edge of the city was turned into a national monument, becoming a popular site for pilgrimages. His face continues to adorn posters and his story is often repeated in speeches and news articles, leading some to describe him as the 'grandson' of the Islamic revolution.[4]

In 2009, the mural was repainted, and given a more abstract form. Hossein's face remains. It is now placed in front of red, black and orange waves in a black frame among grey clouds. Instead of the face of Khomeini and the Iraqi tank, there are now three candles around a single grenade (figure 2.2).[5] Adjacent to the eight-storey-high Enghelab Street mural, celebrating Hossein Fahmideh's martyrdom, there is still a vertical line of air-conditioning units and small windows. These are reminders of the many lives going on behind this imposing and now transformed picture. Like so many other traces from the Iran–Iraq war, this image is embedded into everyday life. While new pictures have been commissioned in the last few years, and some, like this one, have been repainted, many other earlier martyrdom murals have lost their original shine: paint peels and images fade. While most of the murals lasted much longer than the graffiti and paper posters denouncing the Shah's regime in 1979, recently some local authorities have even had visual traces of propaganda from the 1980–8 war whitewashed over. New buildings obscure other depictions, making it hard to catch a complete view. For locals today, many of those remaining portrayals have almost become invisible, easy to pass by, take for granted or ignore. There is a sense in which familiarity breeds invisibility. Many young Iranians, born during or after the war, have little interest in or desire to revisit the conflict.[6] Like many war memorials in Britain, these images in Iran are becoming part of an easily overlooked urban geography shaped by the desire of an earlier generation to commemorate the deaths of their contemporaries. Nonetheless, in Iran some of these depictions of martyrs have taken on a new significance in the light of more recent events.

Following the presidential elections in 2009, thousands of demonstrators took to the streets in Tehran to challenge the results. These protests were confronted

Figure 2.2 Renovated *Hossein Fahmideh* mural, same location as figure 2.1, repainted in 2009. Photograph courtesy of Christiane Gruber.

by increasingly violent suppression. On 20 June, a 27-year-old Iranian woman, Neda Agha-Soltan, was shot in the chest. As she lay dying on the road, at least two bystanders captured her last moments on camera. One of these 'video' clips depicts her falling to the ground; blood comes out of her nose and mouth while several men attempt to stop the wound in her chest. The crying becomes increasingly fraught as the seriousness of her injuries become clear. Within a few hours of her death these images were placed on YouTube and other sites, where they have since been watched by hundreds of thousands of viewers. In subsequent days, demonstrators held pictures of her blood-spattered face aloft and the images of her last moments were set to music on several video sites. The words: 'I am Neda' were commonly used to frame the picture of her blood-spattered face. This was used by demonstrators not only in Iran but by protesters around the world. Western news organisations either repeated this graphic footage or showed stills of her last moments. They followed this up by providing brief details of her life story and death, explaining that she was a non-violent observer who had only stepped out of her car for some fresh air.[7] Since then memorial sites have been set up and publicised through Wikipedia, Facebook and Twitter.[8] Some described her as the 'first YouTube martyr' and others even claimed she had become the martyr of a 'new revolutionary movement in Iran'.[9]

Both sets of images were put to multiple uses, both locally and internationally. Locally, the depiction of the boy martyr Hossein Fahmideh was used to encourage others to give their lives in the fight for the survival of the embattled Islamic republic during the 1980s. Internationally, the writer and presenter of a Channel 4 documentary Robert Baer, a former CIA operative in Beirut, claimed that Hossein's 'suicidal attack' represents one of the foundations for *The Cult of the Suicide Bomber*.[10] Early in this documentary he visits Hossein's family, sees the small shrine they keep in his memory and interviews his mother, who states that her son drank 'the elixir of martyrdom'. The family entirely reject the suggestion that Hossein's action was a form of 'suicide bombing'. In their eyes he was without doubt 'a *shahid*' or 'a martyr'. Beyond their family circles, both Hossein and Neda were turned into national symbols of martyrdom, with international significance. While the government promoted Hossein's clean visage and heroic story, Neda's bloodied face has been used to underline the oppressive violence of the state. Their images became visual metonyms, symbolising contrasting forms of martyrdom. Hossein represents an active form of martyrdom, which includes killing the enemy, while Neda represents a passive form of martyrdom, which was not intentionally sought and which does not result directly in the deaths of others. Her image was used not only in Iran but also around the world as a sign of protest. I was surprised to see demonstrators by the cathedral in Cologne, Germany, holding up placards with pictures of her face the week after her death. The Iranian government, including President Mahmoud Ahmadinejad, contested the claim that she was shot by the police. He questioned who had actually killed her, even suggesting that it was part of a foreign plot to shame the nation.[11] Both inside and outside Iran commentators repeatedly claim that such depictions of martyrs have a particular resonance in Iran. These claims raise questions about why images and stories celebrating martyrdom are apparently able to carry such persuasive power.

Introduction

In *My Life is a Weapon*, Christoph Reuter suggests that in order to understand recent suicide bombing, not only in Iraq, Israel and Lebanon but also in New York, London and Bali, it is important to reflect further upon the willingness of Iranian young men and boys to die as martyrs during the Iran–Iraq war.[12] A similar line of argument is found in Robert Baer's documentary *The Cult of the Suicide Bomber*. If, as Reuter and Baer suggest, the desire for martyrdom found amongst many young Iranians during the war represents the modern starting point for more recent 'martyrdom operations', then it is particularly useful to consider how such beliefs were originally promoted in Iran.

In this second chapter, my central aim is to understand some of the persuasive processes that were used to try to encourage young men and boys to take up arms, as well as convince their families, friends and relatives of the value of their sacrifices both during and after the war. Mobilising a population to fight, while certainly not without precedent, is no mean achievement. It was, according to Roxanne Varzi, the 'largest mobilization ever of the Iranian population, which was achieved primarily by producing and promoting a culture of martyrdom based on religious themes found in Shi'i Islam'.[13] In Iran thousands of 14- to 16-year-olds, and even 12- and 13-year-olds, were enlisted and many were killed in the conflict. The Iran–Iraq war (September 1980–August 1988) is now widely believed to have cost well over a million lives.[14] Both nations still carry the scars of a conflict, which saw the employment of tactics reminiscent of the First World War, including the use of trenches, bayonet charges, poisonous gas and barbed wire.

In Iran it was officially described as an 'Imposed War', with those Iranians who died characterised as 'martyrs'. On one level it was portrayed as a war of national survival that Saddam Hussein had initiated, while on another it was a war of 'Holy' or 'Sacred Defence'. A whole range of different media were used to depict, celebrate and thereby promote martyrdom both during and after the war, including posters, paintings, murals, documentaries and films. These portrayals of martyrdom can be found in many different places: on walls, stamps, banknotes and postcards, on television and at the cinema, as well as in cemeteries, museums and on websites. 'Everything from print to celluloid was used to illustrate the beauty of sacrifice';[15] even chewing gum wrappers and 'primary school textbook illustrations were used to mobilize a people'.[16] As Christiane Gruber has demonstrated, posters emerging in the early 1980s, were the precursors and catalysts for murals'.[17] Numerous billboards were set up close to the front, either exhorting sacrifice or praising the supreme leader, Ayatollah Khomeini.

The ubiquity of these memorials can be observed not only when travelling in Iran but also by studying materials produced by the Iranian government, which continues to preserve photographs, posters, cartoons, printed documents, films, documentaries, books, poems and songs.[18] These are a rich resource for understanding the extensive propaganda that emerged in support of the Islamic Republic of Iran's stand against Iraq. What is particularly striking is how the war is regularly depicted as an 'imposed war' or a conflict of 'holy defence' and is promoted in religious terms. Soldiers killed in action are repeatedly referred to as martyrs or depicted as such. In these official records there are also countless pictures of martyrs' graveyards, memorials and museums, which are now located all over Iran. These were originally sponsored and maintained by several different organizations, including the Martyrs' Foundation (Bonyad-e Shahid) and the Revolutionary Guards (Sepah-e Pasdaran). The Martyrs' Foundation has also begun to preserve and archive some of the propaganda, which emerged during and after the war. These diverse materials also reveal some of the different ways in which martyrdom was characterised, promoted and celebrated.

In the pages that follow, I primarily concentrate upon murals found in urban spaces in order to illuminate how martyrdom was remembered, celebrated and reflected upon in Iran. I begin by showing how many of these depictions draw upon particular Shi'a traditions, beliefs and practices. I then investigate what these images reveal about the processes of resisting, symbolising and grieving. Through these discussions I analyse different kinds of visual rhetoric that were employed in an attempt to incite both the young men to give their lives and the families to encourage their sacrifices. It is beyond the scope of this chapter to consider in detail how posters, cartoons and murals were used to ridicule and to vilify Iran's perceived enemies. At the outset it is also important to underline that some of the martyr images were created after the war to commemorate, to justify and to celebrate acts of martyrdom.[19] Alongside this detailed analysis of the visual representations of martyrdom, I therefore also investigate how these depictions were used, recycled and even interrogated. In the light of these discussions I conclude by considering the ways in which such celebratory representations of martyrdom are now being contested. I reflect on how even cemeteries have become sites of contest.

Remembering Karbala

Karbala is now an Iraqi town about 50 miles south of Baghdad. This was the site of the battle where Muhammad's grandson Husayn suffered thirst and multiple wounds. There he was killed and then beheaded by soldiers fighting in the caliph Yizad's army in 680. Even more than the murder of his father Ali, Husayn's death is commonly seen within Shi'ism as a founding death. Some scholars assert that the 'martyrdom of Husayn is to Shi'ites what the crucifixion is to Christians: the seminal event of the faith, always there to be read and re-read into the changing reality of the communal anxieties'.[20] This claim may blur the distinctiveness of the foundations of both religious traditions but for many Iranians, Husayn's brutal death, over 1,300 years ago at Karbala, has come to be seen as the 'supreme self-sacrifice'.

Artists commonly reference this founding story of Shi'a Islam in their wartime murals and other forms of propaganda. For example, several images include representations of Husayn's headless corpse or his white horse peppered with arrows.[21] Modern martyrs, young Iranian soldiers, are often included in these depictions. In one picture, a young soldier has one hand holding a rifle the other resting on a Quran. He is looking up towards a brightly illuminated white horse, pierced with arrows, rising up towards an even brighter light above. The dazzling light contrasts with the darker greens and blues in the lower half of the picture.

Colours are symbolically important in many of these posters and murals. For instance, in the portrayal of a blindfolded Iranian soldier shot in the heart at 'point-blank range', reds and green predominate. The soldier, in green fatigues, falls back towards Husayn with his white horse. Husayn appears to be holding or pulling a green sheet; it is as if he is drawing the soul of the martyred soldier towards himself. Three headless martyrs clad in red, representing 'martyrs that died alongside Husayn at the Battle of Karbala', provide a further connection point between the martyr from the Iran–Iraq war and the 'original' martyrdom. One holds a green Quran over his heart, as he points towards heaven. The green symbolizes both the prophet Muhammad and the Imam Husayn. The red points to the martyrdoms of Husayn and his followers (figure 2.3).[22]

This resonates with another mural in Tehran that depicts a young martyred soldier. On the tip of his rifle is a picture of Khomeini. Around his head a red band that refers to Husayn by stating: 'O, the shining moon of the tribe of Hashim'. In a way similar to the bright light found in the figure above, one's eye is drawn towards a golden light emanating from clouds behind. They partly encircle the golden dome of a mosque: Husayn's shrine in Karbala.[23] Several pictures draw upon other elements in the story, such as the extreme thirst that Husayn and his followers experienced, the death of Husayn's baby son or women mourning at Karbala. Through such pictures, the battle at Karbala in 680, where Husayn, his companions and many of his family were killed, is inextricably connected with the conflict in the 1980s that claimed hundreds of thousands of lives. These portrayals emerged in a context where Iranian offensives were given titles such as Karbala IV and Karbala VIII. Signposts were erected near to the front pointing in the direction of the battle, with only one word inscribed: 'Karbala'. Battlefields became a place to re-enact or re-experience what happened at Karbala.

For many scholars the 'Karbala event' is for Shi'i Islam a 'defining master-narrative'. Malise Ruthven believes that 'the "massacre" of Karbala, a fight between rival clans that only lasts a day and results in the death of a few dozen dead', became 'the defining myth of Shi'ism, an emblem of suffering and martyrdom'.[24] Many Shi'i Muslims understand Husayn's death at Karbala 'as a fulcrum in the history of the world and which remains to this day as a primary focus of spiritual reflection'.[25] In *Staging a Revolution: The Art of Persuasion in the Islamic Republic of Iran*, Peter Chelowski and Hamid Dabashi assert that the

Figure 2.3 Blindfolded Soldier Shot at Gunpoint, c.1981. Courtesy of the Special Collections Research Center, The University of Chicago Library (Middle Eastern Posters Collection, Box 4, Poster 197).

Karbala story 'has remained at the heart of the Shi'i collective consciousness, to be reinvented for any number of immediate political ends'.[26] The political end in the 1980s was to mobilize a population to fight. One of the ways in which the population was encouraged to go to war was through the production of state-funded murals that resonated with stories believed by many to be at the heart of their faith. Elsewhere Chelowksi claims that 'never in the history of propaganda have the graphic arts systematically played such an important role as they did in Iran in the years 1980–8'.[27] The visual depictions that reference Karbala and Husayn resonate with earlier recitations, processions and coffee-house depictions of Karbala. This wartime art was part of a wider communicative process which sacralised a contemporary conflict by connecting it with commonly repeated collective memories and rituals.

The events surrounding Husayn and his seventy-two companions' deaths are commonly re-enacted through colourful 'passion' plays (*ta'ziya* or *ta'ziyeh*).[28] In his memoir *The Rose Garden of Martyrs*, Christopher de Bellaigue takes his readers to witness one of these passion plays in a poorer part of Tehran, illustrating how these plays continue to attract large audiences to this day. Viewers become passionately involved in what they see. These passion plays originated in earlier cathartic processions of mourning, and are complemented by retelling of the stories (*Rowzehs*) or meditations (*Zekrs*) upon these martyrdoms. The tenth (*Ashura*) day of *Muharram*, when Husayn was killed at Karbala, is the focal point of these dramatic enactments. Within this tradition, Muharram, after Ramadan, is the holiest month of the Islamic year, when fighting is supposedly forbidden. 'During Muharram, what happened thirteen centuries ago on the plains of Karbala is perceived as if it were happening here and now. Shi'ites atone for their failure to rescue Husayn from his entrapment', not only by re-enacting the drama through annual passion plays but also by 'inflicting bodily pain on themselves'.[29] After ten days of mourning, building up to the crescendo of Ashura, audiences hearing or seeing these stories commonly cry out or weep, especially when they are reminded of the sufferings, the thirst and the killing of Husayn, his family and his followers. For his installation entitled *Ta'ziyeh* (first performed in 2002) the Iranian film director Abbas Kiarostami captured the powerful emotional impact of these plays upon rural audiences by filming them as they watched these traditional dramas. This dramatic piece illustrates the powerful connection developed between performers and audiences who, as the tragic tale unfolds, are increasingly drawn into the world created by the *Ta'ziyeh*.

In most Shi'ite villages, many flagellants will process through the streets on the anniversary of Husayn's death, punishing themselves for 'the betraying of the Prophet's grandson'.[30] In some processions women carry water as symbolic reminders of how the Karbala martyrs suffered from agonising thirst, prevented from reaching the Euphrates by Yazid's 'cruel' troops (the evil ruler responsible for the 'butchery' at Karbala). Several murals also draw upon this element of the story, with one depicting a soldier-like figure up to his knees in water pouring out water from a glass jug clutched close to his body. It is reminiscent of pictures of Christ's wounded side where blood gushes from his body, though in this case it is water. In the midst of what looks like a waterfall cascading from the jug, there are petals from a red flower. In some processions women also carry spades, to act as a reminder that Husayn and his followers were initially left unburied.[31] Husayn is widely referred to as 'Chief', 'Lord' or 'Prince of Martyrs', and his picture, along with one of his father Ali, is sometimes carried aloft in these processions. Every year on *Ashura*, in some towns and cities a 'wooden heart-shaped structure covered with a black cloth and with verses embroidered around a central medallion in praise of Imam Husayn' is carried by mourners in the 'heart of the procession'.[32] Known as a *nakhl* (literally translated as 'palm tree'), this represents the coffin of Husayn. It is not only in mourning processions that such representations and symbols are displayed. Pictures of both Husayn and Ali can also be found in many graveyard cabinets of martyrs killed during the Iran–Iraq war. At least one mural in Tehran shows Husayn holding an unnamed war martyr.[33] It is also possible the prostrate figure is intended to evoke memories of Husayn's martyred son, Ali. Even if it is not, the message is clear: the martyr will be rewarded in heaven and welcomed into the embrace of the 'Prince of Martyrs' himself, Imam Husayn. The writing at the bottom, loosely translated, includes the claim that 'the honour of Martyrdom is passed down from the prophetic household', thereby connecting less well-known martyrs with the Prophet's family (figure 2.4).

The significance of Husayn's death over 1,300 years ago is contested both within and beyond Shi'ite Islam, especially within the Sunni tradition. Commonly read and recited texts retelling the story of Karbala, such as Husayn Wa'iz Khwansari's popular early sixteenth-century book *Meadow of the Martyrs* (*Rawdat al-Shuhada*, c.1502), have retained their popularity in many different settings. Several writers have also claimed that Husayn's role has changed within Shi'ite Islam, evolving from an 'intercessor' figure to a revolutionary 'example' who resists unjust rulers.[34] The story of his death has been put to multiple uses. For some it is used to evoke devotion, lamentation and even physical self-harm in an attempt to atone for what happened at Karbala. The awareness of guilt is underlined by the fact that no assistance was sent to the seventy-two men led by Husayn and trapped in the searing heat of the desert. In contrast to this comparatively passive pietism, his story has more recently been used as an example of heroic activism to emulate. Here is a model fighting martyr. This story was put to use before and during the 1979 revolutionary period and was therefore easily translatable into the conflict against Iraq. Moreover, some even suggested that, by following in Husayn's footsteps, contemporary martyrs were helping to atone for the past sin of failing to offer assistance and even to prepare the world for the return of the twelfth Imam.

Husayn is by no means the only martyr from an earlier age remembered and celebrated in Iran. For example, Husayn's father, Ali, may have been the Prophet's son-in-law and cousin, but he was still assassinated in the mosque of Kufa (661). Ali's death is commemorated on the nineteenth night of Ramadan, two

Figure 2.4 Mural, *Imam Husayn Holds an Anonymous War Martyr*. This mural is on one of Tehran's busiest roads: the Modarres Highway at the Resalat Street exit. Photograph courtesy of Christiane Gruber.

days after he was 'struck on the head with a poisoned sword' by an assassin from Egypt as he 'entered the mosque of Kufa to perform the morning prayer'.[35] In Iran, where over 90 per cent of the population are Shi'a, the stories relating to Karbala, especially the martyrdom of Husayn, and to a lesser extent the martyrdom of his father Ali, along with beliefs associated with the hidden twelfth Imam (Muhammed Al-Mahdi), resonate in many people's imagination. This is because reference to these stories regularly found their way into public sermons, political speeches, radio broadcasts, university lectures and classroom lessons. Murals that reference these stories, well known at the time among Iranians, draw upon a rich semiotic reservoir of meaning.

The visual depictions are produced within a particular communicative context, and they stand within these traditions of belief and practice. They are further illuminated when studied alongside the speeches of Iranian leaders such as Khumayni, Khamini'i and Rafsanjani. Saskia Gieling's study, *Religion and War in Revolutionary Iran,* is based upon careful study of numerous such sermons and public addresses. Gieling demonstrates how the leaders repeatedly celebrated Husayn as a 'revolutionary war hero who had fought against tyranny and striven for the preservation and revival of Islam'. In these speeches, the war is also depicted as a 're-enactment of the martyrdom of Husayn at Karbala'. Such accounts stand in sharp contrast to the 'traditional interpretation of Husayn's martyrdom which held that Husayn's sacrifice was a unique and inimitable event in history, beyond the capacity of human beings to follow'.[36] Individual martyrs are celebrated and portrayed as following in the footsteps of Husayn. Martyrdom in *jihad* is glorified as 'the most certain way of receiving God's reward and obtaining a place in paradise'.[37] For Khomeini, martyrdom 'for the cause of God was ... the ultimate perfection a human being could attain'.[38]

Khomeini and other religious leaders (such as Ali Khamenei, Khomeini's successor as supreme leader of Iran) regularly drew upon what Kamran Aghaie described as the 'Karbala Paradigm' in their sermons. For instance, at Friday prayers in Tehran on 13 October 1983, Khomeini included in one of his homilies, 'O Creator. Cause us to be among the people of Karbala'.[39] To which his listeners replied, 'Amen'. These sermons, at the University of Tehran, were widely disseminated by Iranian radio and television, as well as being reproduced in newspapers and books. Aghaie traces the different uses and evolution of the Karbala Paradigm, showing how the post-revolutionary leaders of the Islamic republic frequently referred to Karbala and Husayn's martyrdom in their addresses. They used such references and associated rituals as a way of reinforcing their hold on power, promoting particular kinds of ethical behaviour and encouraging the population towards celebrating martyrdom in the war. While other martyrs, such as those killed by Iraqi bombings of the cities, were recognized, the highest honour or 'exaltation' was reserved for 'battlefield martyrs'.[40] These speeches celebrating martyrdom contributed to the communicative environment in which the murals and posters of related themes were viewed. By connecting contemporary martyrdom stories with sacred narratives, Iranian leaders were able to encourage others to join the fight, and grieving relatives were able to see that the death of their son, brother or father was not a pointless waste in a seemingly endless war, but rather a religiously significant sacrifice.

Resisting enemies

Initially, Iranian resistance against the powerful forces that they faced relied heavily upon many soldiers being willing to sacrifice themselves. At the start of the Iran–Iraq war, the Iranian army faced a better-equipped enemy. Iraq's forces benefited from direct and indirect support from the superpowers of the day, both the USA and Russia. The 1979 revolution was widely seen as a destabilising event in the region, which threatened the security of the entire Middle East. Other local powers, such as Saudi Arabia and Kuwait, provided considerable unseen support to Saddam Hussein's Iraqi forces. For the new and comparatively insecure regime in Iran, the invasion over a 400-mile front was an 'imposed war' by Iraq that allowed the leadership to unify the nation in what was commonly portrayed as a holy war. Some observers believe that after they had regained lost territory in 1982 the Iranian leadership prolonged the conflict in order to secure their hold on power,[41] while other historians believe that the leadership became 'captive to their own rhetoric'.[42] So, by turning this into a holy war where Iranian Muslims had already sacrificed so much to resist the evil Iraqi followers of 'Satan', then nothing short of complete victory was acceptable. The policy to prolong the war and invade Iraq, even after all lost territory was regained, was followed in the face of opposition from within the Iranian religious and military leadership who wanted to accept the comparatively generous terms for peace offered by Iraq and conclude the war.[43]

While they might not have had the military equipment, Iran had a rapidly growing population of around 40 million in 1980, nearly three times larger than Iraq's, who throughout Iran were encouraged in multiple ways to be ready to give their lives as martyrs. The story of 13-year-old Hossein, discussed earlier, is but one of many stories about young martyrs. This is reflected in several posters that were turned into murals and vice versa. For example, one image from the 1980s depicts a young boy with his back to the viewers, facing a host of tanks on the horizon. Like a metallic tidal wave they come crashing towards him, too many to count. Both the clouds above and the tanks below are beginning to encircle him. He stands amidst red, white and golden flowers, with a red 'head-scarf' wrapped around his head. Directly above him, a break in the clouds reveals blue sky; in front of him, on the horizon, golden light beckons him forwards. His arms, out to the side, and his hands, open, speak of his readiness to face what looks like certain death. There is not a hint of fear in the face of such overwhelming odds. It is as if he willingly accepts the storm before him, safe in the knowledge of a brighter future that awaits him as a martyr.

This depiction resonates with the story of Husayn, as he faced a force of overwhelming power in 680. Nonetheless, the anonymity of the single figure, only a back view visible, invites viewers to imagine themselves standing in his place. Such invitations were made real by recruiters who visited schools telling the Karbala story like a 'fairytale adventure' to children barely teenagers, encouraging these young listeners to take their place in the heroic epic. They would be teased by their peers, as well as vilified and threatened by the recruiters, if they refused to join up.[44] Many children and young men needed little encouragement, such was the collective enthusiasm reinforced on many levels. In a similar way to boys during the First World War, many Iranian youngsters lied about their age in order to be allowed to join the army. In the autumn of 1982, Khomeini declared that youngsters did not even need the permission of their parents to join up and go to war.[45]

Numerous other pictures produced during the war have at their centre the peaceful and accepting figure or face of a martyr. Their uncomplaining acceptance of death gives them power over multiple adversaries. The picture by Kazem Chalipa (born 1957), entitled 'Blood Vanquishes the Sword', goes a step further. Chalipa's pictures were commonly reproduced as posters and then murals after the 1979 revolution and during the Iran–Iraq war. At first sight it is difficult to make out what this image represents. On closer inspection it becomes clear that at the centre of the picture is a dark tank. It poses no obvious threat, as this single tank is encircled not by other technological weapons of war, but rather by a spiral of white figures. They are depicted standing shoulder to shoulder, but all are headless. The white robes of the closest circle of figures to the tank are turning red, a sign of blood spilt by martyrs. The technological power of the tank is depicted as worthless in the face of this symbolically charged field of martyrs.

Here is an example of what Imam Khomeini described as 'blood overcoming the sword'. Many members of the Iranian leadership reiterated this point. For Ali Akbar Hashemi Rafsanjani, Supreme Defence Council leader, the 'faith of the Islamic troops is stronger than Iraq's superior firepower'. In blunter terms, 'the "dying power", the willingness to make the ultimate sacrifice, became a stronger force than the "killing power"'.[46] The belief was widely promoted that, through the sheer force of numbers prepared to sacrifice themselves as martyrs, the technological superiority of Iraq could be overcome. 'The Iranians compensated for their inferior equipment by encouraging religious fervour, sustaining a level of casualties not seen since the Western Front during the First World War. In official panegyrics, martyrdom was glorified for its own sake'.[47] After the lost territory was regained in 1982, the objective was no longer defensive resistance but rather conquest and complete victory. Up until 1984, Iranian military tactics included full-frontal assaults by poorly equipped children charging towards the Iraqi lines. The result: thousands of youngsters lost their lives.[48]

The images produced during the war were part of a wider campaign to persuade Iranians that there was no more honourable way to die than to give up your life in a war against the historic Sunni enemy. Their leader, Saddam Hussein, was regularly vilified or demonised in cartoons and pictured as a modern-day Yazid. While the USA, Israel and Iraq were also commonly associated with Yazid, as mentioned earlier it was Hussein (even more than President Jimmy Carter) who replaced the Shah as the figure to hate and fight against. He was a contemporary Yazid whom the Iranians confronted today. Ironically, Hussein's invasion, which had intended to capitalise upon the divisions within post-revolutionary Iran, had the opposite effect, allowing the Iranian regime to consolidate its hold on power. Iranians were united together in a war of supposed self-protection. Several accounts underline the righteous quality of the local martyrs fighting against Iraqi infidels. This characterisation of the enemy as infidels allowed the Iranian leadership to define the conflict as a *Jihad*, or Holy War, and place martyrdom at the centre of the state's wartime policy.

Death on the battlefield, as underlined earlier, was commonly depicted as the ultimate form of martyrdom in such a war. This was not to be a cause of fear, but rather should be embraced fearlessly. Khomeini asked: 'Can anyone who believes in the world beyond be afraid? ... We must thank God if He confers on us the honor of dying in the Holy Battle. Let us thrust our way into the ranks of the martyrs in our hordes ... if we have been afraid, this means that we don't believe in the world beyond'.[49] At school, children were given plastic keys painted gold and told that 'if they went to war and were lucky enough to die', the 'key would get them into heaven'.[50] Many would die as machine gun fodder or human mine clearers on the battlefields, reputedly hoping for heaven. Several of the war posters and murals include glimpses or hints of paradise.

In a related poster the dark cloud-filled sky is opened, revealing golden light beyond. Above the dark debris-filled battlefield a bearded soldier looks as if he is sleeping in the clouds. Like many other pictures, this was replicated on commemorative stamps. Other images contrasted the battlefield with flower and fruit-filled gardens, which are depicted as calm and restful. In one picture the body has vanished (figure 2.5) and all that is left is a helmet in a tulip field. The sun is on the horizon, illuminating banners, which include verses from the Quran.[51] In this way the battlefield is transformed into a place of peace.

Symbolising death

By no means are all of the murals so peaceful. One of the most striking and disturbing images has at its centre a woman, wearing a chador, holding a corpse. Entitled *Devotion (Yaqin)* and painted by Kazim Chalipa in 1980,[52] the corpse's underside is drenched in blood. The blood takes on a form of its own, turning into the shape of a giant open tulip. After the 1979 Revolution and during the Iran–Iraq war, the red tulip became the most common symbol used to represent martyrdom. This is not surprising given the fact that within the Shi'a tradition tulips are commonly used to symbolise martyrdom, based on the longstanding belief that where the blood of a martyr is spilt, a red tulip will grow. The tulip, as symbol of martyrdom, has a long and complex literary history in Iran. The idea is found not only in accounts of Husayn's martyrdom, but also in the vast epic poem *Shahnameh (King's Tales)*. Written around 1000 by Ferdousi, a Persian poet, it comprises over 60,000 couplets. In one of its stories, it recounts how, after one character named *Siyavash* was killed, a red flower grows from his blood. Given the red flower and red tulip's common appearance in Iranian poetry and literature, this means that it is an easily recognisable symbol. At the centre of the current Iranian flag is red Arabic calligraphy, meaning 'Allah', shaped in the outline of a tulip.[53] Tulips are depicted in many other martyrdom murals. They are also to be found in earlier posters produced in support of the 1979 revolution. For example, an Iranian artist, Morteza Momayez, depicted three tulips in the form of clenched fists, with this quotation from a poem: 'tulips have blossomed from the blood of the nation's youth'.[54] Tulips often appear in murals or posters of soldiers killed during the war. They are depicted around the face of a martyred soldier, emerging out of the smoke of battle and even replacing the martyrs themselves with headbands around their petals (figure 2.6).

Figure 2.5 Mural, *Helmet in Tulip Field*. This huge mural is on Taleqani Street, close to the site of the former American Embassy in Tehran. It includes phrases from the Koran, celebrating the oneness of God, as well as an indirect reference to the Karbala story, and common refrains such as 'Hail Husayn' and 'Down with the USA'. Above the picture, Khomeini's successor Seyyed Ali Khamane'i is quoted, roughly translated it declares: 'Every martyr is a banner for independence and an honour to the nation'. Photograph courtesy of Eefje Blankevoort.

Figure 2.6 Devotion (also titled as *Certitude of Belief* or *Altruism*), c.1981. Courtesy of the Special
Collections Research Center, The University of Chicago Library, (Middle

This picture of a woman holding a bloodied corpse goes even further. Beneath the curve of the corpse in her arms, a line of smaller tulips fall away into the distance. The first contains a small curled-up foetus in its womb-like bulb. On the opposite side, a column of soldiers holding guns march towards the viewer. Behind these two processions stand a cluster of four stakes, two on each side, and tied to each is a blindfolded figure. They slump down to the side, presumably executed martyrs. Some scholars believe that the picture is entitled *Yaqin*, meaning 'certitude of belief', while others that it is *Ithar*, translated as 'giving in abundance' or simply 'altruism'.[55] In the lower half of the picture, soaked in various shades of blood red, giving is explicitly depicted. The mother figure gives her soldier son. By producing and then giving her offspring, she is contributing altruistically to the war effort, as they will become soldiers, many of whom will give their own lives as martyrs.

The redness in the lower half of picture contrasts sharply with the white figures above. Directly behind the women is a white horse, with a mounted headless figure holding a scimitar in one hand and presumably the Quran in the other. He represents the leader or 'prince of martyrs', Imam Husayn. Behind him stand three rows of white robed headless martyrs. They are either waiting or moving towards heaven. This is represented by a lighter tulip-shaped set of lines, encompassing a single hand with its index figure pointing upwards beyond the picture itself. All this is set beneath a prayer niche, or *mihrab*, which includes quotations from the Koran such as: 'To him who fights in the cause of Allah whether he is slain or gets victory soon shall we give him a reward of great [value]'.[56]

This depiction therefore celebrates not only the martyrs giving their lives but also the mothers giving their children. Khomeini commonly celebrated this latter generosity in his speeches, where he affirmed both their desire to give their offspring as martyrs and the power of the Ashura rituals in nurturing mothers who would hold onto this vision of martyrdom.[57] Their self-sacrificing actions are validated by the foundational martyr figure of Husayn, who gave his life at Karbala over 1,300 years ago. The blood-drenched realities of birth and death are balanced by the softer white symbolism of a more peaceful end in heaven. The shape of the central part of the picture is reminiscent of Trinitarian depictions, showing not only the Mother holding her dead son but also the Father behind and the Spirit hovering in the background. This is also redolent of Renaissance Pietà portrayals, showing Mary holding the dead body of Jesus, though, unlike the Pietà, this Mother figure does not look overwhelmed by grief.[58]

Several other portrayals appear to be drawing upon the Pietà motif. For instance, consider G.H. Taheree's *Another Birth*. Unlike *Altruism*, this picture contains only a hint of blood. At its centre is the white-robed body of a young man. His eyes are closed. His pale death-like complexion stands in sharp contrast to the red band around his forehead and the longer red scarf tied around his waist. He is held not by Mary, but by his mother – clad all in black. Her eyes, nearly closed, look down on this face. One of her hands supports his forehead. An angel, dressed in white, holds his legs, while another angelic figure hovers behind, taking his hand

and pointing him on towards a heavenly white light in the sky. In the background a tree laden with green leaves flourishes; another branch closer to a second unsmiling woman is beginning to bloom into new life. This is not the 'man of sorrows', of late medieval or Renaissance depictions of the suffering of Christ, but a peaceful corpse being borne towards another world.

Consoling grief

As suggested earlier, a sense of peacefulness pervades many portrayals of those left behind. Many depictions are located in a war cemetery, which could be any of hundreds in Iran, though again the mother figure plays a central role. In this striking depiction, a woman holds a young girl on her lap, and points towards the inscription on the flat gravestone. Above, as is common on many individual memorials, is a picture of the departed – presumably the father of the three children in the picture. The girl concentrates intently, while the two young boys look on. The taller boy has a gun slung over his shoulder, a red flower, perhaps a tulip, protruding out of the barrel of his gun. He looks defiantly out towards the viewer. Here is the new head of the family, hand on his younger brother's shoulder, ready for action and himself carrying a visual symbol of martyrdom. By contrast the other boy looks more forlorn, his shoulders slightly hunched with grief. Wearing a jacket slightly too big for him, his hand grips the frame of his father's picture. He looks disconsolately down towards the bowls of fruit on his father's grave.

In the midst of such grieving and understated defiance the sources of comfort are made pictorially explicit through the figures of five ghostly apparitions standing behind this grieving family. They have halos, but their faces have been left blank. These five phantoms represent the Islamic Holy Family (presumably here made up of Muhammad, Ali, Fatemeh, Hasan and Husayn) and their presence is a way of showing that the human family will not be abandoned. There is a stillness in this picture, reflecting 'Shi'i Muslims' devotional allegiance to the prophet Muhammad and his family', even in the midst of grief.[59] While the setting is a cemetery, there is also a garden-like quality to the environment. Gardens are commonly perceived to be anticipations of paradise. These posters are not simply encouragements to enlist, to fight and to be martyred, they are also visual forms of consolation. Those left behind are not alone. Their loved ones have departed to a better place. In a poster by Hamid Qaderiyan, five women dressed in black, clustering around a grave, are joined by a shimmering white figure. This is Fatemeh, daughter of the Prophet Muhammad and mother of Husayn, who in this picture is bringing 'consolation to the grieving women at the grave of a martyred hero of the Iraqi war'.[60]

Other depictions of grief can be found displayed in public spaces. One of the best known was beside one of Tehran's busiest roads. A small girl holds a red rose, grieving over her dead father, who lies at her feet. She cries out: 'My martyr father – no rose smells sweeter than your memory!' Martyrs will not be forgotten. In the top right corner there is an opening in the sky, revealing a glimpse of heaven. Her father may have left her, but as a martyr he has gone to a better place.[61] There is less comfort to be found in a picture by J. Hamidee. Here a young woman, alone, rests her cheek on the empty uniform of her absent husband. Her fingers touch the sleeve of his green jacket. A grey scarf slung over the shoulder is close to her nose. It has flecks of red, reminiscent of drips of blood. Her mouth is open, her eyes half closed as she grieves the loss of her loved one. She looks as if she is weeping uncontrollably. Behind her a helmet and rifle hang in a cupboard. There is no celebration here of glorious sacrifice or courageous acts; simply an empty jacket on a hanger in the privacy of home. This intimate picture is titled 'The Odor of Paradise'. This title, as Evelijn Blankevoort suggests, 'changes the entire content of the image'.[62] In other words, the title transforms it into a sign signifying the ultimate destination of the killed soldier. Even with this title, there is something haunting about this image, revealing the heartbreak experienced by many who lost loved ones during the war.

While not on the same numerical scale of the First World War, the heartbreak experienced by thousands of people in Iran was no less real.[63] In spite of its title that speaks of 'paradise', this picture of a grieving widow resonates with the common human experience of loss. It invites the viewer to sympathise or identify with the woman's grief. The title may point towards the next life, but for those also grieving it has the potential to stir painful memories. There is evidence that publicly many widows or grieving mothers requested not condolences but congratulations on the martyrdom of their loved ones, but in private there was clearly considerable unstated grief. Khomeini encouraged *public* outpourings of grief: 'Weep, weep, if weeping brings you closer to God!'[64] Such grief was intended to draw followers closer to Husayn's sufferings and to avenge his martyrdom. By contrast, this image captures a rare moment of private grief, which in some cases appears to have fuelled questions about the military tactics employed and even the necessity of so many martyrdoms.

Contesting martyrdom

Roxanne Varzi's documentary film *Plastic Flowers Never Die* (2008), a personal account of her own return to the country of her birth, skilfully captures the way in which martyrdom is contested today within Iran. There are still those who work to preserve and promote the memory of those who sacrificed their lives during the war. In Varzi's documentary a man, employed by the government, is interviewed while repainting a celebratory mural. He states that 'We paint murals so that society doesn't forget'. He admits that he was too young to have fought himself, but he is the son of a martyr killed in the war. This is clearly a personal vocation, supported by the state. He is concerned that 'people are quickly forgetting martyrdoms' and that we are losing the 'aroma' and the 'colours' of martyrs. Another Iranian interviewee declares that the 'war is so important that it must not be forgotten'. By contrast, a young high-school student believes that 'my generation wants to escape anything to do with our war'. In this highly personal documentary, Varzi observes that the martyr museums appear empty while the murals fade.

Even the best-known martyr stories can disappear from collective memory.[65] In the prologue of this chapter I described the mural celebrating the young martyr Hossein Fahmideh, whose story was so widely circulated during and after the 1980–8 war. While his picture is opposite the main entrance of the University of Tehran, even his story is becoming less well known among students. In 2004 and 2007, the researcher Christine Gruber found that many university students who she spoke with had not scrutinised or even noticed the mural, and of this group some did not even know the story of this 13-year-old. Even more striking was the fact that 'these students voiced dismay, even hostility, towards the depicted subject stating that the twin subjects of martyrdom and war are no longer relevant or are of no interest to the young generation of the post-war period'.[66] As more than twenty years have passed since the end of the war, many of these students were born after the conflict was ended and therefore have no direct memories of what happened. Even for those who lived through the war, memories have faded. It is not surprising, therefore, that many people, especially the younger generation, when encouraged to consider the martyrdom murals, 'describe them as inappropriate, distasteful, obsolete, and, quite literally, behind the times'.[67]

In the last decade propaganda murals provoked even more hostile responses. As Pamela Karimi points out, during some street demonstrations they have become targets of vandalism expressing anti-regime sentiments. Sometimes fireworks or explosives have been used to damage murals. While Tehran produced around 33,000 wartime martyrs, only about 140 are found depicted on the murals. The result is that the families of martyrs, both those depicted and those not, 'complain about poor representation'. Even those who lost loved ones during the war have become critical of these depictions. For other Iranians, the use of murals for propaganda purposes is problematic, with many believing that murals 'should only serve to beautify the city'.[68] From 2001, the state-run 'Organisation for the Beautification of the City of Tehran' (known as *Sazman*) has attempted to take over the preservation and commissioning of all of Tehran's murals. The director of this organisation appears to be less than committed to preserving these martyrdom murals, though enthusiastic about beautifying the city through murals which include trees, sky, clouds and even balloons, thereby expanding the visual horizon and sense of urban space. Rather than speaking of death, these pictures become ways to create a sense of the burgeoning of nature amidst a busy cityscape. Recent mural artists are critical of their predecessors' work, going so far as to suggest that it 'poorly' represents 'the martyrs' and disrespects 'their mission'.[69] Symbols such as butterflies, surreal landscapes or even more abstract depictions have appeared in post-Khomeini Tehran, coinciding with the reforming presidency of Mohammad Khatami (1997–2005). While some younger Iranians have little time or interest in commemorating wartime martyrdoms, others do wish to create or preserve their memories, though perhaps in new and less direct ways. Drawing on the more mystical themes found amongst many ancient Persian poets, a 'martyr now is not depicted as a brave young man in battle but rather as a mystical bird'.[70] More permanent even than the murals, however, are the cemeteries. These appear to have had and continue to have a more significant impact upon both locals and visitors.

This is the case for de Bellaigue, whose memoir *In the Rose Garden of Martyrs* draws its title from the martyrs' cemetery in Isfahan (Esfahan). This houses the remains of at least 7,000 men killed during the Iran–Iraq war.[71] Here is a more permanent memorial to martyrs. In *Plastic Flowers Never Die*, Varzi observes how, unlike Western war cemeteries with countless identical white crosses, each memorial in Isfahan is unique. Like the other martyr burial spaces in Iran, an individual photograph marks each grave, acting as a reminder that each man in these rows and rows of graves had a unique life, cut short prematurely. More haunting still is what is revealed on the back of every one of these memorial photographs. A photograph of a single, bearded, unsmiling figure: Ayatollah Khomeini. This once charismatic leader, who himself never fought, is shown to be inextricably connected with the fate of each of these young soldiers, who fought because they were inspired by Khomeini's words and his followers' rhetoric. Varzi may have missed the war, but she appears haunted by the visible reminders of so many deaths.

Western journalists and writers tend to focus on other even more accessible memorials, especially the capital's martyrs' cemetery, which is about half an hour southwest of the centre of Tehran.[72] The *Behesht-e Zahra* cemetery, of which the martyrs' cemetery is only a part, consists of thousands of gravestones, of those who were killed not only during the Iran–Iraq war but also in the 1979 revolution. *Behesht-e Zahra* (*Zahra's* paradise), named after the daughter of the Prophet who was the mother of Husayn, is reputedly one of the world's largest cemeteries (figure 2.7). While some of the gravestones have only the picture of a dove and 'unknown' engraved in Farsi, many more elaborate collections preserved in a glass cabinets. These are made up of fading photographs, plastic flowers or other tattered mementos. In a vivid account entitled 'Iranian Lessons', for the *New York Times Magazine*, Michael Ignatieff describes this space as a 'vast city of the dead', with 'little shrines' that 'seem to go on forever, each one a family's attempt to confer immortality on some young man who died in the trenches at a place like Khorramshahr, the pinnacle of Iranian resistance to the Iraqi invaders'.[73] In many of the cabinets there is also a copy of the martyr's Quran, prayer beads and an Iranian flag. Through these simple symbols, as so often in the Islamic Republic of Iran, the Shi'ite faith and the state are brought closely together.

Journalists from the West have visited and used this graveyard in Tehran as the setting for their reports. During the war, many referenced the fountain in this graveyard that controversially used to flow with red-coloured liquid that represented the pouring out of the blood of martyrs. More recently, in one of a series of reports from Iran, the web journalist Kevin Sites describes and shows

Figure 2.7 Behesht-e Zahra cemetery, Tehran. Photograph courtesy of Eefje Blankevoort.

pictures of this cemetery in a photo essay.[74] He introduces his readers to two mothers who both lost sons in the Iran–Iraq war. On the one hand there is Iran Allahkarami, who states that 'It was for God's satisfaction', as 'our enemies were attacking our country. I say this on behalf of all martyrs' mothers. I'm not angered by the death of my sons'. He contrasts this description with Iran's friend Maryam Tavaghai, 'who has expressed misgivings about the war and the loss of her son, Hooshang'. He was a conscript, not a volunteer. In a couple of paragraphs Sites has turned even the martyrs' cemetery into a site of contest. Admittedly, while these mothers may debate the righteousness of the war, they nonetheless represent a significant body of opinion in Iran which believes martyrdom to be a highly honoured status. His report then goes on to quote the spokesperson of a comparatively new organisation, the Commemoration of Martyrs, which is supposedly recruiting hundreds of volunteers to act as suicide bombers against Israel. This swift move from discussing soldiers who fell in war as martyrs to describing volunteers who will kill themselves as martyrs is noteworthy, as it reflects the common blurring between different kinds of martyrdom. Some scholars have described this move as a development from 'warrior' or 'militant' forms of martyrdom to 'predatory' forms of martyrdom.[75]

With the advent of weblogs and other interactive websites, Western tourists and other visitors to these martyrs' cemeteries are able to record and make public their own personal responses. Some use their photographs to support their assertions and others use their descriptions to make a rhetorical point. For example, one travel review of this cemetery by a British woman had the following headline: 'War! What is it good for? Absolutely NOTHING – say it again!'[76] More experienced Western journalists also use their descriptions of these war cemeteries to contest the value or interpretation of such martyrdoms. Robert Fisk's article on 'Voices from the martyrs' cemetery', in the *Independent*, describes how he encountered a number of Iranian men at the cemetery, such as Mushtara Yussefi, who asserted that 'My dead father and brother fought for the *velayat e-faqih* … for the Imam's Islamic republic' and for the maintenance of specific ways of life.[77] Fisk explained that the '*velayat e-faqih* is the institution of the Supreme Guide – now Ayatollah Ali Khamenei' and then Fisk outlines his own personal response: 'I am stunned by all this. Did the dead of *Behesht Zahra* [sic], did the men whose bones are still crated up here from the old battlefields, really sacrifice themselves to keep Iran's women in chadors, to ensure that no real democracy could flourish amid the autocratic clergy loyal to Khomeini? Was it for this they died?'[78] Even as an outsider Fisk questions the way in which these deaths were and are being used in Iran.

Nevertheless, the power of Husayn's story and the loyalty it evokes can be detected in an extended *National Geographic* report on Iran. This included an interview by Fen Montaigne with Habib Eqbalpour, aged 70, and his wife, Zinat Parvaresh, 63. They lost two of their sons (one 17 and the other 21) in the Iran–Iraq war but were clearly proud of the sacrifice their two children had made: 'We are proud we lost our children … My sons are following in the path of Imam

Husayn, and when they are in the other world, they are helped by Imam Husayn'. Like others who lost family members in the Iran–Iraq war, several 'government foundations, including *the Martyrs' Foundation*, provide them with a free apartment and pay them a stipend of 360,000 rials a month (about $120)'.[79] While the financial support is valued, what gives them real pleasure and pride, is that their sons were martyrs standing in the tradition of a founding martyr, Husayn.

Conclusion

In this chapter I have considered how soldiers from the Iran–Iraq war were portrayed, remembered and celebrated as martyrs. These were some of the means by which men and youngsters were mobilised to fight and mourners were encouraged to hope. Connected to this process we have seen how Husayn's story was repeated and visually elaborated. This was by no means an entirely innovative practice. There is a long history in Iran of the rulers drawing upon Karbala stories, rituals and symbols to bolster their position and preserve the status quo. Some scholars believe that one of the reasons why the last Shah and Pahlavi's regime came to an end in 1979 was because of their inability 'to incorporate these symbols and rituals adequately into its program and ideology'. This stands in sharp contrast to Khomeini and his followers. As early as 1963, ten years previously, 'Khomeini drew analogies between the martyrdom of Husayn and the plight of the Iranian people'.[80] The wartime murals considered above are a more recent visual example of this connective process. A range of other media were used to amplify and to preserve the memories of these contemporary martyrs and to connect them with what is sometimes described in Iran as the 'tragedy' of Karbala, the killing of Husayn and his company. There has not been space in this chapter to consider the films and television programmes (and more recent video games) that were also produced to celebrate martyrdom and to link it with these earlier devotional martyrdom stories.[81] Part of the power of these narratives is the way in which they can be used not only to incite a population to fight but also to console a grieving populace. The visual culture that emerged out of the Iran–Iraq war provides further evidence of both the resonance and the flexibility of these stories.

The designation of 'martyr' is not always clear cut, nor is it without controversy.[82] Contesting who is and who is not a martyr continues to the present day. Some bloggers even deny that Neda, the young woman shot in the demonstrations in 2009, was a martyr, suggesting rather that she was an unfortunate bystander whose death has been commodified. Such debates are not new and they illustrate how quickly the term can become like a magnet for controversy. In this chapter, I have concentrated upon how depictions of 'martyrdom' were used in an attempt to mobilise and to consol the Iranian people during and soon after the Iran–Iraq war. Claiming soldiers are martyrs is not a unique phenomenon found only in Islam. During the Middle Ages, it was not uncommon for the Crusaders to be designated as 'martyrs' within the Christian tradition.[83] Nor are the writers emerging out of the Islamic or Christian traditions alone in using the term as a way of inciting violence. The executed leaders of the Irish Easter Rising in Dublin were also widely described in Ireland as 'martyrs'. In particular, those arrested and then executed in the stonebreakers' yard in Kilmainham jail, Dublin, were soon venerated as martyrs. In the same year, one of the less well-known English First World War poets, Robert Nichols, wrote his poem 'The Last Salute' while serving at Ypres in 1916, claiming that, even though he may die anonymous and alone, 'the soldier is the Martyr of a nation'.[84] In each of these cases, the martyrs celebrated were used not only as incitements to further violence or resistance but also as focal points for expressions of personal and collective grief. It was not long after the end of the First World War that the value and necessity of such martyrdoms were being contested. Similarly, for those commemorating the fallen of the Iran–Iraq war, such a description of a martyr as solely for the good of the nation would not be perceived as an example of a complete description. As we have seen, such Iranian fighters are commonly depicted as far more than simply martyrs for the army or the state; they were inextricably connected with a distant set of earlier martyrdoms. The resonance of these stories may explain why a new generation of Iranian students can overlook or even reject pictorial memorials of the Iran–Iraq war, while they continue fervently to celebrate more recent martyrdoms.

Chapter 3

Cultivating violence

Prologue

Not long ago I found myself in the back of a battered old car, juddering down a long bumpy road in Rwanda. It was dusty and hot. The journey was longer than expected. We were in search of one particular building. When we finally arrived at the small village of Ntarama, barefoot children dashed out of their houses, waving and laughing at us. It was a relief to get out of the car. I felt shaken up by the journey; but I would be far more troubled by what we found.

Large metal gates confronted us, with purple and white ribbons dangling from the railings. Walking into a tree-lined enclosure, we found ourselves facing three buildings. I stooped to go inside the largest of these. The church was smaller than I had expected. Above low wooden benches, drab clothes were hanging from the rafters. There was a musty smell of rotting fabric. As my eyes became accustomed to the darker interior, I could make out flowers on an altar at the front. On the wall, next to where we had come in, there were the remains of a poster of John Paul II. It was in tatters. To the left of this picture, there were ordinary metal shelves, reminiscent of those that you might find at a home improvement store. On these shelves, neatly organised in rows, were skulls. They stared out silently. One still had a metal rod protruding from its forehead. Beneath them were layers of different-sized bones (figure 3.1).

This was one of the many churches in Rwanda where thousands of Tutsis had fled for safety. Here in Ntarama, about 25 miles south of Kigali, over 5,000 Tutsi women, men and children sought sanctuary in or next to this place of worship. That was before many of their Hutu neighbours came, aided by gangs of young men, the *interahamwe*, mostly from Kigali. They carried tools intended for the farm – machetes, hoes or clubs – along with a few guns, tear gas and grenades. These were thrown into the church. Within a few hours, almost everyone was killed. For several years bodies, bones and other debris were left where they fell in April 1994. Like many of the other 'killing churches', it has been 'tidied up' and turned into a genocide memorial.

Figure 3.1 Ntarama Church interior, Rwanda. Photograph by Jolyon Mitchell.

Rwanda, a country famous for its 'thousand hills', its gorillas in the mist and its beauty, is now becoming better known for its hundreds or perhaps thousands of genocide memorials. For many, Rwanda has become inextricably connected with, even defined by, the 1994 genocide. Our guide in Ntarama hardly smiled as she showed us around twelve years later; not surprising, as she had lost her parents, her brothers and her sisters nearby. It is strange how small details can haunt you, shake you, inscribe themselves onto your memory: an open wooden chest full of children's notebooks, pens and rosaries hanging on a line above a pile of shoes (figure 3.2), a woven communion cup lying in the dust.

Walking around this and other memorials in Rwanda, it is hard to appreciate the sheer scale of the killing. Here was a quiet, shaded and tranquil space bearing solemn witness to one among thousands of unimaginable nightmares. Even though pictures of this church, both carpeted in bodies and after it was 'tidied up', are now easily available around the world on the web, there were no obvious signs of global or local media presence. On our way out, I asked the guide what I could do. Her response has stayed with me ever since, resonating with the stated aim of other genocide memorials and museums around the world. Her exhortation to action has informed my own reflection, teaching and research: 'Make sure you tell people what happened here. So it never happens again. Never again'.

Figure 3.2 Ntarama Church, pens and rosaries. Photograph by Jolyon Mitchell.

Introduction

My aim in this chapter is to go beyond simply describing what happened in Rwanda during and after the 1994 genocide, as this has been done in detail elsewhere.[1] My focus is upon the actual communicative process of 'telling', and how certain kinds of telling can contribute to cultivating violence. I will therefore investigate some of the ways that people both inside and outside Rwanda were told about what happened in 1994. Behind this analysis are a number of questions, including: What can be learnt from the uses of the local media in Rwanda at this time and the subsequent global coverage of the Rwandan genocide? As we shall see, the case of 'telling people about' the Rwandan genocide raises a number of important questions, including: What is the role of both local and global media in moments of confusion and violence? Given the importance attributed to religion, especially Catholicism, in Rwanda's recent history, it also raises questions about how religious expression and themes are drawn upon, adapted or ignored in the process of telling and promoting violence. Many churches, such as Ntarama, have not returned to their original use as places of worship. Instead they have been turned into memorials, places to visit, to preserve and remember (figure 3.3).

Figure 3.3 Ntarama Church, landscape sign explains how 'improvements' to the site will 'create a dignified memorial'. Photograph by Jolyon Mitchell.

This has turned some into contested spaces, with government and religious leaders wrestling for control over the memorials. In the discussion which follows, I analyse different kinds of telling: radio broadcasting, subverting and claiming, chatting and singing, publishing and naming, directing and inciting, reporting and interpreting, judging and assessing, and, in the final section, displaying.

Radio broadcasting

Some of the most chilling broadcasts in the history of radio emerged from Rwanda in the 1990s. *Radio-Télévision Libre des Mille Collines* (RTLM), One Thousand Hills Free Radio, which broadcast between July 1993 and July 1994, is frequently blamed for inciting the genocide that claimed over 800,000 lives during a hundred days in 1994.[2] In 'its scale and apparent impact, hate radio in Rwanda seemed to have no parallel since the Nazi propaganda for genocide'.[3] At the genocide's peak there were more than five deaths every minute in Rwanda: the rate of killing was three times as rapid as the murder of the Jews in the Second World War.[4] Unlike in Germany, where people were mostly transported to die in gas chambers away from their home communities, many Rwandan women, children and men died from *masu* (nail-studded clubs) or machete blows at the hands of neighbours in their own homes or nearby in local churches, hospitals, schools and at roadblocks.

What role did radio actually play in these intimate mass murders? Some early accounts claim that much 'of the responsibility for the genocide in Rwanda can be blamed on the media'.[5] More precisely, other scholars and journalists assert that when RTLM 'said it was time to kill people',[6] these orders were 'heeded' by 'hundreds of thousands'.[7] Daryl Li, for instance, suggests that, by 'articulating a coherent language of massacre, bringing listeners together as witnesses and performers, and infiltrating everyday routines, RTLM may even have been the key to transforming the Rwandan genocide from a state-led campaign into a mass-participatory nationwide project'.[8] Another researcher even claims that the existence of RTLM increased the number of killings during the genocide by around 9 per cent.[9]

By contrast, other scholars argue that the Rwandan genocide would have happened without the broadcasts of RTLM, and that blaming radio is one way of denying responsibility for what was an ethnocide.[10] For example, in *The Order of Genocide* Scott Strauss claims, on the basis of six months of interviews with many perpetrators in Rwanda, that, while the radio 'undoubtedly did play a critical role, particularly in tipping the power toward violence in some communities by signalling who had power and in linking genocidal violence to authority', Strauss found that 'the overwhelming majority of respondents said that the radio on its own did not cause them to participate'. Far more common was the claim by perpetrators that 'they joined the attacks because of face-to-face mobilization' and fear of invasion by the RPF (*Front patriotique rwandais*, Rwandan Patriotic Front).[11] The precise role of radio in the genocide remains a contested phenomenon and, while it is neither a new nor unique occurrence, the use of radio to express racial hatred and attempt to inspire ethnic violence remains one of the most disturbing examples of how the wireless can be misused.

This radio station was by no means the only local medium expressing hatred towards an ethnic minority, but it soon became one of the most popular. In the midst of both a civil war and genocide, RTLM offered listeners an account of reality, and increasingly blatant exhortations to act violently, that were profoundly at odds with the encouragement to love your enemy. By stereotyping, scapegoating and demonising the Tutsi and some moderate Hutus, as well as portraying RTLM as the defender of the previously victimised Hutu majority, this radio station helped to legitimise the slaughter of hundreds of thousands of innocent people. Many were murdered simply because they carried one wrong word in their identity card: '*batutsi*'. The role of radio in the Rwandan genocide may sometimes have been overstated as a way of deflecting legitimate criticism of previous colonial regimes, post-colonial governments and the non-intervention of powerful nations in the UN. Nevertheless, RTLM's broadcasters found fertile ground upon which to sow seeds of hatred. Many Rwandans appear, at best, to have turned a deaf ear on the call to hate their neighbour or, at worst, to participate in the killing. Some did this indirectly by providing logistical support, while others did this directly by turning 'ploughshares', or other farming tools, into weapons. RTLM is no more, but hate speech is far from extinct.[12] Religious beliefs are commonly drawn upon and distorted through public expressions of hatred of the 'other'. The problem of how mediated hate speech be resisted remains a pressing one for anyone concerned with the relation between media and religion. Rwanda provides an important case for reflecting on both past and current situations where media are used to incite hatred and violence.

In a country where nearly 50 per cent of the population could neither read nor write, radio was a vital form of public communication.[13] Radio appears also to have been widely trusted in Rwanda, with several surveys in the 1980s showing that the vast majority of the population believed that 'radio tells the truth'.[14] Television was expensive and, given the hilly terrain, it was almost impossible at that time to receive a clear terrestrial signal. By contrast, radio could reach nearly 90 per cent of the country. During the 1980s, the production of radios was subsidised by foreign donors and the MRND government,[15] who both sold sets at a reduced price and gave them away to party administrators, as well as more widely during elections. Some of these radios could only receive FM, thereby preventing many listeners from hearing international broadcasters based outside the country who used short wave. In 1970 there was about one radio to every 120 people, but by 1990 this had increased to one radio to every 13 people.[16] With this greater availability, radio increasingly became a focal point for entertainment, information and discussion in Rwanda.[17] With the founding of RTLM in July 1993, Rwanda's airwaves were filled with a new sound. It soon became Rwanda's most popular radio station, and in the months preceding the genocide radios tuned to RTLM were to be found both in homes and 'in offices, cafes, bars and other public gathering places, even in taxis'.[18] In the midst of what some saw as a civil war and others an invasion, RTLM contributed to the development of an increasingly tense public sphere, which provided a forum for extremist speakers to articulate old grievances and new anxieties.

Subsequent journalistic accounts of the Rwandan genocide pointed to locally produced radio broadcasts as a significant catalyst for the explosion of violence.[19] Other media, particularly the Hutu extremist newspaper *Kangura* ('Wake him up'), were also blamed, but it was the radio broadcasts of RTLM, and to a lesser extent Radio Rwanda, that were deemed to be particularly culpable. One Canadian journalist described how 'Hutus could be seen listening attentively to every broadcast ... They held their cheap radios in one hand and machetes in the other, ready to start killing once the order had been given'.[20] Other journalists in the West also highlighted the part played by RTLM in the genocide. The *Washington Post*, for example, as early as 7 April quoted a RTLM broadcast that warned Tutsi in Rwanda, 'You cockroaches must know you are made of flesh! We won't let you kill! We will kill you!" *Associated Press* on 25 April quoted a UN spokesman in Kigali claiming that 'Radio RTLM is calling on militias to step up the killing of civilians'. Such reports did little to galvanise action against the station in the West. They also reflect a presupposition expressed in many parts of the Western press that the media inevitably have a powerful influence on how people behave. The belief that radio was partly to blame for the Rwandan tragedy has been reinforced in other contexts. For example, a short French film, *Itsembatsemba: Rwanda One Genocide Later* (Alexis Cordesse and Eyal Sivan, 1996) depicts how RTLM began to broadcast with the assistance of the government and then played a central part in 'the unleashing and the coordination' of the genocide. Recent feature films about the genocide, such as *Hotel Rwanda* (2004) also highlight the role of the radio. Nevertheless, the actual role that RTLM played in the Rwandan genocide remains not only a debated phenomenon but also a point of judicial inquiry.

Subverting and claiming

The power of radio to break down barriers of space and time has long been recognised.[21] It is by no means a unique characteristic, but given the dominance of radio in the Rwandan media environment it takes on greater significance. For example, one local politician, Léon Mugesera, made a now infamous speech over sixteen months prior to the genocide, on 22 November 1992, warning his audience to remain vigilant. He referred to the Tutsi as *Inyenzi* (cockroaches) and asserted that they had 'threatened the security of the nation' by sending their children to join the RPF. They should be exterminated, and if the justice system fails to punish them then people should 'take the law into their own hands' and 'we ourselves will take care of massacring these gangs of thugs'. His desire to see them sent home, on an 'express trip' back to Ethiopia via the river Nyabarongo,[22] is particularly haunting given that many Tutsi were killed and then thrown into rivers during the genocide.[23] Mugesera encourages his listeners to overlook Matthew 5.39, so that if they are 'provoked, they should forget the biblical notion of turning the other cheek and instead should meet violence with greater violence'. Mugesera 'corrects' biblical texts to suit his own purposes, asserting that the lessons of the Bible had been transformed: 'I tell you that the Gospel has already changed in our movement. If someone gives you a slap, give him two in return, two fatal ones'.[24] Mugesera's sentiments were later frequently repeated on RTLM. His speech was also tape-recorded and broadcast on national radio, while cassettes of his speech were copied and circulated in Kigali.[25] Through recording and radio technologies, his words attempting to incite violence were able to travel further and last longer. Two decades later the web makes it possible for similar local hate speech to be made available globally. His incitements are captured on a display in the Kigali Genocide Memorial Centre (figure 3.4).

Mugesera's corruption of a specific biblical text by Hutu power propagandists was by no means an isolated incident.[26] The 'ten commandments' published in several extremist newspapers, including *Kangura*, with extracts regularly repeated on air, exemplifies how a biblical text is mimicked, corrupted and reversed in order to heighten mistrust of the Tutsi people. It is an extremist manifesto: any Hutu who marries or befriends a Tutsi woman, or does business with a Tutsi is

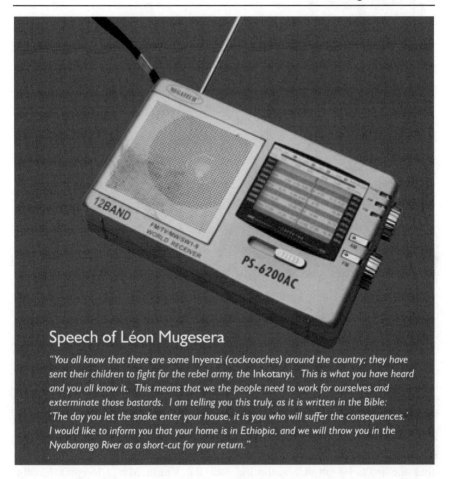

Speech of Léon Mugesera

"You all know that there are some Inyenzi (cockroaches) around the country; they have sent their children to fight for the rebel army, the Inkotanyi. This is what you have heard and you all know it. This means that we the people need to work for ourselves and exterminate those bastards. I am telling you this truly, as it is written in the Bible: 'The day you let the snake enter your house, it is you who will suffer the consequences.' I would like to inform you that your home is in Ethiopia, and we will throw you in the Nyabarongo River as a short-cut for your return."

Figure 3.4 Display of *Radio* and extract from Mugesera's speech as part of the 'Propaganda' display at the Kigali Genocide Memorial Centre. Courtesy of the Aegis Trust.

to be called a traitor. The attack upon intimate relations between ethnic groups also recurred on RTLM, where Tutsi women were often represented as agents for the RPF. They were used to lead Hutu men astray. According to these 'commands', the education system must be dominated by Hutu and the army 'should be exclusively' Hutu. An end to mercy towards the Tutsi, and loyalty to the Hutu cause, are marks of solidarity against the common enemy of the Tutsi.[27] According to the eighth commandment, 'Hutus must cease having any pity for the Tutsi'. Any sense of love or empathy for your Tutsi neighbour is to be erased, and replaced by a cold distance because the Tutsi is the enemy within.[28]

One witness at the so-called 'media trial', who had worked at the Ministry of Information, described hearing the 'ten commandments' broadcast and commented upon several times on RTLM.[29] He believed that the aim of broadcasting them was to encourage all Hutus in Rwanda to unite around 'a single fighting goal' and not to develop relationships with Tutsis. He also thought that these commandments were one of the reasons why some 'men started killing their Tutsi wives, or children of a mixed marriage killed their own Tutsi parents'.[30] One of the journalists who worked for *Kangura* believed that the promotion of the 'ten commandments' actually led to the Hutu 'perceiving the Tutsi as enemies instead of seeing them as citizens, and the Tutsi also starting seeing the Hutu as a threat'.[31] It is not possible to prove that the publication of the 'ten commandments' was such a pivotal moment in ethnic relations, but other local observers recognised that their publication sent shock waves among the people.[32]

RTLM was not the only medium to try to subvert traditional religious belief. For example, one cover of *Kangura* consists of a deceptively peaceful picture of the Holy Family (figure 3.5). Mary looking down at her Son says: 'Son of God, you were just born at Christmas. Do all that you can to save the Hutu of Burundi from death'. A childlike and angelic looking Jesus replies: 'I will tell them to love each other as God loves them'.[33] In response, Joseph on the right of the picture retorts: 'No, rather, tell the Hutu of the world to unite'. The headline above the image leaves little doubt who has won the argument: 'God is mobilized for the worldwide battle of the Hutu'. The encouragement to love your neighbour, on the basis of God's love for humanity, is portrayed as a force not powerful enough to protect the Hutus in Burundi. Joseph's statement, 'tell the Hutu of the world to unite', takes precedence over the words of both Mary and Jesus. Joseph offers Hutu unification as the only real solution to preventing a rerun of the 1972 extermination of over 100,000 Hutus in Burundi. Reminding the reader of past crimes against the Hutu people, the traditional Catholic iconography is subverted by the captions, showing that the male Joseph has authority over the Virgin Mary. Joseph's forceful assertion resonates with the extreme violence perpetrated against thousands of women during the genocide. The headline unequivocally enlists God to the Hutu cause.

Several radio broadcasters would also later claim God's support for the defence of the Hutu regime. In contrast to the image discussed above, Marian piety was sometimes used to support the Hutu cause. 'RTLM announcer Bemeriki maintained that the Virgin Mary, said to appear from time to time at Kibeho church, had declared that "we will have the victory". In the same vein, the announcer Kantano Habimana said of the Tutsi, "Even God himself has dropped them"'.[34] In another broadcast, near the end of the 1994 genocide, Habimana celebrates: 'Come let us sing: "Come, let us rejoice: the *Inkotanyi* have been exterminated! Come dear friends, let us rejoice, the Good Lord is just". The Good Lord is really just, these evildoers, these terrorists, these people with suicidal tendencies will end up being exterminated'.[35] Here name calling and demonising the enemy is fused into a mock liturgical chant. The manipulation of

Figure 3.5 'Holy Family' front cover of *Kangura,* no. 3, July 1990, including the statement by Joseph in Kinyarwandan: 'tell the Hutu of the world to unite'. Courtesy of Kigali National Genocide Archive and Library.

theistic language and religious symbols for violent ends is by no means unique to the Rwandan genocide, but the broadcasting of an inverted 'turn the other cheek', the Hutu 'ten commandments' and claims that God has deserted the enemy and justly supported their extermination, illustrates how religious expression was manipulated for nurturing violent ends.

Chatting and singing

Radio-Télévision Libre des Mille Collines (RTLM) began broadcasting on 8 July 1993, nearly a year before the start of the genocide. At first it was only heard in and around Kigali, by 1994 it could be heard over most of the country. The first three months of RTLM's broadcasting (July until October 1994) was dominated by music. RTLM started by 'endearing itself to the people' by using popular music to help win an audience. This music was referred to as 'hot', and was predominantly Congolese in origin.[36] Also originating from Cameroon and the Caribbean, the music was complemented by some light-hearted and comparatively innocuous comment. The former director of Radio Rwanda, Jean-Marie Higirio, explained RTLM's early success in the following terms:

> The broadcasts were like a conversation among Rwandans who knew each other well and were relaxing over some banana beer or a bottle of Primus [the local beer] in a bar. It was a conversation without a moderator and without any requirements as to the truth of what was said. The people who were there recounted what they had seen or heard during the day. The exchanges covered everything: rumours circulating on the hills, news from the national radio, conflicts among local political bosses ... It was all in fun. Some people left the bar, others came in, the conversations went on or stopped if it got too late, and the next day took it up again after work.[37]

At first RTLM employed eight educated and mostly experienced journalists who skilfully adapted a Western-disc-jockey-style presentation and talk-show format for a Rwandan context. Globalisation was put to local uses. The broadcasters had links with or were members of extremist parties, but initially their approach was far more subtle than the often quoted and possibly mythical cry: 'The grave is only half full; who will help us to fill it up?'[38] RTLM's airtime was filled with a mixture of popular music interspersed with coarse jokes, banter, laughter, personal reflections, extended interviews and phone-ins from the audience. It 'revolutionised radio in Rwanda'.[39] Often eschewing French, RTLM employed the slang of the Rwandan street and the language of Rwanda's two main ethnic groups, Kinyarwanda.[40]

A relaxed, informal approach pervaded the station's output, and as such it had no real competition in Rwanda. They described themselves as 'radio by the people, and for the people'. Given the more formal and somewhat slow style of Radio Rwanda it is not surprising that RTLM rapidly grew in popularity, particularly among the under-20s. It was widely listened to in Kigali, often by workers during office hours. One witness at the media trial described how young people were 'always' to 'be seen on the street with a radio listening to RTLM and that the broadcasts were a common topic of conversation' both at home and in public.[41] In Kigali it appears to have appealed both to office workers and to the jobless youngsters who were drawn into the youth wings of extreme Hutu paramilitary organisations, either the *interahamwe* (this is Kinyarwandan for 'those who work, stand, attack or fight together') or *Impuzamugambi* ('those who have the same or single goal').[42] 'Outside Kigali and other urban centres, the station is reported to have attracted people from urban backgrounds, administrators and teachers, rather than peasants from rural areas'.[43]

Even some fighting members of the Rwanda Patriotic Front (RPF) chose to listen to RTLM over their own Radio Muhabura ('Radio Beacon'), which tended towards being over-formal, explicitly propagandistic and simply countering the claims of Rwanda Radio. RTLM's light-hearted approach was balanced with more serious monologues, as well as interviews with academics or politicians. Throughout RTLM's short broadcasting life many of its broadcasters made skilful use of apparently authoritative sources to endorse their informal commentaries about the problems facing Rwanda. The station also made use of Georges Ruggiu, a white Belgian citizen, who regularly broadcast in French, quoting Machiavelli and playing European classical music. Many listeners believed that he was used to give further international authority to the station.[44]

Tutsis began to be demonized by RTLM through different forms of subtle stereotyping. In the same way that the Jews were accused of owning an 'unjustifiable' share of the wealth in Germany during the Holocaust, so the Tutsi were also inaccurately portrayed on RTLM as 'the ones having all the money'.[45] The kernel of truth here was that socio-economic exclusion had been used by both colonial and post-colonial rulers as a form of control over the majority of the population.[46] With the crash of the coffee market in 1987, a resulting famine in 1989, considerable overpopulation and a 40 per cent currency devaluation in 1990, many Rwandans were suffering from serious economic hardship in the years before the genocide. References to economic disparity in a country where approximately 16 per cent of the people held 43 per cent of the cultivated land in 1991, further accentuated feelings of injustice.

Beneath an apparently peaceful surface lay a growing body of anti-Tutsi rhetoric. Through songs, and later through comments and interviews, it echoed the extremist paper *Kangura*, which suggested that the Tutsi had infiltrated positions of power like 'snakes' in order to restore the old pre-1959 feudal regime where the Tutsi would once again control the country.[47] RTLM would often play songs that highlighted this supposed danger, such as the popular singer Simon Bikindi's *Bene Sebahinzi* ('The Descendants of Sebahinzi').[48] In this song Bikindi affirmed the importance of the 1959 revolution, where the Tutsi leadership was overthrown, as 'a heritage that should be carefully maintained … and transmitted to posterity'. The reason: 'the servitude, the whip, the lash, the forced work that exhausted the people, that has disappeared forever'. He exhorts the 'great majority', the descendants of Sebahinzi to 'remember this evil that should be driven as far away as possible, so that it never returns to Rwanda'.[49] Bikindi's songs distorted the history and politics of Rwanda to advance Hutu unity against the Tutsi. For example, another of his popular compositions was *Twasezereye*, composed in 1987, which meant 'we said goodbye to the feudal regime'. It was regularly played on Radio Rwanda in 1992, as well as on RTLM in 1993. '*Twasezereye* was a public call for Hutu solidarity in opposition to the Arusha [peace] accords'.[50] Accounts of RTLM which pay little attention to songs and music as both a persuasive force and expression of ethnic division are omitting a highly significant component in the station's popular appeal.

Many of Bikindi's compositions have a subtext, and are not explicitly violent, though for Rwandans the intended meaning is clear. For example, one of his songs that was repeatedly broadcast on RTLM, though banned on Radio Rwanda before the genocide, was his *Nanga Ba-Hutu* or *Je déteste ces Hutu* ('I Hate the Hutu'). He sang: 'I hate these Hutus, these de-Hutuized Hutus, who have renounced their identity, dear comrades'. He is referring here to those Hutus who married Tutsis. He then goes on to sing: 'I hate these Hutus, these Hutus who march blindly, like imbeciles. This species of naive Hutus who join a war without knowing its cause'. His target here is almost certainly a Hutu colonel and his force who changed sides and joined the RPF. 'I hate them and I don't apologize for that. Lucky for us that they are few in number … '[51] In short, Bikindi is referring to his own hatred for the Hutu who support the Tutsi. The tune of this song was extremely popular. According to one witness, the lyrics 'broadcast ethnic hatred' and later became a 'hymn' for the killings.[52] In March 1994, '*Interahamwe* and *Impuzamugambi* youth in their uniforms with the radio to their ear were omnipresent, singing songs very loudly, songs of Bikindi and others saying "We shall exterminate the enemies of the country"'.[53]

Publishing and naming

Kangura, described by one reader as 'The Bell of Death',[54] lived up to this name with its front page in the November 1991 edition (issue 26). On this cover there is a question in a vertical black box: 'What weapons shall we use to conquer the *Inyenzi* [cockroaches] once and for all?' This is answered by the stark picture of a machete (figure 3.6).

This cover was analysed and discussed in some detail by the International Criminal Tribunal for Rwanda (ICTR), who concluded that the message is clear: 'the machete should be used to conquer the *Inyenzi* once and for all'.[55] The first President of Rwanda, Grégoire Kayibanda, and one of the leaders of the 1959 Hutu revolution, is in the centre page and occupies most of the space.[56] Beneath the picture of the former President is the text 'How about re-launching the 1959 Bahutu revolution so that we can conquer the

Figure 3.6 'Machete' front cover of *Kangura*, no 26, c. November 1991. This cover was distributed free of charge in Bugesera in the weeks before the Bugesera massacre, which claimed hundreds of lives, in March 1992. Courtesy of Kigali National Genocide Archive and Library.

Inyenzi-Ntutsi?' In 1959 machetes had been used to kill many Tutsis and this cover appears to be calling its readers to a second revolution which will eradicate the enemy once and for all. At the top of the page is a simple headline: 'Tutsi: Race of God?' In this issue the Tutsi were actually characterised not as God's race, but as thieves, hypocrites, liars and killers. This cover was widely distributed in Bugesera, free of charge in February 1992, only a few weeks before the Bugesera massacres in March that claimed hundreds of lives.[57] This was one of four massacres in Rwanda that took place during the three and a half years between the invasion by the RPF in 1990 and the 1994 genocide. Some 3,000 Tutsi lost their lives through these outbursts of ethnic violence, which went unpunished and were commonly misinterpreted in extremist publications such as *Kangura*.[58]

Other editorials, articles and cartoons published in *Kangura* echoed the contempt and hatred for Tutsi found in this notorious edition. Tustis were characterised as 'wicked and ambitious, using women and money against the vulnerable Hutu'.[59] In similar way to many of the broadcasts on RTLM, history was repeatedly used to demonise Tutsis and to underline how Hutus have been victims of their oppression in the past. At the same time the RPF or Tutsis were accused of atrocities, which were in fact often being perpetrated by Hutu groups. These 'accusations in a mirror' were intended to instil fear that the minority Tutsis were planning and attempting to exterminate the Hutu majority.[60]

The tone is a long way from detached or reflective journalism. One striking example is the article 'A Cockroach Cannot Give Birth to a Butterfly'.[61] This article calls Tutsis *Inyenzi*, cockroaches, claiming that, just as cockroaches cannot change, so too Tutsis will always remain wicked.[62] In 1960–3, *Inyenzi* was the name given to the Tutsi guerrillas, both as a term of abuse and because, like cockroaches, they often moved at night. After 1990 it was used for the RPF fighters who invaded Rwanda, and later RTLM and the interim government would use it to refer to the Tutsi in general. In the run-up to the genocide *Kangura* and RTLM regularly employed the word *Inyenzi* to describe the Tutsi people, as the Nazis used the term 'vermin' to describe Jews. This name substitution or name calling was another common technique employed by RTLM broadcasters. Part of the danger of such language is that naming has a descriptive force that dehumanises perceived opponents, turning them into a subhuman species, who also completely lose their individuality. It may be deemed easier to stamp on a cockroach or to poison vermin than to extinguish a human life. During the actual genocide, RTLM claimed that 'the cruelty of the *Inyenzi* [cockroaches] is incurable, the cruelty of the *Inyenzi* can only be cured by their total extermination'.[63] The term *Inyenzi* had come to mean a person or animal to be killed.

A Hutu civil servant who worked for the Ministry of Information, and was responsible for monitoring all private press between September and November 1993, described *Kangura* as 'the most extremist paper'. He suggested that, in spite of the comparatively low literacy rates, it was due to the strong oral tradition in

Rwanda that *Kangura* became a topic of conversation: those who could read discussed its contents with those who could not read. 'Because *Kangura* was extremist in nature, everyone spoke of it, in buses and everywhere. He said, "thus, the news would spread like fire; it was sensational news"'.[64] These popular discussions of the paper and the exposure on RTLM ensured that, while *Kangura* had a comparatively small print run of only about 1,500 to 3,000, both its Kinyarwanda and French editions attracted wide public attention.[65]

These observations about *Kangura* illustrate how RTLM was by no means operating in a communicative vacuum. There were more than twenty other newspapers and journals inciting hatred of Tutsis. It was not the only voice inciting racial hatred. Like Radio Rwanda, the content of RTLM's news broadcasts were often significantly different depending on whether they were broadcast in French or Kinyarwanda, with reports in the local language being more explicit in their incitement to racial hatred.[66] The hate media found in Rwanda in the early 1990s, epitomised by RTLM and *Kangura*, helped prepare the ground for the explosion of extreme violence. They were part of a wider coalition, whose purpose 'was to mobilize the Hutu population against the Tutsi ethnic minority'.[67] Up to this point I have suggested that RTLM's popularity was derived partly through its broadcasting style and partly because its broadcasts resonated with popular anti-Tutsi sentiment. The hate speech found on this station was symptomatic of the growing ethnic fear and abhorrence of the 'other', which the RPF invasion had exacerbated. Many of these broadcasts and writings caricatured the Tutsi as an outsider, an alien, or a settler who was inherently ambitious and wicked, intent on returning Rwanda to a monarchical Tutsi dominated past. This would be a world where Hutu would once again be oppressed or victimised by a cruel returning elite. Listeners were encouraged to be vigilant, to beware or be on their guard against infiltration. In the months before the start of the genocide on 6 April, broadcasters increasingly used language which was intended to fan the flames of fear, anger and resentment against the Tutsi population.

Directing and inciting

> What RTLM did was almost to pour petrol – to spread petrol throughout the country little by little, so that one day it would be able to set fire to the whole country.[68]

Before 6 April some people described RTLM as 'Radio Rutswitsi', which means 'to burn',[69] implying that this was a station that fanned the flames of hatred. Within a few weeks of the start of the genocide on 6 April, other listeners had begun to call it 'Radio Machete',[70] with one person even describing it as 'Vampire Radio', which was 'calling for blood and massacres'.[71] Several accounts, written soon after the genocide, failed to represent the intensification of hate speech being broadcast after 6 April 1994.[72] Later descriptions demonstrate that these and other journalistic accounts also failed to distinguish between broadcasting before 6 April and after the start of the genocide.[73] It was easier to paint RTLM as a station that had always engaged in such patterns of speech, when there had in fact been a rapid evolution of hate speech. Between January and April 1994 RTLM became increasingly vitriolic, inspiring fear among Tutsis and naming specific neighbourhoods and individuals.[74] The station, which had begun as a mouthpiece of political frustration and fears, had evolved into something far more problematic. How then did RTLM's role develop during the genocide itself?

Within half an hour of the shooting down of the Falcon jet carrying the presidents of Rwanda (Juvénal Habyarimana) and Burundi (Cyprien Ntaryamira) on 6 April 1994, roadblocks had been set up in Kigali. RTLM was the first to break the news of his death, less than an hour after the 'plane crash'. This event was not so much the spark as the signal for a highly organised and pre-planned killing campaign to begin. On April 10 RTLM demanded that Hutus should remain vigilantly at their roadblocks.[75] The commands to 'be vigilant' and to 'take action' were repeated regularly. These were places where thousands of Tutsis and moderate Hutus were stopped, questioned and killed. Several witnesses described seeing militia at roadblocks listening to RTLM. A French lawyer and journalist, Philippe Dahinden, described how at roadblocks he frequently came across militia with radios, listening to RTLM. He was particularly struck by how much the militia relied on the radio for directions and information. They were clearly following orders to keep listening to the radio for instructions from the interim government. Radio had become an important tool in the genocide.

One broadcast from a member of the CDR (*Coalition pour la Défense de la République*, Coalition for the Defence of the Republic) militia stated: 'Whoever does not have his identity card should be arrested and maybe lose his head there' (29 May). Other broadcasts encouraged listeners not simply to fight in a battle, but to ravage and to punish. RTLM would congratulate listeners for their 'heroic' efforts, affirming the efforts of women alongside men.[76] On 23 May, for example, Kantano Habimana promised rewards after the war was finished for those who helped on the roadblocks. 'Those very active within the government and the army and who really "work" are well known. They will get very nice rewards. Those who do not 'work' will receive no reward at all. This is not the time to fall ill'.[77] Rewards were often promised, so too were punishments for those who failed to carry out what was euphemistically known as the 'work'. Several of the monologues or conversations on RTLM included explicit encouragement to fight: 'take your spears, clubs, guns, swords, stones, everything, sharpen them, hack them, those enemies, those cockroaches, those enemies of democracy, show that you can defend yourselves'.[78] Repeated calls to action were based upon the impending threat of the 'enemy', which was combined with the claim that everybody was involved in this war against these 'foreigners', 'terrorists' or 'wrong-doers'.[79]

One of the survivors from the Ministry of Information stayed at home after 6 April, monitoring RTLM's output:

> RTLM was constantly asking people to kill other people, to look for those who were in hiding, and to describe the hiding places of those who were described as being accomplices. I also remember RTLM programmes in which it was obvious that the people who were speaking were happy to say that there had been massive killings of *Inyenzi*, and they made no difference between *Inyenzis* and Tutsis. And they said that they should continue to search for those people and kill them so that the future generations would have to actually ask what *Inyenzis* looked like, or, ultimately, what Tutsis looked like.[80]

The blurring of descriptive terms became far more acute during the genocide. It was clear that *inyenzi* and *inkotanyi* had in many cases come to mean Tutsi. These broadcasts also helped to highlight the imaginative divide between 'us' and 'them'.

Even with its laidback style of presentation RTLM was perceived by many rural Rwandans as a station for the educated urban elite, though many of those without radios were aware during the killings of its exhortations to join in 'the work'. Through informal conversations and gossip, the 'hot news' from RTLM was spread around the country. Rwandans outside the cities remembered 'agrarian metaphors' where 'the radio told us to clear the bushes', to 'separate the grass from the millet' and 'to pull out the poison ivy together with its roots'.[81] Interviews with killers after the genocide highlight how many of the perpetrators perceived the role of radio in inciting killing. For example, in *Valentina's Story*, a *Newsnight* documentary discussed in chapter 4, one of the killers, Denis Bagaruka, described how 'We heard the radio telling us to be strong and to cut down the tall trees. Our local leader explained these trees were the Tutsis. We were listening to the radio and, because of that and what the soldiers were urging, we started to kill our neighbours'.[82]

Many broadcasts would go further than simply these generalised incitements to kill, or simply naming or vilifying individuals, and provided specific details of where particular individuals were to be found. For example, during the 'first week of the genocide, RTLM described a red van which it claimed was "full of accomplices", and provided its number-plate'.[83] It is believed that it was stopped the same day and all its occupants were killed on the spot. Similar accounts of ambulances, cars and buses being stopped following announcements illustrate how RTLM worked closely with the militias. After 6 April, names and locations of Tutsis in hiding, especially in Kigali, were also frequently broadcast, with fatal consequences. 'Urgent! Urgent! Calling the militia members of Muhima! Direct yourselves to the Rugenge area'.[84] This broadcast referred to Dr Gafaranga, a leader of an opposition party, the PSD (*Parti Social Démocrate*, Social Democratic Party), who was hunted down, arrested and executed later the same day. Early in the genocide RTLM appears to have been used to encourage Tutsis to leave their hiding place, either to show their loyalty by going to the roadblocks or to protect their property by returning home. Those Tutsis who followed these instructions were invariably killed.[85]

The priests who actually took a stand against the killing also became a target for RTLM, who claimed that churches were being used by RPF troops as military bases. For example, on RTLM (20 May 1994), Valerie Bemeriki named several priests as being involved in the armed conflict:

> we know that in God's Place, there is a place where the body of Christ is kept, which is known as the tabernacle. So? Could Father Ntagara explain to the Rwandan people the reason why the Eucharist has been replaced by ammunition? And the sacristy? Isn't it there that good priests – the ones we swamp with praise – keep their sacred vestments when they go to say mass, and also keep their consecrated items? Therefore, since when have these items been intermingled with guns? You, Father Modeste Mungwarareba, I have seen you ever since you were rector of Karubanda Minor Seminary. God looked at you and said: "No. What belongs to me cannot be mixed up with all these instruments, which are used for shedding blood!" Can you therefore tell us a little bit about the small secrets in the sacristy? So all of us Hutus must remain vigilant.[86]

Bemeriki's broadcast both questions the peacefulness of specific priests and identifies churches as places where arms might be hoarded. In fact, thousands of people around the country fled to them as places of sanctuary. Tragically, 'many of the largest massacres took place in churches because, rather than waiting to be attacked in their homes, people fled there looking for sanctuary, religious comfort, solidarity with others in danger and the opportunity to defend themselves in numbers'.[87] Several other churches and a mosque were named on RTLM and soon afterwards became sites of extensive killing.[88] When able to receive its broadcasts the semi-private Hutu youth gangs and many members of the presidential guard used RTLM not only for specific information and directions, but also for inspiration and entertainment. During the first ten days of the genocide, RTLM were broadcasting twenty-four hours a day and, despite conveying all these murderous details, they mostly maintained their informal, relaxed speaking style and mix of African music.

Reporting and interpreting

Up to this point, I have concentrated upon local media work before, during and after the genocide. From early April 1994, and the beginning of the genocide, the interim government developed a practice of feeding the international media with a regular diet of misinformation. This led to many global news channels initially portraying the killings as emerging out of tribal conflict, which had a long tradition in Rwanda. The interim government appealed for international aid and, most dangerously, blurred the distinction between the genocide and the war against the RPF. Both Radio Rwanda and RTLM were used in its propaganda war of disinformation. Some foreign journalists did not accept the government line uncritically, 'however, a disturbingly large number of foreign correspondents swallowed the "tribal violence" line either in whole or in part. "Anarchy" and "an orgy of violence" were favourite terms'. In the foreign media, 'references to "ethnic bloodbath" and "ancient tribal hatred" persisted into mid-August'.[89] The underlying assumption in many radio, television and newspaper reports was that Rwanda had fallen into an anarchic civil war, where Hutu fought Tutsi in a bloody resurgence of an ancient enmity.[90] 'Everyone was killing everyone else; it was uncontrollable violence',[91] rather than the reality: Rwanda was held in the grips of a government-supported genocide.

Some newspapers offered more accurate accounts and by late May UN interviewees were more explicit in their condemnation. The then Secretary-General of the UN, Boutros Ghali, admitted: 'We are all to be held accountable for this failure, all of us, the great powers, African countries, the NGOs, the international community. It is a genocide ... I have failed ... It is a scandal'.[92] With tragic consequences, many radio, television and newspapers failed to heighten public consciousness about what was happening in Rwanda.

Unfortunately, for many weeks editors were desperately short of 'good' pictures, as camera crews and most photojournalists would only travel with international troops for protection. These UNAMIR (United Nations Assistance Mission for Rwanda) forces were primarily looking after foreign nationals, with the Rwandese being left to fend for themselves. The result was that many pictures and reports initially concentrated on Europeans being evacuated. There was nothing equivalent to the gripping television pictures of planes flying into skyscrapers, or missiles hitting their targets, to awaken international consciousness. It was not until the genocide was effectively over that many foreign television crews ventured to cover the story.

Another related issue was that there were no international journalists in the rural areas witnessing the massacres first-hand. Most reporters relied instead on the accounts of non-governmental organisations, survivors and local media, many of which were distorted or initially unable to comprehend the vast scale of the killings. This was exacerbated by the fact that the vast majority of senior Western and African journalists were not in Rwanda, but in South Africa, covering Nelson Mandela's triumph in the historic election and the related threat of extremist right-wing violence. Many news organisations relied instead on inexperienced stringers (a kind of freelance journalist) or young journalists with little knowledge of this area to cover the Rwanda story. While it received regular coverage, it was limited in terms of depth, accuracy and length. Unfortunately, not until it was too late was there anything comparable to Michael Buerk's unforgettable pictures and reports from Korem on the Ethiopian famines of 1983.[93] Nor was there anything to compare with Bob Geldof's charismatic leadership of the telegenic Band Aid, which assisted in galvanising public opinion in the West to care about the starving population of Ethiopia. In comparison to the initial treatment of the genocide, there was far more international television coverage of the Rwandan refugees struggling to survive in Goma, Zaire, and the ensuing cholera epidemic in July and August. The unfolding tragedy during April, May and June in Rwanda effectively remained a closed book for many international audiences for several weeks, while the reports of RTLM and Radio Rwanda continued to cultivate and even incite violence around the country itself.

Judging and assessing

> RTLM is instrumental in awakening the majority of the people ... today's wars are not fought using bullets only, it is also a war of media, words, newspapers and radio stations.[94]

This claim was made by RTLM's mastermind and sometime director, Ferdinand Nahimana, during an interview on Radio Rwanda at the height of the killing. The popularity of RTLM, the continued use of the radio to express hatred and the cry heard at that time on the telephone out of Rwanda – 'Stop that Radio'[95] – raises several questions connected to what is the best way to counter hate radio. Is it, as some suggest, to electronically jam racist stations?[96] Or does this set a precedent that allows authoritarian governments to clamp down on the expression of free speech? Is it better to wait before embarking on blocking the airwaves until the station becomes an explicit tool of the violence, as RTLM did after 6 April 1994? Or, if this is a 'war of media', is it most effective to follow in the footsteps of RPF and actually bomb the offending radio station? Alternatively, is it more valuable in the long term to use powerful transmitters to broadcast peaceful messages, as was done in Cambodia by the UN in 1992 to out-broadcast the Khmer Rouge's radio propaganda? At first sight, for those intent on stopping 'that radio', these instrumental options appear to offer several possibilities. However, simply concentrating on how to physically halt hate radio fails to address some of the more foundational issues that have been highlighted by the role played by the media in the genocide.

It is, of course, impossible to predict what would have happened if RTLM had been sanctioned or jammed as some commentators recommended, if Radio Rwanda had offered alternative perspectives and if there had been a greater diversity of local and global broadcast media in Rwanda. The genocide would almost certainly still have gone ahead, but with perhaps a little less efficiency and possibly even less fear-motivated anger. Some still assert that 'the fundamental reality, which cannot be stated too often, is that genocide is not caused by the mass media. At worst they may abet the process, but inflammatory media coverage is essentially a symptom of a process resulting from other causes'.[97] The roots of evil and what actually causes the inversion of morality are extremely difficult to untangle.[98] While many claim that the 'massacres would have taken place with or without the RTLM broadcasts',[99] one strand to my argument in this chapter is that radio may well be more than just a symptom of listeners' mistrust and prejudice: RTLM did broadcast many words and much music which generated fear and hatred, in an attempt to incite violence.

This conclusion is supported by the observation from the 700-page Human Rights Watch report on the Rwandan genocide: 'It is difficult to overstate the importance of the mass media in whipping up popular sentiment. Most rural people in Rwanda could only obtain their news from radio broadcasts, and the incessant propaganda, to exterminate the Tutsi, and the claims that the government was winning the war, made many ordinary people believe that the future belonged solely to Hutu extremism'.[100] As suggested earlier, it is almost impossible to demonstrate conclusively that the local media actually galvanised people to violence; in fact, motivations for participation in the genocide clearly varied from individual to individual. 'Some were moved by virulent hatred, others by real fear, by ambition, by greed, by a desire to escape injury at the hands of those who demanded they participate, or by the wish to avoid fines for non-participation that they could not hope to pay'.[101] Part of the skill of RTLM's broadcasters was to tap and even heighten many of these emotions and motives, thereby exacerbating an already explosive situation. Add to this radio's leading role in Rwanda as a means of disseminating information, and it is reasonable to conclude that radio played a significant part in contributing or reinforcing many listeners' fearful and violent imaginative world as well as directing the killers to their victims.

Some scholars have drawn comparisons between RTLM's broadcasts in Rwanda in 1993–4 and a certain radio broadcast in the USA in 1938. *War of the Worlds* is perhaps the most famous dramatic adaptation in the history of radio. The Mercury Theatre Company's rendition of H. G. Wells' story derives its fame from the extreme responses it provoked from many listeners. Out of an estimated audience of six million, some one million are believed to have been frightened, with many taking panic-driven action on hearing the broadcast. For example, in New Jersey 'in a single block, more than 20 families rushed out of their houses with wet handkerchiefs and towels over their faces'. In Birmingham, Alabama, 'many gathered in churches and prayed', with some students in a South Eastern college 'huddling round their radios trembling and weeping in each other's arms'.[102] While there are clearly significant differences between the USA in 1938 and Rwanda in 1994, there are according to Kellow and Steeves several intriguing parallels. First, many people in both countries put 'great faith' in radio as a reliable and authoritative form of news. Second, at a time of political and economic turmoil radio played an important role in providing 'information and guidance'. Third, Orson Welles and his company created a believable imaginative soundscape through the skilful use of 'on-the-spot reporting', interviews with experts and references to real places. RTLM's broadcasts may have been of a very different style, but they also created a sound environment which was both enjoyable to listen to and believable. Kellow and

Steeves' conclusion is that, in both cases, in the USA in the 1930s and Rwanda in the 1990s, listeners 'acted on what they believed to be true and real'.[103]

One important qualification is rooted in the observation that over five million people in the USA were not frightened and did not panic. They resisted believing what they heard for a number of reasons, including the realisation that the timescale of the drama was impossible, or after checking with other sources they discovered that what they were listening to was a play. On the basis of such critical verification they were able to resist being sucked into the extreme responses of others around the country.[104] Simply hearing a credible radio programme, and being surrounded by people who are frightened, does not absolve the listener from individual moral responsibility in how they themselves respond; nor does the listener's moral agency absolve broadcasters from responsibility towards their audiences.

This was also part of the conclusion of the International Criminal Tribunal for Rwanda's so called 'Media Trial'.[105] On 3 December 2003, the International Criminal Tribunal for Rwanda (ICTR) judged two of the founders of RTLM, the academic Ferdinand Nahimana and the lawyer Jean-Bosco Barayagwiza, as well as the owner and editor of *Kangura*, Hassan Ngeze, guilty of genocide, conspiracy to commit genocide, public incitement to commit genocide and crimes against humanity. The judges concluded that the 'RTLM broadcasts exploited the history of Tutsi privilege and Hutu disadvantage, and the fear of armed insurrection, to mobilize the population, whipping them into a frenzy of hatred and violence that was directed largely against the Tutsi ethnic group'. The tribunal declared that the former history professor, Nahimana, acted 'without a firearm, machete or any physical weapon', but 'caused the deaths of thousands of innocent civilians',[106] through helping to create 'a climate of harm'.[107] All three wielded not machetes but words against many of their neighbours. Nahimana and Ngeze were sentenced to imprisonment for the rest of their lives and Barayagwiza received a thirty-five-year sentence.[108] Not since the Nuremberg trials in 1946, where Julius Streicher, the publisher and editor of the virulently anti-semitic *Der Stürmer* (*The Attacker*), was sentenced to death by hanging for crimes against humanity,[109] have media practitioners been found guilty of such wrongdoing. The actual trial provides valuable additional evidence for helping to assess accurately the broadcasting practices and audience uses of radio prior to and during the four months of genocidal violence. Reading through more than 300 pages of judgement and sentence, based upon over three years of legal proceedings, it is clear that words of peace were overwhelmed by expressions of hatred.

The December 2003 judgment at Arusha is too late, of course, for many of the victims. It is crucial to understand more clearly how RTLM was able to operate with such freedom. Alexis and Mpambara's report on *The Rwandan Media Experience from the Genocide* (2003)[110] emphasises how there were no effective external institutions to counter RTLM's flagrant transgression of its original agreement with the government, which stated that it would not 'broadcast any programs of a nature to incite hatred, violence or any form of division', and would 'refrain from telling lies or giving out information that may mislead the public'.[111] With powerful supporters and close links in the government, RTLM was able to ignore the Minister of Information's orders and avoid sanctions.[112] Legislation will not always protect the airwaves, particularly when powerful vested interests are determined to protect the channels, which are expressing their own extremist views.

It is sometimes argued that the spread of global media and the fragmentation of local media is an entirely problematic social and communicative trend. But given what we know of what happened in Rwanda, surely it is reasonable to suggest that access to more than simply government run channels or state-backed local broadcasting stations will be an advantage to citizens in search of a just peace? Consider how demonstrations by Buddhist monks in Myanmar, by students in Tehran and by protesters in Syria provoked violent repression by the government of independent media as well as an even stricter clamp-down on global networks trying to tell the story of their repression. Similarly, though in a very different setting, it is hard not to wonder, had there been more diversity of media outlets and greater access to international media channels in Rwanda, whether the slide towards hatred and ultimately genocide would have at least been exposed more swiftly and questioned more rigorously both in Rwanda and around the globe.

Displaying

I began this chapter with a personal prologue: a brief description of one of my own visits to a genocide memorial in Rwanda during 2007, the church at Ntarama. The form of telling is comparatively understated there, with a guide to show you around, answer questions and even point out what you might miss. There is now additional covering to protect the three small church buildings (figure 3.7). The intention is clearly to preserve this as a monument for visitors from all around the world, who leave their marks in the visitors' book. There is also a long memorial wall with many victims' names. What is striking here is that there remain extensive blank spaces for the anonymous or forgotten victims. Nearby, hanging on the outside of the church is a purple sheet on which is written in white letters and Kinyarwandan: 'If you knew me and you knew yourself you wouldn't have killed me'.

In the capital, the Kigali Memorial Centre tells the story of the genocide in far greater detail. One is greeted in the garden by a map of the globe with a flag piercing the heart of Rwanda. This map is intended to be a place where visitors can reflect on 'genocide both past and present' across the world.[113] There are simple signs recording survivors' stories. It is easy to forget, while walking around the displays, that the place where the centre is located, the district of Gisozi, is also the resting place of about 250,000 victims of the genocide in Kigali. Outside the centre are eight mass graves, made up of concrete crypts, filled from floor to

Figure 3.7 Ntarama Church exterior, Rwanda. Photograph by Jolyon Mitchell.

ceiling with coffins containing the remains of up to fifty victims. Situated by a memorial garden, these are usually silent spaces, apart from the sounds of the city drifting across the valley (figures 3.8a–d).

The covered graves, horizontal presences, are less obviously expressive than the media inside the centre, which tell part of the genocide's story. These varied media include photograph after photograph of victims during their lifetime, recorded interviews of survivors, images of the immediate aftermath of the genocide and photographs of neatly ordered skulls and bones. One display shows how local radio, newspapers and magazines were used as tools for propaganda to incite hatred. Another wall displays the limited international press coverage preceding the genocide from papers such as *The Times* or the *New York Times*. Put side by side they reveal the sharp contrast between local media and global media coverage of the Rwandan genocide: a divide that I have highlighted through my earlier discussions.[114]

There are several elements in the exhibition that highlight Rwanda's religious history and in particular its connection with the Catholic Church. For instance, one photograph depicts several Western priests dressed in white standing surrounded by young Rwandans. Such images illustrate the perceived influence of the Church on education during the later part of the Belgian rule (1916–62). The commentary alongside several other pictures portrays a church that had a divisive influence, initially favouring Tutsis to be leaders, but then supporting the

Figure 3.8a Kigali Memorial Centre, Rwanda. This acts as a museum, a memorial and an education centre, as well as a tourist destination. Photograph by Jolyon Mitchell.

Figure 3.8b Kigali Memorial Centre, world map, Rwanda. Photograph by Jolyon Mitchell.

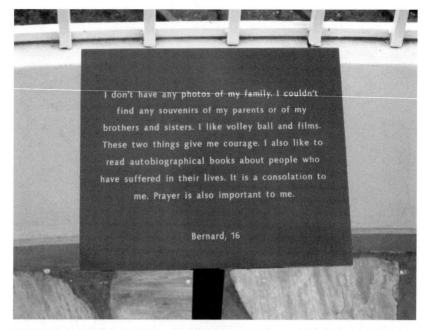

I don't have any photos of my family. I couldn't
find any souvenirs of my parents or of my
brothers and sisters. I like volley ball and films.
These two things give me courage. I also like to
read autobiographical books about people who
have suffered in their lives. It is a consolation to
me. Prayer is also important to me.

Bernard, 16

Figure 3.8c Kigali Memorial Centre, plaque. Photograph by Jolyon Mitchell.

Figure 3.8d Kigali Memorial Centre, graves. One of several mass graves, housing around 250,000 bodies, including the 'unknown victim'. Photograph by Jolyon Mitchell.

Hutus after 1959. In the sections on the actual genocide there are several photos of the 'killing churches', such as one image from Ntarama, Bugesera, showing photos taken soon after the genocide of bodies carpeting the inside of the church I had visited. The descriptions are without adornment: 'People ran to churches for shelter in large numbers. But churches were not sanctuaries of safety. The genocidaires moved into the pews and altars and massacred thousands at a time. Believers ended their lives piled in the aisles in pools of blood'.[115] Next to harrowing photographs of these events, there are contrasting accounts of the role of local religious leaders during the genocide.

The ambiguity of the role of the churches and their leaders are highlighted through two contrasting stories. On the one hand, Father Wenceslas Munyeshyaka priest in charge of St Famille, Kigali, a priest who according to witnesses discarded his priest's cassock and took to wearing a flak jacket and carrying a pistol. He not only colluded but also actually committed acts of violence against Tutsis. And on the other hand, Father Célestin Hakizimana, who at considerable personal risk helped to turn St Paul's Pastoral Centre, close to the parish of St Famille, into a haven for around 2,000 people. The ambiguous role of religion displayed in the museum was expressed, as we saw earlier, through RTLM by the appropriation of religious language while also encouraging direct attacks on 'troublesome priests'. This ambiguity is also to be found visually expressed in several of Rwanda's 'killing churches', which have now been turned into memorials. A torn poster of John Paul II visiting Rwanda in 1990 can be seen not only on the wall at Ntarama, described in the prologue of this chapter (figure 3.1), but also pinned to the wall in the former church at Nyamata (about 22 miles from Kigali), where some 10,000 people were massacred in 1994. On this poster the face of the pope is easier to make out, as is the crucifix that he carries in front of him.

It is impossible to remain unmoved by what you see and hear at such memorials and at the centre in Kigali, which acts as both a memorial and a museum. Unlike the Jewish Museum in Berlin, reminiscent of an unravelling Star of David and designed by Daniel Libeskind, where visitors walk through into disorientating voids, visitors in Kigali walk around a series of displays. Responses vary. Some visitors are silent, while others more vocal. I saw a young woman from Europe burst into tears and crumple to the floor after listening to a video-recorded story of one survivor, who lost all of her extended family in the genocide. Alongside this exhibition is a children's memorial, dedicated to 'the memory of the many thousands of children whose lives were cut short cruelly and intentionally' in Rwanda. Part of the power of this mediated memorial space is the way it leads visitors beyond the bounds of the local to the global. The Rwandan genocide is not depicted as an isolated phenomenon. Situated above the memorial museum, which documents some of the causes and consequences of genocide, is an exhibition entitled 'Wasted Lives', which displays other examples of twentieth-century genocidal violence in Namibia, Armenia, Nazi Germany, Cambodia and the Balkans. By locating the Rwandan genocide in a wider context, it offers visitors a global and historical perspective to reflect on the similarities and dissimilarities between what happened in Rwanda and what has happened elsewhere. This is far more explicit than the map in the garden. It is a form of 'global telling' in a local setting. It underlines that promoting genocidal violence through different media is by no means a phenomenon isolated to Central Africa.

Conclusion

In this chapter, I have shown through an examination of RTLM, Radio Rwanda and *Kangura*, how 'telling', describing well and remembering wisely is globally significant. A broadcaster may sound friendly and innocuous, but easy-going banter and singing may mask more sinister intentions. Publishing biased news, naming enemies, directing violence and cultivating hatred are examples of 'telling' inadequately. Reporting can tell the truth, revealing hidden violence, or it can overlook or obscure violence. Visiting and then walking round the comparatively untidy remains of a devastated former church may speak more memorably about a genocide than watching a news report or even traipsing around another well-ordered gallery which points back to a moment of chaos. Displaying can keep memories fresh and heighten the desire to make sure genocide will never happen again, but, if too neatly or gratuitously laid out, it can transform viewers into little more than voyeurs who feel powerless under the weight of the promotion and cultivation of violence.

Part I Conclusions

What has emerged from the first part of this book? At first sight, the situations of 1994 Rwanda (chapter 3), 1980–8 Iran (chapter 2) and 1919 Britain (chapter 1) appear to be very dissimilar. They are obviously significantly different cultural, historical and religious contexts. There are clearly many dissimilarities, especially between genocidal violence and wars of perceived national survival. Nevertheless, there are a number of striking similarities. First, these cases illustrate how a range of media can be employed to remember the fallen, to comfort the living and to inspire the fighting forces to turn their 'ploughshares into swords'.[1] Coloured glass, passionate sermons, vast wall paintings, colourful posters, relaxed radio broadcasts and simple cartoons have all been used in an attempt to encourage populations to fear, to fight the 'other', or even to kill their neighbours for an apparently greater good. Not only words but also images can be used to highlight communal suffering, to commemorate violent killings and to celebrate heroic martyrdoms. Again and again, through different media communities remind themselves of past hurts, 'we have been wronged and we are victims'; of heroic sacrifices, 'we have given our lives fighting for others'; and of evil enemies, 'we face immoral and demonic forces'. Through such verbal or visual representations, wrongs are remembered, local heroes are glorified and enemies are vilified.

Second, these processes can inspire imitation, sometimes known in this context as mimesis. Imitating the friend who fights, the martyr who sacrifices or the neighbour who kills can bring short-term benefits. The French scholar René Girard argues that violence is rooted in mimesis (imitation). Girard believes that imitation can move from mimetic desire and acquisitiveness to mimetic rivalry and competitiveness, which can lead to mimetic conflict and violence, which in turn leads to the desire for vengeance. In this way violence and conflict can escalate out of control. According to Girard, this can become 'a vicious circle' and 'an interminable, infinitely repetitive process'.[2] Even the most active and dynamic audiences can participate within these destructive communicative circles. One possible cumulative result of participating within this mimetic process is for individuals to join the ranks of those who are ready either to sacrifice scapegoats within their own communities or to sacrifice their own lives as they attempt to destroy the feared 'other'. As Girard suggests, these kinds of sacrificial processes have a tendency to break down and ultimately prove unsustainable for bringing peace. In fractured environments, breaking these communicative cycles, remembering wisely and re-imagining enemies are difficult practices to develop.[3] The remembrance, celebration and escalation of violence is driven not only by those who *imitate* earlier fighters, or by those who have suffered previous hurt, or by those who fear for their own safety, but also by those determined to grasp more material possessions and to hold onto power.

Third, as with so many other wars and organised killings, it is commonly older men who use many different approaches to try to persuade younger men, or even boys, to risk their own lives, to fight and to kill. At the same time these leaders seek to persuade mothers, wives and sisters, along with other family members, of the value of the sacrifices made and the actions to be taken. These gendered generalisations are not watertight—women can also fight and kill—but it is striking to observe how in Western Europe, in Iran and in Rwanda how it is normally men who have dominated the public incitements to violence. There are, of course, exceptions, with examples of women giving white feathers to those who did not fight during the First World War, of mothers boasting of their son's martyrdom in Iran and of spouses encouraging partners in Rwanda to complete their genocidal 'work'. The hidden encouragements within families, of contemporaries to their friends and of individuals to themselves are likely to be more persuasive than, or at least reinforce, the more public exhortations of leaders to their followers to join the 'bandwagon'. In the case of child soldiers, who are often cut off from their closest relatives, it is their fellow fighters who can become replacement families, exerting considerable influence on the actions of these militarised youngsters. Immediate loyalties combined with the 'need to belong', and even the pleasures derived from violence are powerful forces within incitements to fight.

Agitation towards violence can also be rooted in the desire to seek vengeance for past hurts, to try to diffuse fear of the 'other' and to counter paranoia about future attacks. As observed earlier, it may often also reflect a hidden desire to preserve the status quo, to gain more land and to grasp more resources. With increasing competition for shrinking resources such as good water, fertile land and clean air, environmentally precipitated conflicts are likely to increase. As we saw in each of the first three chapters, it is not only powerful elites or individuals, but also peer pressure, that can incite others to pick up weapons to defend, to attack and to kill. The cry 'kill or be killed', the whisper 'fight or watch your loved ones be butchered' and the insinuation that 'we *must* fight to remain safe or to survive' are to be found behind many calls to communal violence. Conflicts where perceived national survival is at stake, such as in Britain, Iran and Rwanda, allow political, religious and other community leaders to step up their verbal and visual rhetoric as they attempt to justify past violence, to manufacture consent and to mobilise populations.

Fourth, media can be used to communicate distorted religious beliefs. For instance, generalised religious language, the 'ten commandments' or selected sayings of Jesus were manipulated through different media in Rwanda to serve extremist ends in the early 1990s. As we saw, Rwandans were encouraged to forget what Jesus had said and use violence against their neighbours. The use of a trusted source, such as a radio broadcast or a political speech, added authority to distorted beliefs. Recall the different ways in which statements were recycled, such as the claim that 'the Gospel has already changed in our movement' and that, 'If someone gives you a slap, give him two in return, two fatal ones'. This is an inversion of Jesus of Nazareth's call to turn the other cheek, found in both the Sermon on the Mount (Matthew 5.38–42) and Sermon on the Plain (Luke 6.27–31). Whether one interprets the original sayings as an exhortation to non-retaliation, and even openness to further attacks, or a more subtle form of non-violent resistance, this affirmation leaves little room for violent aggression.[4] The exhortation to pay back one act of violence with more than twice as much in revenge is the equivalent of 'two killings for one slap'. This is a way of death. The challenge to 'Love your enemies and do good to them which hate you' (Luke 6.27; see also Matthew 5.44, *KJB*) is in direct opposition to the repeated exhortations to fear your enemies, to fight your opponents and even to kill your neighbours found both in RTLM broadcasts and extremist papers, such as *Kangura,* in Rwanda. The uncritical celebration of active martyrdom, the recycling of demonising wartime propaganda and the portrayal of the necessity of fighting to create or to preserve an ideal peaceful world are common rhetorical devices. Fighters can be sanctified and the enemy can be vilified. These practices illustrate how it is possible to simplify, to distort and to transform more peaceful religious visions in order to incite violence.

The more subtle transformations are often harder to detect. Memorials, stained-glass windows, sermons, murals, posters and radio broadcasts can all be transformed into both a source of inspiration and a resource for persuasion towards violent acts. Individual and communal belief can reinforce trust in the rightness of one's own cause, confidence in the truth of one's own ordering of the world and a desire to bring peace on one's own terms. In some settings violence is portrayed unambiguously as a redemptive, even a peacemaking, force. The 'myth of redemptive violence', the idea of using violence as a way to bring peace, can be woven into national narratives and used to justify future violence.[5] Incitements towards violence are commonly couched in remembrance of past victories, atrocities and the language of bringing peace to the world.

One of the most dangerous threats to those who seek to incite vengeful violence are those who are prepared to risk bearing witness to violence's devastating effects, who search for truth and reconciliation even when the dominant powers wish to hide the troubling past and avoid the long road towards reconciliation. Such builders of peace, often themselves motivated by religious belief, commonly dare to imagine a world where resorting to violence is the last rather than the first option, where remembering violence wisely is a craft to be nurtured and where promoting peace can become a troubling and uncomfortable practice. Chapters 4–7 will explore how these processes of bearing witness, searching for truth and reconciliation and promoting peace through different media are far from simple, safe and easily embodied options.

Part II

Promoting peace

Chapter 4

Bearing witness through film

Prologue

When we arrived at the school we found the gates wide open. As we stepped out of the taxi, I was struck by the soft sand underfoot and the noise of children playing in the distance. This was the only sign of life in what otherwise appeared like a deserted compound. A number of single-storeyed classrooms were close by on our right. Doors and windows were shut. Looking behind I recognised the large dark gates; I had seen them before, though on a screen back home in Britain rather than in real life here in Kigali, Rwanda. The difference was that in the film *Shooting Dogs* (Michael Caton-Jones, 2005) the gates were a dirty off-white and, for most of the movie, firmly shut. It was strange to be standing in what was now a quiet, still space, which in the film had been teeming full of people creating noise, arguments and action. Looking carefully at the actual gates it was possible to make out three letters in the metalwork at the top: 'ETO'. A reminder that, while the central characters are fictional, *Shooting Dogs* is based upon the true story of a large group of Tutsis who sought refuge in April 1994 in this Kigali secondary school (*École Technique Officielle* or ETO), which was briefly protected by UN troops.[1] Once the Belgian soldiers withdrew on 11 April, however, the waiting militia (the *interahamwe*) massacred many of the defenceless men, women and children left behind. They then marched the remaining refugees about an hour away up the road to Nyanza, where another massacre took place. Around 2,500 people lost their lives in these two related massacres.[2] *Shooting Dogs* was mostly filmed at the school, on the actual site of the first set of killings.

Standing there, one scene from the film came back to mind. I watched it again on my return to the UK. In *Shooting Dogs*, over twenty-five men and women stand looking through the closed gates. All that can be seen of them is the backs of their heads, some covered by hats and caps. One man has his arms raised in the air and another clutches his own head. Even from behind it is possible to detect their fear. They are straining to see through the bars of the gates, all are looking in one direction: down the tree-lined sand-coloured drive. At its end, and at first out of focus, are a group of youths waving their clubs, machetes and knives,

Figure 4.1 Still from *Shooting Dogs* (also known as *Beyond the Gates*), 2005. Courtesy of Crossday Productions, UK Film Council, and The Kobal Collection.

while shouting and blowing on their whistles. Their gesticulations speak of hatred and rage (figure 4.1). By contrast, when I visited there was no menacing threat and no danger. It felt smaller, emptier, peaceful. Even when the head-master appeared, greeted us and graciously explained in French that the *école* was still operating as a school and in future we would need formal permission to visit, the calm was not shattered. He reminded us that this was the site not only of a feature film, but also of an actual massacre during the genocide. We were to tread carefully.

A few months later, after my return to Edinburgh, I began a lecture by asking the participants what their favourite film was. I was genuinely surprised when several, out of about fifty students, put *Shooting Dogs*, filmed some ten years after the 1994 genocide in Rwanda, at the top of their list. I was intrigued to find out from this group of mostly British nationals in their twenties studying religion or theology why they rated a film about the genocide in Rwanda so highly. There ensued a fascinating discussion about the merits and difficulties of making a film about genocide. It emerged through this conversation that several other students named *Life is Beautiful* (*La Vita è Bella*, Roberto Benigni, 1997), a comedy partly set in a concentration camp behind locked gates, as one of their 'favourite films'. While for some genocide was a depressing topic and made for a 'difficult viewing experience', for many others films such as *Shooting Dogs* (also known in the USA as *Beyond the Gates*) raised profound ethical and religious questions. For many of these young viewers this was their first glimpse of what had happened during the 1994 genocide. They trod carefully. Several questions stand out, pertinent to both feature and documentary films, including: What is it that films about the genocide in Rwanda bear witness to? What are the different kinds of bearing witness found in these films? And how might such cinematic forms of bearing witness promote peace?

Introduction

In this chapter I investigate the ways in which films have been used to bear witness to genocide, in particular the genocide in Rwanda. Elsewhere, I have discussed the process of 'witnessing' through news reports about distant suffering.[3] Like journalists, film-makers take on a number of roles. They can record, preserve and screen the testimony of eyewitnesses to atrocities, they can act as witnesses themselves and, through their cinematic productions, they can then bear witness to traumatic realities. Film-makers can investigate, reveal and even distort what they see and discover. Their experience is commonly peripatetic, travelling between 'the field' and 'the editing suite' (however mobile that has now become). They can capture different kinds of witnesses expressing their testimonies in contrasting physical spaces. 'Witnessing', as John Durham Peters suggests, is to be found in the 'procedures of the courtroom, the pain of the martyr and the cry of the survivor', as well as through the 'borrowed eyes and ears of the media'.[4] Viewers may not be able to be physically present, but they can witness at a distance thanks to the screen.

Through my discussion here I will consider several feature films which bear witness to the genocide in Rwanda, focusing particularly upon *Shooting Dogs*, I then I will move on to examine in more detail a range of documentary films.[5] I consider how these documentaries investigate, interpret, evaluate and commemorate. More attention is given to documentaries, partly because there are few detailed studies of this kind of bearing witness.[6] In chapter 3, we saw the role of different media prior to, during and after the 1994 genocide in Rwanda. In the pages that follow, I consider how the genocide has been re-presented through a range of films and how far such depictions can contribute to building peace.

Apart from *Shooting Dogs*, the 1994 genocide in Rwanda has already inspired over half a dozen internationally produced feature films, including *100 Days* (Nick Hughes, 2001), *Hotel Rwanda* (Terry George, 2004), *Sometimes in April* (Raoul Peck, 2005), *Un dimanche à Kigali* (*A Sunday in Kigali*) (Robert Favreau, 2006), *Shake Hands with the Devil* (Roger Spottiswoode, 2007), *Munyurangabo* (Lee Isaac Chung, 2007), *Kinyarwanda* (Alrick Brown, 2011) and the locally produced *Matière Grise* (*Grey Matter*) (Kivu Ruhorahoza, 2011). Not only feature film-makers, but also documentary producers from all over the world have attempted to bear witness to what happened in and after April 1994. There have been many more documentaries produced than feature films. This is not surprising, given the lower costs involved in this kind of film-making and the nature of the subject matter.

Bearing witness to genocide through feature and documentary film is by no means a new phenomenon. There are numerous cinematic precedents where film-makers have attempted to highlight what happened in the ghettos in Warsaw, in the concentration camps in Central Europe and in the killing fields of Cambodia. Up to this point the vast majority of academic studies have focused on the film-makers who attempted to bear witness to the mass murder of Jews during the Second World War.[7] In *Remembering to Forget*, Barbie Zelizer suggests that the widespread recycling of images from the concentration camps, taken immediately after their liberation in 1945, ensures that many viewers have points of visual reference when confronted by new images of later atrocities, such as the genocide in Rwanda. Reflecting upon the category of 'bearing witness', she suggests that the 'insistence of remembering earlier atrocities may not necessarily promote active responses to new instances of brutality', as 'we may remember earlier atrocities so as to forget the contemporary ones'.[8] This claim is worth bearing in mind as we turn our attention to consider the ways in which documentaries bear witness, using images that are redolent of earlier genocide portrayals. Given how many of the documentaries and several of the films about the genocide in Rwanda resonate with these earlier depictions, especially of the attempted extermination of the Jewish people which often took place behind locked gates, it will be useful to reflect briefly on attempts by film-makers to shed light upon other genocides before turning our attention to Central Africa.

Bearing witness to genocide through film

Film-makers have largely ignored the claim that genocides and their aftermath should not, or at least cannot adequately, be represented cinematically. Adorno's oft-quoted statement 'to write poetry after Auschwitz is barbaric' has sometimes been broadened to include other forms of literature, visual arts and film.[9] Could the same be said after what happened in Rwanda in 1994? Adorno would later qualify this claim, admitting in *Negative Dialectics* that 'it may have been wrong to say that after Auschwitz you could no longer write poems', while claiming the experience of Auschwitz had radically transformed the nature of art.[10] Nevertheless, for those whose own knowledge has been mediated by documentaries, photographs and other visual arts, it is not surprising that some have turned to film-making as they attempt to bear witness to events they did not directly experience themselves. 'Since the 1980s, the question is no longer *whether*, but rather *how* to represent the Holocaust in literature, film and the visual arts'.[11] The historian Tim Cole claims that 'from a position of relative ignorance' or 'silence', the 'Holocaust has emerged – in the Western World – as the most talked about and represented event of the twentieth century'.[12] While it may not be, as Cole suggests, the 'ruling symbol in our culture'[13,] it is possible to trace the Holocaust's emergence as one of the most emotive symbols in Western cultural contexts by reflecting on the wide range of cinematic depictions. How do feature films or documentaries bear witness to this 'defining' genocide? This ranges from visual quotation within fictional film to investigative documentaries via fictional reconstruction of historical events and personal narratives of actual events.

First, visual quotation: Orson Welles' *The Stranger* (1946) is often cited as the first feature film to include documentary footage of the concentration camps. The film depicts the hunt for a Nazi war criminal (played by Orson Welles) who supposedly masterminded the Holocaust and has now escaped to America. He has taken on a new identity (as Charles Rankin) and a new job as a college professor, marrying the local judge's daughter, Mary Longstreet (played by Loretta Young). While the film is now commonly referred to as an example of film noir, at the time of its release it was interpreted as a horror film. In 1946 the *New York Times* review castigated Welles for overacting his part as the 'brains' behind the Holocaust.[14] The horror is to be found not so much in Welles taking 'pleasure out of playing [another] villainous role' as the 'inventor' of the Nazi's 'monstrous murder machine', but rather in his wife discovering that she has married a murderer with a hidden history of orchestrating genocide.[15] In a memorable scene, the UN War Crimes investigator, Mr Wilson (played by Edward G. Robinson), shows footage to Mary and her father of piles of corpses, gas chambers and lime pits where hundreds were buried alive. Wilson's commentary explains how showers were used to open the pores so the gas could be more easily absorbed. In between shots the camera lingers on Mary, with the flicker casting shadows across her face. At one moment Mary declares: 'Why do you want me to look at these horrors?' This question has been both posed and answered cinematically in different ways by other film-makers.

Second, investigative documentary: compare Welles' fictional *Stranger*, which embeds actual footage into the story, with Claude Lanzmann's nine hour *Shoah* (1985), which eschews showing historical footage or dramatic re-enactments, and relies primarily upon interviews with actual survivors, bystanders and perpetrators set in present-day settings.[16] Unlike many other documentary filmmakers, he does not use the photographs taken by the Nazis or the pictures taken by the concentration camp liberators of bulldozers piling up emaciated corpses. *Shoah* is a good example of an investigative documentary which allows victims, observers and killers to speak in their own words. Lanzmann saw his film as a kind of 'resurrection' of the victims.[17] The quotation from the book of Isaiah 56.5, 'I will give them an everlasting name', appears at the start of the film. Here is a very different kind of memorial compared to those discussed in the first half of this book. It took Lanzmann eleven years to produce this documentary, collecting over 350 hours of interviews in fourteen countries. Annette Insdorf, herself the daughter of a concentration camp survivor, writes in *Indelible Shadows: Film and the Holocaust* that 'The achievement of *Shoah* is that it contains no music, no voice-over narration, no self-conscious camera work, no stock images – just precise questions and answers, evocative places and faces, and horror recollected in tranquility'.[18] Given its subject matter and inclusion of numerous interviews with survivors, *Shoah* has taken on an almost sacred quality for some viewers, which has meant that writers have tended to be reticent in their critical evaluation. Nevertheless, it is one example among a 'staggering' number of documentary and fictional films produced on the subject.[19]

Third, dramatic reconstruction: contrast this approach to the recreation of concentration camp life found in the almost entirely black and white drama of *Schindler's List* (Steven Spielberg, 1993), which recreates the world of the ghettos, the forced labour factory and the concentration camp.[20] After many years ruminating, Spielberg decided to direct the film after hearing news about Holocaust deniers and atrocities in Bosnia.[21] Based on a true story that was turned into a novel, *Schindler's Ark* (1982) by the Australian Thomas Keneally, it famously depicts how Schindler (played by Liam Neeson) changes from being a crooked German businessman to the rescuer of over 1,000 Jews. Spielberg set aside the normal tools of his trade, such as the crane, the Steadicam and colour, replacing them with hand-held, more improvised shots. Behind these apparently rough images is crafted cinema. *Schindler's List* was a considerable production, with 126 speaking parts, 30,000 extras, shot on 148 sets with 35 locations.[22] For some critics 'Spielberg transforms Schindler into a Christ-like figure' or a 'contemporary Holocaust saint'.[23] Lanzmann, director of *Shoah*, was even more critical, claiming that *Schindler's List* 'commits a transgression by trivializing the Holocaust, thereby denying its unique character'.[24] Nevertheless, for some viewers the semi-documentary style and rapid storytelling in *Schindler's List* 'provides pain but also catharsis',[25] bearing witness not only to genocide, but also to a more hopeful story amid the loss of over 6 million lives.

Bearing witness is a significant practice in a number of religious traditions, but it can prove to be a difficult undertaking when the subject matter is so bleak. Recalling mass murder through the visually powerful medium of film can be a painful task, especially as retelling or showing again may reopen old wounds. Nonetheless, in the shadows of the attempted extermination of the Jewish people, remembering genocide through film has become a topic regularly attempted by film-makers.[26] When handled with sensitivity and skill, both documentaries and feature films can provoke profound ethical and religious questions. They can also reveal to wider general audiences some of the histories of violence beyond Europe, sometimes overlooked in the West.

A fourth characteristic of these depictions is the way in which film-makers focus on personal narratives. For example, Roland Joffé's Oscar-winning drama *The Killing Fields* (1984) introduced many Western audiences to the horrors of what happened in Cambodia under Pol Pot's Khmer Rouge-led regime. It is estimated that approximately 1.7 million people, of a population of 8 million, died because of the policies of the Khmer Rouge.[27] Joffé focused on two characters. Based on the actual experience of several journalists, *The Killing Fields* portrays the friendship between American journalist Sidney Schanberg (played by Sam Waterston), who escapes Cambodia, and his local apprentice Dith Pran (played by Haing S. Ngor), who is incarcerated by the Khmer Rouge. The last thirty minutes of the film concentrates upon Pran's escape from his captors in

Cambodia. In several sequences devoid of dialogue, we see him tumble through trees and muddy fields, once falling into a waterlogged hole filled with skeletons. He looks lost among the Cambodian 'killing fields'. Unlike the documentary *S-21* (Rithy Panh, 2003), which reveals through interviews how over 14,000 men, women and children were killed by the Khmer Rouge, after being interrogated and tortured at Security Prison 21 in Phnom Penh, *The Killing Fields* dramatically reconstructs the story of two men from very different cultural contexts.

More recently two other semi-autobiographical documentaries stand out. In *New Year Baby* (2006) the documentary film-maker Socheata Poeuv investigates why her own family were so reticent about surviving the genocide in Cambodia.[28] In *Enemies of the People* (Rob Lemkin and Thet Sambath, 2009) the journalist Thet Sambath, who lost his father and brother during the genocide in Cambodia, succeeds in drawing out both the local killers and the Khmer Rouge's second in command, Nuon Chea, also known as Brother Number 2. At times 'Sambath suggests a one-man Cambodian Truth and Reconciliation Commission. Instead of affixing blame, he seeks the healing power of confession'.[29] It is striking how Sambath seeks not vengeance but simply to bear witness to hidden truths through his investigative film.

Forgotten individual narratives embedded in histories of violence have also become the subject of feature film portrayals. By comparison to the *Shoah,* or what most film-makers more commonly describe as 'the Holocaust', far fewer films or documentaries have been made about the Armenian genocide.[30] There are several notable exceptions. Probably the first ever 'genocide film', *Ravished Armenia* (Oscar Apfel, 1919) was based on the experiences of a 16-year-old survivor, Arshalouys Aurora Mardiganian, who played the leading role in this film that was also known as *Auction of Souls*.[31] It depicts the cruelty, through forced marches, beatings, rapes and killings, meted out upon the Armenian population. Only about twenty minutes of the film has survived, but this extract includes the controversial and commonly recycled images of young women crucified. The film, and the book that it was based upon, raised awareness and significant funds in North America for support of the Armenian cause.[32] Over eighty years later, Atom Egoyan's complex *Ararat* (2002) explores the Armenian genocide and its impact on several contemporary lives. While it received a mixed critical reception, some reviewers found it to be a 'thought-provoking film' that 'compels us to experience the toxicity of genocide and the ways it continues to cast shadows on the lives of Armenians and others years after its bloody unfolding'.[33] Films do not provide an antidote to the poison of genocide, they can even wallow in and exploit images of cruelty, but they can at least bear witness to distant audiences both forgotten histories and the longer-term ramifications of violence.

An increasing number of scholars are now turning their attention to cinematic portrayals of the genocide in Rwanda.[34] As with the films discussed above, they can be categorised into a number of related groups, including investigative documentaries, fictional films that make use of actual visual quotations, films that reconstruct historical events and films that are built upon personal narratives. Several writers have been particularly critical of attempts to depict what happened in Rwanda during April 1994 through fictional feature films. It is common for both academics and reviewers to criticise the use of white 'rescuer or saviour figures', the stereotyping of tribal violence, the implied diminishment of Western failures, the romantic narrative or plot structure and the semi-happy endings. Through such films, reminiscent of other Holocaust and Hollywood action or disaster films, Africa is once again shown to be a place of exotic dangers. The result, according to this line of criticism, is that the genocide in Rwanda is divorced from its historical context, romanticised and domesticated.[35] As we shall see, several of the documentaries about the genocide in Rwanda have suffered similar criticisms. If such criticisms are accurate, if only partially, how far does this undermine a film's ability to bear witness? In order to answer this, and the questions posed at the end of the prologue, my intention in the remainder of this chapter is to analyse the different ways in which films have attempted to bear witness to the genocide in Rwanda.

Bearing witness through feature film

Shooting Dogs (aka *Beyond the Gates*, 2005, Michael Caton-Jones) has a Catholic priest, Father Christopher (played by John Hurt), as the central protagonist. As observed earlier, this fictional story was based upon real events and was largely filmed at a secondary school in Kigali where several thousand Tutsis were actually killed. *Shooting Dogs* draws the viewer into a world reeking of death, where law and order is breaking down. Gradually the horror of what is happening outside the school gates is revealed. When the young idealistic British teacher Joe Conner (played by Hugh Dancy) or Father Christopher venture 'beyond the gates' and outside the apparent safety of the compound, they encounter bodies littered on the roads or at checkpoints, and see former pupils wielding machetes, in the midst of gangs who kill without hesitation. *Shooting Dogs* is more explicit in its depiction of violence than *Hotel Rwanda* (2004, Terry George), though the hotel's manager Paul Rusesabagina (played by Don Cheadle) and a colleague do venture beyond the safe haven of the hotel. In a haunting scene from *Hotel Rwanda*, they drive along a bumpy road in semi-darkness and fog only to discover that the bumps were not a sign of going off the track. Rusesabagina steps out of the car, stumbling onto several dead bodies. The viewer is briefly shown a close-up of a lifeless and bloodied face. The fog begins to dissipate and the extent of the horror becomes clearer. Rusesabagina is sick as he realises what is littering the road as far as he can see: piles of corpses.

Through these cinematic revelations, which take place 'beyond the gates', viewers become eyewitnesses of film fictions that point towards actual events. In *Shooting Dogs*, Father Christopher pays his weekly visit to a nearby convent, only to discover the door off its hinges, a smell that makes him retch, and the bloodied corpses of nuns, who also appear to have been raped. The camera does not linger on such scenes but reveals enough to bear witness to a recent atrocity. One result of witnessing the results of such violence is that he begins to question the value of his thirty years of work in Africa. In the face of so much killing, Christopher's hope is 'running dry'. When there is no more fuel for the fires he suggests that they 'use the bibles', as they can share those left over. This moment, set in his chapel, is symbolic of Christopher's growing sense of despair, which is reflected later in the distracted way in which he performs a baptism.

After witnessing the brutal murder of a young mother and baby as they tried to flee, the young teacher Joe asks: 'How much pain can a human being take? If you feel enough pain does everything just shut down before you die?' Father Christopher replies: 'I don't know'. Looking into the middle distance Joe says: 'God knows … maybe we should ask him. If he's still around'. Joe, who earlier in the film had struggled to explain to the children in his class whether Jesus was in the bread during communion, highlights a more profound struggle with the perceived absence of God. This is some distance from a formal discussion of *Deus Absconditus* ('the Hidden God'), and perhaps has more resonance with Elie Wiesel's account of 'those flames which consumed my faith forever' in his memorable book about life, death and a 'world without God' at Auschwitz and Buchenwald, *Night*.[36]

In spite of his own doubts, Father Christopher still attempts to assist the victims, physically, by risking his life to obtain drugs for a sick baby, and spiritually, by trying to ensure that these 'children do not die without taking communion'. Scenes of the communion are juxtaposed with pictures of the Belgium peace monitors lowering their flags, packing up their equipment and preparing to leave as quietly as they can. On one level, the liturgy acts as a distraction to the men, women and children who are relying on the protection of these soldiers, while on another it highlights the divide between what is said and what is happening. While Christopher states, 'Happy are those who are called to this supper', the faces of his communicants look more pensive than joyful. His closing statement, that 'the burden we have set down at the door of the Church for this Eucharist, we know we must bear again', resonates more closely with the actual situation. His final words, with arms raised, carry with them much dramatic irony – 'Go in Peace'– as is highlighted by the fact he immediately looks down and is lost in thought, presumably as to what is likely to happen to those in the church.

At least one critic observed how this film bore witness to the abandonment of Rwanda by the international community. In the context of a largely positive review, Geoff Andrew, writing in London's *Time Out*, observed that *Shooting Dogs* 'doesn't entirely avoid the pitfalls traditional to heroic drama (occasional expository dialogue, the odd tidily convenient climax)', but that the director Michael Caton-Jones, 'orchestrates the spiralling violence with considerable dexterity, revealing a keen understanding of how, in the wrong circumstances, human beings can and do inflict the most barbaric cruelties upon one another'. Andrew also applauds how 'the Hutu are not presented as pantomime villains; nor are the UN troops. Rather, we're kept aware of an absence: the rest of the world, abandoning the Rwandans to their fate'.[37]

There is a sense in which, even more than *Hotel Rwanda*, *Shooting Dogs* bears witness to multiple abandonments. The French soldiers leave, the journalists leave, the white Europeans leave, the UN peace monitors leave, and even the young idealistic teacher Joe leaves in one of the last lorries to depart the compound. The presence outside the compound of a gang of machete-waving youths, blowing whistles and shouting drunkenly, is a visual reminder of the threat prowling beyond the gates. By contrast, the fact that Father Christopher remains almost to the very end expresses a different kind of presence. His staying highlights the departure of so many others, and raises the question of why he stayed and so many others left. Father Christopher's parting words to Joe articulate his own experience of moving on from despair at the horrors he has witnessed: 'You asked me, Joe, where is God in everything happening here, in all this suffering? I know exactly where he is. He's right here, with these people, suffering, his love is here, more intense and profound than I have ever felt'.[38] Even staring directly into the sun, John Hurt delivers these lines with understated force and it is hard not to believe him when he goes on to say, 'And my heart, my soul is here ... If I leave, I think, I might not find it again'. Father Christopher's loyalty for his 'flock' is manifested by his continued presence even when all the other Europeans have left.

Unlike in *Hotel Rwanda*, where the protagonist Paul Rusesabagina acts like a Rwandan Oskar Schindler, providing a safe haven for endangered Rwandans, Father Christopher's character performs smaller-scale roles. Action, for this priest, is partly about being present with those who suffer and performing the liturgies of the church, along with welcoming hundreds of strangers into his school, trying to organise their protection and then, when all else fails, successfully attempting to help several children to escape. This will cost him his life. When he is stopped and confronted at a roadblock by a drunk and enraged former pupil, instead of fighting or running away, he affirms: 'When I look into your eyes, the only feeling I have is love'. The creation of a heroic lead character, especially as a white European priest who ultimately dies a martyr's death, was criticised by a number of commentators.[39]

Several other reviewers were equally uncomfortable that the story was told through the eyes of two white characters. According to Kirk Honeycutt writing in the *Hollywood Reporter*, 'the greatest failure' of the film is 'its inability to enter into the lives of the Rwandans, Tutsi and Hutu alike. The movie never moves beyond the tragic facts to show us the human face of either victims or perpetrators. All we get are white people shaking their heads and cursing Western governments'.[40] Taken out of context this is an overstated criticism, which does justice neither to the film's narrative nor to its characterisations. Out of sixty reviews on the *Rotten Tomatoes* site, over fifty were defined as 'fresh' – in other words they were largely positive – with many providing evidence of how some viewers recognised *Shooting Dogs'* weaknesses while also affirming its ability to bear witness dramatically to aspects of what had happened in Rwanda.[41]

The film's producers also, unsurprisingly, defended the film's ability to bear witness to actual events and individuals. As the producer, co-writer and former Rwanda-based BBC journalist David Bolton states in the commentary to the DVD, this film does not intend 'to give all the answers' and he hopes that the audience will 'go away with further questions' about what actually happened in Rwanda. There are several scenes in the film that do this particularly success-fully, for example, the conversation between Joe, the young teacher, who hoped to 'make a difference' and Rachel, the seasoned television journalist (played by Nicola Walker), who admits that she felt far more emotion in Bosnia seeing bodies of European women than she did in Rwanda witnessing Africans being killed. This memorable and shocking discussion explores motivations, memories and responsibilities associated with bearing witness. In a similar fashion, the value of showing Western viewers what was happening in Rwanda is inter-rogated in *Hotel Rwanda*. A cameraman, Jack Daglish (played by Joaquin Phoenix), has captured graphic scenes of killing on film and Rusesabagina believes such footage will bring help from the international community, asking: 'How can they not intervene when they witness such atrocities?' Daglish's response is pessimistic: 'I think if people see this footage, they'll say Oh, my God, that's horrible. And then they'll go on eating their dinners'. The Westerner here is no hero, like Father Christopher, but a sceptical journalist.

The screenwriter of *Shooting Dogs*, David Wolsencroft, based his characterisa-tion of Father Christopher upon an actual Croatian Franciscan priest, Vjeko Curic (1957–98). He was one of the few Europeans who refused to leave the country during the genocide, despite being ordered to by his superiors. Curic sheltered numerous Tutsis, saving hundreds of lives. Curic's actual practices were more nuanced than those of his cinematic counterpart. For example, during 'the genocide and a number of months later, he refused to provide the sacraments to his flock, finding it inappropriate to do so while they were in the throes of madness; and then after the genocide, only once they had under-taken such acts of collective penance and reconciliation as, for example, rebuilding the houses of their victims'.[42] Curic himself survived the genocide, only to be shot by unknown assailants in 1998. His life story illustrates how some religious leaders neither fled nor supported the genocide, choosing instead to stand up against the mass killing.[43] By drawing a historical reality to the atten-tion of viewers intrigued by the brave actions of Father Christopher in *Shooting Dogs*, this film encouraged viewers to think through the diversity of responses to the genocide, found even among religious leaders.[44] It also encouraged some to consider the difference between the actual life of Curic and the fictional depiction by John Hurt of Father Christopher.

Shooting Dogs, and other feature films based upon the genocide in Rwanda, are sometimes described as 'docudramas', drawing together both fictional and his-torical settings, events and characters. For example, in *100 Days* a Hutu Catholic priest is portrayed as a treacherous rapist, who confines the protagonist, Josette, as a concubine and rapes her nightly. This fictional cleric's actions are based on a number of clerics who actually aided or participated in the genocide.[45] This character stands in sharp contrast to Father Christopher, in *Shooting Dogs*, who is killed as he attempts to smuggle out a number of Tutsi children past the road-blocks of the *interahamwe*. These contrasting portrayals put religion into the foreground of these two feature films, raising questions about the role of religious leaders during the genocide. More recently *Kinyarwanda* (2011) focuses not only on the role of some local Christian leaders but also reveals the less well-known fact that some Muslim leaders provided sanctuary during the 1994 genocide in their mosques. With these notable exceptions, religion is more commonly kept in the background in most feature and many documentary films.

Shooting Dogs, like most of the other feature films on the genocide, focuses on personal stories rather than attempting to put the genocide into a broader his-torical context. *Sometimes in April* (2005) is an exception to this observation. The film does offer a brief history and geography lesson at the beginning of the movie. Directed by the Haitian film-maker Raoul Peck, it memorably begins with the picture of an ancient map of Africa. Slowly the focus narrows and the viewer is offered a closer and closer view of Central Africa and then of Rwanda. During this opening sequence, the 1994 genocide is put into context, with an overlaid text providing a short historical summary of the fall into genocide. This is followed by pictures of a white Belgian soldier in a pith helmet standing over and shaking hands with a tribal king. These grainy colour pictures are overlaid by haunting music and commentary critical of the entire colonial enterprise. There is no direct answer to the question: 'When did paradise become hell?' Instead, the off-screen narrator claims that 'It was never about tribe or race. It was always about greed, arrogance, power … When we finally grasped the horror it was too late'. Unlike *Shooting Dogs*, there is little explicit depiction of religion in *Sometimes in April*, with the exception of the portrayal of a church in Kigali being used as a refuge by large groups of Tutsi survivors. In contrast to Father Christopher in *Shooting Dogs*, the senior priest's role in these scenes from *Sometimes in April* is shown to be highly ambiguous, as he appears to be colla-borating with the killers. Here is a film made by an outsider to Africa, but which nevertheless provides a scathing critique of the misuse of both religious and colonial power.

A good number of local survivors supported the making of *Shooting Dogs* on the grounds that it helped to preserve the memory of what had happened during the genocide beyond Rwanda. For many local people who lost relatives, friends or their own limbs, these are memories that can never be fully erased. For instance, some extras participating in the filming of *Shooting Dogs* in Kigali found the pro-cess revived too many traumatic memories and had to receive medical atten-tion.[46] What the producers described as the 'World Premiere' of the film was on 27 March 2006, at the Amahoro National Stadium in Kigali. In spite of a heavy rainstorm disrupting the event, over 1,500 people saw the film and, according to some observers, it provoked strong emotional responses among many of the survivors. For instance, Speciose Kanyabugovi, a 55-year-old, admitted to an Associated Press journalist that, after seeing *Shooting Dogs*, 'I have no words to explain what I feel. We were abandoned. I hope this film explains the reality to the world'.[47] The desire here is rooted in vivid memories and the belief that a film can bear witness to what happened in Rwanda to the rest of the world.

For all their limitations, *Shooting Dogs* and the other feature films considered briefly here attempt to bring, with varying degrees of success, the story of what happened in Rwanda in 1994 into the popular public domain. Like earlier genocide films from other parts of the world, they also draw upon various kinds of personal narratives, visual quotations and dramatic reconstructions. Religious practices and language are among a number of symbolic resources drawn upon by film-makers. Imaginative elaboration may heighten the dramatic tension, but at the same time it limits the ability of a film to bear witness precisely to actual events. Documentary precision and historical accuracy are rarely the objective of feature film-makers, even when working on such a troubling topic. Instead, small-scale personal stories are used as cinematic metonyms, largely intended to awaken distant audiences to violent histories.

Bearing witness through documentary film

In the previous section we saw how a feature film such as *Shooting Dogs*, even if flawed, is able cinematically to bear witness to and raise awareness of the genocide. Documentaries may not attract such large audiences but, at their best, they have the potential to offer both more detailed and immediate analysis. As we shall see they can investigate, interpret, evaluate and commemorate. As the reality of what had happened in Rwanda became clearer, increasing numbers of journalists, editors and film-makers grasped its significance. The result is that international news organisations, independent producers and more recently local film-makers have been making documentaries on topics related to the 1994 genocide.

Given the scale and speed of what happened in Rwanda it is not surprising that this genocide attracted a large number of documentary film-makers and journalists. Most wrestled with the tension between two sides of witnessing: seeing and showing. This was exacerbated by further common tensions relating to pragmatics: keeping safe while producing a documentary on time and on budget; aesthetics, that is, respecting the victims while crafting a 'beautiful' and magnetic film; veracity, making it accurate while uncovering hidden truths.

Documentary productions can roughly be divided into several groups, which have evolved since the 1994 genocide in Rwanda. While I am neither proposing an evolutionary model of understanding documentary films about the genocide in Rwanda nor drawing directly upon Nichols' well-known categorisation of the different 'modes' of documentary film,[48] it is useful to observe a number of different ways in which these documentaries bear witness to a range of topics which include the initial devastation, survivors' memories of the killings, the return of killers to their own communities, attempts at bringing justice, and moves towards reconciliation and forgiveness.

Investigating: 'A country still in shock'

The first group of documentaries were those made immediately after the genocide in Rwanda (1994–9). These films largely attempted to investigate and to bear witness to what had happened and, in the immediate aftermath, offer some explanations for what had taken place. These were produced by visitors to Rwanda working for international news agencies. For example, consider the BBC current affairs programme *Panorama*, which produced at least half a dozen programmes, and in particular those presented either by the Irish journalist Fergal Keane or by the British reporter Steve Bradshaw. Religion in these documentaries played a recurring rather than a dominant theme, with churches providing the backdrop for many of their investigative accounts.

The first *Panorama* on the topic was *Journey into Darkness* (27 June 1994). In this documentary, Keane visited massacre sites, interviewed victims and even pursued a mayor, Sylvestre Gacumbitsi, accused of 'orchestrating the slaughter of thousands of Tutsis in the village church'.[49] Keane understates the fear, uncertainties and difficulties faced by film-makers and journalists in a country where killing had almost become normalised. This was the first documentary in the UK to show piles of decomposing corpses, many around a single church complex. The documentary challenges ethnic stereotyping, beginning with interviews of moderate Hutus whose families had been murdered. Johan Pottier, who is deeply critical of Keane's appropriation of the RPF (Rwandan Patriotic Front) version of history in his book *Season of Blood*,[50] nevertheless commends Keane for his courageous journalism in this documentary and for 'effectively' challenging 'all received wisdom on the nature of the killings'.[51] For the first time British viewers were able to see and to hear from prisoners who confess that they knew many of their victims and that they killed in order to be rewarded. *Journey into Darkness* won the International Current Affairs Award of the Royal Television Society, though it was only aired after most of the killing of Tutsis and moderate Hutus had taken place. In *A Culture of Murder* (22 August 1994), the reporter Steve Bradshaw focused primarily upon the refugees who had fled the country in the wake of the civil war and genocide. Nearly a year later, in *The Bloody Tricolour* (20 August 1995), a *Panorama* team investigated the role of the French government in the genocide, a topic that other British, French and Canadian documentary makers would investigate in subsequent years.[52]

Two years later, Fergal Keane returned to Rwanda to meet some of the victims he had interviewed for his 1994 documentary. The result was another award winning film: *Valentina's Story* (10 February 1997). This documentary bore witness to the story of an 11-year-old girl who had seen her father and brother murdered, and had been left for dead under a pile of bodies at the church in

Nyarubuye. In a later interview Keane reflects that: 'The programme had one of the most minimalist scripts I'd ever written. It was all told in Valentina's words, a kid who had had her head hacked in, her hand chopped off'. Keane was surprised that 'it had an amazing impact on the British public. People were writing in to get in touch with her. They were sending money for her education. And, nearly 15 years since that film was broadcast, she is studying in the United States'.[53] Note how Keane sees the apparent consequences of this film as a form of vindication for focusing upon Valentina. Towards the end of the documentary Keane, who won several other awards for his coverage of the Rwandan genocide, asserts that: 'it is in parishes like Nyarubuye that Rwanda's future will be decided. Here the Government and the Church tell Hutus and Tutsis to become one people but in Nyarubuye memory is a stronger weapon than any speech or sermon'. Not surprisingly, memory is a recurring theme in many documentaries about the genocide in Rwanda. Back in the church where many of her friends and neighbours were killed, Valentina Iribagiza explains how she feels angry being back in this church. Later she demands revenge, while a perpetrator hopes for forgiveness one day. Keane's final words bear witness to the wounds to be found among the survivors, such as Valentina, 'who survived the unspeakable'. For her, Keane believes 'forgiveness seems impossible. This child and her country face a future that is threatened by the memory of blood'.[54]

This documentary bears witness to the way that 'memory of blood' is brought back to life for this survivor by revisiting a place of trauma, which is still used as a church. This memory is now preserved both through this documentary and in several different forms on the internet. So too are Keane's personal reflections on the experience of covering this story:

> There comes a point in the telling of this story where the existing vocabulary of suffering becomes inadequate, where words wither in the face of an unrelenting darkness. As a reporter I found this the most difficult story of my career to tell. As a parent I listened to Valentina's story with a sense of heartbreak. I marvelled at her courage but felt deep anger that this should happen to any child.[55]

Keane describes here both the limitations of bearing witness as a journalist and the emotional impact of coming close to another's suffering. Keane uses one story to represent an entire season of killing. For some critics, Keane's commentary lacks historical contextualization and 'verges on tendentious oversimplification in setting Tutsi victims against Hutu villains'.[56] This is a common criticism of other documentaries, which all too easily slide into an oversimplified equation of Tutsi = Good and Hutu = Evil. Keane certainly doesn't go as far as a BBC 1 news report (broadcast on 1 January 1996), broadcast at the time of the 1996 refugee crisis in Zaire, which referred to a 'deep-seated tribal conflict' and was accompanied by a visual that described the Tutsi as cattle owners, rich elite and tall, and Hutus as peasant farmers, lower class and small.[57] *Valentina's Story* is a more nuanced account, partly because it allows survivors to bear witness to their experience. Even if it does offer viewers a limited interpretative frame, the recording and broadcasting of these eyewitness accounts bring the story to life in a way that more academic, comprehensive or 'polished accounts of international chicanery and internal rivalries might mask'.[58] Keane is far from a detached observer and is himself an eyewitness revisiting sites of trauma, oscillating in his reports between pained empathy and controlled rage.

In *When Good Men Do Nothing* (7 December 1998), BBC reporter Steve Bradshaw investigated why the West failed to intervene and effectively stood by as the last genocide of the twentieth century took place. This highly critical account of internal UN and US politics was recut for PBS's *Frontline* series and entitled *Triumph of Evil* (26 January 1999). Apart from a brief recycled clip of Valentina speaking about her horrific experience in the Catholic church in Nyarubuye, there is no obvious mention of religion. The programmes describe in detail how UN peacekeepers were ordered to abandon Tutsi civilians pleading for protection in ways reminiscent of the feature film *Shooting Dogs*. The two titles of these documentaries come from the well-known phrase 'All that is necessary for the triumph of evil is that good men do nothing'. While this quotation is widely attributed to the Anglo-Irish politician Edmund Burke (1729–97), there is no exact original textual source. Nevertheless, both phrases capture the essence of these closely related documentaries. Bradshaw later explains how they could also 'have called it "And Who Is My Neighbour?"' recalling 'the sardonic question a lawyer asks in Saint Luke, a question that prompts the Parable of the Good Samaritan'.[59] Bradshaw's film reveals how many political and UN leaders 'crossed over to the other side', ignoring their international neighbours, rather than become embroiled in trying to halt the killing in Rwanda.

Explaining: 'Why did they kill their neighbours?'

These *Panorama* productions are not the only documentaries produced during the 1990s about the genocide in Rwanda. Film-makers and journalists from around the world attempted to bear witness to what had happened. There are a number of French and French language documentaries.[60] Even when many of the bodies were not yet buried, film-makers not only investigated, but also attempted to explain the causes of the genocide. For instance, the short French film *Itsembatsemba: Rwanda One Genocide Later* (Alexis Cordesse and Eyal Sivan, 1996) combines pictures of mutilated corpses and skeletons littered on the ground with a soundtrack dominated by hate speech and songs from the local radio. This film, like several others, bears witness to the role of Radio Television Mille Collines (RTLM), discussed in chapter 3. The Japanese film-maker Kumiko Igarashi's film *Why Did They Kill Their Neighbours?* (1998) also points to the apparently persuasive power of local hate media. This film shows how there were other forces at work, focusing on the story of one man who was forced by his neighbours to murder his sister's children.

After the genocide many NGOs (Non-Governmental Organisations) returned or set up projects in Rwanda. These groups were also keen to try to bear witness to what had happened. For example, Amnesty International supported the production of *Forsaken Cries: The Story of Rwanda* (Andrea Torrice, 1997), which attempted to highlight the colonial roots of the genocide. Alongside these early attempts at explanation, there are films that also attempted to point towards reconstruction. The Canadian documentary *Rwanda: in Search of Hope* (Peter Raymont, 1999) follows a group of Canadian teachers and community workers as they meet a number of survivors. In one scene, the group meets a 15-year-old, Adelphine Umutesi, who lost both her parents in the genocide and is now responsible for bringing up her four younger brothers and sisters. Even though these Canadians are clearly a thoughtful and sensitive group, it is hard not to think of disaster tourists as the film captures them taking photographs of vulnerable youngsters, who are used to represent 'a country still in shock, still reeling from the genocide and its aftermath, still struggling with the consequences – a people trying to find a way to rebuild their shattered nation'.[61]

Religious imagery is once again integrated within many of these and other documentaries. This is not surprising given the ambiguous role that the churches played before and during the genocide.[62] For example, within the first two minutes of *Chronicle of a Genocide Foretold* (Daniele Lacourse and Yvan Patry, 1996) the viewer is shown a statue of Mary in a deserted church. In her arms there is a bunch of drooping pink flowers, fluttering in a gentle breeze. The camera scans down her body to reveal she is damaged: almost snapped in half at her womb. This shattered religious image is allowed to speak for itself. So too are the empty pews and an incomplete stained-glass window. This sequence is part of the first of three sections and is entitled: 'Kibuye – Blood Flowed Like a River'. Up to this moment the viewer has been offered scenic views of hills and lakes, birds crowing as they circle like vultures, all accompanied by discordant music. Then inside the church a lone figure limps uneasily towards the camera; speaking in French, Louis Rutaganira describes how he likes to come to this church to remember those who were killed. Unlike Valentina in Fergal Keane's documentaries, this survivor does not reveal his anger, even though he lost eighty-six members of his family. From his comments we learn that his losses include his wife, by machete, and youngest son, by grenade. He recalls how as Catholics they had gone to this church for refuge. He recalls how their parish priest had been encouraged to escape to safety in a boat to Zaire. An offer he refused, because he declared: 'I'm the shepherd of the flock. I can't abandon 9,000 people just like that'. The result, according to this eyewitness who survived by hiding under a pile of bodies, was that their priest remained to pray and to die with his people.

Visit Kibuye today and you can hear how this head priest, Boniface Senyenzi, a Hutu, did indeed stay with his 'flock' and 'helped seal up the doors and windows against the militias. He is believed to be one of the 11,400 people killed in the attack on the church that lasted two and a half days'.[63] The film skirts over what a later newspaper account reveals. In the *Guardian*, survivor Louis Rutaganira is reported to reveal his sense of betrayal and how, like many other survivors, 'I cannot go back to that church. It betrayed all of us. The Catholic church has never apologised for supporting the killers'. According to this report Louis Rutaganira has since joined the American evangelist Pat Robertson's church, the Assemblies of God.[64]

As documentary drama, the testimonies of Louis, Adelphine and Valentina have heightened authenticity because they have endured hardship, suffered loss and experienced heartbreak. As explanatory accounts they suffer from the limitations of having to create dramatic narratives and being produced so soon after the events. As a first rough draft of broader history, unsurprisingly, these early documentaries commonly overlook significant details and lack historical contextualisation.

Understanding: 'How history can lead to genocide'

Nevertheless, several other film-makers during the second half of the 1990s did attempt to offer viewers a sense of historical perspective. For example, the argument in the film *A Republic Gone Mad: Rwanda 1894–1994* (Luc de Heusch and Kathleen de Béthune, 1996) is that there originally had been peaceful relations between the Tutsis and Hutus, who had shared a common language, religion and 'sacred' king. The film suggests that one reason for the later violent divide in Rwandan society is to be found in the way in which the European missionaries initially singled out Tutsis for favourable treatment by the Belgian colonial powers, resulting in better education and jobs. The seeds of ethnic divisions were sown and nurtured when the Hutu majority received colonial support in the late 1950s. The presidencies of Grégoire Kayibanda (1961–73) and Juvénal Habyarimana (1973–94) poured further fuel on these ethnic divides.

Robert Genoud's *Rwanda, How History Can Lead to Genocide* (1995) develops a similar line of argument, suggesting that the genocide in Rwanda had its roots in 'the early colonization of the country'. As we shall see, this is a far from uncontroversial reading of Rwanda's history. The account offered in this film once again observes how the divided society was 'perpetuated' by both the Belgians and the French missionaries' who initially supported the 'Tutsi minority governing class' and then embraced the Hutu majority.[65] Taken together these programmes bear witness to perpetrators' atrocities, victims' experiences, governmental inaction and even historical background. They illustrate the fact that no documentary can offer a complete picture, and how in the rush to move from investigation to explanation narratives can be simplified or even distorted. Nevertheless, many of them performed a vital role in bearing witness in uncompromising terms to the unimaginable.

Interpreting: 'Threatened by the memory of blood'

The second group, mostly produced ten years after the genocide in 2004, retold aspects of the genocide story and also investigated how Rwandans attempted to both live with and even exorcise the ghosts of the past. Once again, it was largely visitors to Rwanda that produced these films. In many cases, these outsiders only visited the country briefly, to produce programmes to mark the tenth anniversary of the genocide. With greater historical perspective, several of these documentaries attempt to offer more detailed interpretations of what happened. These documentaries also reveal the difficulties and emotional costs of bearing witness and remembering, as well as the place of religion. One of the most widely viewed, whose legacy is preserved through an extensive website, is PBS's *Ghosts of Rwanda* (2004). This time Fergal Keane is one of the interviewees, describing his experience in late May 1994 at the church in Nyarubuye.

> I just remember looking up at the church itself, and there's this white statue of Christ standing with his arms open. And as you look down from him, there's the remains of a human body underneath. And I was – you know, I was raised as a Catholic, and I kind of drifted away, big-time, from religion. But I really – I prayed so hard. I said, 'Our father, who art in heaven, hallowed be thy name. Give us thy kingdom come'. I needed to believe in something.[66]

The full interview, not included in the original documentary, reveals how this experience has changed his view on the world and undermined his optimistic beliefs about humanity and a good force keeping evil at bay. The genocide in Rwanda was clearly a 'defining story' for Keane, as he makes clear both in his own book, *A Season of Blood,* and in the documentary *Ghosts of Rwanda*:

> I think going to Nyarubuye, seeing what had happened there a few weeks earlier and coming face to face with the human capacity for evil on a scale I just hadn't imagined – you can imagine it in your mind, but until you experience it and smell it, until you walk there, in that, that changes you. But I don't welcome the fact that I was changed.[67]

Witnessing the mass killings had a transformative impact upon witnesses from outside Rwanda, such as Keane.

For the tenth anniversary of the genocide, *Panorama* also returned to the story, producing *Killers* (2004). This was first broadcast on BBC 1 on 4 April 2004. Fergal Keane again presented this documentary. With the advantage of historical distance this documentary described both what happened in 1994, using earlier films, and what was happening now regarding the search for justice. It is not always clear which is current and which is old film. The church at

Nyarubuye once again provides the backdrop for several scenes in this documentary.

In *Killers*, one survivor, Flora Mukampore, describes how they knew their killers: 'We used to go to church with them and they taught us together that committing murder is a sin, and God punishes those who kill'. In the previous times of unrest, as we saw earlier, the churches had been used as places of sanctuary, so thousands of Tutsis again sought refuge in these places of worship. Flora's belief was commonly held: 'We thought that no one would dare come to attack us at the church because the church is a holy place'. Later in the programme Keane interviews one of the killers, called Rwamuhizi, who provides a different perspective: 'It was as if we were taken over by Satan. When Satan is using you, you lose your mind. We were not ourselves. Starting with me, I don't think I was normal. You couldn't be normal and start butchering people for no reason. We'd been attacked by the devil.'[68] As we shall see, this kind of explanation recurs in testimonies found in a number of documentaries. For some, this explanation is an excuse and an abrogation of personal responsibility. For others, it is ultimately the only explanation that can finally make sense of what happened. Viewers are left to make their own judgement about such claims of Satanic involvement, though other reasons, such as fear, poverty or hatred, emerge in this and other films.

As with his other *Panorama* films, the reporting and editing is often brisk, moving on from one witness to another, interspersed with Keane's observations. Viewers learn that the 'church at Nyarubuye is a place of worship again but also a memorial. Hutu and Tutsi play together here once more. But Nyarubuye is a place haunted by the memory of what neighbour did to neighbour'. These swift assertions are supported by the reflections of another killer, Renzaho: 'The worst thing for me was killing my neighbour. I used to share a drink with him. His cattle used to graze on my land. It was like I killed a relative'.[69] Keane was not himself a direct witness of the actual killings but the power of these documentaries is partly rooted in the fact that we hear from actual participants and eyewitnesses, often speaking in the places where they had witnessed scenes of cruelty hard to imagine. In this way these films become platforms for bearing witness to what has gone on before. Many of these films serve a similar function to the memorials discussed in chapter 3 and expressed at the University of Butare memorial, which includes a large purple sheet with white lettering: 'You are the loss that shall never be replaced' (figure 4.2).

Observing: 'Determined to be a witness'

Increasing numbers of documentaries in this second group of productions have attempted to tell the story of individuals who actually bore witness to the genocide. For instance, Roméo Dallaire, the retired Lieutenant General in charge of UNAMIR (United Nations Assistance Mission for Rwanda) during the 1994 genocide, has been the subject of several films (including Roger Spottiswoode's

Figure 4.2 Banner at National University of Butare Genocide Memorial, Rwanda, which displays photographs of about 60 victims. Over 500 staff and students were killed. Some students were murdered by their own teachers. Photograph by Jolyon Mitchell.

2007 feature film, *Shake Hands with the Devil*) and documentaries (Steven Silver's *The Last Just Man*, 2001 and Peter Raymont's *Shake Hands with the Devil: The Journey of Roméo Dallaire*, 2004). Both films reveal the post-traumatic difficulties that the Canadian Dallaire experienced. Even though Dallaire 'didn't have the resources to stop the killing, he was determined to be a witness'.[70] This is a paraphrase of Dallaire's own statement in Raymont's documentary, which makes clear that he had originally gone to Rwanda not to be a witness but to lead an international peacekeeping force.

Raymont's film is particularly striking in its ability to create a double witnessing effect. Dallaire becomes the central witness to both the past and the present. Through skilful editing (Michèle Hozer, editor) viewers are taken from images of Rwanda in 2004 and images of Rwanda ten years before. Early in the documentary Dallaire is filmed on a plane returning to Rwanda. He looks down over Lake Victoria, confessing hesitation about what for him would be like 'going back into hell'. Dallaire is conflicted by what he sees and what he remembers: 'I'm seeing the differences but can't get past pictures out [of my mind]'. As he is driven through the streets of Kigali and beyond, we hear how remembered images are 'just exploding in front' of him. For Dallaire they are 'digitally clear' and 'in slow motion'. These comments are brought to life for viewers by the juxtaposition of 1994 shots of corpses lining the streets. Later in the film he revisits his former UN headquarters, as well as the stadium where he created an overcrowded 'safe haven' for several thousand survivors. He declares that 'All I can see is the past'. Through this film it is as if we are seeing Dallaire's memories. Towards the end of the film he and his wife, Beth, visit the Bisesero (renamed 'the Hill of Resistance') genocide memorial, which for his wife is 'a revelation'. In a film that hardly touches on the role of religion during the genocide in Rwanda, one phrase stands out. As they look over beside hundreds of neatly arranged skulls, their local guide declares in Kinyarwandan that: 'nobody protected them … just the hands of God'.

This phrase resonates both with the title of the film and title of Dallaire's book written with Brent Beardsley, *Shake Hands with the Devil: The Failure of Humanity in Rwanda* (2003). The final paragraph of Dallaire's preface is more explicit than most documentaries in its engagement with religious issues. In response to a question posed by a Canadian forces padre whether he could 'still believe in God' after all that he had witnessed, Dallaire's answer provides an insight into his worldview: 'I know there is a God because in Rwanda I shook hands with the devil. I have seen him, I have smelled him and I have touched him. I know the devil exists and therefore I know there is a God'.[71] Like Raymont's documentary, Dallaire's book is more concerned with the failures of humanity than the presence or absence of God.

With a title such as *God Sleeps in Rwanda* (2005), it might be expected that Kimberlee Acquaro and Stacy Sherman's twenty-eight-minute documentary would deal explicitly with religious topics. Instead, it powerfully charts the stories of five women who survived the genocide and are now courageously going on with their lives in spite of their experiences of multiple-rape, losing many of their closest relatives in the genocide and in some cases living with HIV. Their persistence and empowerment bears witness to a more hopeful future for Rwanda. Given the title, *God Sleeps in Rwanda*, it is surprising that religion plays little role in this documentary, with the exception of a brief reference by one survivor to her hope being in God. At first glance the title evokes a passive deity who sleeps through the anguished cries of the women featured in this film. This film is more subtle, as at the end we are reminded of a Rwandan trope, also used in the opening of the feature film *Sometimes in April*: 'They say my country is so beautiful that although God may wander the world during the day He returns at night to sleep in Rwanda'. This documentary may not explicitly deal with religious issues, but like many others it does raise religious questions through its choice of language and its bearing witness to the courage of individual survivors. It is also noteworthy how all of the films in this section draw, to differing degrees, upon religious language, symbols and explanations to tell their stories.

Screening justice: when 'Our killers have returned'

A third group of documentaries produced between 2000 and 2010 focuses on questions relating to justice. Several documentaries covered the International

Criminal Tribunal for Rwanda (ICTR). The South African director Mandy Jacobson's *The Arusha Tapes* (2000), which concentrates on several different trials held in Arusha, was part of a larger project ('Genocide on Trial: the Arusha Video Project') that had at its centre the belief that 'peace and reconciliation will only be possible in Rwanda when those who suffered sense that justice has been done'.[72] The aim was to bear witness to how some of those behind the genocide were being brought to justice in an international court in Arusha, Tanzania. More recent films have revealed the difficulties of bringing the thousands of perpetrators to justice. The French documentary *From Arusha to Arusha* (Christopher Gargot, 2008) explores whether the ICTR contributes to reconciliation, and the limitations of these trials. On the basis of four years of work on this over-long but beautiful film, Gargot believes that 'the ICTR has failed to establish a genuine bond with Rwandan citizens' and that for most people in Rwanda the ICTR means little more than 'footage of trials shown in the evening news, especially when emblematic figures of the former regime are convicted'.[73] His film bears witness to the difficulties of a slow-moving elite justice system, taking place outside Rwanda, which is unable to address some of the injustices that continued to be committed after the genocide by the victorious RPF.

Contrast these films that primarily bear witness to the work of the ICTR with documentaries that portray the work of the local *Gacaca* courts and two very different worlds emerge. In one we see lawyers and judges in gowns peering into computer screens in a courtroom full of desks. In the other we are shown villagers sitting on the grass, protecting themselves from the sun with umbrellas, listening to the stories of their neighbours. For several years large posters promoting the new *Gacaca* process as a way towards truth, justice and reconciliation adorned roadsides in Rwanda (figure 4.3).

Several films highlight the practical reasons for the establishment of *Gacaca* courts. Over 110,000 people were incarcerated in overcrowded jails in 2001 on charges relating to the genocide. An Amnesty International report, *Rwanda Gacaca: A Question of Justice* (2002) suggested that around 11,000 prisoners died between the end of 1994 and end of 2001, from preventable diseases or malnutrition brought about by overcrowding. The local formal genocide courts were only handling just over 1,000 cases a year, leading some to observe it could take about 100 years to clear the backlog of cases. The use of non-professional local courts was an attempt to accelerate the legal process and contribute towards post-genocide justice and reconciliation in Rwanda.[74] It was part of a process that attempted to break the 'culture of impunity', which had ruled in Rwanda for many years before 1994. The Kinyarwanda word *Gacaca* is sometimes translated as 'short grass', 'justice in the grass' or 'lawn justice', and refers to the idea of justice taking place outside. This process is a revival and adaptation of a pre-colonial tradition, where *Gacaca* courts were used to settle local land, familial or village disputes.[75]

Figure 4.3 Gacaca roadside poster, outside Kigali. *Ukuri, Ubutabera, Ubwiyunge* are normally translated from Kinyarwandan as truth, justice, and reconciliation. Photograph by Jolyon Mitchell.

Covering justice: 'Living together again in Rwanda?'

Four films by the French film-maker Anne Aghion provide a detailed insight into the *Gacaca* process. These documentaries are set in the remote rural village of Gufumba, in the Ntongwe district, within the Gitarama region, over two hours' drive southwest of Kigali. The films within Aghion's trilogy on *Gacaca* justice are entitled *Gacaca, Living Together Again in Rwanda?* (2002), *In Rwanda We Say ... The Family That Does Not Speak Dies* (2004) and *The Notebooks of Memory* (2009) (figure 4.4).

This trilogy captures the evolution of the process in one situation. They reveal not only how the *Gacaca* process was explained and undertaken, but also the stories of individual perpetrators and survivors. Narration and explanation are kept to a minimum as locals are allowed to tell their own stories. For example, we are shown a victim accuse, a defendant deny, while dozens of neighbours sit on the grass watching and listening. Finally, viewers are shown the non-professional judges (known as *Inyangamugayo*; in Kinyarwanda, 'people of integrity') taking notes, weighing up conflicting accounts, confessions and delivering appropriate sentences. These films have already been put to use in Rwanda. For example, the documentary *In Rwanda We Say ...* , a film depicting the return of a prisoner to his community, 'was shown to 30,000 or 40,000 prisoners throughout Rwanda as an example of what they might expect to find

Figure 4.4 Production still from *Gacaca, Living Together in Rwanda?* (2002). James Kakwerere (Cameraman) and Anne Aghion (Director) interview *Gacaca* participants. Courtesy of Gacaca Productions, the Kobal Collection, and Marco Longari.

when they return home'. It was used as a way of dissipating fear among prisoners who were 'terrified they'd be terrorized or killed if they came home to their communities'. This film was therefore used to demonstrate that, even though returning was 'not going to be easy', returnees would nevertheless survive.[76]

Aghion's feature length film *My Neighbor, My Killer* (2009) draws on material from her earlier three films. This independent film-maker has spent some ten years working on these films. She may not speak Kinyarwanda, but with the help of a local translator she is clearly able to act as careful witness, collecting over 350 hours of footage. Unlike many of the documentaries discussed up to this point, Aghion does not show a single image of the 1994 massacre. We only hear the cutting down of banana trees for wood. She relies instead upon testimonies. The results are films that lay bare 'memories of blood' and feelings of anger, fear, remorse and acceptance. Jeanette Catsoulis, in the *New York Times*, observes that the women who have witnessed and lost so much are in 'no mood for the group hug of reconciliation' and they 'disdain categorization' and use 'as symbols of suffering: tough, wise and sorrow-forged, they address the camera with a forthrightness' that challenges the viewer.[77] In the words of another reviewer, '*My Neighbor, My Killer* isn't a preachy film. Aghion's pure cinema verité style lets the scenario and players deliver the message by example', because the 'camera is used in such a purely, passively and intimately observational way' viewers take on the role of 'witness', which in turn can even lead to 'self-examination'.[78] In a pivotal scene, two survivors who lost many members of their own families discuss both the *Gacaca* and the process of being filmed. 'It's true our killers have returned'. Their pensive reflections bear witness to their own uncertainties: 'What can we do? Why speak of it?' and stoicism in the middle of trauma: 'I am already dead' and bemusement with the filming process: 'These whites ask the strangest questions'. This scene offers a critical response both towards the film-makers and towards the *Gacaca* process.

This cinematic series of testimonies is interspersed by Radio Rwanda head-lines, which provide a brief moment of historical contextualisation, which is otherwise largely absent. Other critics, while commending the avoidance of 'sensationalism', find that 'its beaten-down, nearly toneless low key, with not a voice raised in righteous anger, grows repetitious'.[79] Even though the govern-ment is demanding local justice and reconciliation as a way to build national unity this documentary explores whether, in a small village, it is possible to live beside the murderer of your family. Alongside the cry 'Forgive us lord' is a sur-vivor who asks, 'My brother's murderer lives just near my home ... why hasn't he come to ask for forgiveness?' Some discussions take place outside the *Gacaca* and depict a survivor encouraging a perpetrator to speak the truth and so allow a weight come off his heart. This was the result of bringing eight people from the one community together and recording four hours of their discussion, resulting in about seven minutes of screen time. Having the camera and film crew bearing witness to their discussions for several years clearly allowed survi-vors to become accustomed to their presence and reflect together on the process. Aghion's films make it clear that the 'Truth becomes an outcome of negotiation between the actors', illustrating how bearing witness to 'Truth in *Gacaca* is both relative and social, and is therefore distinguished from theoretical judicial truth based on an inquiry by an impartial third person'.[80] This negotiated truth is provisional, and it interrogates the value of the expression of painful memories if it does not lead to justice.

Truth telling: the difficulties of speaking out

Other films highlight some of the difficulties inherent in uncovering the truth through the *Gacaca* hearings. For example, the Belgian documentary *Rwanda, les collines parlent* (Bernard Bellefroid, 2005) brings together three stories of perpe-trators searching for pardon and forgiveness. One appears to use the process of bearing witness to bring his release, another shows no remorse, and a third, who killed his brother, seeks reconciliation with his sister. The narrator of *In the Tall Grass* (J. Coll Metcalfe, 2006) claims that success in the *Gacaca* process will set Rwanda on 'the road to reconciliation', while failure will 're-open the gates to a living hell'. This film, like *My Neighbor, My Killer*, primarily concentrates on a single village as a way of bearing witness to the *Gacaca* process. The primary focus of the film is upon a single survivor of the genocide. Joanita Mukarusanga, whose husband and four of her five children were murdered, declares that 'I will never be able to erase it from my mind'. The other central character of the film is one of her neighbours, Anastase Butera, who she believes was among the killers, though he denies having killed anyone. Joanita believes that, since the genocide, 'We are different people, we are suspicious of everybody. We can't trust anyone because we saw so many people murdered'. Some scholars have found a 'dissonance between gacaca courts in theory and in practice' in other parts of Rwanda.[81] One strength of this film is the way that it captures this dissonance, contrasting the ideal: 'Everyone in the village is a lawyer, is a judge, is a prosecutor, and the ordinary people including victims, perpetrators, witnesses are working together ... ' with the actual experience of Joanita and her friends. While they recognise that 'gacaca is a place for us to talk about what we saw', they find that 'some killers would harass witnesses or even hurt them for telling the truth'. This leads them to confess that 'Lying in bed at night you ask yourself if it's even worth it to tell the truth'.[82]

The costs of telling the truth are rarely critically investigated within these documentaries. The 'everyday acts of resistance', often subtle and unnoticed, performed as indirect opposition to the *Gacaca* process are normally overlooked.[83] This is not surprising, as there are no incentives to speak out against the government-promoted reconciliation process. There is evidence to suggest that some film-makers put the search for capturing truth on film above the responsibility to interviewees. This manifests itself by some film-makers, who briefly parachute into people's lives, stir up traumatic memories through their investigations, and then depart with their material, leaving further unresolved trauma behind once they have uncovered the 'truth'. By no means all film-makers fall into this trap, some returning over months or years, such as Aghion. Others find that they cannot be passive witnesses, and they themselves become involved in reconstruction work. For example, consider the director of *Intended Consequences* (2009), Jonathan Torgovnik.[84] He set up a foundation to assist the subject of his documentary. His film provides an insight into the living memories of mothers of children conceived by rape during the genocide. Some speak of their lack of love for their children, while others that they live for their children; another mother (Stella) describes her son as being like a tree without branches and claims that because of its inaction during the genocide, the International Community has a debt to the nation of Rwanda. The voices of the children are also heard, alongside some striking photographs of mother and child. Some describe themselves as hating themselves, as 'left-overs of the militia's sexual appetite', while others are more hopeful. The film itself ends evocatively with a series of beautiful photos of individual children.

The search for truth is at the heart of *Rwanda: A Killer's Homecoming* (Daniela Völker, 2004). It took over a year to make, was broadcast on 22 February 2004 and was part of the BBC *This World* strand of programmes. In sharp contrast to those songs that were used to incite violence, discussed in chapter 3, this film includes part of a song that states: 'This land was cursed. Rwanda, I pray for you. We welcome back the refugees who fled. We reach out to everybody'. Through the retelling of a complicated story, this documentary questions how realistic it is to 'reach out to everybody'. It does this by focusing on the story of Odette and Theophile. Before the genocide they were married and had two children. During the genocide Theophile killed his mother-in-law and other members of her family. He claims he was made to do this. In general terms Odette is unhappy that prisoners have been released and now live close by, 'when they've killed your whole family, looking at you mockingly, that doesn't make me happy at all'. More particularly she appears understandably unable to forgive Theophile: 'he should pay for the suffering he has caused me, for my people whom he killed. I think someone who kills should never be forgiven. The one who has killed should be killed'. In contrast, Theophile, after nine years in prison, wants to return home to his children, and declares that 'I knew that killing was a sin. I seek forgiveness from God all the time. Those who killed should ask to be forgiven. And those who lost their loved ones should forgive, that's the only way forward'. Theophile will have to ask Odette's forgiveness in the *Gacaca* court. His hope for forgiveness is further complicated by the fact Odette has remarried, though without divorcing him, and Theophile is attempting to use the courts to win her and his children back. This tangled story is not fully resolved by the end of the documentary, demonstrating the difficulties brought about as killers attempt to reintegrate into or close to traumatised families or individuals.

Portraying forgiveness: 'They have forgiven me'?

A fourth group of films, produced after 2004, have focused even more sharply on the related themes of forgiveness and reconciliation. In comparison to *Rwanda: A Killer's Homecoming* the documentary *Rwanda: Living Forgiveness* (Ralf Springhorn, 2005) is less ambivalent about the journey towards forgiveness.[85] Viewers hear not only from survivors who bear witness to the killings they have seen, but also from several convicted prisoners. On release they return with some trepidation to their communities, discovering to their surprise that they are apparently accepted and forgiven. While the pain and trauma is not denied, there is a definite movement towards hope and closure. This is most clearly seen in the final sequence, which oscillates between a perpetrator, Kamuzinzi, and a survivor, Jean-Claude. Kamuzinzi describes how he heard on the radio that the president's plane had been shot down by Tutsis, that he was 'required to separate the wheat from the tares', and that the authorities then furnished machetes and other weapons to eradicate the Tutsis. Kamuzinzi and others arrested and killed people at Lake Kivu on 7 April. This testimony of violence juxtaposes with Jean-Claude's description of how he had lost members of his family in that very same location. From talking heads to a roaring motorbike, we are then shown the two of them driving together: the narrator steps in, explaining that Kamuzinzi and Jean-Claude, sworn enemies, now 'relentlessly' tour the country preaching forgiveness and restoration in 'churches and remote places'.

What has brought about this extraordinary change? According to Kamuzinzi, it was hearing 'the word of God' in prison. This led him to a change of heart: 'I deeply regretted what I had done. I confessed everything'. Throughout, his words are translated into American English. Kamuzinzi had killed fourteen members of Jean-Claude's family. Nevertheless, Jean-Claude forgave him, believing that 'We should not judge him, since it's clear that evil forces were at work within him'. The film reveals how Jean-Claude believes that he is called 'to preach to perpetrators'. He believes that the combination of telling his own story of forgiving those who killed his family and showing *The Jesus Film* (1979) results in his listeners being deeply moved. Jean-Claude perceives that when people hear his story they acknowledge that they too must forgive. The stated result for Kamuzinzi is that 'I feel genuine peace. People accept me. They have forgiven me. Now I will have to face *Gacaca* justice, where I will have the opportunity to confess my guilt openly. I have been forgiven, which is why I can live in peace with people'. As a climax to the documentary we see them both outside, dancing and singing worship songs together in front of a rapidly assembled film screen. The moments include a gathered crowd in the semi-darkness viewing *The Jesus Film*. A crowd watches another celluloid crowd. On the screen is Jesus, surrounded by people, welcoming the tax collector Zacchaeus out of his tree (Luke 19).

The detail of this sequence raises several significant issues. These include, first, how this documentary shows *The Jesus Film* (1979), which was largely funded by supporters of Campus Crusade for Christ, being used to reinforce a message of forgiveness in post-genocide Rwanda. The final shot of the documentary is a close up of Jean-Claude's face, his glasses glinting in the light of the flickering projector as he stares towards the screen. His reflective absorption speaks how, for Jean-Claude at least, these moving images have a magnetic attraction. Second, in the English version of *Rwanda: Living Forgiveness* the narrator's deep, rich and resonant American accent and the theology that is celebrated makes it clear that this version was produced with a North American audience in mind. As well as English, the DVD offers German and French versions. It was originally produced for presentation at a Christian conference in Basel, Switzerland, in 2004, and then turned into a DVD. It was also broadcast on some television stations in Switzerland and beyond.[86] Third, as in other documentaries discussed earlier, several interviewees assert that the killers were possessed 'by an evil spirit'. In a context where evil spirits are understood to be real, this is a logical explanation of what drove neighbours to acts of apparent madness. Understanding brokenness like this certainly simplifies the prospect of, if not the reality of, reconciliation.

It is striking how the makers of *Living Forgiveness* go further than many documentary film-makers, framing the killings and cruelty with spiritual categories. The divisive legacy of colonial rule and the contemporary demands from the current government for reconciliation are overlooked. The survivors and perpetrators explore the nature and function of forgiveness apolitically. *Living Forgiveness* offers less than ninety seconds of a simplified history of Rwanda near the start of the film. Viewers are informed that 'this land of a thousand hills is one of the most densely populated nations in the world' and it 'has a turbulent and bloody past'. The narrator then controversially asserts that this is 'owing to the age-old power struggle between the Hutu and Tutsi tribes, which has lasted over centuries' and was reinforced by the colonial German and Belgian over-lords. This is touched on in *Living Forgiveness* and highlighted further in many other documentaries, which highlight that the Belgian authorities introduced identity cards in 1933, which made the ethnic designation between Hutu, Tutsi and Twa clear. The precise extent to which the colonial powers created or reinforced the ethnic divides is an area of ongoing debate, which is ignored in *Living Forgiveness*.[87] Historical context is therefore largely, though not completely, absent. The result is a spiritualising of the genocide.

Categories blur in this short film. Reconciliation between neighbours comes through prayer and personal forgiveness, reconciliation workshops, and the local *Gacaca* system. Little film time is given to explaining the *Gacaca* system of community justice in Rwanda. The narrator declares that 'whoever confesses his guilt here can expect not to be punished'. This is not strictly accurate, though perpetrators may well receive a less severe sentence. Unlike the films discussed earlier that focus on the *Gacaca* system, *Living Forgiveness* does not dwell on the complexities and difficulties of this system of killers of your family returning to live as your neighbours. By contrast, *Living Forgiveness* appropriates the local *Gacaca* system, making it synonymous with reconciliation and forgiveness.

Overall, *Rwanda: Living Forgiveness* appears to divide viewers and critics. Some have found it moving. For example, one viewer in Florida wrote: 'What took my breath away was the ability of these particular victims of unspeakable horror and betrayal to forgive the very people who slaughtered their families and children. The bravery of these loving souls will stay with me forever'. The film even won a Golden Crown Award in 2005 in the USA for being 'Best International Con-tribution' at the International Christian Visual Media Association.[88] For many other viewers, the lack of historical context, the spiritualising of the genocide and the desire to reflect positive and complete closure, like a Hollywood movie rooted in Christian faith, is deeply problematic. One Canadian viewer writes, 'I was not impressed with this film, clearly presented from an evangelical per-spective'. They are particularly critical of how 'several victims talk about the "devil" entering the hearts of the Hutu. As long as the Devil is blamed for this appalling genocide, how much progress is really made – for, in the end, no human responsibility is actually taken for it'. For this viewer, 'the reconciliation that occurs seems hollow and untrustworthy'.[89] These contrasting responses illustrate how a film can become like a mirror reflecting the presuppositions and beliefs of the viewers themselves.

Rwanda: Living Forgiveness is by no means the only film that bears witness to the processes of justice, reconciliation and forgiveness in post-genocide Rwanda. For example, *As We Forgive* (2008) is a film that explores forgiveness in Rwanda following the release of many of the killers back into their communities in 2005. *As We Forgive* was produced by a young film student (Laura Waters Hinton) as her Master's thesis,[90] was narrated by Mia Farrow, and went on to win the student Oscar for Best Documentary. The director herself relies on spiritual categories to explain what happened in Rwanda,[91] though the journey towards forgiveness is depicted as somewhat more complex than it is within *Rwanda: Living Forgiveness*. This is also the case in *Flowers of Rwanda* (David Munoz, 2008), where we hear survivors describe that they can only forgive if a perpetrator actually asks for forgiveness; otherwise there is a lurking fear that they may have it in them to kill again. The subtitle of this film is an unsettling phrase, 'Making Peace with Genocide'. At first sight it is impossible to make peace with genocide, though in this film it becomes clear that the 'older generation in Rwanda feels responsible to forgive the perpetrators of the genocide in order to lay a foundation of peace for the next generation'.[92] Through interviews and shots of inflatable film screens being set up, this documentary also underlines the significance of both education and film in this process of moving towards reconciliation. *Flower in the Gun Barrel* (Gabriel Cowan, 2009) is another example of a film that explores the struggle between 'memories of blood' and the government's encouragement to forgive.

Film-makers are more drawn to individual stories of survival and forgiveness than to collective acts of reconciliation. At the centre of *The Diary of Immaculée* (Peter LeDonne, 2006) is the story of one of Rwanda's best-known survivors of the genocide: Immaculée Ilibagiza. Viewers learn how Immaculée hid in a tiny, three-by four-foot bathroom with seven others for ninety-one days. They could not talk, for fear of being discovered. They were hiding in the home of a Hutu pastor, Simeon Nzabahimana, who is one of the film's interviewees: 'During the killings I saw them coming and could not turn them away. They were the children of my friends'. Immaculée's Catholicism is downplayed in this documentary, though we do see her light a candle in St Patrick's Cathedral in New York, where she has settled. We hear an observer suggest that in the Divine she found the 'power to love and power to forgive'. Her story is also briefly used in another documentary, *Uganda: Ready to Forgive* (Ralph Springhorn, 2008), which she presents. Once again the film overlooks Immaculée's Catholicism, so, for example, her praying with the rosary while in hiding is not mentioned. She does, however, provide a bridge into the world of Uganda by asserting that 'Rwandans are not the only people to suffer and forgive'. Like *Living Forgiveness*, both these documentaries appear to have different parts of the North American evangelical market in mind.

Remembering: "the process of witnessing the past ... the present ... the future"

Who bears witness in the films and documentaries considered up to this point? In many films it is an outsider who is one of the most significant witnesses within the film, including a white Catholic priest, a British teacher, a Canadian general, an American Adventist aid worker, a French politician, a Swiss Red Cross director and an Irish journalist. These figures interview, comment upon or act as the interpreter of the stories of the local survivors. In the words of the local film-maker Eric Kabera: 'It's through other people's eyes that the Rwandan genocide has been discovered'.[93] This is not surprising given that up to this point we have largely considered documentaries produced by visitors to Rwanda. Many of these films, produced by outsiders, have as their primary target audiences from outside Central Africa. This process continues.[94] There are, however, an increasing number of films made by Rwandans with local audiences in mind. The large number of international documentaries produced in Rwanda over the last years partly explains why there has been a growth in locally produced films. Some productions used and even trained local film-makers. Kigali's film centre and the touring 'Hillywood' film festival have also contributed to this dynamic growth. One of the leading forces in this developing Rwandan film industry is Eric Kabera, who sees himself as a 'socially conscious film-maker' who can 'actively contribute to keeping peace' through his film-making, which includes bearing witness to what has happened, is happening and could happen.

> When I started all this I don't think I fully appreciated how important and how crucial the filmmaker is to the process of witnessing the past here, witnessing the present life, and indeed witnessing the future.[95]

Kabera is the founder and current president of the Rwanda Cinema Centre. He has acted as producer on two feature films, Nick Hughes' *100 Days* (2001) and *Africa United* (2010), and he directed *Keepers of Memory: Survivors' Accounts of the Rwandan Genocide* (2005).

This documentary focuses on how memories of the genocide are being preserved. Kabera's film takes the viewers around a number of memorial sites, including several of the killing churches. On one level, he was attempting to 'portray a country full of graves' and introduce audiences to those who tend these memorials: the 'memory keepers'.[96] On another level, making this film for Kabera, who lost many of his own family in the genocide, was 'like a self-discovery process – digging into my own soul through the souls of the survivors'. This is clearly a painful process.

> I think it is very difficult to truly portray the madness of the suffering of the Rwandan population and what they have seen and experienced, especially with regard to the genocide, which affected the Tutsi communities. All a filmmaker can do is to try to present the sheer magnitude of the experience. We've seen it done with the *Shoah*. The pain is so deep and there are so many layers. There's so much; it's beyond any human being's strength, because evil is so powerful.[97]

This was 'a very personal investment' for Kabera and it took him about 'four years to recover' from making this film and 'to move to other subjects or even to film similar topics'. The power of Kabera's *Keepers of Memory* is rooted in the fact that it relies almost entirely on locals narrating their own stories. This creates what Roger Bromley describes as an 'aesthetic of ethical respect' challenging the reductive stereotyping of other Western representations which rely on the 'spectacle of the dead African body'.[98] Memory keepers, survivors, witnesses and perpetrators provide contrasting testimonies. We hear one perpetrator asking for forgiveness from the Rwandan people and from God. We see Veneranda, who appears to tend the Nyarubuye monument alone, laying flowers on bones both calling on God to 'punish the perpetrators' and then praying for them.

This film subtly bears witness to the complexities of a government attempting to assert unity and reconciliation from above, when so many local survivors remain traumatised and often impoverished. One of the keepers poignantly asks:

> I have the impression you are journalists ... you come and ask us questions and then you go back ... many of us are dying ... why do you ask all these questions ... the way I see it, you are not of any help to us ... when will you come to be of help ... can you not see how old we are ... do you want to wait until it is too late?[99]

Here the local rural residents interrogate the urban visitors who come to bear witness to their story, but do no more than observe. Kabera is a confident enough film-maker to include this in his final cut, and the result is that the interrogation goes beyond the screen to the audience itself. As with Aghion's observational film *My Neighbor, My Killer*, the 'proscenium arch' or 'fourth wall' is broken as the interviewees interact with the film-makers.

Kabera is by no means the only local film-maker who finds producing such documentaries both painful and at the same time cathartic. The director of *Behind this Convent* (2008), Gilbert Ndahayo, describes how 'Rwanda has suffered a lot. I have suffered a lot. I want to express it'. When he was only 13, he returned home to discover the corpses of his family and some 153 bodies of his neighbours 'in a pit in the back garden where he played as a boy'.[100] For Ndahayo, who lost over fifty members of his family in the genocide, including his parents, grandparents and sister, the making of his fifty-five-minute documentary *Behind this Convent*, which became the longer hundred-minute film *Rwanda: Beyond the Deadly Pit* (2010), 'was a really hard thing to do', but he admitted that: 'I used it to try to heal myself'.[101] From this perspective the making of the film became a way of searching for interior peace and reflecting through a semi-autobiographical film the search for justice and reconciliation. Several interviewees interrogate the role of the Catholic Church before the genocide, which according to one woman became a 'vehicle for genocide ideology'. Another interviewee, a young man, questioned the danger of outsiders after the genocide coming in and encouraging people to sing '"forgive, forgive" without it coming from the heart'. The film bears witness to the complexities of a wounded film-maker using film production as a therapeutic space, a memorial and a place to investigate the real difficulties of embracing forgiveness. 'The only cure for my sickness is to tell my Father's story', though he admits he couldn't tell how his mother was raped or his 11-year-old sister was murdered. He had to allow other survivors to speak on his behalf. His own story is to be found beyond this documentary in an interview on *YouTube*, where he explains that, 'When confronted by the repentant killer of his Father he confesses that he had to forgive him, though for Ndahayo "forgiveness is not above the law".[102] Filmed over a three year period, collecting over 600 hours of film testimony, eschewing narrator and music, this film is an attempt to "haunt the souls" of viewers and "inspire new hope"'.[103]

The experience of film-makers as they both bear witness to and bear witness against the genocide resonates through their films. Léo Kalinda dedicated his documentary *Mothers Courage: Thriving Survivors* (2005) to his own 'massacred family'. At the heart of this film is Athanasie Mukarwego, a woman who lost her husband in the genocide and, in view of her four children, was repeatedly raped over three months. She has helped to set up groups to assist other rape victims and traumatised survivors, to deal with feelings of guilt, anger and shame. It is not just stories of survivors that have continued to be produced.

Daddy Ruhorahoza's *Confession* (2008) is an example of a locally produced low-budget short film, made for only $350, which borrows the language of documentaries to tell its semi-fictional story. As with *Behind the Convent*, the director Ruhorahoza's experience during the genocide shaped the content of this film. Unlike Ndahayo, his own family were unexpectedly protected. This was by a man who raped and killed over thirty women in his neighbourhood, who apparently protected them because Ruhorahoza's mother supplied him with a meal every Friday. In the light of this and other experiences, he wanted to make a short film that illustrated that there is 'humanity left in every criminal'.[104] How does he achieve this? One way is that he places the perpetrator in a still, interior, darkened space, a side-light gently illuminating half of his face. A paper cross is stuck onto the semi-translucent material, creating a setting reminiscent of a confessional. Most of the time the man stares intently towards the camera, confessing his rape, his 'sinning' and how the woman he raped was never seen again. As viewers we are also shown a simple purple flower lying on her foot. The flower is reminiscent of those used in cemeteries in Rwanda. For local audiences this would be a clear sign that she died. He explains how he now prays for her every 6 April, together with her family. The formal confessional may not work for him, but the end result for viewers is memorable: looking away from the camera, he declares that 'I ask for God's mercy. I want peace in my soul'.

The search for peace also found in another locally produced film entitled *Icyizere: Hope* (Patrick Mureithi, 2009). This film concentrates upon the stories of ten perpetrators and ten survivors meeting together at a three-day reconciliation workshop. Mureithi, a Kenyan film-maker, reflects moments of trauma and tentative steps towards reconciliation. He uses the camera creatively, sometimes focusing on an individual's face and other times almost absent-mindedly looking out of the window. Mureithi screened this film to audiences of several thousand during Rwanda's touring Hillywood film festival. Like many others he set up an inflatable screen to facilitate outdoor showings. Piotr Cieplak uses this film's production, content and display as an example of the development of an alternative African Cinema.[105] He also draws on Debs Gardner-Paterson's *We Are All Rwandans* (2008) to support his case. This documentary tells the story of a group of Rwandan teenagers whose school is attacked by militia in 1997. They are ordered to separate into Hutus and Tutsis, but refuse, declaring, 'We are all Rwandans'. Some of them paid with their lives because of their bold refusal to be ethnically determined.

This story of non-violent resistance gestures towards a future where ethnic divides will not necessarily lead to victimisation. Increasingly both local and international film-makers are attempting to bear witness to a more hopeful vision of Rwanda's future by focusing on some of its young people. *A Generation After Genocide* (Torey Kohara and Jonathan Weiman, 2009) shows how three young orphans from different ethnic backgrounds are brought together through football. Not only sport but, according to other films, also the arts are being used to promote peace. In Kabera's *Through My Eyes: A Film About Rwandan Youth* (2006), viewers are shown how a number of teenagers, who lost many within their families during the genocide, are now using the music, dance, painting and poetry to come to terms with both the physical and emotional trauma that they have lived through. More recently, locally produced feature films have been produced exploring life and love in the aftermath of the genocide. For example, in Dushimirimana Thierry's *Une Lettre d'amour à mon pays (A Love Letter to My Country*, 2006) a young Tutsi survivor of the genocide falls for a Hutu, whose family was involved in the killings. It does not slide into a tragic *Romeo and Juliet*-type ending, it also avoids tumbling into a celebratory crescendo to be found in a film such as *Africa United* (Debs Peterson, 2010), which depicts several Rwandan youngsters making an epic journey from Rwanda to South Africa for the World Cup. *A Love Letter to My Country* may lack the production values of some of its international, and more costly counterparts, but this feature, like many of the documentaries discussed in this chapter, explores how forgiveness and reconciliation might emerge between individuals divided by memories of blood.

'Determined and Fragile Witnesses'

Close to the *école*, where so many were killed after the UN troops left the compound, there is a different kind of gate than the one described at the start of this chapter. It provides both access and protection to the cemetery where many of those who had sought sanctuary in the ETO are buried (figure 4.5).

The doors are green, and painted in white capital letters at the top is the word *IBUKA*, Kinyarwandan for 'remember'. Below this, on the doors of the gate, is the French statement translated here into English:

> You cannot respond to such a determined and terrible crime, except with an equal determination to bear witness ... [106]

As we have seen in this chapter, one of the recurring elements within the films that focus on Rwanda before, during and after the 1994 genocide is a determination to bear witness.

Since 1994, dozens of documentaries have been produced bearing witness to the genocide and its aftermath in Rwanda.[107] No end is in sight of this prolific film-making as both local and visiting film-makers continue to attempt to represent Rwanda's evolving story from different perspectives. We have considered how numerous documentary films bear witness to a wide range of related topics, including the actual 1994 genocide, its historical roots and social causes, survivors' memories of the massacres, the return of *génocidaires* to their own communities, attempts at bringing justice through local *Gacaca* courts, and attempted moves towards reconciliation and forgiveness. This has been a far from an easy journey. It is difficult to put a frame around any genocide. Inevitably, important details are left outside the cinematic or documentary frame. For instance, the relation between the genocide in Rwanda and the subsequent civil war in the Democratic Republic of Congo is rarely explored. Like the feature films about the 1994 genocide, such as *Shooting Dogs*, we have seen that, while many documentaries have limitations, they mostly succeed in bearing witness to aspects of the troubled past, or the complex present or even the hopeful future of Rwanda. To achieve these ends we have seen how film-makers have employed a range of cinematic and documentary devices to investigate, to interpret, to evaluate and to commemorate.

As has become clear through this chapter, the most commonly used device is personal testimony and narrative. These personal stories are becoming increasingly accessible. Clips and entire documentaries are now available online. For example, *Raindrops over Rwanda* (Weingarten, 2010), whose producers attempted to attract an online audience of over 50,000 by July 2011, is no exception when it comes to revealing personal narratives. It focuses on the experience of the reporter and the story of Honoré Getare, the 28-year-old 'head tour guide' from Kigali Memorial Centre, enabling him to tell part of his story and affirm that 'we need to tell the truth to each other'. For him, the result of forgiving is confession and apology by perpetrators leading to new forms of interaction and the healing of community.[108] While the official narrative of reconciliation and unity is presented largely uncritically in this short documentary, it remains a tale moving towards hope. For José Rabasa, a scholar of recent Mexican history, testimonial documentaries are 'political interventions in the context of disputed truth'. Rabasa recognises that they are not unbiased, but that by mixing verbal testimony and visual information, close-ups, clips and music they can contradict claims made by authorities in different context that deny the reality of state killings.[109] Documentaries whether in the Americas or Africa can also, of course, unintentionally reinforce narratives promoted by the regime in power.

The French journalist Jean-Christophe Klotz was in Rwanda during much of the genocide, until he was badly injured and evacuated to France for medical treatment. Returning some ten years later, he produced *Kigali, des images contre un massacre* (2006). Reflecting on the experience of working as a journalistic witness, Klotz metaphorically contrasts the moth and the butterfly. The moth that is exposed to the flame: too close to reality, it burns; too far from reality, it remains permanently outside, with the butterfly. For Klotz the butterfly is the witness who helplessly watches the execution of an entire population.[110] Klotz clearly perceives himself, and several other figures within the documentary, like a butterfly, little more than a fragile and powerless witness. This sense of powerlessness pervades many of the testimonies found within the documentaries considered in this chapter.

This powerlessness is not always complete, especially when the central protagonist is undertaking a journey of discovery, which has the potential to draw the viewer into the unfolding narrative. Consider *True Stories: Rwanda After Genocide* (Deborah Scranton, 2011), which follows a Rwandan, Jean-Pierre Sagahutu, who goes in search of those who killed his father. He is motivated by the desire to uncover the truth. He eventually finds and then confronts his father's killer, who confesses to the murder, explaining how he was motivated by fear and that he had lost his own Tutsi wife during the genocide. While he is not immediately ready to 'forgive', Sagahutu's final response is particularly striking: 'The cycle of hatred and violence stops with me. I will not pass it down to my children'.[111] The film's original title was *Earth Made of Glass* (2010), which is drawn from Ralph Waldo Emerson's assertion that 'There is no den in the wide world to hide a rogue. Commit a crime, and the earth is made of glass'.

Documentaries, however, are not as translucent as their producers would always wish. Alongside this personal narrative *Earth Made of Glass* provides viewers with extended opportunities to hear from Rwandan's current president, Paul Kagame. He comes across as a thoughtful and dignified leader who even requested his 'men to stop taking him to inspect yet more scenes of slaughter'. His stated reason is that 'The more that you see ... the more it will impair your judgement'. Nevertheless, this former military leader bears witness in a persuasive fashion to what is sometimes described as the 'RPF version' of Rwanda's history.[112] This assumes that there was a harmonious situation in Rwanda before the colonial invasion, suggesting that the ethnic divides which led to the genocide are almost entirely caused by colonial rulers. When history is covered, this narrative is to be found in many of the documentaries already considered in this chapter. There is no reference to the detailed scholarly claims that the ethnic divides, while significantly reinforced by the European invaders, have a longer pre-colonial history.[113] Documentaries also downplay, or even completely overlook, the claims that the RPF themselves carried out atrocities or revenge attacks upon the Hutu majority. Film-makers who are too reliant on local fixers or the government of the day can all too easily acquiesce to repeating the commonly accepted government account of historical reality.

Whatever the precise historical background, many *génocidaires* literally got away with murder in 1994. Film footage that bears witness to the actual process of killing in Rwanda is extremely rare. The most widely viewed sequence, out of three known, shows a woman kneeling in the middle of a road, surrounded by bodies, pleading for her life. Nearby, a group of people talk, apparently oblivious to her cries, a young boy passes her with little more than a backward glance, a truck passes with the passengers in the open back apparently taunting her. Finally, two men approach her. First they beat a man next to her and then the other with a violent swipe knocks her to the ground. Unlike in *Hotel Rwanda*, where the video footage taken by Jack Daglish and discussed earlier leaves little to the imagination, it is hard to discern precisely what is happening, as the figures are distant and the branches of a tree partly obscure the shot. A freelance cameraman, Nick Hughes, filmed this from the comparative safety of a high building nearby. His batteries were running out, so the film is interrupted as he switches off his camera in an attempt to save power. This rare film record, used in several of the documentaries discussed in this chapter, also became the subject of *ISETA: The Road Block* (Juan Reina, 2008) a documentary co-produced by Eric Kabera. This film shows Hughes meeting up with those caught on the film and relatives of those killed. The sequences of him showing these films to the relatives are both memorable and painful as we witness moments of recognition as they realise their loved ones' last moments were captured on film. The emotional force of such a moment is impossible to deny. As I have argued, bearing witness can be a painful and complex exercise.

Conclusion

Nevertheless, as we have seen in this chapter the process of bearing witness through documentaries has been put to many different uses. A significant number have operated within an *investigative* mode, investigating what actually happened during the hundred days of killing. Others have embraced an *interpretative* mode, attempting to explain both what happened and why Rwanda slid into a genocide. The failure of the international community, especially the UN and the former colonial powers, have led some film-makers into *evaluative* descriptions, pointing the finger at those who could have acted but did nothing. It is noticeably rare for this critical evaluation to turn against the international media and its failure to cover the story effectively, especially in the early days of the killing. As time has passed, some documentaries have taken on a *commemorative* role, preserving the memories of those who died and marking anniversaries since the genocide.

Bringing dangerous memories back to life is a recurring difficulty for many film-makers. The return of former killers to their original communities and the subsequent local *Gacaca* hearings have allowed some film-makers to re-present and interrogate restorative forms of justice. By focusing on individual stories, some documentaries have even become critical vehicles against a top-down approach to reconciliation, which ignores the traumas that individuals are struggling to live with.[114] Some documentaries use local processes for their own rhetorical ends, promoting particular kinds of forgiveness or religious belief. Others put it to political ends. In a manner reminiscent of the exhibition on the top floor of the genocide memorial museum in Kigali, where the genocide in Rwanda is placed alongside other earlier genocides, some programme makers place the genocide in Rwanda alongside other genocides, even using it to warn about the dangers of history repeating itself in Darfur.[115]

Whether attempting to investigate, to interpret, to evaluate or to commemorate, it is striking how every documentary discussed in this chapter makes use of at least one emotionally charged account by a survivor. Haunting music or images, which encourage viewers to 'feel deeply' about what they are witnessing, amplifies the emotional force of what is being shown. When confronted by a survivor who has lost dozens of family members, it is hard not to be drawn into the narrative, leaving behind critical distance and rational reflection. In these contexts, it is all too easy to overlook the fact that viewing will often take place in the comparatively comfortable and secure setting of the West, that the violence did not end in 1994, that Hutus can also be demonised or marginalised, or that religion is playing, and continues to play, a part in the task of rebuilding a nation and helping to heal some of the all too present wounds. Simply bearing witness through film is not enough to build sustainable peace.

Chapter 5

Searching for truth and reconciliation

Prologue

Some people are hard to forget. Our guide on Robben Island, the notorious prison for political opponents of the apartheid state in South Africa, was one such person. Modise Pheknonyane spent over five years (1977–82) incarcerated on Robben Island for his protests against the Bantu segregated education system.[1] Modise was one among many in the youth wing of the ANC who demonstrated against the apartheid regime, refusing to speak Afrikaans at school and protesting for better education for black youngsters.[2] Like well over 200,000 opponents of the regime, he was imprisoned for his resistance. Modise speaks with a quiet passion, which is hard to resist: 'I despised apartheid. I was not a human being in apartheid. I was humiliated during apartheid. I was degraded'.[3] It is not just his words that illuminate his trauma. He used his whole body to communicate and bring the 1970s back to life (figure 5.1).

At the start of our visit, as we entered the prison, he gestured down to the spot where he was made to sit naked as a teenager on the cold floor. Then he told how he and his inmates waited for their prison uniforms. Leading us from the entrance hall into one of the small dormitories, he there described in greater detail how he, and his fellow inmates, were abused and tortured. Gesturing with his hands he recalled when a gun was thrust into his mouth and he was ordered to 'confess'. If he didn't, his tormentors claimed they would 'blow his brains out'. He was also held upside down by a river, threatened and then beaten until his face swelled up. The abuse he received drove him to contemplating suicide on several occasions. I remember his story and his demeanour all the more clearly because I recorded him on film and have watched him several times since returning to Europe.

Given how he was treated both before and during his confinement it was not surprising to hear him admit that as a teenager: 'I was so hateful when I came here. Really, truly I hated white people inside'. He explained that he was even angry with fellow inmate Nelson Mandela who he felt had 'sold out' to the regime, reflecting how the prisoners of different ages and parties were not as united as sometimes depicted. Gradually his attitude changed: 'Today, I live,

Figure 5.1 Modise Pheknonyane. Robben Island, South Africa. Photograph by Jolyon Mitchell.

I walk, I sleep – everything about me is about peace, reconciliation and justice. I cannot see any other way … ' He mused on what would be the case if he had not followed the path of reconciliation: 'I would still hate, I would still be angry, bitter and a victim'. Even if apartheid had vanished he would 'still be left angry and hateful', he would still be full of 'hate' and 'unmanaged anger', still 'a victim'. Modise reflected on what happens when anger and hatred is unchecked: 'Think of Burundi and Rwanda, think today of the poor Somalians, think today of Zimbabwe'. It was noticeable how he connected his own journey towards reconciliation with national traumas. His celebration of reconciliation was not rooted in wishful thinking or a yearning for an African utopia:

> Life today makes sense to me. It does not mean because I forgave and reconciled there are houses for everybody. It doesn't mean we don't have an HIV problem, it doesn't mean crime is not a problem. It doesn't mean necessarily that there are people who still don't like me. Or in my world black people still don't like white people.[4]

For Modise, forgiveness and reconciliation are not magic pills that will cure all of South Africa's ills. From his perspective they do, however, have the potential to help to transform a landscape previously dominated by violence. Modise names the rifts and the wounds in today's South Africa, recognising the need for change. Modise's personal account was striking not simply because of his manner and passion, but also because of where he tells his story – an island where he had experienced regular brutality, and because of his realism: 'reconciliation and forgiveness was a very tough pill to swallow but once it was down in the system it did a good job. And it's worth it, trust me'. Modise is now a published poet and has an infectious charisma, which makes his vision for building peace all the more convincing.[5] His primary media at the time we visited were his forceful voice and his passionate words. He is a convincing performer. He has obviously recounted these stories many times to numerous visitors, but there is a freshness, energy and passion that are hard to resist.

On return to the UK I found that his tour of the prison, his story of personal transformation and his highlighting of Mandela's experience has affected many others.[6] For instance, one academic from North America wrote on her weblog after her visit how Modise had singled her out and said:

> "I have the key to Mandela's cell. Today we will unlock it together". Tears filled my eyes ... Modise spoke directly to me in a tone for everyone to hear, "It usually was white men who locked up black men in this prison. You cannot help it that you were born white and I cannot help it that I was born black. But, today, we will together unlock Nelson Mandela's cell as a symbol of future possibilities together". I was so overcome by emotion that I could hardly place my hand over Modise's hand to grasp the key.[7]

This dramatic moment was not repeated on our tour, but Modise did theatrically use a large jailer's key to unlock cell 5 in Block B, Mandela's tiny cell. This small, sparse space has room for little more than a mat to lie on, a waste bucket and a tiny table. My own film and photographs do not capture the mundane smallness of the space (figures 5.2a and b). Of the twenty-seven years Nelson Mandela spent in prison, he was incarcerated on Robben Island for over eighteen years. Mandela wrote part of his autobiography in secret there. Modise showed us the places in the exercise yard where Mandela had hidden some sections. In *Long Walk to Freedom*, Mandela describes Robben Island as 'without question the harshest, most iron-fisted outpost in the South African penal system'. For Mandela, 'journeying to Robben Island was like going to another country'.[8] For our mixed race group of visitors, seeing the cells, learning the history, listening to and filming the stories of the Island's violent past was a bracing reminder of a sharply divided nation.

Mandela's story was singled out above those of the many other incarcerated political prisoners. It is intriguing how many of the cells had been repainted, becoming both monument and museum. As a visitor, I found stepping inside this claustrophobic cell a physical reminder of Mandela's long and difficult road to freedom. At the time, and reviewing my own brief film recordings afterwards, listening to Modise describe his journey from hatred to reconciliation was even more memorable.

Figure 5.2 (a) Corridor leading towards Nelson Mandela's prison cell.

Figure 5.2 (b) Nelson Mandela's prison cell. Robben Island, South Africa. Photographs by Jolyon Mitchell.

Introduction

As I was to find out myself, the move towards reconciliation can be a process difficult to capture on film. Nevertheless, at the heart of this chapter is this question: How far can films help in the search for truth and the building of reconciliation? In order to answer this question I primarily analyse feature films, though I will also consider several documentary films. I focus on films that search for the truth about what happened during the apartheid regime, and what is happening in the reconciliation process in post-apartheid South Africa. My argument is structured around three movements, which reflect my own brief journey to Robben Island. First, moving towards apartheid, I use the film versions of *Cry, the Beloved Country* (1951 and 1995), based upon Alan Paton's 1948 novel, as the focal point of my discussion. Second, moving within apartheid, I analyse how films, such as *Cry Freedom* (1987) and *Sarafina!* (1992), produced both during and after the regime's demise, were used to reveal some of the realities of apartheid. While state subsidies were available for films that supported or promoted aspects of the apartheid regime, my primary focus will be upon anti-apartheid films. Third, moving away from apartheid, I consider in greater detail both portrayals of and responses to the Truth and Reconciliation Commission (TRC). As will become clearer through this third section, both 'truth' and 'reconciliation' are contested terms and goals, around which a number of debates have emerged. The same is true of the results and practices of the TRC itself. I compare and contrast Western films such as *Red Dust* (2004) and *In My Country* (2004) with largely locally produced productions such as *Zulu Love Letter* (2004) and *Forgiveness* (2004). In the light of my discussion of feature films I turn my attention to how selected documentaries (e.g. *Long Night's Journey into Day*, 2000) have covered the search for truth and reconciliation.

There is a growing body of literature reflecting on the history of South African film,[9] but less attention has been paid to the role of religion in these films. While my argument is largely structured chronologically, my aim is to investigate the different ways in which such films about South Africa's recent history might be able to contribute to the process of searching for truth and building reconciliation. This is not to suggest that through skilful portrayal of the truth and reconciliation process audiences will necessarily be turned into more peaceful or forgiving citizens. In other words, it is not my intention in this chapter to endorse the notion that dramatic and powerful films will transform the beliefs and actions of passive audiences. My aim is rather to use these films as a way of reflecting critically on some of the ways in which film can reveal aspects of the search for truth, and depict the long road towards reconciliation.

Moving towards apartheid

The boat trip from Cape Town to Robben Island normally takes about thirty to forty minutes and the sun was shining as we crossed nearly seven kilometres of the South Atlantic Ocean. It was a smooth crossing taking us from the busy, noisy, world of Cape Town to the isolation of Robben Island. I had not anticipated that it would be so quiet. The move towards apartheid in South Africa, during the middle of the twentieth century, was far less serene.

There are numerous historical accounts of South Africa's slide onto the rocks of apartheid,[10] and several reference one of South Africa's most famous novels: Alan Paton's *Cry, the Beloved Country* (1948).[11] The cinematic adaptations of Paton's book, like the book itself, shed light not only on the move towards apartheid, but also the tentative search for different kinds of truth and reconciliation.

Both Zoltan Zorda's 1951 black and white production (released in the USA in 1952) and Darrell Roodt's 1995 colour version of *Cry, the Beloved Country* largely follow the narrative of the novel. Both films draw upon the novel's dialogue, though the 1951 version follows the novel particularly closely. This is not surprising, given that the author Alan Paton wrote the 1951 screenplay himself. The screenwriter for the 1995 version, Ronald Harwood, states in an interview on the DVD that he was keen to use Paton's language. The result: both films are easily recognised as offspring of the novel, even though they emerged out of significantly different historical contexts, with the first produced towards the start and the other after the end of the period of apartheid law. One anticipates apartheid from the early 1950s, while the other is looking back at its emergence from the vantage point of the mid-1990s. The 1951 version 'depicts the social and economical degradation of black South Africans in a way never done before'.[12] The 1995 version was the first major Hollywood film on South Africa produced post-apartheid. As in Paton's book, aspects of the truth are gradually revealed. These two films illustrate how a cinematic story can explore in concrete narrative both different layers of truth and the gradual move towards personal reconciliation.

At its heart *Cry, the Beloved Country* is a tale of two grief-stricken fathers. The first part of the novel centres on the search by an elderly black Anglican priest, Stephen Kumalo, for his lost son, Absalom (aka Absolom). Slowly he discovers that some of his worst fears have come true. The second part initially focuses on a white farmer, James Jarvis, following the murder of his son, Arthur. Through reading his deceased son's writings and learning of his tireless work for justice he gradually awakens to new ways of looking at and living in his homeland. For both Kumalo and Jarvis, discovering the truth about their sons and their country is a painful process. The two films intermix the stories of these two men and their respective sons. The result is that, like the novel, both movies reflect some of the tensions rife within South Africa on the eve of the formal introduction of *apartheid* (the Afrikaans word for 'separateness').

Both films begin with a small girl bringing Kumalo (addressed respectfully as *umfundisi*, meaning 'parson') a letter telling how his sister is 'very sick' and needs his help. He travels by train from his small village in the countryside to the noisy metropolis of Johannesburg. Kumalo (played by Canada Lee) is particularly fearful and deferential in the 1951 version, though in court he retains a dignity, even as he hears evidence pile up against his own son (figure 5.3). We learn from the second film that this is a journey he has 'always feared', across a 'lovely land' divided by racial inequality 'where the white man has

Figure 5.3 Still from *Cry, the Beloved Country* (1951, Zoltan Korda). Reverend Msimangu
(played by Sidney Poitier) and Stephen Kumalo (played by Canada Lee) await
the judgement in the courtroom scene. Courtesy of British Lion and the Kobal
Collection.

everything and the black man nothing'. Once in the sprawling city he finds his
sister is not sick but has become a prostitute. She agrees at first, with little resistance, to return home with him. Searching for his son, however, in the poverty
of Sophiatown, one of Johannesburg's satellite cities, is more complicated. His
lengthy search, accompanied by another priest, Theophilus Msimangu (played
by Sidney Poitier in the 1951 version), takes him first to his carpenter brother,
John Kumalo, who is involved in local politics as a mesmerising public speaker.
In both films we are shown how his hunt then takes him via a dilapidated
boarding house and reticent taxi driver to a reformatory. There he finds Absalom
has been released a month before, partly because of his good behaviour and
partly to care for a 16-year-old girl who is pregnant with his child. Even finding
the girl does not lead them immediately to Absalom. He has disappeared for
several days. It transpires that Absalom is now in prison charged with the
murder of a liberal white engineer, Arthur Jarvis, who, unknown to Absalom,
has tirelessly fought for the rights of the black majority. Unlike his two accomplices, Absalom immediately confesses and, following a brief trial, finds himself
facing a death sentence for his crime. Father and son are reunited in prison and
reconciled. Kumalo's journeying brings him to an unintended face-to-face
meeting with James Jarvis, the father of the murdered Arthur. They come from

the same area of the country but have never met before. It is a pivotal moment in the novel and in both films.

Both movies depict Kumalo's fear at facing Jarvis. Here is the father of the man his son shot. The truth of that is hard to bear. Kumalo drops papers, stutters and hesitates before responding to Jarvis' request to reveal what it is that is between them: 'This thing that is the heaviest thing of all my years, is the heaviest thing of all your years also'.[13] He then reveals that 'It was my son that killed your son'. In both the novel and the 1951 film, Jarvis (played by Charles Carson) walks away 'into the trees of the garden' to look 'out over the veld'. In the 1995 version Jarvis (played by Richard Harris) simply turns away to face the house. As the truth sinks in, he is silent for over ten seconds. A shot of his back is replaced by a medium-close-up of his face, with Kumalo (played by James Earl Jones) in the background. The silence speaks volumes. Moving closer, Jarvis confides: 'I understand what I did not understand. There is no anger in me'.[14] *New York Times* film critic Stephen Holden rightly observes that this is a highly 'risky' moment, because 'movies have become so invested in the unleashing of violent emotion and the escalation of hostility, that expressions of restraint, reconciliation and forgiveness can easily be read as a corny cop-out'. For Holden this film is neither 'corny' nor a 'cop-out'.[15] It is believable partly because of what has happened in the lead-up to this transformative moment. The story has been adapted not only for the screen but also for the stage, with the musical entitled *Lost in the Stars* (lyrics by Maxwell Anderson and music by Kurt Weill, 1949), which was adapted for a far from successful film (Daniel Mann, 1974). This film version was widely criticised for its static production and because it overlooked this transformative process, downplaying the reconciliation between 'the black preacher and the wealthy old white bigot',[16] thereby undermining the heart of the narrative's dénouement.

Discovering the truth about a violent act does not always provoke peaceful reconciliation. Earlier in the 1995 film, after Jarvis identifies the body of his son in the morgue, he exclaims: 'bloody *kaffirs*, whoever did this, find them, hang them, bastards, bloody bastards'. Later, after his son's funeral, Jarvis is portrayed with an immobile face, refusing to shake hands with a black man. He thereby blocks his fellow mourners' offer of condolences. This moment comes in the midst of a montage sequence where viewers are shown uniformed police with dogs raiding a series of houses, dragging out innocent-looking black men and women. Some are beaten, others are bundled into waiting cars. The 1995 script in this section, very close to the original text of Paton's novel and narrated by Kumalo, overlies this montage.

A number of quotations from the book are compressed into this short sequence. There is 'fear in the land' and 'fear in the heart' of all living there.[17] This fear, which 'rules the land', leads to a breakdown of understanding which in turn will make it hard 'to fashion' the land, as out of fear the white man 'put more locks on his door and get a fine fierce dog'. A longer section is then quoted from the book:

Cry, the beloved country for the unborn child that is the inheritor of our fear. Let him not love the earth too deeply … Let him not be too moved when the birds of his land are singing, nor give too much of his heart to a mountain or a valley. For fear will rob him of all if he gives too much.[18]

This is the moment when in the film Jarvis, frozen in grief, refuses to shake hands with the blacks who respected his son. The narrator then repeats the title of the book and film: 'cry, the beloved country'.

The gravity and semi-biblical quality of the language of the novel has been transposed into the 1995 film. Jarvis does not cry at his son's funeral. Richard Harris, playing Jarvis, dominates the screen here. It is as if he is frozen in grief and anger. His refusal to shake hands with a black mourner reveals his prejudice and heightens the contrast with his later generosity towards the black rural priest Kumalo. Towards the end of the film Jarvis provides for the repair of the leaky church roof. As in the novel he is awakened to the injustice dividing the land through reading his son's writing: 'it is not native crime, but it is white crime that is the problem'. He is clearly shocked to the core when he reads: 'What sort of memorial do we want … what sort of memorial do we deserve … we call ourselves a Christian people when posterity comes to judge us … it will consign us to the, the sewers of history as tyrants, oppressors, criminals … We called ourselves Christians, but are indifferent to the suffering of Christians'. Whether the truth of these words ever fully dawn upon him is unclear from the 1995 film, but he is clearly struck by the discovery of his son's leadership of a boys' club, emblematic of his investment of time with the black communities and 'his belief in a better future'.

In the black and white version from the 1950s, Jarvis's gradual transformation comes earlier in the story. Even more is made of Jarvis's reading of his son's writings. He is absorbed and challenged. After the funeral he simply pauses and then, unlike in the 1995 film, shakes hands with a number of black well-wishers. The novel makes it clear that this is 'first time he's ever shaken hands with black people'.[19] In the earlier film this is a simple sign of his growing openness towards communities beyond his own. Facing the truth about both oneself and one's own community can be more than a little painful. The novel, more even than both of the films, captures what it is that holds back divided communities from embracing one another: fear. This emotion recurs again and again. For example, Kumalo is fearful of the big city, Kumalo's sister is fearful of her brother's anger and many whites are fearful of black violence and criminality. As an internalised emotion fear is hard to depict on screen, but is sometimes revealed through dialogue. In a much-quoted passage, used in both films, Msimangu, the priest who accompanies Kumalo on his journeying, admits to a 'great fear' in his 'heart that one day when the white man turns to loving, he will find that we have turned to hating'.[20]

The themes of loving and hating are evoked through the final minutes of the 1995 film. In one of the most memorable sequences from the movie, viewers are

Figure 5.4 Still from *Cry, the Beloved Country* (1995, Darrell Roodt) brings together James
Jarvis (played by Richard Harris) and Stephen Kumalo (played by James Earl
Jones), two fathers who have lost their sons. Courtesy of Videovision, Miramax,
Distant Horizons and the Kobal Collection.

shown through a three-way montage the fathers briefly together in the hills, at
the same time as the execution of Absalom (figure 5.4). The hanging of Kumalo's
son is also juxtaposed with the birth of his grandson. Once again the narrator's
script draws upon Paton's novel. This time the questioning of the purpose of
human hardship combines with Paton's use of the King James Version (1611) of
the Bible:

> Who knows for what we live, and struggle and die. Who knows what keeps
> us living and struggling, while all things break about us. Who knows why the
> warm flesh of a child is such comfort, when ones own child is lost and
> cannot be recovered. Wise men write many books, in words too hard to
> understand. But this, the purpose of our lives, the end of all our struggle, is
> beyond all human wisdom. O God, my God, do not Thou forsake me. Yea
> though I walk through the valley of the shadow of death, I shall fear no evil,
> *if* Thou art with me.[21]

Kumalo intones the script in such a way that the end of fear affirmed in Psalm
23 is interrogated by his emphasis upon 'IF', questioning 'if' God is present. This
doubtful moment is qualified by the final shot. Kumalo kneels praying in the
midst of a stunning mountainscape and on the screen Alan Paton's final words
from the novel appears: 'For it is the dawn that has come, as it has come for a

thousand centuries, never failing. But when that dawn will come, of our eman-
cipation, from the fear of bondage and the bondage of fear, why, that is a
secret'.[22] This hope of freedom from fear is made more real through the transformation of the older Jarvis and his understated reconciliation with the frail
black priest, Kumalo.

Both of these films attempt to engage with different kinds of truth. First, they
reflect the difficulty of discovering the 'forensic' truth in a court of law. Absalom's
truthfulness is rewarded with a death sentence, while his two accomplices lie and
escape punishment. Second, these two movies are far more successful at revealing the truth of small-scale violence than of the far more insidious structural and
hidden violence. The overlooking of dispossession, forcible removals and repeated injustices against the non-white population, while the 'two fathers were
embracing on their hillside', led film critic Roger Ebert to assert that the 1995
film was only a 'gentle parable when an angry exhortation might have been
more appropriate', and that ultimately this film fails 'as a portrait of what it used
to be like in South Africa, what happened and what it's like now'.[23]

Nevertheless, such criticisms are overstated, as third, both films illustrate how
even if a story only concentrates on a few individuals' lives the narrative can still
reveal wider fractures within society. For those living within South Africa, the
1951 version 'was seen as a very significant moment for local black audiences',
with magazines such as *Zonk!* celebrating its 'use of local black talent'. The
portrayal of the elderly priest Kumalo as an over-deferential black man
'cow-towing' to the white 'master', however, attracted criticism in the magazine
Drum and even parody in the less well-known docudrama *Come Back, Africa*
(Lionel Rogosin, 1959).[24] For these writers the priest Kumalo became similar to
an anti-hero, the absolute antithesis of the more radical resistance espoused by
the Sophiatown intellectuals who co-wrote *Come Back, Africa*. They are equally
critical of the portrayal of the other black leader in the story: Stephen's politically active brother, John, who encourages deception for the benefit of his own
son while damaging the case of his nephew. The reception of the 1951 version of
Cry, the Beloved Country clearly varies, with some of those living outside South
Africa finding that it 'served as an unforgettable introduction to the evils of
apartheid, and had inescapable application to the still heavily segregated United
States of the early '50s'.[25] More recently, film critics such as Philip French celebrate it as a 'vivid and moving portrait of a cruelly divided society of exploited,
uprooted black people and troubled, guilty white people' with 'strong biblical
undertones'.[26]

The 1995 version, described by its producers as 'the first major film produced
in post-apartheid South Africa', marked the end of an era and, in the words of
Nelson Mandela, it 'evoked strong emotions about a terrible past', provided
'bitter-sweet memories of our youth' and was a 'monument to the future'.[27]
There is a sense in which Mandela welcomes this film as a form of cinematic
'nation-building'.[28] While it may not have looked back in anger, it did look
forward in hope. By evoking dangerous memories and revealing the fissures

which divide a community, a film, however flawed, can become a site of dialogue for reflecting critically upon past and present injustices. Despite their limitations and the fact they are set over fifty years ago, by portraying how individual reconciliation can be achieved, both films do at least gesture towards the possibility of wider forms of reconciliation.

Moving within apartheid

There are numerous visual reminders of the apartheid regime on Robben Island. Several large black and white photographs are mounted close to or on the grey and white stone prison walls. One photograph shows a line of about fifty black men in flimsy shorts and shirts, standing without shoes, awaiting an order to move on (figure 5.5). It looks as though the prisoners have small manacles constraining one of their legs. Running would be hard. Surrounding them are several better-dressed men with hats, rifles and footwear. Somewhat incongruously, a shiny Volkswagen Beetle is parked adjacent to the line of prisoners. In South Africa, the so-called 'people's car' was not for everyone.

Figure 5.5 Captivity. Photograph of poster depicting prisoners on Robben Island. Photograph by Jolyon Mitchell.

This single photograph speaks volumes about movement and constraint within apartheid South Africa. Prisoners were obviously constrained, but millions of non-whites were not allowed to move into white-only spaces and were also forcibly evicted from their homes. Meanwhile, a white minority were able to move more freely and to live lives isolated from or ignoring these and other manifest injustices.

Several films have attempted to represent life in South Africa during the apartheid years. What is revealed through these depictions? One recurring theme is the awakening of an individual character to some of the harsh truths about apartheid. In several films the protagonist enacts a process that resonates with what Paulo Freire (1921–97) described in Portuguese as '*conscientização*' ('conscientisation'). Drawing on the work of other educators and his experience of working within impoverished communities, Freire described how individuals could move from 'magical' or 'naïve' consciousness to 'critical' consciousness.[29] Freire developed this theme in his later books, showing how this was an evolving process which through action and reflection allows an individual to probe beneath surface appearances, to 'unveil' what remains hidden[30] and end 'cultures of silence'.[31] A number of films from the late 1980s provide portrayals of characters moving towards critical consciousness.

Representing apartheid

Richard Attenborough's *Cry Freedom* (1987) is one of the best-known cinematic tales emerging out of the apartheid era (figure 5.6). Attenborough's aim was 'to reach the unknowing and uncaring' through *Cry Freedom*.[32] Many claim that it is 'Hollywood's first anti-apartheid movie'.[33] Coming over thirty years after apartheid's beginning, it is set between 1975 and 1977 and is based on the journalist Donald Woods' biography *Biko* (1978) and his autobiography *Asking For Trouble* (1981). In *Cry Freedom*, Woods, a liberal white editor-in-chief of the *Daily Dispatch*, develops an unlikely friendship with the leader of the black consciousness movement, Steve Biko. Accepting Biko's invitation to see how and where blacks live, Woods is taken through an impoverished township, the like of which he would never have seen before, where he meets other young activists and sees and hears about the daily injustices of apartheid. He becomes increasingly uneasy about a regime that allows him to enjoy well-paid employment and have neatly tended lawns, a swimming pool and a black maid. Following Biko's arrest and subsequent death at the age of only 30 in 1977, Woods becomes even more critical of the apartheid regime and its political leaders. In the film, Woods uncovers that Biko died after twenty-one days of incarceration not because of a 'hunger strike' but because of serious injuries to his head while in police custody. Twenty years later, five police officers confessed their responsibility for his death to the Truth and Reconciliation Commission. In a memorable scene from *Cry Freedom*, reminiscent of *Cry, the Beloved Country* (1995) where Jarvis identifies the body of his murdered son,

Figure 5.6 Cry Freedom poster (1987, Richard Attenborough), featuring Denzel Washington (playing Steve Biko) and Kevin Kline (playing Donald Woods). Courtesy of Marble Arch Productions, Universal and the Kobal Collection.

Woods and his photographer surreptitiously take photos of the battered corpse of Biko in the morgue. The viewer is shown apartheid primarily through the eyes of a liberal white journalist, who awakens into critical consciousness.

Woods' investigations and outspokenness ensure that he becomes a 'banned person' who was limited in his travel and forms of public expression. His movement was constrained, though obviously not as much as those imprisoned on Robben Island. The final hour of the film becomes more like a chase thriller as Woods, disguised as a priest, hitchhikes his way towards freedom, with his family following closely behind. Some reviewers outside South Africa were euphoric, claiming that the 'performances are excellent, the crowd scenes astonishing, and the climax truly nerve-wracking'. For the same reviewer from *Time Out*, it is an 'implacable work of authority and compassion, *Cry Freedom* is political cinema at its best'.[34] Such positive reviews overlook the film's inherent bias towards a white perspective, offering only partial truths about apartheid. Some viewers were deeply critical of the focal point of the film being the white Woods, and observe that it is only when he himself 'is the banned person', '*his* friends are arrested and die in detention', *his* 6-year-old is seriously injured by putting on an acid-covered T-shirt that 'suddenly South Africa becomes unbearable for him'. Victoria Carchidi goes on somewhat ironically to compare the Woods' family adventure with the escape of the Von Trapps in *The Sound of Music* (Robert Wise, 1965).[35] Like several other films produced during and soon after the apartheid regime 'it devotes very little time to the day-to-day indignities created by apartheid'.[36] Some critics are even harsher, suggesting that *Cry Freedom* encourages viewers to fly from South Africa with Woods in his 'Light Airplane of Political Awakening'.[37] Other critics are more precise, asserting that 'Attenborough filters out the radical political discourse of the Black Consciousness Movement, replacing it with the more palatable liberal discourse of moral decency and human rights'.[38]

From this evidence it is clear that the reception of *Cry Freedom* was mixed, with some commentators observing how even Woods would have been the target of Biko's criticism and others wondering, like Carchidi, why a film about Biko spent so much time covering Woods' story. After an initial showing, it was, unsurprisingly, banned in South Africa. *Cry Freedom* is clearly aimed at a predominantly white audience and at its heart the central character is not Biko (persuasively played by Denzel Washington) but Woods (played effectively by Kevin Kline). For Roger Ebert the 'problem with this movie is similar to the dilemma in South Africa: Whites occupy the foreground and establish the terms of the discussion, while the 80 percent non white majority remains a shadowy, half-seen presence in the background'.[39] Part of the reason for this is that, as Attenborough reiterated on several occasions, he wanted *Cry Freedom* 'to reach people who were indifferent, who didn't know what was going on and didn't care'.[40] In short, he was aiming to move viewers outside South Africa towards critical consciousness of what was happening in South Africa.

The film attempts to do this by concentrating upon the transformation of one individual in the wake of Biko's brutal murder, set against a larger background of violence.

The cinematic portrayal of the Soweto riots is widely regarded as 'packed' with a 'powerful emotional punch'.[41] Several months are compressed into a day's action, with white police replacing the largely black force. According to official estimates, between June 1976 and February 1977 at least 574 people, including 134 younger than 18, lost their lives. In the film, as nameless children scream, flee and are shot, viewers are offered a momentary glimpse of a scene that embodied the riots: the photograph by Masana Sam Nzima of the small boy Hector Pieterson being carried by his brother as a lifeless corpse. It is striking to see how this iconic image, used first in the black-run paper the *World* (16 June 1976), and then in newspapers around the world,[42] loses some of its force when it is embedded in this fast-paced ten-minute film sequence. There is an unforgettable particularity about the photographic image: a teenage boy in overalls cradles his brother's limp body, holding back a cry, while alongside his sister screams silently with her palm raised, like a futile attempt to stop the pain and the past. Looking again at this image, over thirty years on, it is clear why many viewers found it evocative of a Pietà. It contains elements that can still 'pierce' like Roland Barthes' 'punctum',[43] thereby awakening viewers to one aspect of South Africa's recent history. By subtly including this momentary scene, Attenborough's film also acts as a reminder of how this photograph captured a split second, yet represented a sustained period of violence.

In film, too, it can be the particularity of a story that contributes to its originality. The sheer scale of *Cry Freedom* obscures the hidden, harsh, everyday details of apartheid. By contrast, *A World Apart* (Chris Menges, 1988) offers 'smaller details of specific lives' reflecting how 'individual lives are affected by a legal system in which one's rights depend on one's race'.[44] It does this from the perspective of Molly, a white 13-year-old (played by Jodhi May) whose father has fled the country and mother is in prison, both for their anti-apartheid activities. The story is based on Shawn Slovo's autobiographical account of her childhood as one of the daughters of anti-apartheid activist Joe Slovo and Ruth First. Set in Johannesburg in 1963, it reveals how for Molly living in South Africa was not like participating in 'some sort of permanent passion play' and how it was possible to 'fall into a workable, even comfortable, routine'. For 'those who do not rock the boat', South Africa could 'be a very pleasant place to live'.[45] The awakening of Molly to what was going on beyond her life of birthday parties and swimming pools provides another example of a cinematic transformation. Molly remains enraged, however, by her mother's desertion due to her political activism and incarceration. The film moves towards a 'powerful reconciliation scene' where Molly's mother declares, 'You deserved to have a mother, you have one, just not the one you wanted', and the 'closing shots of their joint attendance at the funeral of an activist friend'.[46] Notice how the film focuses on a personal reconciliation, this time it is between two whites, with the apartheid struggle providing the background to their story. For Vincent Canby, 'A World Apart, like Sir Richard Attenborough's Cry Freedom, suggests that the white man's burden, which once was trade, education and the propagation of the Christian faith, is now to suffer selflessly on behalf of the world's benighted. In whatever way you look at these films, the white man still shoulders the burden, and still receives most of the sympathy'.[47] In other words, the power of particularity found in this film has not inoculated it from criticism for focusing almost exclusively on the story of the transformation of a white protagonist.

Another transformation is found in A Dry White Season (Euzhan Palcy, 1989), based on the novel by the Afrikaans writer André Brink, which portrays the gradual political awakening of a middle-aged white teacher Ben Du Toit (played by Donald Sutherland). For one reviewer it is 'not so much a sweeping political statement as an exploration of one man's moral fibre'.[48] The director Euzhan Palcy, a black film-maker herself, wanted to make it from a 'black point of view', but found this was 'impossible' because 'the people who have the money here to make films are not interested in black leads'.[49] Nonetheless, Palcy believed that film was the 'perfect medium for enlightening people about apartheid',[50] and that Brink's novel provided her the opportunity to explore cinematically not only white but also black perspectives on apartheid. Set in the 1970s, again at the time of the Soweto riots, it shows how Du Toit's comfortable and cocooned existence is challenged as he delves into the disappearance of his gardener and the gardener's son after the Soweto riots. Drinks on the patio with Du Toit's family are juxtaposed with bloodied graphic moments of torture in the police cells.

A turning point for Du Toit is when he travels illegally into one of the townships to look at the body of his battered gardener, Gordon, in an undertaker's casket. As a result, he persists in confronting cultures of silence and is alienated from most of his family for his troubles. He becomes a 'traitor to Afrikanerdom'.[51] This is an 'effective, emotional, angry, subtle movie', which also attempts to 'show daily life in the townships'.[52] A Dry White Season is, as Lindiwe Dovey correctly suggests, one of a number of examples of 'post-apartheid exilic films', which 'erode an insider/outsider dichotomy primarily through their alternative form, a subversive combination of documentary and fiction'.[53] The blurring between fact and fiction is commonly found in films where the protagonist awakes to the realities of apartheid.

Nevertheless, for other writers, A Dry White Season, like Cry Freedom, fails to 'present the felt texture of South African life' and 'provides no insight into the vexed political situation of South Africa, nor into the conditions under which blacks live'. The portrayals and the depictions illustrate 'how ingrained the patterns of thinking fostered by apartheid are', how they are to be found in films about apartheid that concentrate upon white protagonists, and even how these films reveal how the 'habits of oppression underlying the South African

Government remain in effect in the very countries that decry apartheid'.[54] This claim, by Carchidi, is rooted in the belief that these films shed more light onto the historical and cultural context out of which they are produced than the historical events upon which they are based.

Such an interpretation overlooks the fact that these films were a cinematic attempt at revealing the truth of what was happening in a country where foreign television cameras were excluded, as a result of the state of emergency, in 1987. They offered striking pictures when few moving images were emerging out of South Africa. Subsidies and strict censorship ensured that the state was able to control film production and distribution. Most official films ignored the history of apartheid, promoting South Africa as a heaven for tourists and a haven for investment, a land where even multiculturalism was celebrated.[55] The films considered in this section can be seen as attempts to challenge such political propaganda, standing in the tradition of those who attempted to appropriate the camera as a tool to fight non-violently against apartheid. Each provides a window, however incomplete, on individuals who are trying to come to terms with the truth of apartheid. These three films, *Cry Freedom*, *A World Apart* and *A Dry White Season*, were produced in the turbulent late 1980s, looking back to earlier moments in the recent history of apartheid. They did not attract huge audiences, with limited success at the box office. *Cry Freedom*, for example, cost over $21 million to create but took only about $6 million at the box office, while *A Dry White Season* cost over $10 million to produce but only raised under $4 million in ticket receipts. Nevertheless, for those who did see these films, they were a vivid introduction to or reminder of the 'terrifying impact of South African police repression' used to uphold the apartheid system.[56] Many people may not have seen these films, but the story of *Cry Freedom*, especially when banned in South Africa, attracted wide public debate and is still used on educational sites promoting peacemaking.[57]

Resisting apartheid

While these three films primarily focus on white liberal resistance during the 1960s and 1970s, other kinds of anti-apartheid films emerged in South Africa with the advent of video films. These 'Third Cinema' films, which unlike 'First Cinema' movies that were supportive of the 'dominant ideology' or 'Second Cinema' productions that were largely apolitical, revealed the 'experience of oppression'.[58] According to Keyan Tomaselli, who also draws on this theoretical frame, the late 1980s can be seen as a pivotal moment for South African Cinema.[59] A number of films were produced that sought not only to educate white audiences outside South Africa, but also to reflect some of the realities of apartheid to local audiences. This was to be found in both feature and documentary films. Censorship made production and distribution of many films difficult if not impossible, but in some cases films found their way to audiences.

Mapantsula (Oliver Schmitz, 1988)

Consider *Mapantsula*, which has already attracted considerable scholarly atten-tion.[60] It is arguably the 'most significant anti-apartheid film to emerge prior to the first democratic elections in 1994'.[61] On the basis of the false script that they were shown, the censorship authorities originally approved the making of this film as merely another gangster movie. At the heart of the film is the radicali-sation of the protagonist, called Panic (played by Thomas Mogotlane), from being an over-confident crook to a visibly shaken and more politically aware prisoner.[62] The film begins with Panic asleep in the back of a police van, dif-ferentiated from the other occupants, who are wearing political slogans on their T-shirts, by his attire: a crisp dark suit. Once in jail the police try to force him to incriminate others. Through several flashbacks Panic is portrayed in different Soweto settings. His life of crime and somewhat tortured relationships are revealed. We also see how he was inadvertently caught up in a demonstration against rent increases, and then shot at, chased, captured, interrogated and finally tortured by the police. The film concludes as this onetime cynical hood-lum turns down the offer of signing a false incriminating document to protect his own life. His refusal is a dramatic form of resistance against apartheid and symptomatic of his personal conscientisation.

A diverse cast of characters surround Panic. Judith Maingard claims that the 'multiplicities' of these 'characters open up many avenues for South African audiences to feel a sense of personal immersion in the unfolding narrative'. She goes on to suggest that 'geographies of the film', such as the 'contrasting heat and dust of Soweto', the 'tightly packed ... small red-bricked dwellings' juxta-posed with the 'cool, arboreal, spacious white suburb', contribute to the reality of the depictions. Experiencing these contrasting worlds and seeing those close to him arrested, beaten, or even killed, contributes to his transformation. For Maingard, not since *Cry, the Beloved Country* (1951) has a film had such an impact on 'black audiences', who, following the Emergency Media Regulations in the mid-1980s, lived 'visually impaired' lives where coverage of strikes, demonstra-tions, riots and other public disturbances were prohibited.[63] 'In addition, the propaganda of the state-owned South African Broadcasting Corporation (SABC) produced an extremely limited visual landscape of South African realities, while access to national broadcasting by oppositional groups was blocked'.[64] *Mapantsula* was banned almost immediately after it was first released, because it was deemed likely to 'incite violence', though over-18s were allowed to watch video versions in cinemas holding no more than 200 people. The major South African film distributors would not screen this or other anti-apartheid films.

Even though the film received limited formal public exposure, it attracted considerable attention. One reason for this is because the ANC and PAC were supportive, facilitating its filming in Soweto and its circumvention of the inter-national boycott of South African products. It was circulated, exhibited and viewed in unconventional settings. Like several other locally produced videos in the 1980s, *Mapantsula* was screened 'at alternative venues like community halls, churches in the townships, selected progressive film festivals and even at private homes'.[65] It also appears that the armed wing of the ANC in one of the Zambian 'insurgent camps' and even the prisoners on 'Robben Island had their own copy'.[66] Exiles, prisoners and insurgents watched and debated the film's value. Litheko Modisane traces the biography of this film from 'perilous production' through to 'clandestine distribution' and unplanned reception, suggesting that the 'militant gestures' within the film were 'critically appreciated' by many viewers.[67] The local production, circulation and reception of *Mapantsula* and other anti-apartheid films stands in contrast to more widely known films, such as *Cry Freedom*, *A World Apart* and *A Dry White Season*, which were largely made by outsiders for international audiences.

Last Grave at Dimbaza (Nana Mahomo, 1974)

Up to this point I have concentrated upon feature films. There are also a significant number of groundbreaking documentaries, produced during and after the 1970s, which revealed some of the realities of apartheid to audiences outside South Africa. Nana Mahomo's *The Dumping Grounds* (1973) and *Last Grave at Dimbaza* (1974) are two of the best known.[68] The South African government banned them both and attempted to counter these clandestine productions with their own documentaries, such as *Land of Promise* (South African Information Service, 1974), which defended the establishment of the apartheid regime and celebrated a South Africa where there was supposedly 'a roof for everyone and clothing and enough to eat'. *Last Grave at Dimbaza* was broadcast on PBS in the USA in October 1975, as well as on Canadian and British television. It revealed how the black communities suffered under apartheid, enduring overcrowding, poor health care and grinding poverty. It is full of poignant images, such as a 'black nurse feeding her white employer's child' with the commentator revealing 'that her own son died of malnutrition'. The conclusion of the film is particularly painful, taking the viewer to a township called Dimbaza, in the 'homeland' of Ciskei, and a special 'children's graveyard', where the camera lingers on some of the 450 graves of 'African children marked with plastic feeding bottles', most of whom 'died before the age of two'.[69]

Short films and documentaries became increasingly popular and significant forms of anti-apartheid expression. Over 200 short fiction and non-fiction documentaries were produced in South Africa between 1980 and 1995.[70] Barry Feinberg directed some of the most memorable, such as *Any Child is My Child* (1988), a film about the severe hardships of children under apartheid, or another about the life and work of Archbishop Trevor Huddleston. Feinberg's work and many other films were funded by the IDAF (International Defence and Aid Fund for Southern Africa).[71] Production companies from outside South Africa also produced documentaries, which acted as *Witness to Apartheid* (Sharon I. Sopher, 1986). Like other international films this documentary combined news footage with interviews and speeches of leading activists such as Desmond Tutu, who declares in this film that 'the primary violence in this land is apartheid' and 'no country can afford to bleed like South Africa'.[72] Graphic images of television reporters being beaten by police combine with an artist's impressions of the time the American production team were arrested and detained for carrying out interviews in the townships. Producing films was a way of both retaining visual records of what was left out of the official accounts and educating international publics about some of the truth of what was happening in Southern Africa. These films largely bear witness to the 'truth' of what was happening rather than highlighting the need for 'reconciliation'.

Remembering apartheid

This tradition of using film not only to entertain but also to educate international audiences continued during and after the dismantling of apartheid in the early 1990s. Once again the central protagonists undergo personal transformations, but now it is beyond purely awakening to the evils of apartheid. Several post-apartheid films attempted to bear witness to the truth of what went on behind locked doors and when cameras were prohibited to record civil disturbance, as well as the moves towards individual reconciliation.

Goodbye Bafana (Bille August, 2007)

In *Goodbye Bafana* the viewer is taken back into the world of Robben Island, though largely from the perspective of the jailors. At the centre of this film is one of Nelson Mandela's prison guards, James Gregory (played by Joseph Fiennes). The plot is based upon Gregory's controversial book *Goodbye Bafana: Nelson Mandela, My Prisoner, My Friend* (1995).[73] The film uncritically follows the account of Gregory, which suggests that a good friendship developed between Mandela and himself. The depth of this relationship has been questioned.[74] Nonetheless, Mandela wrote respectfully of this trilingual warder who had first arrived on Robben Island in 1966, and who even embraced him just before his release in 1990. This scene is recreated in the last moments of *Goodbye Bafana*.

By concentrating upon the journey of Gregory from racist guard to enlightened guardian, the film provides few in-depth insights into life on Robben Island or in apartheid South Africa. The injustices, the boredom and the cruelty experienced by the prisoners are hardly touched upon. Outside the prison we catch glimpses of everyday apartheid – with blacks confined to the back of buses and banned ANC literature kept in restricted sections in libraries. When Gregory's daughter witnesses the vicious beating of blacks and the violent separation of a mother from a baby by white police in the streets of Cape Town, she is traumatised. After this event a close-up shows this young girl lying on her grandmother's sofa, clutching a white doll, and looking troubled by what she has just witnessed. Her parents attempt to comfort her by justifying segregation. On hearing that only blacks are required to have passes she asks: 'but is that fair?' In response, her mother (played by Diane Kruger) claims that apartheid is 'God's way, just like he doesn't put a sparrow with a swallow, or goose with a duck, or cow with a buck. It's just not natural. And we don't question God'. The questioning in this film is expressed through Gregory's own journey within and ultimately away from apartheid.

Mandela's story and the political realities of apartheid are eclipsed by this tale of a white guard's transformation. Partly because of his regular contact with Mandela (played by Dennis Haysbert), he finds that Mandela is not what he was led to expect: a murderous terrorist. Nonetheless, 'Mandela is reduced to a background prop as Gregory launches a quest to educate himself on the principles of egalitarianism after years of being drip-fed Apartheid propaganda'.[75] While the film received several lukewarm reviews, being described as a 'rose-tinted homage' (James Christopher, *The Times*, 10 May 2007), one of the more memorable elements in the film is Gregory's *volte-face* and his questioning of 'the apartheid regime that pays his wages'.[76] The film shows that, while Gregory is free to leave Robben Island and visit Cape Town, it is several years before he is free of the ideological shackles of apartheid.

Goodbye Bafana depicts the constricted lives not only of the guards, but also of the prisoners. In one brief prison visit, Winnie and Nelson Mandela are shown separated by glass, talking intensely by phone, with their conversation carefully monitored to ensure that it is free from political reference. Several first-hand accounts offer a different perspective on what actually transpired in real life, for example, inmates commonly 'had to yell and scream to be heard on the other side'.[77] The movie also shows something of how Mandela actually had to argue over a period of months and years for fairer treatment, better food, and other bare necessities such as long trousers or a simple table and chair.[78] The film provides brief glimpses of how Mandela and his fellow prisoners were forced to carry out 'tedious and difficult' tasks, such as carrying and crushing heavy stones. Less obvious is how they suffered many other indignities at the hands of largely unsympathetic and sometimes cruel guards.[79] *Goodbye Bafana* is a flawed and yet moving attempt to embody former political prisoner, island inmate and ANC leader Ahmed (Kathy) Kathrada's hope that, in spite of the unforgettable 'brutality of apartheid', Robben Island will not become a 'monument' of 'hardship and suffering' but rather a monument of 'freedom and human dignity over oppression and humiliation' as well as the 'triumph of courage and determination over human frailty and weakness',[80] a sentiment quoted on one of the posters on the island, which shows a group of inmates waving triumphantly on a boat as they leave the prison for the last time (figure 5.7).

Catch a Fire (Philip Noyce, 2006)

Human frailty and weakness is made explicit in *Catch a Fire*. This film, based on the real-life story of Patrick Chamusso, tells the tale of an initially apolitical man

Figure 5.7 Freedom. Photograph of poster depicting prisoners on boat having left Robben Island. Photograph by Jolyon Mitchell.

(played by Derek Luke) who is incorrectly detained and tortured by the apart-heid police. His experiences radicalise him and lead him towards joining the ANC and attempting to blow up an oil refinery. He is only partly successful and is later given up by his wife and captured. He is sentenced to twenty-four years and sent to Robben Island. After his early release, while he can forgive his ex-wife, he cannot bring himself to forget or forgive the policeman who caused him and many others so much pain. He appears trapped by the pain. In the last moments of the film, he spies Nic Vos (played by Tim Robbins) on the other side of a small lake. A long shot shows the 'monster' sitting alone, drinking wine by his fishing gear. Patrick creeps up behind Vos. The camera shot closes on his neck as Patrick says to himself, 'you can end it now … kill him … break his neck'. One moment the viewer is shown a grey-haired and bearded face, an aged Vos (Robbins); the next, in a reduced frame, the face of the real Patrick Chamusso reflecting on an actual moment in his own life: 'As I was walking towards him. I said no, oh no. Killing him is not going to help me. Revenge is not good … It's going to carry on war for this generation and the next genera-tion. Let him live and then I will be free'. As Vos is a composite figure, Chamusso is reflecting on a moment of hatred towards one of a number of his oppressors. The film ends revealing that Chamusso has overcome his hatred and has adop-ted over eighty AIDS orphans and provided them with housing. The reconciliation is an interior act that has external ramifications. The film is rarer in that it depicts the transformation of a black South African who endures apartheid and then, like our Robben Island guide Modise, refuses to take revenge.

Sarafina (Darrell Roodt, 1992)

In contrast, this is a film produced over a decade earlier, after Mandela's release (11 February 1990), and as 'the book was being closed' on apartheid following the referendum vote that supported President De Klerk's reform process (17 March 1992). Set in Soweto, the musical *Sarafina!*, based on a stage musical of the same name (written and directed by Mbongeni Ngema) shows the trans-formation of a young girl from a daydreaming teenager to a defiant and then tortured activist. It is an ambiguous film, which depicts events similar to the June 1976 Soweto riots, though the precise historical context is hard to place. On the one hand, there is the teacher, Mary Masembuko (played by Whoopi Goldberg), leading the school in a dramatic version of the Lord's Prayer, hiding a gun in her kitchen and asserting that 'I hate the killing. I hate the violence'. On the other hand, a group of youngsters (with Sarafina watching) throw a tyre around a local policeman's head, pour petrol all over him and set him on fire. The failure of the film to deal adequately with this action leads Roger Ebert to assert that the film-makers have 'taken a wonderful musical and turned it into a confused and misleading narrative quagmire'.[81]

More memorable are the set-piece songs, which dramatically capture the power of music to challenge the powers that be. Youths march as they sing: 'You can wound us, but you can't stop us. We are coming. You can kill us. But we will live again. We are coming. Sharpen your spears. The war is at your door. We are coming'. Sung among flames, it is a striking contrast with the Lord's Prayer song, which takes place in a school playground. More heart-wrenching is the number sung from inside four police vans: 'The nation is crying, the cattle are gone, the old men are prisoners, the young men have fled, only women and babies in Soweto, weep for the pain of Africa'. Sarafina (played by Leleti Khumalo) begins the film dreaming of being a film star, while talking to Nelson Mandela's picture on her bedroom wall. As the film progresses, she awakens to the endemic violence around her. In prayerful tones she exclaims despairingly to Mandela: 'you're not there, you can't hear me, you can't hear anyone, been away too long, your children are dying'. This leads to another bleak song: 'The Black Nation is dying. Who will lead us to the day of peace? The Black Nation is dying. Oh, Mama, I am crying for the day of peace'. The film reveals how children and teenagers were abused, interrogated, beaten or taken to rooms full of dead bodies in prison, following the Soweto riots. And only in the final sequences do more hopeful statements emerge: 'The day is coming when we all be free from hatred, free from fear, free from killing'. The last words on the screen are telling: 'On February 11th 1990 Nelson Mandela was released. On June 17th 1991, South Africa's Apartheid laws were repealed. The struggle continues ... FREEDOM IS COMING!' In different ways, all of the films considered here – *Goodbye Bafana, Catch A Fire* and *Sarafina* – reveal not only personal transformations, but also aspects of the struggle, and the hope that freedom from the oppression of apartheid was coming.

Moving away from apartheid

Robben Island may be physically close to Cape Town but, measuring little more than five square kilometres, it was like a distant country cut off from the mainland for the prisoners sent to live there. Even in films set largely on Robben Island, such as *Goodbye Bafana*, little is made of its history. We were told the history both on the island and, in more detail, as we headed back to Cape Town. Prior to being a maximum-security prison for political prisoners (1961–94) during the Apartheid Republic of South Africa, it had served a number of purposes, including as a hospital for lepers (1846–1931), as a 'lunatic asylum' (1846–1921), as well as a site for Xhosa political prisoners (1855–69) and a naval and military base (1939–59). Named after the Dutch word for 'seal', it was known by many locals simply as 'the island' (*Esiquithini*) or place of 'forlorn hope'. *Goodbye Bafana* does, however, manage to bring to life the fact that its 'isolation made it not simply another prison, but a world of its own'.[82] Mandela may have described Robben Island as 'the University' for future leaders, and, while it may have had striking views of Table Mountain, this was a mountain that could be seen but not touched or visited, symbolic of the prisoners' isolation from the city and indeed from the rest of South Africa. My own trip back, moving away from the Island to the mainland, was far from smooth. The sun vanished, a squall blew up, and the sea became rougher. I felt sick. But unlike the prisoners, who when they were transported were locked below deck, I was at least able to breathe fresh air as I looked back at the Island and forward, longingly, towards the mainland.

The long road to reconciliation

Leaving apartheid behind was never going to be a simple journey, and many predicted that what was becoming a low-grade civil war during the 1980s would erupt into something far more bloody with the move towards the first democratic elections in the 1990s. The Canadian–South African film *The Bang, Bang Club* (Steven Silver, 2010) reflects the violent transitional period from 1990 to 1994 in South Africa and how four photojournalists risked their lives in an attempt to capture newsworthy pictures. In the year following the election of Mandela as president, the Promotion of National Unity and Reconciliation Bill formally established a Commission in 1995,[83] with much of its work being undertaken between 1996 and 1998. Rather than following the Nuremberg model of retributional justice or offering a general amnesty, the Truth and Reconciliation Commission attempted to develop a third way, rooted in restorative justice. For some commentators its central aim was to help South Africa come to terms with its apartheid past rather than let it 'live with us like a festering sore'.[84]

Before turning to consider cinematic depictions of the Truth and Reconciliation Commission (TRC) it is useful to reflect on the actual process within South Africa. The TRC itself was made up of seventeen members and consisted of three committees. First, there was the Human Rights Violations Committee, which investigated the 'accounts of victims through hearings and investigations'. In the words of the final 3,500-page report of the Commission: 'One of the main tasks of the Commission was to uncover as much as possible of the truth about past gross violation of human rights', between 1 March 1960 and 10 May 1994.[85] In order to do this, the Human Rights Violations Committee organised public hearings and collected over 21,000 statements. Up to the present time, it is probably 'the largest survey of human rights violations undertaken anywhere in the world'. [86] Second, there was the Amnesty Committee, which evaluated amnesty applications. They received over 7,100 applications for amnesty. It was the first commission in the world to be 'given the power to grant amnesty to individual perpetrators'.[87] This process continued after the submission of the five-volume report and it took over five years to complete. The Committee's work was the most controversial aspect of the entire process. Fewer than one in seven applicants were eventually granted amnesty. Third, there was the Reparation and Rehabilitation Committee (RRC), which attempted to 'formulate a reparation policy to restore and rehabilitate the lives of victims and survivors of human rights violations'.[88] Unlike the Amnesty Committee, whose decisions were legally binding, the RRC provided recommendations for financial support for the victims, which were only partly followed some years later.

In the first volume of the report, the terms of truth and reconciliation are defined. Four kinds of truth are identified. These are first, factual or forensic truth, second, personal or narrative truth, third, social or 'dialogue' truth, and fourth, healing and restorative truth.[89] This typology was outlined about eighteen months into the proceedings and reflects what was already happening in the different committees, rather than providing a definitive vision for the work of the commission. Megan Shore persuasively argues that different kinds of truth were dominant in different committees.[90] For example, through its public hearings the Human Rights Violations Committee (HRVC) was particularly adept at drawing out personal stories from victims, which were commonly couched in Christian language. In other words, the HRVC was particularly good at drawing out personal and narrative truth. The Chairperson of the Commission, Archbishop Desmond Tutu, made this very clear early on, stating that at the hearings 'everyone should be given a chance to say his truth or her truth as he or she sees it'.[91]

In sharp contrast, the longer-running Amnesty Committee, initially chaired by three external judges and two lawyers from the commission itself, followed more legal protocols and was dominated by judicial language. In this context, if perpetrators confessed their misdemeanours and these confessions were determined to be factually accurate, they could be granted amnesty. The result was that this committee operated under a more forensic or factual vision of truth. Even with the investigative units, the lack of wholehearted support from the NP (National Party), the IKFP (Inkartha Freedom Party) and the criticism from the ANC contributed to the fact that overall the TRC appears to have been less successful at drawing out the factual and forensic truth.[92] Several critics go further, suggesting that the TRC operated with an incomplete view of truth because it concentrated upon 'gross violations of human rights', rather than the 'everyday violence of the apartheid system' and wider recurring injustices. These included 'the forced removal of over 3.5 million people, forced labour, the educational and social deprivation of the non-white communities combined with 'the institutional and psychological violence that was integral to the apartheid system'.[93] People who had suffered these were the hidden victims of apartheid. 'The TRC created a diminished truth that wrote the vast majority of apartheid's victims out of its version of history'.[94] While the TRC has been the subject of many criticisms, 'few doubt that the TRC enabled South Africa to avoid a great deal of bloodshed'.[95]

What is meant here by reconciliation? Reconciliation is described in the final report of the TRC as both a 'goal and a process', which operates at different levels. These include 'coming to terms with painful truth', reconciliation between 'victims and perpetrators', reconciliation at a community and national level, and redistribution of wealth and resources.[96] Shore argues that 'two different and at times competing streams of thought regarding reconciliation in the TRC developed, namely the religious moral understanding of reconciliation and the legal, political understanding of reconciliation'.[97] The ambiguity concerning what was meant by 'reconciliation' within the TRC has contributed to the 'fragile and liminal' state of reconciliation to be found within South African society.[98]

Zapiro's (aka Jonathan Shapiro) well-known cartoons capture the perceived necessity of searching for the truth, the difficulties of finding the truth and the chasm between the search for truth and for reconciliation (figures 5.8 and 5.9):

Figure 5.8 SA's Past (published in *Sowetan* on 23 May 1995). This Zapiro cartoon depicts the then Minister of Justice, Dullah Omar, heading towards 'the haunted house of South Africa's murky and violent past'. Zapiro Cartoons © 2011 Zapiro (All rights reserved). Printed with permission from www.zapiro.com.

Figure 5.9 Truth and Reconciliation (published in *Sowetan* on 27 May 1997). Zapiro Cartoons © 2011 Zapiro (All rights reserved) Printed with permission from www.zapiro.com.

Some contemporary commentators are even more outspoken, observing that 'the majority of black people remain at the bottom of the food chain, wallowing in poverty' and claiming that reconciliation 'has been shown' to have 'been very superficial'.[99] Given such claims and the history of the TRC, my original question – How far can films help in the search for truth and the building of reconciliation? – takes on a sharper meaning and greater urgency.

Romanticising reconciliation

Film-makers were swiftly attracted to the drama of the TRC hearings. At least one film romanticised the process. *In My Country* (John Boorman, 2004) tells the story of an Afrikaner journalist and poet, Anna Malan (played by Juliette Binoche), and an African American reporter for the *Washington Post*, Langston Whitfield (played by Samuel L. Jackson), who are sent to cover the TRC hearings. Their interactions are at first stormy. Langston, carrying his own experience of North American racial discrimination, believes the entire TRC process is flawed, allowing the whites to escape justice for the atrocities they have committed. He becomes an outspoken voice of criticism at press conferences, asking: 'How can there be any reconciliation when whites control 90 per cent of the country's wealth?' By contrast, Anna is torn between guilt and belief in the TRC process. Even though she is deeply disturbed by what she hears at the hearings, she passionately defends the Commission's search for truth and reconciliation, which is portrayed as an embodiment of *ubuntu*.[100] This idea, which the script somewhat simplifies, is reflected through the portrayal of the TRC attempting to create 'harmony among all people by absolving transgressions rather than seeking retribution for them'.[101] Their conflicting positions do not always ring true. Ann Peacock, who adapted the story from the radio journalist Antjie Krog's haunting memoir *Country of My Skull*,[102] 'makes the fatal mistake of turning characters into mouthpieces'.[103]

While *In My Country* has scenes of 'undeniable power', such as when victims tell their stories, perpetrators plead for forgiveness or when the black Langston encounters the brutal white racist torturer Colonel De Jager (played by Brendan Gleeson), this remains a film which is 'more didactic than dramatic' and which is 'told too much from the outside'.[104] In between several harrowing scenes of TRC hearings, Langston and Anna's differences are reconciled and they slide into an affair. They may have enacted what would have been illegal under apartheid due to the Immorality Act (1950–85), but most reviewers were unconvinced by this turn. For one thing, there was 'something too calculated about the movie's pairing up of the political and the personal'.[105] The result is that it fails to be emblematic of a possible reconciliation between black and white South Africa. Langston returns home changed by the experience. Anna's reconciliation is more painful. The final scene, as Lucia Saks observes, shows Anna's tired face accompanied by her voice-over quoting Krog's text: 'Forgive me, forgive, forgive me'. There is no answer except for shots of the 'lush, green beauty' of the country, leading Saks to assert that this symbolises how the country 'has indeed forgiven her and that her healing, and by extension the country's, has begun'.[106] Given the casting of an American film star, Samuel L. Jackson, and its limited global distribution, this was a film that was intended to reveal the TRC to a primarily North American market. The search for truth and reconciliation in this film, however, had little impact on the people whose story it aimed to portray. There were 'only seven prints distributed', making little more than $20,000 at the box office, in South Africa.[107] There are few signs of critical awakening in this film. The concentration upon two characters and their search for truth, tenderness and personal reconciliation belittled what could have provided a richer and larger story: the TRC's search for truth and reconciliation in the face of the actual traumas perpetrated and experienced.

The same year saw the release of *Red Dust* (Tom Hooper, 2004), based on a novel of the same title by Gillian Slovo. This is a more nuanced account of the TRC than *In My Country*. At its centre is the story of a lawyer from New York,

Sarah Barcant (played by Hilary Swank), who returns somewhat unwillingly to her native South Africa to act on behalf of a former victim and politician Alex Mpondo (played by Chiwetel Ejiofor), as he faces one of his torturers at a local hearing of the TRC. Alex has repressed many of his most painful memories and these are cinematically brought back to life through darkened and rapid flash-backs. Many locals appear more concerned with what happened to Alex's friend Steve Sizela, who was not only imprisoned and tortured, but also disappeared. This is essentially a courtroom drama, which has its origins in the real-life experience of Gillian Slovo when at some TRC hearings she faced the men responsible for killing her mother, Ruth First, by a letter bomb. While Slovo found it unnerving to be 'put on a level of intimacy with her mother's killers',[108] Alex is re-traumatised by facing his torturers and he is nervous that he himself might be accused of being a traitor to the cause because he was unable not to reveal Sizela's involvement in the struggle against apartheid. Saks, drawing on David Bordwell's work on thrillers, identifies the states of 'curiosity', 'suspense', and 'surprise', as the truth is gradually and painfully revealed. The discovery and exhumation of Steve's body, with incriminating evidence, is a powerful scene in a film, which remains a memorable metaphor of the difficulties faced when trying to dig back into the past.

It is striking how both *In My Country* and *Red Dust* compress many of the pro-cesses of the TRC. In an attempt to entertain and to hold their audience, these films, not surprisingly, simplify and heighten the drama of the lengthy hearings. While religion is not entirely excluded, the original Christian framing of the proceedings are commonly reduced and only briefly referenced. Both *In My Country* and *Red Dust* depict the revelation of hidden narratives and search for forensic forms of truth, though the narrative forms tend to dominate the plot. As the journalist Anna and the lawyer Sarah discover truths about apartheid and themselves, they are challenged by hidden violent histories. The form of recon-ciliation represented is a personal one. For the perpetrators, the immediate reward for telling the truth to the TRC is neither reconciliation nor forgiveness, but simply amnesty as a repayment for honesty. The scale and complexity of both these melodramatic stories are limited in an attempt to make the process more accessible to audiences who had little or no knowledge of the TRC. Both films ultimately celebrate the overall process, leaving little space for criticism of the TRC.

Contesting reconciliation

The claim, by Saks, that there is 'no film yet made which investigates critiques of the TRC',[109] is open to qualification. Several cinematic accounts raise significant questions about the results of the TRC. *Ubuntu's Wounds* (Sechaba Morojele, 2001), described by Martin Botha as a landmark in 'post-apartheid cinema', is a good example of a film that highlights such questions. Only about thirty minutes long, *Ubuntu's Wounds* is 'the first attempt outside documentary film making to examine the effectiveness of the [TRC] process', questioning 'whether real forgiveness is possible in response to truly inhuman acts'.[110]

The aim of the film, according to its director Morojele, was to interrogate assumptions 'widely held' outside South Africa that 'black people are very forgiving, very religiously forgiving' and that they 'have little or no anger about apartheid or the atrocities committed against them'. Morojele wanted to show that the victims of apartheid 'have not really been allowed to vent their anger' and that the TRC 'does not address the individual's dilemma to deal with the past'. For Morojele, the TRC and the nation puts pressure on individuals to say 'we do forgive' and as a result many people succumb to alcohol or drug abuse and 'fail to deal with it'. The film depicts this by showing how Lebo, the main character, has, according to Morojele, 'become a wound',[111] and has moved away to America, leaving his daughter and his family behind. Lebo remains haunted by the fact that the TRC gave amnesty to an ex-secret police officer Venter, the killer of his wife, whom he meets some years later in Los Angeles. Lebo dreams of exacting revenge on Venter, and in one nightmare he even hangs him upside down naked, only to be interrupted by a friend from the TRC, who pleads with him to hold back from revenge. Later in the dream he ignores these pleas, killing Venter in the same way that his wife was murdered.

Back in real life, in his apartment, he replays a video of Venter's testimony at the TRC, and from what we already know it is clear that Venter lies, and yet he was still granted amnesty. Venter now appears to live an untroubled life, unlike Lebo who has been psychologically wounded. Lebo decides to take the law into his own hands, and goes to the church where Venter and his wife worship. He orders them to kneel and looks set to kill them when he is unexpectedly reminded of the importance of respect for his ancestors. The result: Lebo does not follow through with killing them, though he does grab a statue of Jesus asking: 'Is this your God? Does he visit you? Does he tell you what to do?' For Cara Moyer-Duncan this moment 'effectively aligns Christianity with the evils of the apartheid state. In contrast he [Morojele] aligns traditional African belief systems with forgiveness and understanding'.[112] As Moyer-Duncan observes, this storyline highlights some of the difficulties raised through the TRC's dispensations of amnesty, but ultimately depicts a protagonist who 'embraces the TRC as the only viable process for moving forward in South Africa'.[113] It is striking how this moment in the film provides an alternative to the Christian discursive world that recurs in many of the Human Rights Violations Committee hearings.

Questioning the TRC is found in other films. In *Zulu Love Letter* (Ramadan Suleman, 2004) a journalist, Thandeka Khumalo, seeks to repair her relationship with her estranged 13-year-old daughter, Simangaliso (Mpumi Malatsi), who was brought up by her grandparents. Thandeka is still haunted by flashbacks from a traumatic past. She witnessed many brutalities and some killings, and was beaten and tortured herself, resulting in her daughter being born deaf.

The film itself is not easy to watch and some reviewers found it confusing. Martin Botha believes that 'ultimately the film fails because it raises too many issues without dealing with all of them adequately and thus becomes quite muddled'.[114] Nonetheless, the six flashbacks or 'interludes' bring to life her painful memories. They illustrate, in a more sustained fashion than *Ubuntu's Wounds*, how trauma and grief can continue to haunt.

Alongside Thandeka's journey is the story of another mother who is searching for the body of her lost son, murdered by the security services. Like the two fathers in *Cry, the Beloved Country*, these two mothers are traumatised by the separation from their offspring, but their wounds are more vividly manifested and the truth appears far more complex to discern. As demonstrated by Maingard in an essay accompanying the film's script, *Zulu Love Letter* is significantly different from other TRC films such as *In My Country* and *Red Dust*. The plot is not easy to follow, eschewing Hollywood narrative conventions. It has neither a 'happy' conclusion nor an 'easy closure'.[115] While there is a degree of reconciliation between mother and daughter, in the words of the film's writer, Bhekizizwe Peterson, 'as far as the larger socio-political questions are concerned, the unfinished and messy business of apartheid does not lend itself to any tidy solutions'.[116] The 'bones of the slain' may be unearthed and reburied, a priest may quote from Ezekiel's valley of dry bones speech in closing act of memorial but it is not clear for the writer, Peterson, how the TRC will breathe life into 'racial, gender and class inequalities and inequities which remain intact', nor what impact it will have when 'perpetrators are still free, victims are still in limbo, reparations are still under consideration and debate'.[117] *Zulu Love Letter* is 'a complex "treatise" on questions of truth', which illustrates that 'while the quest for truth plagues those who have been traumatised, "truth" can never be discovered or revealed as a singular set of facts'.[118]

In *Zulu Love Letter* Thandeka scales a fence and avoids guards to confront a TRC councillor. There is a sense in which the entire film does something similar, as through its narrative it indirectly questions the TRC process. For the director, Suleman, the TRC was 'fraught with problems' and did not provide an opportunity for healing for the vast majority who had suffered and were traumatised because of apartheid. Nevertheless, such limitations do not undermine the fact that the TRC was the 'beginning of the healing process' and at least it ensures that 'never again will South Africans be able to say "we did not know"'.[119] For all their cinematic complexities and limitations, both *Zulu Love Letter* and *Ubuntu's Wounds* act like cinematic memorials for both victims and traumatised survivors.

Searching for forgiveness

Questioning voices are also found in Ian Gabriel's *Forgiveness* (2004). This South African film portrays a policeman, Dirk Coetzee (played by Arnold Vosloo), who has confessed to having tortured and killed a young man, Daniel Grootboom, and is granted amnesty by the TRC. In the film he has travelled west to a small fishing village, Paternoster, to meet with Daniel's family and request their forgiveness. Using a local priest, Father Dalton, as a go-between, Coetzee finds a family still devastated by their eldest son's death. At first he is met by silence and by anger. Sannie (played by Quanita Adams), Daniel's sister, is full of rage, later phoning his former comrades for whom he kept silent and paid with his life. Sannie is told to keep Coetzee in town so they can come and take revenge. He is allowed back to the house, is given tea and is asked to retell how Daniel died. Facing Daniel's family, Coetzee details how Daniel was picked up, taken to a farm outside Cape Town and tortured. He wouldn't talk, even though he was made to stand on a brick, beaten with a hosepipe, electrocuted and almost drowned by having a wet towel tied around his head. When Coetzee reveals his request to die, Daniel's brother Ernest (played by Christo Davies) smashes a teapot against Coetzee's head. He falls to his knees, hardly reacting and declares Ernest has done nothing wrong. Instructed by her father, Daniel's sister Sannie tends to his wound, using a tea towel as an improvised bandage. Coetzee later invites the family to share Sunday lunch at the local hotel. The meal and wine draws out stories and a little more openness towards Coetzee, who has ordered a headstone to mark Daniel's grave. Sannie's view towards Coetzee softens as she gradually realises that his repentance is genuine, but she is unable to contact and avert the three brothers-in-arms, and unable to persuade Coetzee to flee before the gravestone is erected.

The final scene, full of dramatic tension, takes place in a windswept graveyard. While the bleached colouration remains, some colour has returned. The landscape, which had initially looked so unforgiving, now has hints of a different tone. The dialogue is equally telling. The word 'forgiveness' is spoken at least four times. The family have gathered around Daniel's grave. Just as the priest says 'forgive us our trespasses as we forgive those … who trespass against us', the battered car of the three 'avenging angels' drives into the graveyard. Their car windscreen glints in the sun. To their surprise Coetzee approaches them, inviting them to come and join them to pray for Daniel. They uneasily come out of their car. Daniel's father declares: 'Perhaps you also need to ask forgiveness for our son'. They are silent. After the prayers, each member of Daniel's family shakes hands and says goodbye to Coetzee. Even the priest declares to Coetzee: 'Forgive me, I misjudged you when you came'. Sannie fails in her attempt to send the 'avenging angels' away. When one of the three comrades, Zuko, is confronted by his betrayal of Daniel, he appears to be overwhelmed by 'sorrow and rage', and he shoots Coetzee. In this scene 'forgiveness clashes with the unforgivable'.[120] A low camera shot captures the car's wheels as they screech out, throwing up dust over Daniel's grave. This pans across to reveal Coetzee's bullet-ridden body lying next to the stones and netting that covers the body he once tortured. There is no happy ending and no forgiveness from these three, though perhaps there is a personal reconciliation with the family and eventually a kind of reconciliation with his former prisoner through his death. In order to create dramatic stories,

Forgiveness, along with *Red Dust* and *In My Country*, oversimplify South Africa's traumatic past, ignoring the day-to-day effects of a minority oppressing a majority who 'tended their gardens and cleaned their homes'. For Martha Evans, these films also lack 'self-awareness of the fragility of the truth they present'.[121]

Such criticisms, while partly accurate, fail to recognise the dramatic, sometimes melodramatic, forms of narrative that these films employ.[122] They are not setting out to provide political tracts or social analysis. They are not trying to represent the whole truth and, for all their limitations, they are effective at revealing the fragility of the human form. Rather, they are endeavouring to tell small-scale, personal stories in the context of the work of the TRC. The final frame of *Forgiveness* is powerful and is simply a quote from Archbishop Desmond Tutu:

> Having looked the beast of the past in the eyes, having asked and received forgiveness … let us shut the door on the past – not to forget it – but to allow it not to imprison us.[123]

Representing reconciliation

After the end of apartheid numerous documentaries investigating aspects of the truth and reconciliation process have been made. It is noticeable how the content of many of these documentaries is far more explicitly religious than many of the feature films discussed earlier. One reason for this is because documentary film-makers tend to use actual extracts of video recordings from the public hearings, which were commonly saturated with Christian language. Desmond Tutu's dramatic communicative style in both interview and as chair of the TRC was particularly appealing. It can be found in a number of documentaries, from the fifty-four minute *Stories My Country Told Me: Tutu and the Rainbow Nation* (Tim May, 2000) to the forty-one-minute film *This Crazy Thing Called Grace: Desmond Tutu and the Truth and Reconciliation Commission* (Joëlle Chesselet, 1997). So we see and hear Tutu declare: 'I have sometimes asked how much truth we can tolerate … ' Or from another setting early in the process he confesses that he is 'amazed at the things that have already happened', citing an example from their first hearing in East London where a white woman who was a hand grenade victim stated: '"I want to meet the perpetrator in a spirit of forgiveness, I want to forgive him and I hope he will forgive me". For Tutu this is a sign that there was an 'incredible alchemy … happening in our country'. Later in the same documentary he opines that the TRC could become a 'symbol of hope for the world' and provide insights for many other countries to deal with the past 'effectively … so that you can go with integrity forward together as one people'.[124] This documentary, while depicting some of the wounds of history, is a largely positive account of the Tutu's leadership of TRC, reiterating Tutu's claim that there is *No Future without Forgiveness*.[125]

Few, if any, films about Tutu and the TRC reflect the perspective of Thomas Brudholm, who celebrates *Resentment's Virtue*.[126] In the first half of the book Brudholm provides a detailed critique of the TRC's promotion of forgiveness, and in particular Tutu and his colleague's exhortation, almost coercion, to victims to put away their anger and their resentment and forgive. For Brudholm anger, resentment and the desire for just punishment can be creative forces. He cites almost approvingly the documentary *A Cry from the Grave* (Leslie Woodhead, 1999), where a 'survivor from the Srebrenica massacre' declares: 'I want these murderers to be arrested and punished. Otherwise, I will never find peace in my life'.[127] Brudholm wishes to see 'more nuanced and fair representations of victims who refuse to forgive or who call for justice and punishment'.[128]

Tutu, while regularly cited, is only one voice among many. Like many feature films, documentaries tend to focus on small-scale individual stories of awakening, resistance or reconciliation. A Canadian documentary, tells the story of *Gerrie and Louise* (1997). These newlyweds have very different backgrounds: Gerrie, working for the military, sought through violent means to uphold apartheid, while Louise, a journalist covering the collapse of apartheid, acted as the principal investigator for the TRC. Bringing together individuals from different backgrounds is a popular filmic device. In *The Unfolding of Sky* (Antjie Krog and Ronelle Loots, 1999), Antjie Krog, who covered the TRC proceedings, is brought into conversation with a victim of apartheid. This is the third of four films from the *Landscape of Memory* series. Another film in the same series, *Nda Mona* (*I Have Seen*, Richard Pakleppa, 1999), reveals contrasting experiences and views about how the SWAPO (South West Africa People's Organization) liberation movement operated. Both films raise critical questions about the personal search for truth and the difficulties of reconciliation.

There are other more direct criticisms of the actual TRC process in several documentaries. For example, in the seventy-minute *We Never Give Up* (Cahal McLaughlin, 2002) a small support group from the Western Cape, eleven survivors of apartheid violence tell of their tussle with the South African government to be paid reparations. Not all documentaries restrict themselves to telling the stories of individuals. The two one-hour documentaries on *Facing the Truth* (1999) provide a broader account, in which several wounded and critical voices are heard. Journalist and poet Don Mattera explains to broadcaster Bill Moyers that 'Sorry is not just a word … It's a deed. It's an act. Contrition is not, "Bless me Father for I have sinned". Contrition is, "I have taken from thee, therefore I give thee back. I have hurt thee, therefore, I help to heal your pain"'. The apparent lack of contrition by many perpetrators of violence who put themselves forward for amnesty caused many victims to question the justice of the TRC.

Dramatising reconciliation

Up to this point I have suggested that such critical questioning about the TRC process is to be found embedded not only in a number of documentaries but also in several locally produced films such as *Zulu Love Letter*, *Ubuntu's Wounds* and *Forgiveness*. In *Forgiveness* the request of the perpetrator to be reconciled is met with a shattering blow to his head. This fictional moment speaks volumes and resonates with a moment in the documentary *Between Joyce and Remembrance* (Mark Kaplan, 2003). This is an extended version of his thirty-minute *Where Truth Lies* (1999). It focuses on one case from 1982 that was brought before the TRC. Siphiwo Mtimkulu was tortured, poisoned and later brutally murdered by several members of the security forces. Gideon Niewoudt was one of the killers who later requested amnesty. His disclosure of the 'shocking' truth of what happened to Siphiwo and his friend Topsy Madka earned him and his colleagues amnesty, but not release from jail, where he was serving a sentence for a bombing attack. On his release, Niewoudt sought forgiveness from Mtimkulu's family at a meeting organised and filmed by Mark Kaplan as if it was happening at this moment: The parents will not accept his plea for forgiveness. They will not be reconciled. The mother memorably declares, 'I have no idea what reconciliation is'. The conversation is intense, but is interrupted when Siphiwo's younger brother, Sikhumbuzo, leaps out of the shadows and smashes a vase against Niewoudt's head. For one commentator this is an unsurprising, even satisfying, moment.[129] It does make for a memorably dramatic moment. By contrast, Simon Bright, one of the producers of the Zimbabwean film *Flame* (Ingrid Sinclair, 1996), questioned the ethics of creating a dramatic situation where further violence can take place and the victim's relatives are so publicly exposed.[130] In the documentary, we learn that Niewoudt's skull is fractured but the parents instinctively go to his aid. This surprising reversal, parents helping to tend their son's murderer's bloodied head, embodies how immediate suffering can temporarily, at least, obscure painful memories.

Compare this film with another documentary, *Long Night's Journey into Day* (Deborah Hoffmann and Frances Reid, 1995) (figures 10a and 10b). In this documentary, unlike many of the feature films already discussed, there is no single protagonist upon whom the spotlight is focused; instead, there are four stories that emerged out of South Africa's Truth and Reconciliation Commission. The first is about the 1993 killing of an American student during a riot in Cape Town. The second story is an account of the disappearance and subsequent murder of two teachers and their friends by South African security forces in 1985. Next is a bombing in Durban in which three white women died in 1996. In the fourth and final story, viewers are taken to Guguletu, a township near Cape Town, for a detailed description of a shootout in 1986 where local police killed seven young men. Some commentators are critical of how the narrative structure that leads towards the concluding scene of this documentary oversimplifies 'a highly contested and contradictory process of negotiation', representing it 'in patently optimistic and perhaps even romantic terms'.[131] Other critics are even more outspoken, describing it as 'little more than a propaganda film that shows mainly the bright side and little of the dark side of the [TRC] process'.[132]

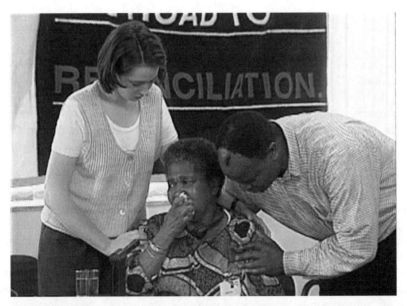

Figure 5.10a Still from *A Long Night's Journey into Day*. Eunice Miya, a Guguletu 7 mother, being comforted at the TRC hearings.

Figure 5.10b Still from *A Long Night's Journey into Day*. Audience members at the TRC hearing in Port Elizabeth, South Africa. Both photographs courtesy of Frances Reid and Debbie Hoffmann, Iris Films. Online. HTTP: <*irisfilms. org/longnight/index.htm*>.

The final scene is more nuanced than such critical accounts claim. It focuses upon Thapelo Mbelo asking forgiveness from the mothers of the Guguletu Seven. In response, one mother observes how they are impoverished and have had no one to support them since their sons were killed. Another stands, drawing attention to her emaciated body and how she has lost so much weight since the loss of his son, declaring she can never forgive him. For a moment it appears he will leave 'unforgiven', but then another of the mothers, Cynthia Ngwe, asks the meaning of his name – which is 'prayer'. She ruminates upon this aloud, saying it is destructive to hold onto anger, declaring, 'It is as if you are my son – you are the same age as my son'. The scene ends with some remaining seated, but most stand to embrace him. There is optimism, but little romanticism in this scene and through the rest of the film. Part of the power of this documentary is that it does not end with the violence and its immediate consequences; instead, it explores how different people respond to hearing the truth about the killing of their nearest and dearest. Some forgive, some are unable to. It is noticeable that those who are unable to forgive or who demand justice for victims and punishment of perpetrators, before being able to talk about forgiveness and reconciliation, are not given as much airtime as those who try to forgive. Nevertheless, the different responses are recorded with little commentary. Searching for truth and building reconciliation are shown to be complex, painful and slow processes. As Dawson correctly asserts, this documentary reflects some of the limitations of the TRC.[133] In particular, by concentrating upon the most obvious victims and their suffering and sacrifice, there is much that is left out of this film's frame, though it does illustrate how dramatising reconciliation can illustrate the possibilities for healing a divided community.

This illustrative and educational potential is to be found not only in the documentary films, but also in many of the feature films discussed in this chapter, depicting the move towards, within and away from apartheid. The film *Invictus* (Clint Eastwood, 2009) is another example of a movie that concentrates on a single story, romanticises and, like most films, simplifies it and then presents it, excluding many other aspects of post-apartheid South Africa. The film, based on John Carlin's book, *Playing the Enemy: Nelson Mandela and the Game that Made a Nation* (2008), depicts how Mandela worked hard to bring the nation together through supporting the Springboks, South Africa's almost exclusively white rugby team. The captain of the Springboks, François Pienaar (played by Matt Damon), takes his team on a visit to Robben Island. Like so many other visitors to the Island he steps into Mandela's tiny cell, and expresses astonishment that someone can be imprisoned in such a place for so long and 'come out ready to forgive'. The film also reflects the reality that Mandela refused to descend into hatred of his oppressors, seeing his guards as 'victims of apartheid'. In his *Long Walk to Freedom* he writes of how in prison his anger towards white guards decreased, though his hatred of the system increased.[134] For Mandela, 'the oppressor must be liberated just as surely as the oppressed. A man who takes away another man's freedom is a prisoner of hatred, he is locked behind the bars of prejudice and narrow-mindedness'.[135]

Invictus sheds light on one of the many ways in which, after his release, Mandela went out of his way to work with his former enemies. He also invited one of his former jailers to his presidential inauguration, and invited the former Robben Island commander, General Johan Willemse, to dinner.[136] These are examples of a number of 'highly publicised symbolic acts' aimed at illustrating how, in spite of a violent past, different races could live together peacefully in one 'rainbow nation'. In the film he embraces former members of the security police who act as his bodyguards. *Invictus* depicts Mandela (played by Morgan Freeman) taking tea with the Springbok captain, Pienaar. Unlike most of the other films discussed in this chapter, *Invictus* attempts to portray forms of communal reconciliation. This is achieved through a number of crowd scenes, where blacks and whites together cheer on their own national team in search of the rugby world cup. This Hollywood account reflects a genuine, though far from lasting, reality, given the continued discrepancies in wealth and resources within different ethnic communities. While rooted in historical events, there is an aspirational fairy-tale quality to this film, as for example the once divided bodyguard team turn to hug each other as South Africa wins the World Cup. The more intimate reconciliations between a mother and a daughter, a father and a son, a victim and an oppressor are more dramatically contained, and therefore simpler to capture cinematically.

Conclusion

My argument in this chapter is that the expressing of small-scale reconciliations and small-scale narrative truths are simpler to depict cinematically than the arduous tasks of uncovering forensic forms of truth or building peace between divided communities. By concentrating upon harrowing individual stories, and individual attempts to build reconciliation out of the remaining ashes, films' horizons are commonly constrained. With the exception of *Invictus*, many of the films we have considered mix together 'forgiveness, repentance, apology, justice, truth, peace' and 'reconciliation itself' in small-scale film narratives, creating what could be called a cinematic 'reconciliation stew'.[137] Even if repentance and apology tend to be marginalised, film-makers often want to bring about a simple harmonious resolution, thereby ignoring the cyclical nature of reconciliation. While some films do reflect the reconciliation process, others highlight reconciliation as an individual goal to be achieved. The result of these approaches is that films overlook the structural and hidden violence of apartheid South Africa.

There is no space on the screen for the 'prophetic' Soweto-based theologians who wrote *The Kairos Document* in 1985, criticising both 'state' and 'church' theologies, which promoted 'superficial forms of reconciliation'.[138] Nor is there room to wrestle cinematically with the claim by South African theologian John De Gruchy that 'reconciliation is about the restoration of justice',[139] even though several do attempt to bear witness to some of the small-scale injustices experienced under apartheid. Films also tend to skate over the significant role of religion in the move towards reconciliation. The films considered in this chapter almost exclusively concentrate upon an individual's horizontal interactions with other people as opposed to vertical forms of reconciliation, which emphasise an individual's search for reconciliation with the divine.

Nevertheless, many of the most successful films, artistically and economically, use a small-scale story as a cinematic metonym to illustrate a wider insight. Films that deal in generalities or broad-brush observations tend both to tire audiences and to oversimplify the fault-lines which continue to divide South African society. More recent films, such as *Tsotsi* (Gavin Hood, 2005), adapted from Athol Fugard's 1980 novel,[140] *Jerusalema* (Ralph Ziman, 2008), *Disgrace* (Steve Jacobs, 2008) and even the science fiction story of *District 9* (Neill Blomkamp, 2009), focus on one or two individuals' stories, often setting them in the commonly overlooked worlds of impoverished post-apartheid South Africa. The background landscape and surrounding characters reveal much about the divided world that many South Africans still have to endure, nearly two decades after the official end of apartheid. As we saw in chapter 4, films, however flawed, can help to bear witness to troubling histories of violence, can awaken audiences to divided worlds and can even help viewers to imagine the possibility of reconciliation. Despite this educational role, films still have to entertain, and therefore they inevitably provide limited perspectives as they attempt to reveal the truth about apartheid and the long road towards reconciliation.

Chapter 6

Promoting peace on screen

Prologue

It was an entirely new experience to have to sit through nearly fifty films in ten days. As a member of one of the many juries at the 59th International Berlin Film Festival I was convinced that *London River* (2009), a film relating to the 7 July 2005 bombings in central London, should win an award. After a vigorous discussion on the last day of the festival, we voted and our jury was equally divided. The casting vote went against *London River*. I was surprised how disappointed I felt. Why? Like many others, if I had made an earlier connection I could all too easily have been travelling on the actual underground train where twenty-six people lost their lives on the Piccadilly Line near King's Cross. Moreover, one of my colleagues had lost a brilliant, young, former student, Helen Jones, in that attack. The film therefore evoked personal memories and mixed emotions. Back at the awards ceremony in Berlin, apart from our brief 'runners-up' commendation, *London River* would only garner one acting award. Disappointed, I assumed that this cinematic drama would vanish, like so many other festival films, without trace into an ocean of forgotten moving pictures. It was a surprise to find that the film had an afterlife, not only after the festival, but also after its limited screen release. Like many other movies, this film now has multiple other incarnations online. Trailers, clips, stills, interviews, reviews and discussions about *London River* are easily accessible to readers, whether sitting by the Thames in London or by the Tigris in Baghdad.

With access to the World Wide Web it is possible to discover the production history, distribution trail, plot synopsis and critical reception of the film without having to go to the cinema, buy the DVD or interview the Algerian director, Rachid Bouchareb. Without seeing the entire film, though, it is hard to glean online that the opening scene of *London River* takes viewers into a church where the priest reads an extract from the Sermon on the Mount, including the statement 'Love your enemies'. In retrospect this text could be seen as a somewhat obvious interpretative key for this film. The next scene depicts a tall African man kneeling in a field as he prays. These are the only two scenes that deal explicitly with religious practice. More commonly described online is how Bouchareb's film brings together a Christian, Mrs Sommers, and a Muslim, Ousmane. She resides in the Channel Islands and he in France. Brenda Blethyn and Sotgui Kouyaté play these roles with sensitivity and skill, with Kouyaté receiving a Silver Bear in Berlin for his performance. In the film she has a daughter and he has a son; both are students in London. After hearing news of the 7 July 2005 terrorist attacks, but having no subsequent contact from their children, they travel to London independently. They unexpectedly meet and eventually go in search of their offspring together. Gradually, mistrust and suspicion are replaced by their united hope and common task. While the depiction of actual terrorism is kept off the screen, the implications of facing violence peacefully are deftly explored. Bouchareb's intention was to depict how the two protagonists 'each live with their own faith serenely'. It does not take long to find out online that this film received many positive reviews in papers at the Berlinale and beyond, especially for the way in which it showed how prejudices can be overcome and mutual respect developed in the midst of tragedy. Sites such as *Rotten Tomatoes* allow viewers to read and compare a whole collection of reviews online, and then add their own reviews and contribute to discussions about the value of a film such as *London River*.[1]

There are some investigations that are hard to undertake when simply staring at a screen. A few months after the attacks, I visited Tavistock Square in London where at 9.47am on 7 July an 18-year-old, Hasib Hussain, had detonated his bomb on a double-decker bus killing himself and thirteen passengers. I was expecting to find flowers near the site. When I looked, there were no obvious markings remaining. At the centre of the square, however, I found a statue of the Indian leader who had so vigorously promoted non-violence, Mahatma Gandhi. The steps up to his statue, where he passively sat cross-legged, were strewn with flowers. Nevertheless, it was only when I was later searching on the web that I discovered that Tavistock Square is home to a small plaque, 'In memory of those who were killed in the bomb attack on a route 30 bus near this spot on 7th July 2005'. Thirteen names are inscribed, along with a simple line drawing of a plant emerging out of the ground. There are thirteen small green leaves. Online, I discovered how the nearby BMA (British Medical Association) had commissioned and dedicated a commemorative sundial for their private physic garden. Without visiting central London, I also saw the official memorial: fifty-two tall stainless-steel pillars in Hyde Park, one for each person who had lost their life that day. I found numerous other sites on the topic, including transcripts of the detailed coroners' hearings and extensive news reports, some casting doubt on the official version of what had happened. Some sites I trusted, while others I was more sceptical of. Online it is possible to find out where individuals were standing or sitting on the three trains and the bus and to read survivor testimonies and victims' obituaries. These interactive and visual memorials provide far more personal details than the post-First World War stained-glass window memorials discussed in chapter 1 and in the film *London River*.

Poignantly, I found online that there was a 1994 plaque that I had missed when I had walked around Tavistock Square, to commemorate not the victims of the bombings but Conscientious Objectors, dedicated 'To all those who have established and are maintaining the right to refuse to kill'. In smaller, more obscure lettering is the claim that 'their foresight and courage give us hope'. One of the striking elements of *London River,* implied in several of the online reviews, is that the story of grieving relatives, from very different religious and cultural backgrounds, who have every reason to withdraw into their own worlds and descend into hatred, are instead brought together by their search for the truth about what happened to their children. The result is ultimately a hopeful story as the two heartbroken protagonists move towards mutual respect and trust.

Introduction

In the second half of this book I have so far examined different ways in which feature films and documentaries bear witness to and search for truth and reconciliation. While reflecting on these processes it is important to understand some of the ways in which the communicative environment in which films are now watched is radically different from that of twenty years ago. One significant reason for this is the advent of the internet and, as observed above, the ability of viewers both to watch and to download trailers, extracts of films and even entire movies. Audiences can research the background 'history' behind film stories and read reviews written by critics from all around the world. With the development of the 'mobile internet' viewers can interact with this material on the move and especially easily where there are wireless technologies.

Moreover, individuals can themselves now become creators and producers of their own films, and can post these online. Viewers can refashion or 'remediate' what they see.[2] They can mix their own recordings with the sounds and furies produced by others. The result is that all kinds of different creations are available on websites such as YouTube. Some clearly celebrate or incite forms of violence. Some simply use new forms of social media to both encourage and orchestrate violence. During the August 2011 riots in the UK, more people used the BlackBerry smartphone messaging service than Facebook, Twitter and other social media sites to communicate and even to try to incite further rioting and looting.[3] Nonetheless, two men were even sentenced to four years in prison for attempting to incite another riot via Facebook, even though they were unsuccessful.[4]

Violence and terror on the internet have become the focal point for a number of academic studies, which have investigated the different ways in which new media are used to incite or to promote violence.[5] 'Martyrdom videos' of suicide bombers or even of beheadings of hostages are often only a few clicks away. News agencies commonly recycle such images to embody the faceless people behind the bombings. A home video of one of the London 2005 bombers holding his baby daughter with the television news on in the background, stating he hopes she will remember him, is easily available online.[6] The face of his daughter is blanked out to preserve her anonymity, while the faces of the journalist Andrew Marr, George Bush and Condoleezza Rice on the television screen behind are easier to discern; so too are images of the life-changing effects both of suicide attacks and the impact of governmental-sponsored violence upon local citizens. For instance, it is comparatively simple to find Kevin Sites' videos of the shooting of a wounded man in a mosque in Fallujah by an American marine (November 2004)[7] or, more recently, images from Bahrain, Cairo, Tunis, Tripoli and Tehran of demonstrators either being beaten or celebrating victory. As we saw in chapter 2, martyred demonstrators or bystanders are commonly remembered and brought back to life online. It is noticeable how many times sites and reports in 2011 repeat the words of demonstrators: 'We are not afraid, we're not afraid, we are afraid only of God'.[8]

Less common is critical reflection on the ways in which the internet is used as a way of responding to violence in a non-violent fashion and even promoting peace. At the heart of this chapter is an investigation of how the web was used for the visual expression of non-violent resistance in the wake of the July 2005 bombings in London.[9] In particular, I will show how several websites became digital galleries for displaying and viewing responses to the attacks. I will look at the communicative ripples caused by these sites, including the development of an Islamic site which accepted the posting of more explicit religious imagery, as well as the development of other related groups on Facebook. These atrocities, which not only killed 52 people but also injured over 700, inevitably provoked a wide range of responses. Every conceivable form of medium carried the story, offering a host of interpretations. The revelation that these explosions were caused by religiously motivated and 'home-grown' suicide bombers led to considerable soul searching in Britain. In both the international and local news media they received far more attention than the 'daily' bombings in Iraq or the ongoing fighting in Central Africa. Many religious leaders used sermons, radio broadcasts, television interviews and newspaper articles to condemn the London bombings.

It was the World Wide Web, however, that provided the opportunity for the most extensive and longest-lasting form of popular response. With its open and easy access it became an ideal location for thousands of people to express their feelings about these suicide attacks and other forms of terrorism. In a few rare cases, some even took the chance to do what was very rarely permitted on the mainstream media: offer support for the bombings. In the cases that we are about to consider, I will show how the web became a place where a vast number of people could express powerful emotions, including fear, anger and defiance, through a creative combination of images and words. While they are not always entirely peaceful, these were often highly imaginative and sometimes comic expressions of non-violent resistance to terrorism. There are intriguing parallels to the responses after other terrorist attacks. For example, in 2001, following the

11 September attacks, 'hundreds of thousands of people began posting online prayers, lighting virtual candles, and entering into religiously based dialogue in an attempt to cope with the tragedy'.[10] There were also diverse reactions within 'Cyber Islamic Environments', where a few extremists celebrated, while many others unequivocally condemned them on religious grounds.[11] In this chapter, I will primarily consider less explicitly religious online responses to another series of terrorist atrocities.

There is a rapidly growing body of research into religious uses of the web.[12] While several researchers have found that boundaries between religions and within religious traditions can be both asserted and blurred on the web,[13] other researchers have claimed that increasing numbers of people use it as a space for defining and moulding their own identities,[14] as well as affirming old communities and forming new ones.[15] How to detect the presence of a 'virtual community' or 'community online', however, is a contested practice. Some studies have suggested that 'virtual communities are nothing more than pseudo-communities', while others assert that 'it is simply assumed too often that "community" is present, without really specifying why or how'.[16] There are increasing numbers of insightful investigations into the relationship between community and identity in online religion. Some of the most significant studies are to be found in Lorne L. Dawson and Douglas E. Cowan's *Religion Online: Finding Faith on the Internet* (2004),[17] Morton Højsgaard and Margit Warburg's *Religion and Cyberspace* (2005), Heidi Campbell's *Exploring Religious Community Online* (2005) and her more recent *When Religion Meets New Media* (2010). Grounded in detailed empirical data, they provide a wide range of nuanced accounts of how different religious groups use the internet for both identity construction and community formation.

I will analyse how people from all over the world left their own distinctive visual marks on the web as a way of expressing resistance to terrorism. How non-violent are these postings? How far do they promote peace? I also ask: To what extent can this posting of images, and words, be described as the formation of a new online community of peaceful defiance? Or is this practice merely like using a supermarket notice board to pin pictures of a bike for sale or a lost cat? The only differences being electricity, global reach and the seriousness of the subject. Or is this something between these two extremes? Perhaps it might be more accurate to see it either as a virtual art gallery, which has few regulations and never-ending walls openly available to amateur digital artists, or a virtual gathering point, with posted images becoming catalysts for debate and discussion? Even if it is not a fully fledged community attempting to build peace, does this collective enterprise go beyond what Wellman and others have described as 'networked individualism'[18] to become a network promoting peaceful resistance? My contention is that to describe this either as the creation of a fully fledged online community or simply as an electronic notice board is to over-simplify what is both a fluid and a social network built upon a set of practices, which is better described, borrowing a Durkheimian phrase, as a 'collective representation' in the face of shared trauma.[19] It is important to underline that the collective nature of this representation does not undermine the diversity of responses that this site attracted. As we shall see, some are violent in tone, others promote peace and others are ambiguous.

In order both to test this thesis out and to understand the dynamic phenomenon, it will be useful initially to set out a taxonomy of visual postings. The aim here will be to establish a nomenclature for describing the different ways in which primarily visual posting sites are used and how they function. Users absorb, interpret, process, adapt and post their own images at these sites. What are the different uses that images are put to on the web? We shall see how they are used to defy, to console, to encourage, to explain, to exhort and to promote peace. It will become clear that these images are put to a number of different rhetorical uses, from expressing heartfelt emotion, via asserting identity, to promoting peace. In this context, we shall see how the visual signs of identity and the markers of community become far less fixed and stable through their exposure in the public domain of the World Wide Web. They are highly elastic signs. With the advent of digital technologies, it has become easy to manipulate pictures and photographs and to send them rapidly around the globe. In the age of sailing ships, to transport a framed picture between continents would have taken several weeks of costly and potentially dangerous travel, while today, for those with access to the appropriate technology, it can be transported in a few seconds across thousands of kilometres, by no more than a few taps on a keyboard and several clicks of a plastic mouse.

In this chapter, I examine a selection of specially created pictures, which were posted from all over the world to several websites to affirm forms of defiance against these attacks and other forms of terrorism. In particular, I describe in detail the different kinds of images that were posted up on the groundbreaking *We're not afraid* site. I then consider how another more explicitly religious site was used to affirm popular forms of non-violent resistance against terrorism. Some became the electronic home for photographs, while others housed written opinion pieces or poems. Given that religious beliefs were inextricably connected with these attacks, it is not surprising either that some users tried to employ religious imagery, nor, given the constraints imposed by the site organisers, that others posted a vast kaleidoscope of secular imagery to express their resistance. The merging of sacred and secular symbols is not a particularly new practice, but the use of digitally altered photographs as non-violent statements against terrorist violence is more original. They clearly emerge from a diversity of social settings, where different 'doxas' and 'sets of dispositions' are to be found.[20]

The origins of the *We're not afraid* site

We're not afraid (figure 6.1) rapidly grew into a website that attracted thousands of images of resistance against terrorism posted from all over the globe. Within two

Figure 6.1 Globe: We are not afraid. Courtesy of Shutterstock.com and with thanks to Brian Fischbacher. The pictures in this chapter are, as close as possible, replicas of those found on the two original websites: 'We're not afraid' and 'Not in the name of Islam'.

months it had received over 33 million hits. It began when Alfie Dennan,[21] a London-based web developer, received a photo from a friend, Adam Stacey, showing how he had escaped the smoke caused by the bomb on the King's Cross train with a sock covering his mouth. Within thirty minutes of the London bombings on 7 July 2005, Dennan posted this photo on his web log (or blog). In a little over two hours the BBC and other news organisations started to use this image. The result was that Dennan's web log rapidly received numerous messages of support. Encouraged by these responses Dennan, along with several of his friends, set up a website on 7 July called *We're not afraid*. Initially, it was simple images of themselves, their families and friends with the copy of either 'We're not Afraid' or, not contracted, 'We are not Afraid' imposed onto the digital pictures. Within days the site was overwhelmed with images at first from within the UK, and later from all over the world.[22] With an estimated 4 million hits in the first few days of its existence the site swiftly snowballed into a global phenomenon. It was possible for several years to purchase, through this avowedly non-profit site, a wide selection of merchandise, including hats, mugs and T-shirts with 'We're not Afraid' emblazoned on the product. An exhibition of selected images was held in central London in the autumn of 2005 and a book was proposed. The site itself now has well over 20,000 images, with an additional 20,000 not making it up onto the web. It is now no longer being added to but remains a virtual memorial of individuals' desire to post and create, and it continues to find expression in new digital settings.

The statements still to be found on the About *We're not afraid* page are revealing and worth citing at length as they appear online:

> We are not afraid to ride public transportation.
> We are not afraid to walk down a crowded street.
> We are not afraid of each other.
> We are not afraid to say that terrorism in any form is never the answer.
>
> *We're not afraid* is an outlet for the global community to speak out against the acts of terror that have struck London, Madrid, New York, Baghdad, Basra, Tikrit, Gaza, Tel-Aviv, Afghanistan, Bali, and against the atrocities occurring in cities around the world each and every day. It is a worldwide action for people not willing to be cowed by terrorism and fear mongering.
>
> The historical response to these types of attacks has been a show of deadly force; we believe that there is a better way. We refuse to respond to aggression and hatred in kind. Instead, we who are not afraid will continue to live our lives the best way we know how. We will work, we will play, we will laugh, we will live. We will not waste one moment, nor sacrifice one bit of our freedom, because of fear.
>
> We are not afraid.[23]

The site's credo is outlined in 186 words. The cities named are noteworthy, going beyond the West and being inclusive in nature. The tone is assertive but not explicitly aggressive. The promotion of a 'better way', which does not 'respond to aggression and hatred in kind', highlights one of the aims of the site. Alongside these peaceful sentiments are statements of non-violent defiance. Arguably these are expressed more articulately through hundreds of the pictures posted on the site.

Images of defiance

Many of the images were sent in as acts of defiance against the London bombers. In the first few days the earliest postings were often, though not exclusively, sombre. The founder of the site, Alfie Dennan, stares impassively out from the screen holding a piece of white A4 paper, bearing the words in blue felt pen, 'We are *Not* Afraid!' 'Not' is double-underlined. The practice of posting images onto the web as an act of defiance can clearly be seen in several of the pictures sent in by actual victims of the attacks. One survivor posted a picture of himself lying bandaged in a hospital bed. On 12 July 'Mark M. from Finsbury Park, London' wrote: 'I was on the tube on the first carriage at Russell Square. I am not afraid'. The words are almost overwhelmed by the striking photo of his face with small strips of white medical tape on his forehead and cheek. The previous day a red tinted picture was posted, showing a young woman with glasses, her eyes lowered, with the words typed in black over the image: 'Yesterday I lost my friend in London, today I am not afraid'. Through such statements and depictions victims were able to assert their courage in the face of heartbreak. Other early postings included pictures of babies, children, pets and, later, large animals at the zoo. While images of dogs and cats were particularly popular, other more exotic creatures, such as photographs of kangaroos bounced their way onto the site. Alongside pictures of suffering, images of innocence were used as non-violent statements of defiance (figures 6.2a and 6.2b). Precise spelling varies, though 'We're not afraid' is the most common phrase.

It was not long before some contributors to the site became more adventurous and creative in their depictions. Tube signs and maps were adapted to incorporate the four key words. An electric meter was adapted into an 'Afraid-o-meter', measuring zero. One woman is photographed sitting on the tube reading a paper, whose headline is digitally changed to 'We are not afraid'. Buses, taxis and even a yacht were also adorned with this simple statement. While the images of the vehicles were digitally altered to incorporate the statement, the yachtsmen claim to have actually painted the logo on the side of their boat for the Cowes race in the Solent (UK). Following the failed bombings a few weeks later, on 21 July, an old tube ticket is apparently embossed with the claim 'We are still not afraid'. Like many of the submissions, this is a sophisticated piece of forgery, as the typescript looks identical to the font used in the unaltered parts of

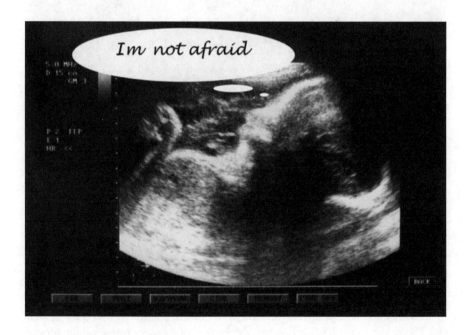

Figure 6.2 (continued)

the ticket. The word 'still' is added to the text on a number of postings after the abortive 21 July attacks. Again the site became a space to express words of defiance in an original visual guise. Intemperate language is rarely permitted on the site, though some participants portray themselves literally 'flipping the finger' or making a 'V' sign to the camera. This non-verbal communication epitomises the response to the attacks that is at the heart of many of these examples of web art. The desire to hit back is beneath the surface of some pictures, which appear to be used to sublimate aggression. Some posters rely on more military images. While the editors sifted out pictures of weapons being used threateningly or in anger, one person sent in an image of an aircraft carrier in the middle of the ocean with jets flying in formation above. Another person chose Joe Rosenthal's famous 1945 photograph of the marines raising the American flag over the Pacific Island of Iwo Jima during the Second World War. The sky is filled with six words: 'We have never been afraid, never'. To suggest that these posters are promoting non-violence would be stretching a point. They are using images of military might or past heroism as statements of defiance.

Almost a month later, a British man sent in the hazy photo of people in the smoke-filled tunnel walking down the tube line in semi-darkness, emergency lights barely illuminating their way to safety. The usual headline of 'We are not afraid' is adorned with a series of exclamation marks. In the foreground a man is holding a mobile phone up as he is also trying to capture the scene digitally. The merging of communication technologies and the ability of mobile phones to be used as cameras has turned every phone user into a potential amateur photo-journalist. The phones themselves have become objects used to express defiance and resistance. One user sent in a picture of his Nokia phone; on it the following message could be seen: 'We are still not afraid: we will never let terrorism dictate the way that we live. We refuse to live in fear. Terror will never win'. In a further example of playful defiance, familiar Microsoft Windows pop-ups were changed to ask the question 'Are you Afraid'; a boxed 'No' makes the response clear.

Here then is an interesting qualification to the suggestion that this site was dominated by pictures of the self, or those people or animals closest to the sender. Technological extensions of personality, redolent of McLuhan's theory about the 'extensions' of humanity through media,[24] are also found posted at the *We're not afraid* site. These images of defiance draw upon a range of visual resources to make their point. The human face recurs again and again: sometimes smiling, sometimes angry and sometimes quizzical. It is as if these mostly anonymous faces are making a demand on the viewer, reminiscent of the French philosopher Emmanuel Levinas' reflections on 'face-to-face' ethics, which begins with the naked face making a simple command: 'do not kill me'.[25] Compared to images of faces, pictures of new media or other technological objects are rarer and often make use of additional words to reinforce the visual impact of the picture. Defiance takes on many guises and appears to be a driving force behind the posting of many of these images.

Images of solidarity

Closely related to a rhetoric of defiance is an assertion of solidarity. Several contributors sent in images of the Twin Towers in Manhattan, sometimes in pristine condition and sometimes following the terrorist attacks. In one case, above the towers was not only the 'We are Not Afraid' statement but also this list of cities: New York, Madrid, Moscow and London. The obvious attempt here is to locate the London attacks in a history of recent terrorism. In passing it is worth noticing which cities are excluded from this list and that an apparently Western frame is provided for understanding where terrorism is happening. Another hauntingly picturesque shot of a marina in the foreground and smoke billowing from the Twin Towers in the background is supplemented with the declaration: 'This did not make us afraid. It made us more compassionate more loving & more unified!!!!'

Experience of terrorist attacks allows contributors to go beyond statements of sympathy to assertions of solidarity. In the highly visual world of this site, whereas we shall see religious imagery is normally not allowed, numerous non-religious images are used to try and speak of peaceful solidarity. This could be described as an expression of civil religion, which emerges from the grassroots and where in this case the symbols of nation are intertwined with the symbols of faith.[26]

Images to counter fear

Many of these pictures reflect on the nature of fear and bravery itself. Some attempt explicitly to encourage the viewer's self-confidence in themselves. For instance, a man from Newcastle (UK) sent in a picture of a kitten looking into a wooden framed mirror, who sees not itself, but a lion with a large mane. Consider the statement to the left of the mirror: 'Look inside yourself. You are brave. You are strong. You are courageous'. This sounds almost as if it has been taken from a course on 'the power of positive thinking'. The assumption here is that courage appears to come not from an external source but from within. At the bottom of the picture the claim of individual strength is qualified: 'together we will be unafraid'. Given that confidence is a fragile commodity, which terrorists aim to undermine, this kind of picture is a humorous visual reflection upon the belief that positive thinking can transform the timid viewer into a lion-heart. This makes an intriguing contrast with late medieval Western imagery, which frequently shows several devotional figures kneeling in prayer, not before a figure of strength such as lion, but beneath a suffering and bloodied semi-naked man. Nevertheless, vulnerable images have their own attraction and are also to be found all over the website. As observed earlier, the figures that are used almost like totems to counter fear are often children, partners or pets. They do not obviously suffer and they are without obvious political power; their charisma is heightened partly through their weakness and innocence in the face of terror.

Images of popular encouragement

Such encouraging sentiments are also to be found in pictures that appropriate images from popular culture. More specifically, the creative use of cultural icons is to be found in visual quotation from popular television programmes. For example, images of superheroes, the *Teletubbies* and characters from *The Simpsons* are used several times. As if he is writing punishment lines, Homer Simpson's son, Bart, is pictured writing 'We are not afraid' again and again on a school blackboard. A still from the popular British soap *EastEnders'* title sequence, the aerial photograph of the city of London is adapted to read 'Not Afraiders'. These are two examples, chosen from many, of how television is used as a visual resource, which is mined for creative and rhetorical purposes. Several publicity posters from films are adapted. Three days after the first attacks in London a man from Milan adapted the famous picture of a large shark, bearing teeth and heading for a female swimmer, promoting *Jaws* (Steven Spielberg, 1975). He digitally scrawled in red on either side of the shark two words: 'not afraid'. The poster and opening titles from *The Matrix* (Wachowski Brothers, 1999) are adapted to include multiple repetitions in green lettering of: 'We are not afraid'.

From the early Middle Ages to the nineteenth century a common reference point for most Western viewers was biblical narrative. Frescoes, stained-glass windows and canvas paintings, unsurprisingly, drew upon stories from Jewish and Christian scriptures. These tales were known and repeated. Given the decrease in scriptural knowledge and the global reach of cinema it is not surprising that films have become one popular resource for those making visual statements on the web. Actual stills from films are used to good effect. Yoda, from *Star Wars,* is particularly popular. In small white capitals over a picture of the cinematic character, with his distinctively pointed ears, is the statement 'Fear is the path to the Dark Side. Fear leads to anger. Anger leads to hate. Hate leads to suffering'. In large bold red capitals is the statement, mimicking the character's speech patterns, 'Not Afraid I am'. Here parody and playfulness with language sharpen the point.

In another picture, and in what is an extremely rare statement for this site, one cinema's illuminated publicity board not only adds the 'We are not afraid' statement but also gestures towards revenge: 'Be prepared: We will get you for this'. More common are pictures of superheroes such as the Incredible Hulk, Captain America and Superman, who make appearances in other photos, though the usual face of Christopher Reeve has been replaced by the sender's own bespectacled visage. Here identity has been momentarily transformed. Once again humour is used as a non-violent defence against terrorism. Even more ironically, a tiny child faces a vast Japanese Sumo wrestler. While there is every reason for him to be fearful, underlined in white, next to the boy, are the words 'I am not afraid'. There are several moments where the creator of the image is offering an image with an ironic wink to the viewer, so a Marmite (vegetable spread) jar, a Carlsberg (lager) and a vodka advert, an iPlayer poster and on several occasions a Coke bottle's famous red label, are altered to 'Not Afraid' statements. Material culture is plundered and adapted to make the point. Humour is used not only to encourage viewers, but also to mock the actions of the terrorists.

Images to provide historical and global perspectives

A further rhetorical device is to use pictures from the past, which encourage viewers to step away from the immediate and look backwards. Older pictures from London's history are used. For example, the famous image from the Second World War of St Paul's Cathedral surrounded by clouds in the Blitz is given the headline 'We fought Terrorism Before and We Won … ' The bottom right corner has the adapted underground logo with the familiar four words. Scottish history is also plundered. A stained-glass window featuring William Wallace holds a double-edged sword with two words added: 'Never Fear'. Famous paintings are also transmogrified. Munch's *The Scream* is adapted several times, most memorably with the figure now placed in front of the House of Commons in London and a red double-decker bus with the statement 'Smiling not Screaming'.

This website provides valuable evidence for some of the visual resources people from all around the world reach for when the traditional forms of religious expression are made off limits. Some scholars might describe this as an expression of 'implicit religion', particularly if this term is understood with reference to 'intensive concerns' for 'commitments' that touch 'human depths'.[27] As we have seen, the majority of the images emerge out of people's closest circles of intimacy: close family, partners or favourite pets. When faced with the threat of violence, many people unsurprisingly use images of their 'nearest and dearest'. Beyond the intimate sphere, there is evidence, from the multitude of images provided, of the significance of friends, colleagues at work and of other members of a sports team. These images speak of solidarity in the face of news of terror. The sphere of memory is drawn upon through the imaginative use of historical posters, family photos from tourist sites, trips abroad or postcards. The communicative environment also provides a rich source for contributors. As we have seen, images from popular culture, films and the actual tools of communication are all woven together to create this vast digital tapestry. The presenting statement 'We are not afraid' may in many cases actually be saying 'Yes, we are afraid', but we will not change how we travel, who we care for or what we do. We will try to act bravely. Given these sentiments it is not surprising that there are many pictures of people sticking out their tongues at the camera, and by extension at the viewer and at those who promote violence against defenceless women, men and children.

Images to promote understanding

This site celebrates individuals' creativity, sense of humour and right to express themselves through creating a transitory virtual network. The comedy sometimes has an edge, as suggested earlier, with mockery of the terrorists being a common device. While the website organisers admit to welcoming 'images of fearlessness from all people', such as firefighters or rescue crews, they will 'not publish images of military or police personnel' if 'there are guns visible or un-holstered in the image'. The reason given for this is that the team do not want 'to send an aggressive message'. They refused several pictures of dead Muslims with the statement 'You should be afraid'. They did not permit hateful, indecent or religious iconography. There are, however, several examples of pictures rich in religious symbolism. A Japanese Buddha with smiling children sitting in front, the steel sculpture of the *Angel of the North* (by Antony Gormley) in Gateshead (figure 6.3b), UK, the vast Art Deco statue of the arms outstretched Christ with a couple beneath in Rio, Brazil, and the statue of huge praying hands from Tulsa, Oklahoma, all carry the usual statement but point towards different religious traditions. There is even a picture of Nostradamus (1503–66) with a playful title: *Notafraidus*. There is also a simple line drawing of a cross, accompanied by the statement: 'Not Afraid, Just disappointed with Mankind'. Alfie Dennan justified the use of these images, and not other explicit religious ones, on the grounds that the dominant theme was not religious and the sentiments could be expressed in any setting (figures 6.3a and 6.3b).[28]

There are a number of representations of Muslims in peaceful settings or poses. For example, several women in Islamic attire are pictured holding candles, as are two walkers on a hill in Iran. In this case, as in some other postings, 'We are not afraid' is translated, this time into Farsi. Perhaps most strikingly, a week after the 7 July attacks a young Muslim woman posted an image of herself wearing a hijab with the unexpected words: 'We are afraid'. This is, according to the site's founder Dennan, the only picture out of over 20,000 posted with these words. Her explanation was as follows: 'This pic is to highlight my concern as an INNOCENT Muslim and to raise awareness about the increase in racial hate n [sic] crime because of the atrocity in london [sic] last week'. As with much of the text on this site, the spelling, sentence structure and use of capitals follows the informal pattern of texting, appearing more colloquial than grammatical. This reflects the increasingly wide use of 'textese', abbreviated writing influenced by text messaging on mobile phones. Far more care appears to have been paid to the creation of the images (figure 6.4). The vast majority of the images found on this extensive site do not use explicit religious imagery. There are resonances with religious texts, such as the young faced man with the simple phrase, which is also found in Psalms, 'Fear No Evil'. There are subtle visual allusions, which are redolent with belief in the afterlife, such as the picture of a woman walking towards a bright light emanating out of a London Underground tunnel.

Images to promote peace

One posting draws on a photograph of an angelic-looking figure to promote peace. A black man dressed in white with vast white wings reaches towards the sky. At the centre of the picture is his face looking out into the middle distance. Hands of many colours encircle him from below, also reaching upwards.

Figure 6.3a Christ the Redeemer, Rio, Brazil. The original shot has a man and woman in front of the statue. Courtesy of Shutterstock.com and Brian Fischbacher.

In bright red letters are the statements 'No fear', 'I am not afraid' encircled by red, and the words 'Live on – in Peace♡✗'. Another striking image, also attempting to promote peace, is composed of over twenty photographs containing some thirty-five faces. These faces of men, women and children, civilians and soldiers have one thing in common: they are all crying. There is the face of Sergeant Ken Kozakiewicz weeping in a helicopter beside a soldier with a

Figure 6.3b   The Angel of the North, Gateshead. Courtesy of Gordon Ball LRPS/Shutterstock. com and Brian Fischbacher.

bandage covering his eyes and the body bag of his dead friend, Andy Alaniz, who was killed by 'friendly fire'. This well-known image is juxtaposed with a series of other less well-known but grief-stricken faces. Interspersed between these lines of faces are three questioning statements: 'You want that!? You don't want that!? Your bombs won't change that!!!' The creative use of punctuation marks heightens the interrogative tone of the sentiments. What will bringing tears, fear and anguish achieve? Will bombs bring an end to crying? This mosaic of grieving faces has a clear answer to these questions and overall it asserts that setting off bombs, whether in 1991 in Iraq or London in 2005, is not the way to bring about peace.

In the wake of the London bombings and following the extraordinary success of the *We are not afraid* site, several other sites were created. One of the most interesting was the Islamic site *Not in the name of peace*, also set up only a few days

Figure 6.4 We are afraid. Courtesy of Shutterstock.com and Brian Fischbacher.

after 7 July. The site's creator was a young British Muslim, Muhammad Ridha Payne. His opening statement to the site is passionate: 'We need to show these maniacs that none of us think what they are doing is right, justified or Islamically based'. Payne believes that 'Islam has very clear guidelines as to what is right and what is wrong'. He acknowledges that 'Of course we all feel aggrieved by actions in Afghanistan, Iraq and Palestine but this does not give anyone the right to kill further innocent people'.[29] The site attracted far fewer images than 'We are not afraid' and appears to have now been taken off the web, but nonetheless the several dozen pictures posted make powerful points. Some seek to reassure viewers. For instance, the words 'Don't Panic I'm Islamic' surround a man as he steps out of his British looking house. He is wearing a simple black and white rounded cap, a *taqiyah*, pointing one finger and gently smiling. There is nothing threatening about his appearance. These images stand in sharp contrast to the more widely disseminated pictures found on extremist websites or in videos sent to television stations of masked men holding guns standing behind blindfolded kneeling hostages. Equally unthreatening here is another image, a well-groomed young-Asian looking man, this time sitting on rocks with a harbour in the background: 'Don't EXPLODE, STRIKE a POSE! ... because terrorism is never pretty'. The comic twist here is found in several other postings such as one of a baby with the statement 'I want to grow up not blow up'.

Images to exhort and to teach

There are more serious religious depictions, from individuals reading sacred texts to crowds praying to Allah. A young girl in a white robe kneeling on a prayer mat with supplicatory hands and an open Quran in front of her is accompanied by a phrase that through repetition emphasises 'the name': 'Not in the name | the name of Islam'. More daringly an image of a woman wearing a face-veil (*niqab*), with only her eyes visible, states simply: 'I am not a terrorist'. In a different picture, a young man kneels, reading a Quran: 'Seek knowledge not war'. Several other pictures show people in prayer. For instance, above two men kneeling with bowed heads touching the prayer carpet of a mosque, are the words 'the proverb says "slaughter your ego with the dagger of self-discipline"', below them three words are added: '"not slaughter people"'. In another picture of rows of men at prayer, nearly fifty Muslims kneel, and over the front row is the exhortation typed in white: 'stop the slaying and get down to some praying'. There is also a picture from Mecca with thousands of pilgrims at prayer with the white words 'not in our names' superimposed in small letters at the bottom of the photograph. Among a number of Shi'ite Muslim young people I spoke with in Tehran about these sites (Iran, November 2007), it was this image that proved the most popular. They were more critical of the images described above which identified terrorism with Islam, suggesting that these images should be addressed against 'Talibanism', not Islam as a whole (figure 6.5).

On the *We're not afraid* site several contributors had digitally daubed words upon a photograph of the new dividing wall in Israel, or at least a wall that looks strikingly similar to it. This image is recycled again on the *Not in the name of peace* site, but used for more explicitly religious reasons. The first line states: 'Islam means peace" the second, 'not in the name of Islam'. The same sentiments are expressed on a skilful adaptation of a London street sign found on the *We're not afraid* site (figure 6.6). The *We're not afraid* team were so impressed, they did something they very rarely do: comment on the image.[30] 'We received this terrific photo along with a link to an online petition which condemns terrorist acts committed in the name of Islam, which can be found and signed here. We urge people to check it out!' On the connected site is a similar image, along with a quote from the '*The Holy Quran* (5.32)' in English: 'to kill one person is like killing the whole of mankind ... And

Figure 6.5 Mecca: Not in our names. Courtesy of Shutterstock.com and Brian Fischbacher.

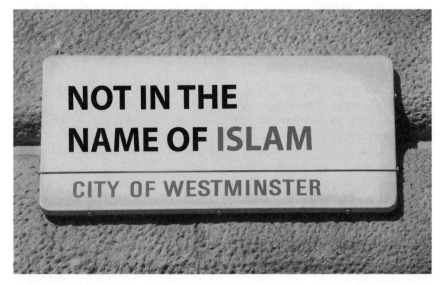

Figure 6.6 Street Sign: Not in the name of Islam. Courtesy of Shutterstock.com and Brian Fischbacher.

to give life to one person is like giving life to the whole of mankind'. Many of these images assert that 'true' Islam is a peaceful and life-bringing faith. One overhead shot of a blurred man, apparently rapidly rotating, reading the Quran is overlaid with the claim, 'Islam "is a way of life" NOT "a way of death"'.[31] 'Life' is written in green and 'death' is written in red.

The colours are striking in many of these pictures. In another picture, five ethnically diverse babies, in only their nappies (diapers), clamber over a white long-haired woolly sofa towards a two-dimensional blue and green depiction of the world. Multi-coloured letters spell out 'One World', while the globe itself simply has in black: 'One God'. In italics and in smaller letters is the catchphrase of the site: *'not in the name of Islam, not in the name of peace.'* Unlike images from the 'hate' sites which position texts behind hostages, here the text is brought to the foreground, highlighting the peaceful intention of this posting.

While it is no surprise that images connected with Islam dominate this site, it is not confined entirely to images of Muslims. One posting has a picture of Pope John Paul II respectfully kissing a large green Koran in the presence of a Muslim religious leader. The heading is 'united we can defeat terror'. Another posting is a photograph of U2 playing at the Arrowhead Pond arena in Anaheim, California, on 1 April 2005. In the original picture, projected in red lines above the band is the word 'Coexist'. This was created with a combination of normal letters and the major religious symbols of Islam (crescent in place of 'c'), Judaism (star in place of 'x'), and Christianity (cross in place of 't'). The inspiration for this powerful linguistic image was drawn from graffiti that the lead singer, Bono, saw somewhere in the Midwest of the USA. Notice how the added copy, which frames the image, reinforces what the picture itself communicates: 'All GOD'S people MUST and U2 can … C⊙E✡ıs✝!' Taken together, the use of the pictures of John Paul II kissing the Quran and U2 performing beneath this single word, partly composed of religious symbols, these are examples of how visual signs are recycled in new contexts to promote peace between religions.

Images to remember

While the original site survives, it is largely dormant. It has become a digital memorial to an international response to the attacks. There is what looks like a final posting from the organisers, dated 17 July 2007, explaining that while the URL would remain active, 'we simply do not have anyone who has the time to keep everything running and dynamic. We are pleased however that the site will remain online as a permanent reminder of the terrorist attacks here in London in 2005, and the incredible response from around the world'.[32] Unlike the ever-expanding social-networking site Facebook, 'We're Not Afraid' peaked within several months of the attacks and is now no longer growing. This is partly because, as is clear from the statement above, the original designers did not have the time to maintain the site and because, unlike Facebook, it is effectively a single-issue website. Nevertheless, the assertion that *We are not afraid* continues to echo through cyberspace and beyond. There are several groups within Facebook which appear under the titles of *We're not afraid*, *We are not afraid* and even one to commemorate five years since the attacks, *We are still not afraid*.[33] Some point back to the original site through links and some through quoted images. These groups attract sparse numbers of supporters, little more than two or three-dozen, but they do explicitly point visitors back to *wearenotafraid.com*.

Others use the 'We're Not Afraid' title as a way of responding to more recent terrorist attacks. One Facebook group was established soon after the June 2007 foiled attacks in London and on Glasgow airport. Here a picture of Big Ben and the Houses of Parliament in London are used to assert strength in the face of these attacks. Another group was set up after the attempted car bomb attack in Times Square, New York (May 2010). This provoked a North American to set up a 'Common Interest – Beliefs and Causes' group on Facebook entitled 'We are not afraid'. Its defining image is that of the crowned light green face, with torch held aloft, of the Statue of Liberty. Alongside is the assertion that 'I, for one, would rather die in an attack than walk the streets of my own country scared of the lunatics that hide among us. This has nothing to do with political parties or ideologies. Nor do I seek the use [of] hatred to build hatred for others … I refuse to be afraid; I refuse to be limited by the hate of others'.[34] Embedded within these statements is a celebration of those who toiled to build 'this nation' and who 'didn't sacrifice for our generation and our children to live in fear'. Here religious language is used to highlight previous civil efforts. These sites offer no analysis, neither religious reflection nor ethical discussion, and appear like 'knee-jerk' digital responses in the face of perceived or actual threats.

Contrast these two largely Western Facebook groups with others established within predominantly Islamic settings. For instance, one 'student – political group' on Facebook was established by a Pakistani, Omer Farooq, who lives in Saudi Arabia, and is entitled 'We want peace not war but we are not afraid'. It appears to have begun on 1 January 2009 and has as its defining image a single illuminated word: 'Peace'. At first sight this group appears to be unequivocally promoting peace, but if you look more carefully at the discussion a more complex picture emerges. Two writers disparagingly agree that India would be unlikely to cope with the Pakistan army given the difficulties it was caused by ten terrorists in the 2008 Mumbai attacks (sometimes known as 26/11). As with the original *We're not Afraid* website, proclaiming peace does not necessarily mean everyone associated with the site solely embraces peaceful practices.

The peaceful eighteen-day 2011 Egyptian uprising, known by some as 'the Facebook revolution', found digital expression on countless sites, many beyond the bounds of Facebook. Consider the YouTube video sequence posted under the title *The Egyptian Uprising, We're Not Afraid*.[35] This 'mashes' together stills of protesters and videos of demonstrators in Tahrir Square and beyond. Like many other digital creations on the same topic, it celebrates those who risk their lives demonstrating largely peacefully against Hosni Mubarak's thirty-year rule. The American rap artist Eminem's hit song 'Not Afraid' (2010) is easily discernible in the background, holding together the core of this sequence. The original Eminem video has been watched over 200 million times on YouTube, as opposed to this montage, which has so far attracted only about 10,000 viewers. In Eminem's version, with the help of CGI (computer generated imagery) he flies through the streets, whereas in its Egyptian, adapted counterpart, the demonstrators are rooted to the ground, some holding flags, banners and others facing police defiantly. Eminem's words take on a new meaning as viewers are shown courageous and largely non-violent forms of resistance. As in his song, they are standing together in the midst of a storm.

Memorably, in a scene reminiscent of the unknown man who stood in front of a line of four tanks in Tiananmen Square (April 1989), a man stands in front of, and by doing so halts, an army truck with a water cannon. Even when the jet of water knocks him over, he is not deterred and another demonstrator joins in the protest, hurling an object at the truck. It is hard to trace the creator of this YouTube video, as they use a pseudonym. Nevertheless, this scene brings to life the claim that 'We're not afraid'.

Conclusion

It is difficult to discern the precise relationship between these more recent digital creations and the original *We're Not Afraid* website. It is as if the term has ricocheted around the web over the last years and has continued to be used in different places, carrying different meanings and resonances. The phrase has a history prior to the attacks in London, as it was one of the lines from a well-known civil rights song in the USA.[36] There are not always direct links or precise quotations between sites. Several sites, reflecting on the self-immolation of the 26-year-old Mohammed Bouazizi,[37] which sparked off the riots in Tunisia that toppled the president,[38] quote protesters who exclaim 'We're Not Afraid Anymore'. There is not evidence to suggest that this is a direct quote or has any connection with the London based website. Likewise in Egypt in early 2011, many protesters and web posters spoke of how through the peaceful protests in Tahrir Square and beyond 'the fear barrier has been broken down'.[39] Breaking down the fear barrier, without resorting to the natural animal responses of either flight or fight, appears to be a common thread through many of the sites examined in the preceding pages.

In this chapter I have considered in detail the visual content of a range of websites, primarily created in the wake of the London terrorist attacks. More specifically I have demonstrated how images have been put to a wide range of rhetorical uses. As I have highlighted, the *We're not afraid* site became an extraordinary web phenomenon, which has now had over 20 million hits, and well over 18,000 images posted. This site has attracted participants and viewers from all over the globe. It has allowed people of many different countries, holding a broad spectrum of beliefs and using different symbolic sign systems, to protest against acts of terrorism. As we have seen, these protests take on many forms, with images used to express defiance, encouragement, solidarity and consolation. Both on this site and other less well-known posting locations, the images are used to promote peace, to teach tolerance, to encourage fearlessness, to mock the bombers, and even to satirise the contributors themselves. These practices can be described as unitive, generative and elastic. Such sites are not only uniting many different people in new independent associations, but also generating new patterns of global pictorial discourse, which are both flexible in their meaning and constantly changing. The *We're not afraid* site initially became a space in which trauma, rage and grief could be articulated visually, though in the weeks and months that followed its creation the emotions expressed have widened. In some cases angry defiance is softened through the use of irony, satire and even celebration of what makes for the good life.

Sometimes contributors used the space to make sense of their own sufferings, with the text 'We're not afraid' referring not only to terrorism but also to overcoming fears of cancer or domestic abuse. The site has extended beyond its original intention, with users stretching the meaning of the words and the images they send in. The *We're not afraid* site, and many of the images found there, also became catalysts for conversations in cyberspace. Some critical voices can be found circulating on the web. A very small number of critics see *We're not afraid* as being used for propaganda purposes, even suggesting it implicitly supports the military. Others claim, accurately, that there is no criticism of state terrorism or governmental violence.

This is not the case in many of the sites or Facebook pages created during the 2011 political upheavals in Egypt, Tunisia and Libya. Phrases on the street were repeated online and beyond. 'We Are All Khaled Said', on Facebook, became one of Egypt's most popular dissident websites. It was established in June 2010, soon after the death of a 28-year-old computer programmer named Khaled Said. It was widely believed that he had died at the hands of two detectives outside the cybercafé he had been in. It was not long before a graphic shot of his severely battered face was circulating the internet. Social media became the forum for explicit and vigorous criticism of Mubarak's regime as well as a place for Islamic prayers and reflections. It was also one of the most significant places where Egyptians learnt not only about the ever-growing crowds in Tahrir Square but also about the suicide of Bouazizi in Tunisia (January 2011).

Tragedy can strengthen ties of solidarity. Just as pictures of the devastation caused by the Indian Ocean tsunami (2004) and the earthquake in Haiti (2010) galvanised individuals and governments to offer aid, so news of the London bombings led to the expression of shared values and, notably on the *We're not afraid* site, an assertion of common humanity through the creation of pictures. The question that arises is whether the posting of images on a website is merely resistance without action, a safe form of protest. Compare digital posting in the safety of one's own home with those who hacked into the Egyptian government's computer system, protested via Facebook and then took to the streets in

Cairo and beyond. There they found thousands of other demonstrators, but they were clearly risking their 'offline' lives. They were protesting not against a single day of attacks but against thirty years of oppression. The web was another public space in which to set up camp, to facilitate and reinforce what was happening in Tahrir Square.

In both settings individuals wanted to rally round and express their passionate feelings, and by doing so they involved themselves in a dynamic action of digital solidarity. In response to both the London attacks and the Egyptian protests there was a multi-layered response, where the people themselves took expressive power. The silent lurkers on the web were not quite so silent, articulating not necessarily what they felt, but what they wanted to feel: we are not afraid. The way in which the *We're not afraid* site was used, according to its creators and explicit evidence on the site, illustrates how surfing the web is a connected process, with users relying not only on search engines but also on friends' recommendations circulated by emails, text messages or mobile phone calls. The same was true of the Egyptian Facebook pages. Combined with television and newspaper reports, they were guided to these websites: a virtual gallery and a protest space. They bookmarked their chosen site, contributed and then watched the sites on a daily basis in the early days and, later, on a weekly basis. The discussion lists on the *We're not afraid* site illustrate that it also became a place of interaction. The same was also true of the more recent 'We Are All Khaled Said' on Facebook. In this way, wherever they originate, websites become focal points, meeting places and resources for both friends and strangers. For some people they even become spaces of visual cooperation and conversation, based upon fellow feelings between people, regardless of their differing cultural and social worlds.

What else, then, does this multifaceted web phenomenon demonstrate? First, many contributors to such sites have become adept at handling digital image producing technology. A lot of the *We're not afraid* images took time and effort to make, but this was not simply about users demonstrating their technological skills: many simply wished to communicate their own resistance to violence. Photos, paintings and drawings are adapted to make this point. Here is evidence of the democratisation of communication among those with access to these technological resources. With the digitisation and subsequent convergence of phones, cameras and computers, more and more people are becoming photojournalists and web artists, skilled in creating their own icons. This partly explains how the simple claim that 'We're not afraid' appears to have crossed over language barriers. For instance, following the Sharm al-Sheikh bombs (22–23 July 2005), which claimed at least eighty-eight lives, hundreds of Egyptian demonstrators marched through the streets in protest, several carrying a banner. Written not in Arabic but in English were the words 'We are not afraid'. Here is a visual hint of digital connection. The web is not a formal community in the traditional sense of the word, but this visually composite site does provide the opportunity for cross-cultural discourse, at a grassroots level of exchange.

Second, the *We're not afraid* site also appears to have provided the space for implicit and understated forms of religious communication. For instance, one picture on the predominantly non-religious site shows ten middle-aged Catholic nuns. The words at the bottom of the picture explain who they are: 'Indian Ursuline Missionaries working in Africa among Muslims and Christians'. Here, inter-religious service is not preached about, but shown. There is a sense in which co-existence is enacted at this site. This phenomenon goes beyond 'networked individualism'[40] to a more cumulative form of interaction. From the debates on the web surrounding the images it is clear that this practice is more than simply individuals connected through the network. Part of its power is that it temporarily brings together a global network of virtual resistance, far more expressively powerful than a single voice or even a peace demonstration. *We're not afraid* is an example of a transitory and visually dominated network of resistance.

Third, the *We're not afraid* site appears to have inspired the development of more explicit religious sites, which have used the format to assert their own religious identities and communities as peaceful. It has allowed some Muslims, who are tired of being portrayed as masked terrorists or merciless hostage-takers, to show themselves in a different light: as peaceful, prayerful people, hospitable to other religious traditions. These amateur web artists appear to be unified by a common desire to provide alternative responses to terrorism to those normally provided by the mainstream news media. These images also represent a contrasting approach to the posters and murals discussed in the chapter 2 celebrating martyrdom.

Fourth, the *We're not afraid* site's core theme resonates with other more recent social network sites. These emerged not in response to attacks by terrorists but as forms of resistance against brutal regimes. They are often far more explicitly religious, containing prayers and theological reflections emerging from different religious traditions. Nevertheless, several recent writers have challenged the utopian claims that the internet would be part of a process that would liberate subjugated people all around the world. For example, Evgeny Morozov's *The Net Delusion: How Not to Liberate the World* is a work of 'cyber-realism', which points to ways in which governments in Iran, China and Russia use what he describes as the 'spinternet' to censor, to survey and subtly to promote their own propaganda.[41] This is a valuable qualification to the views of those 'cyber-optimists' who even nominated the internet for the Nobel Peace Prize in 2010 and who point to sites such as *We're not afraid* as signs of how peace can be effectively promoted and the world changed through the Internet. While scholars such as Lev Manovich are more positive about the role and evolution of new media, while exploring cultures embedded in digital form they are also critical of the difficulties involved in searching through the unprecedented amount of material that has been digitised.[42] It is impossible for the public to see all the pictures on *We're not afraid*, as several thousand were never posted up online. It also takes hours to view several thousand, let alone the entire collection.

Finally, this raises important questions about how some people make use of the sign systems of their own religion, and the symbols of popular culture, to re-interpret their own fears for their communities, their families or themselves. Part of the draw of these sites is rooted in the fact that news about terrorism, or direct experience of terrorism, has the power to cause fear. This fear is hard to name and can even be 'decoupled' from its original cause. Zygmunt Bauman describes this as *Liquid Fear*, which it is at its 'most fearsome when it is diffuse, scattered, unclear, unattached, unanchored, free floating' and becomes a general 'deriva-tive' sense of danger and fear.[43] (This is reminiscent of the atmosphere of fear described in Alan Paton's *Cry the Beloved Country*, see Chapter 5). Both a terrorist attack and a government's use of force can provoke terror. Yet here is a form of mass popular resistance to specific and hidden acts of state violence. Deep feel-ings can be aired. Emotions can be not only heightened, but also dispelled. These sites, emerging after a terrorist attack or in the midst of governmental violence, have the potential to act like a safety valve, where people are free to express their fears, violent gut feelings, their own anger, as well as creative and imaginative insights. In the vast majority of postings, individuals offer their own faces. It is as if these mostly anonymous faces are making a demand on the viewer, reminiscent of the French philosopher Emmanuel Levinas' reflections on 'face-to-face' ethics, which begins with the naked face making a simple command: 'do not kill me'.[44] This process of digital self-revelation is clearly often informed by a participant's residual anxieties combined with their imagination of a different world. The conversations and postings around the images show how artistic creations and written interaction can sometimes sublimate or even dispel negative emotions. Later video creations provide a 'moving' venue for 'facing' violence, for creative expression and for peaceful political protest. They thereby have the potential to allow participants to use creative patterns of digital discourse to promote more peaceful forms of protest and communicative interaction.

Chapter 7

Conclusion

'Swords into Ploughshares'

A tree and a chair made out of decommissioned weapons, described at the start of the book, illustrate how artists and religious leaders in Mozambique chose to imagine a world that was not defined by violence. These sculptures point back to a land devastated by civil war and point forward to communities working towards peace. Both the *Tree of Life* and the *Throne of Weapons* act as idiosyncratic war memorials that commemorate not the 'heroes of the armed struggle but those who suffered at its hands, including thousands of child soldiers'.[1] Both objects silently bear witness to the suffering that violence can bring. As memorials rich in symbolism both pieces have acted like cultural magnets, attracting extensive journalistic interest and curatorial attention. Chris Spring, curator of the British Museum's African Galleries, bought the *Throne* and later commissioned the *Tree of Life* for the British Museum. The *Tree* was given pride of place in the Museum's Great Court for the Africa 2005 season. It is ironic how some of the weapons of war created and sold in the West have now been brought back to their birthplaces as powerful artistic symbols of peace. The *Tree of Life* and *Throne of Weapons* were not produced in a vacuum. They are emblematic of a broader creative and imaginative response to a land and a people broken by an imported war. The experiment to exchange arms for useful tools, and then to turn some of the arms into art, originated not among the political elite but among local religious leaders and local artists, who were supported by Christian Aid and local Mozambican churches.

News reports commonly focus on high-level peace negotiations between political leaders, leaving out of the news frame middle-level religious leaders and grassroots groups. A number of different national and international non-governmental organisations were also involved in the Mozambican peace process. For example, the lay Catholic Sant' Egidio Community hosted all twelve rounds of the peace talks in Rome during the late 1980s and early 1990s. The community, who also see that 'war is the mother of all poverty', helped to create a 'neutral' environment where opposing groups were able to negotiate and then move slowly towards the 1992 Rome peace accords. In *A Different Kind of War Story* anthropologist Carolyn Nordstrom persuasively qualifies the assertion that peace in Mozambique was solely brought about by the peace accords brokered in Rome by political elites. On the basis of her ethnographic work she argues that 'average citizens unmade the possibility and the power of violence, and in doing so set the stage for peace'. It was not through the efforts of United Nations troops or international news organisations but through their own, locally produced plays, prose, poetry and pictures that people 'created the conditions for peace. They made war an impossibility. And it was on this work that the peace accords were built'.[2] Nordstrom wrote this a couple of years after the religiously inspired Transforming Arms into Tools project was being established. Put into this context, the *Tree of Life* and *Throne of Weapons* are not isolated memorials: they are emblematic of a broader turn away from violence that emerged out of 'vast networks of creative resistance'.[3]

Webs of relationships play an important role in John Paul Lederach's approach to breaking 'cycles of violence', as discussed in the introduction of this book. Creative networks go beyond interacting with friends to stepping imaginatively into the world of enemies. Part of the reason for my detailed analysis of First World War memorials, Iranian martyrdom posters and Rwandan radio broadcasts is my belief, with Lederach, that in order to build peace it is important to imagine the enemies' world and to 'understand and feel the landscape of protracted violence and why it poses such deep-rooted challenges to constructive change'.[4] Through this book I have suggested that creatively employed documentaries, feature films and even postings online can assist audiences to set their 'feet deeply into the geographies and realities of what destructive relationships produce, what legacies they leave, and what breaking their violent patterns will require'.[5] Even if they are flawed, biased or highly selective, these different media still have the potential to become catalysts for critical reflection and communal interaction.

In chapter 6 I focused on several other 'vast networks of creative resistance'. These were digitally connected webs of relating together. Both the bombings in London (2005) and the demonstrations in Cairo (2011) became focal points not only for terrestrial, satellite and online news services, but also for informal forms of digital expression and dialogue. Even though the two events emerged out of very different cultural and communicative settings, online discussions allowed individuals, with access to the internet, to offer their faces online, to express feelings of grief, rage, defiance and hope, as well as to discuss in detail the significance and implications of these events. While the associations may be looser than the collective of Mozambican artists who transform weapons into art, the digital communication described earlier has the potential to draw together individuals from a diversity of religious and cultural backgrounds. Examples from a diversity of countries such as Egypt, Mozambique, Rwanda and South Africa, or of different times, such as the First World War in Europe (1914–18) or the Iran–Iraq war (1980s), have been used in this book not to put the spotlight onto the 'exotic other' in 'distant lands' and 'times', but in the hope of deriving translatable insights into promoting peace and inciting violence.

As we saw earlier, the conflict and sculptures from Mozambique are not as distant to the rest of the world as they may first appear. The *Tree of Life* uses imported weapons from an even wider range of nations than the *Throne*, sometimes endearingly known as the 'armschair'. Part of these sculptures' enduring power is that they can unsettle, unnerve and challenge assumptions about responsibilities for distant wars. They also commemorate 'not so much the bravery of those who fought with guns, but more the bravery of those who were prepared to stand up, unarmed, against a culture of violence', along with 'those who were prepared to break their addiction to the gun, whatever the consequences'.[6] The four artists who together created the *Tree of Life* observed how the process itself was full of mixed emotions. While they used some of the lighter parts of the AK-47 for the branches on the *Tree*, they observed how each cartridge took thirty-six bullets (in fact it is normally thirty), each with the potential to take a life. Working with weapons that could kill, and perhaps had killed, proved to be understandably difficult for the artists. This is one of the ways in which the *Tree* became like a 'tree of knowledge'. Unlike trees that can bring life through fruit, through shade and through fresh air, here is a single tree that both points back to violent histories and forwards towards peaceful futures. The picture on the front cover of this book was taken just before the *Tree* made its long journey from Mozambique to the British Museum. The photograph is of children playing under the *Tree of Life* in Maputo's peace park. It is a sign of how 'swords' can be 'transformed into ploughshares'.

Facing violent histories

Through one of her best-known poems, *On the Pulse of Morning*, Maya Angelou underlines the importance of facing history with courage to ensure that it does not repeat itself.[7] Different media can be creatively employed to face violent histories with courage. Some histories can be dangerous to remember. Recalling violence can both promote peace and incite violence. Media can highlight non-violent responses to acts of violence. Alternatively, media can re-present the 'wrenching pain' of violent histories in such a way as to escalate tensions and further conflict. They can be too dangerous or difficult to touch. However much a cliché it might be to claim that history can help explain most, if not all, current conflicts, there is much to learn from studying how histories of violence are re-presented through different media. While in the words of the poet Maya Angelou violent histories 'need not be lived again', it is all too easy for painful historical memories, unless they are faced with courage and truthfulness, to be used to incite further violence.

In chapter 1 I showed how memories of the perceived brutality of the enemy were promoted and lived on after the First World War. I suggested that once an opponent is demonised it is hard to transform them back into a peaceful stranger, let alone a friendly neighbour. Some memories became fossilised in unexpected locations such as a stained-glass window or a book of sermons. Even within ecclesial settings there are traces of the vitriolic propaganda and the painful memories that would haunt Europe through many decades of the twentieth century. Peaceful memorials may actually mask unresolved grief and anger as well as violent feelings towards neighbouring peoples. Closely connected with demonisation of the enemy is glorification of the community's defenders.

Many of the Iranian posters considered in chapter 2 provide examples of such glorification. There I explored some of the persuasive processes that were used to encourage young men and boys to take up arms in Iran during the 1980s, as well as to convince their families and friends of the value of their sacrifices. Mobilising an entire population to fight is not without precedent and commonly draws upon religious beliefs as a rhetorical resource. While 1980s Iran is obviously a very different religious and cultural context, the sanctification of soldiers, the celebration of sacrifice and the glorification of martyrdom have clear resonances with some First World War European propaganda, sermons and memorials. Nevertheless, there are distinctive ways in which Iranian martyrs were used not only as incitements to involvement in a war of perceived national survival but also as focal points for expressions of personal and collective grief. These incitements in Iran drew upon foundational Shi'a religious beliefs and practices.[8] We saw that, while memories of the war in Iran are becoming increasingly distant, the idea of martyrdom continues to carry considerable cultural capital.

When a nation lives with strictly controlled or limited communicative resources, then the few available media outlets take on greater significance. This was the case in Rwanda in the early 1990s where a handful of radio stations dominated the airwaves.[9] As I showed in chapter 3, the use of religious language and beliefs on local radio, before and during the 1994 Rwandan genocide, contributed to an environment of hatred. In the extremist paper *Kangura* the cartoons and commentary commonly appealed to readers' sensibilities as they attempted to sanctify Hutu leaders and demonise the Tutsi.[10] 'Accusations in the mirror', where RTLM broadcasters accused Tutsis of atrocities, which had in fact been perpetrated by the supporters of RTLM, were commonplace. 'Truthful' accounts were obscured, manipulated and distorted. On RTLM even ostensibly innocuous, easygoing banter and singing masked more sinister intentions. Distorting history, reopening old jealousies and wounds, heightening fears of invasion and publishing biased news are all ways of inciting hatred. The result can be toxic, especially when combined with religious language. There is a sense in which journalists, editors and programme makers, echoing teachers, political and religious leaders, can contribute to the 'heating up' of a communicative environment. The result is that words of hatred can become normalised and acts of ethnic violence can go unpunished. Even though broadcasters and religious leaders may even speak of 'peace', their words can easily have the opposite effect.

There is a long history of leaders drawing on visions of peace to encourage violent actions. Consider, for instance, how taking up arms to fight in a holy or just war was promoted in the past within different religious traditions, often as a way of supposedly bringing peace. Within Christianity, for example, various media were used to promote the medieval crusading ideal: from the sermons of Urban II to the repeated use of visual aids by the preaching friars.[11] Medieval and Renaissance art was sometimes enlisted to promote a vision of peace being brought through divinely sanctioned crusading violence. More recent popular renditions in the West have tended to dramatise and even to sanitise the crusades.[12] While there are obviously significant historical discontinuities, bellicose verbal and visual expressions from medieval times resonate with later uses of media and religion to incite violence for the supposed sake of peace. In other words, the sermons, the pamphlets and the posters promoting the call to arms on religious grounds employed in the First World War, the Iran–Iraq war and the 1994 genocide in Rwanda may have distinct characteristics but they were by no means without precedent. Sometimes these calls are drenched in religious language, while in other settings they draw upon religious metaphors more sparingly.

As we have seen, particularly in the first half of the book, there are many different ways in which images and broadcasts have been used to promote war as a holy, sacred or divinely inspired venture. Posters and newspapers, as well as videos and web sites promote violent forms of holy war in many parts of the world. Visual references to memories of both distant defeats and more recent hurts are recycled in popular media and increasingly commonly online. Even graphic depictions of the brutal sacking of Jerusalem at the end of the First Crusade (1099) or the defeat of the Serbian army by the Ottoman's forces at the Battle of Kosovo (1389) are put to rhetorical uses.[13] Photographs of more recent atrocities such as the Sabra and Shatila massacres in Beirut (1982) or the Srebrenica massacre in Bosnia-Herzegovina (1995) are now recycled online and accessible within a few seconds. The appropriation, creation or recycling of such imagery or stories reflect a desire by some to try to bring these historical wounds back to life, and thereby strengthen contemporary incitements to violence.

As well as historical atrocities from the past, mythological stories drawn from sacred texts can be used in an attempt to galvanise a majority to exclude the outsider. The way in which one of the world's most successful television series was used illustrates this claim. In India between 25 January 1987 and 31 July 1988 many parts of the country came to a halt every Sunday morning as an estimated 80–100 million people, about one eighth of the population, watched the dramatisation of the religious epic the *Ramayan* on television. Trains were delayed as passengers refused to stop watching the sets on platforms until an episode was finished. In many rural villages, with only one television, dozens of people gathered outside to watch. The television itself was often garlanded with flowers or incense, as some viewers engaged in prayers or purificatory washing before watching the programme. Viewing had itself become a sacred ritual. During and after this series, electronic shops in India reported a significant increase in the number of televisions sold. In India, local critics expressed anxiety about the impact of Ramanand Sagar's seventy-eight-episode adaptation of the *Ramayan*. They argued that the televising of this 2,000-year-old epic trivialised the sacred narrative. More specifically some commentators were concerned that the depiction of Ram, as a particularly warlike God, might actually increase violence against the Muslim and Christian minorities.[14] It is hard to demonstrate conclusively whether such anxieties were well founded, but it is worth noting how the soap opera was put to use by both supporters of the Hindu nationalist BJP party and by critics of the BJP's vision of a Hindu-dominated peace for India. My point here is that not only histories of victim-hood but also mediated mythological stories drawn from sacred texts can be used to incite violence.

From violent histories to peaceful futures

How can painful memories of actual or mythical violence be handled wisely? These 'dangerous memories' are often kept alive through the recycling of images and stories.[15] Different media arts can 'instead of healing the past perpetuate its wrongs'.[16] The claim that different media and religious beliefs can be used to incite violence is not a new one: what is rarer is the claim that they can be used to promote peace. While 'the conflict-resolution' potential of various media is 'largely underutilized' in many settings, there are instances where media have been used to help 'rebuild a society after the conflict has passed'.[17] For increasing numbers of scholars, mediators and other practitioners, building sustainable peace goes beyond peacemaking and peacekeeping to peacebuilding.[18] Insightful media productions can illuminate how the waging of violence and peace commonly goes in cycles, with conflict transformation taking place in unexpected settings and initiated by unexpected figures. The roles of comparatively unknown religious peacebuilders and media artists are commonly underexplored within interpretations of cycles of violence and peace.

As we have seen, media can be used not only to incite violence, but they can also be used to encourage peace. Different media can be used to play a vital role in conflict transformation and peacebuilding. This can take many years.[19] Peacebuilding commonly develops through a number of stages in a range of contexts. We have seen the ways in which creative media use can contribute to each of these stages. First, media can be used to bear witness to the suffering caused by violence. Second, through media, individuals and communities can conduct enquiry that leads towards searching for and establishing the truth. Third, media creations can highlight good practice, portraying patterns of reconciliation, and thereby potentially help dissipate the desire for revenge, even, arguably, promote more lasting peace. Finally, media productions can help people to envision and to imagine a more peaceful future. The ways that different media can be, and are, involved in each of these stages of peacebuilding underlie the second half of this book.

There are many risks associated with building peace. As I suggested in chapter 4, bearing witness can be a painful and complex task. Even for experienced feature and documentary film-makers, representing a genocide is fraught with difficulty. As one film-maker journalist observed (chapter 4), the witness is as vulnerable and fragile as a butterfly. In the immediate aftermath film-makers commonly find themselves in difficult, dangerous and confusing situations where they are able to do little more than observe and survive. We saw that the process of bearing witness through documentaries has nevertheless been put to many different uses, including investigative, interpretative, critical and commemorative ends. Several documentaries, for instance, investigated the role of 'Hate Media' in Rwanda during the early 1990s, even implying that RTLM should have been jammed. Other documentaries not only investigated but also critically interpreted the role of local *Gacaca* courts in the justice and reconciliation process. Many other films went beyond this, commemorating the roles of individuals and critically describing the failures of the UN, Western governments and religious leaders in 1994 Rwanda. These films evolved from immediate description of what had happened during the genocide, via covering attempts to bring about local justice and reconciliation, to exploring attempts to reconstruct a nation with a 'memory of blood' and move towards a sustainable peace.

What is missing from this body of films about Rwanda? First, only a few documentaries, and no feature films, concentrate upon the ways that different media have been used to promote peace. Unlike the many films that reference or analyse the use of RTLM, they largely overlook the establishment of 'peace' radio stations, by the Hirondelle Foundation, such as the short-lived Radio Agatashya ('little swallow' in Kinyarwanda) in the Great Lakes region,[20] or studio *Jambo* ('wise words' in Kirundi) in Burundi. These stations attempted to bring together Tutsi and Hutu journalists and producers, 'cool down' ethnic tensions by providing accurate, non-partisan reports on the war and on the 'fragile peace' that reigned after the 1994 genocide in Rwanda.[21] The documentary film *Radio Okapi, radio de la vie* (Pierre Guyot, 2006), is an exception, bearing witness to the work of Radio Okapi, a UN- and Hirondelle-funded station, and one radio journalist in particular, Breuil Munganga, who worked for peace partly by trying to cover the news truthfully in the Democratic Republic of Congo.[22] How to create soundscapes that can contribute to building peaceful communicative environments is a topic worthy of careful attention by both scholars and film-makers.[23]

A second absence within these films about Rwanda is their lack of self-criticism. Few film-makers interrogate the visual representation of the genocide in Rwanda. Some artists are more insightful. Consider, for example, the Chilean Alfredo Jaar's haunting *The Eyes of Gutete Emerita* (1996). Rather than showing pictures of the rotting corpses from Ntarama church, he simply displays a picture of the eyes of a single survivor, Gutete Emerita. In *Eyes* and *Real Pictures* (1995) he documents how Gutete was participating in mass at the church when the killing began. Jaar's display names each of the victims. Viewers learn that she witnessed the murder of her husband Tito Kahinamura (40) and her two sons Muhoza (10) and Matirigari (7), only just escaping with her daughter Marie-Louise

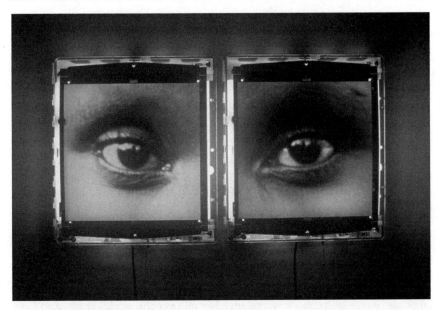

Figure 7.1   The Eyes of Gutete Emerita. Courtesy of Alfredo Jaar, NY. With thanks also to the Hood Museum, Dartmouth College. For the internet version see <http://alfredojaar.net/gutete/gutete.html>.

Unamararunga (12), and then surviving by hiding in the nearby swamp for several weeks.[24] While one set of the original photos are now in the USA at the Hood Museum at Dartmouth College, New Hampshire, there is also an internet version of *The Eyes of Gutete Emerita* (figure 7.1).[25] In the original, a mountain-like pile of photographic slides of the survivor's eyes bears witness in a peaceful but haunting fashion to the land and people of a thousand hills that suffered so much trauma. Whether this visually reticent artistic interpretation of the 'unpresentable' enables viewers to move forwards towards a secure peace is less clear than the fact that it raises significant questions about re-presenting the trauma that is commonly left out of films covering the topic.[26]

Alongside these two absences within films about Rwanda, it is possible to make a third broader generalisation. The portrayal through local media of the role of religiously inspired individuals in peacebuilding is also a rarity, though some films based on events in other parts of Africa do celebrate those who attempt to build peace. Consider *The Imam and the Pastor* (Alan Channer, 2006), which is a widely used and watched documentary that depicts the surprising friendship between a Christian pastor and a Muslim preacher in Nigeria. Both men were passionate advocates of their own religious tradition. In the 1980s, tension between the Muslim and Christian communities in Nigeria exploded into violent bloodshed, with hundreds killed, and churches and mosques burnt to the ground in the town of Zangon Kataf in 1992. As leaders of opposing militia groups Imam Ashafa and Pastor Wuye suffered personal losses through the fighting, Ashafa losing several close family members, and Wuye, his right hand. Relying on their personal testimonies, the documentary tells of their journey towards friendship and reconciliation, which has led them to work together to build peace in Nigeria and beyond. This documentary narrates their story, acknowledging their religious differences, while showing how their respective faiths enrich their desire to act as unexpected peacebuilders. Part of the strength of this documentary film is that it reveals the complexity of their evolving relationship. In many ways *The Imam and Pastor* provides a more nuanced account of two people being reconciled than the final story in *Rwanda: Living Forgiveness,* one of the documentaries discussed in detail in chapter 4, which moves towards a largely happy and uncomplicated ending of reconciliation.

Personal interviews in Edinburgh with Imam Muhammad Ashafa and Pastor James Wuye revealed how the documentary has developed an extensive real and digital 'after-life'.[27] Their story of reconciliation and peacebuilding has been shown in schools, colleges, universities, mosques, churches and town halls, not only around Nigeria, but also in many other parts of the world. The two protagonists have spoken and lectured together all over the world. It has also been used extensively on the web and in other forms of communication. *An African Answer* (Alan Channer, 2008), the sequel to *The Imam and Pastor,* is becoming increasingly well known. This short documentary covers Imam Ashafa and Pastor Wuye's visit to the Rift Valley area of Kenya in the wake of post-election violence and killings at the end of 2007 and start of 2008. For both of them, the solution to this ethnic violence will not be imposed from outside but will emerge from within the divided communities. They are shown listening, teaching and imploring local residents to put down their weapons and move towards reconciliation. It is striking to see how they both appeal to a divided but predominantly Christian Kenyan audience on the basis of their listeners' faith. It is not only filmed stories about past violence but also contemporary narratives about peacebuilding that can take on a life of their own as they are repeated, amplified, elaborated upon and as they reverberate in different cultural settings.

Similar processes take place around some of the films considered in chapter 5. Even a flawed feature film can reveal aspects of the search for truth about apartheid and the difficult journey towards reconciliation in South Africa. As we saw, critical questions about the TRC process are embedded not only in a number of documentaries but also in several locally produced films. The portrayal of small-scale reconciliations and narrative truths appear simpler to depict than the arduous tasks of uncovering forensic forms of truth or building peace between divided communities. We saw how reconciliation is a contested, multi-layered and often-gradual process, which is hard to capture comprehensively on screen.

Sometimes local 'home-grown productions', while not expensively made with the highest production values, wrestle creatively with the often-difficult road towards reconciliation. For example, in the short fictional Rwandan film *A Love Letter to My Country* (Thierry Dushimirimana, 2006), the viewer is shown how there is often real ambiguity embedded within the move towards reconciliation. This movie portrays a 'burgeoning love affair' between a 21-year-old Tutsi, Marta, whose family were murdered during the genocide, and Rukundo, a 27-year-old Hutu, whose relatives are in prison for participating in the genocide.[28] As the truth of their violent personal histories becomes clearer, their initial attraction, which began in church, is put under severe pressure. This is heightened when their families become involved and demand that they separate. They decide to elope. On the bus Marta dreams of reconciliation, including between her families, but awakens to the reality of being alone with her partner she is to marry. She has left behind a divided community, and communal reconciliation still remains a dream.[29]

Memories often inspire dreams, both of a violent past and a more peaceful future. Several of the South African films on events relating to apartheid (discussed in chapter 5) include dream sequences, such as Sarafina imagining herself as a liberated Nelson Mandela, or flashbacks, such as the protagonist Alex Mpondo (played by Chiwetel Ejiofor) in *Red Dust* remembering his brutal torture by the apartheid police. Both cinematic devices can evoke empathy for the character, but also some confusion as to the precise 'truth' being celebrated. In the short South African-produced film *The Tunnel* (Jenna Bass, 2010), dreams, flashbacks and stories are brought together to give a glimpse of the atrocities of Robert Mugabe's 5th Brigade during the 1980s. It sheds light on a time 'known as *Gukurahundi*: the rain that washes away the chaff before spring'.[30] The young girl at the heart of *The Tunnel* concludes: 'it gets so I don't know what is truth and what is not truth'. While films can dramatically portray the search for truth and reconciliation, they can also blur that search by leaving out of the frame crucial details and offering vivid alternative perspectives on violent histories.

Memories of violence, experience of trauma and dreams of a better future can nevertheless contribute towards creative production. It took film-makers some time to catch up with the creative outburst that emerged soon after the 1976 Soweto uprising and continued in the final years of apartheid. In South Africa film was a relative latecomer compared to the art of resistance such as the 'colourful posters, T-Shirts, graffiti (alongside township poetry and street-theatre), along with some remarkable photography' that all emerged out of the townships.[31] Films are commonly flawed or delayed, but in spite of their inadequacies they still have the potential to help awaken audiences to divided worlds. This is especially the case if watched within communities committed to transforming conflict, alongside imagining and building peace. In this role, films can still be used to educate, to entertain and to inspire, as they reveal aspects of the truth about apartheid and the long road towards reconciliation.

A documentary about the Moroccan truth commission, *Our Forbidden Places* (*Nos Lieux interdits*, Leila Kilani, 2008) included a local elderly woman who compared the traumatic past of her nation to a bees' nest, that would best be left alone and undisturbed; otherwise, if it is opened up, the bees will swarm angrily out and sting anyone nearby. Re-presenting the harsh and painful truth of the past will not necessarily bring more peace, and can even make the situation worse. Nonetheless, as Desmond Tutu suggests, 'forgiving and being reconciled are not about pretending that things are other than they are', or 'turning a blind eye to the wrong. True reconciliation exposes the awfulness, the abuse, the pain, the degradation, the truth'.[32] My argument through this book is that films, and other media, have a role to play in exposing aspects of the 'truth' even if it is awful to learn about and even if there is a risk of disturbing the bees' nest of the buried past. In the long run, facing violent histories honestly has the potential to contribute to more lasting forms of peace in the future.

The revelatory potential of different kinds of films and other media should not, however, be overstated. Alongside the potential of films to reveal, to interrogate and to confront elements within violent histories, it is important to bear in mind the limitations of documentary and feature films, discussed in chapters 4 and 5, which in turn underlines the dangers of over-claiming the significance of such media in the process of building peace. It is hard to predict an audience's response to a film's attempt to bear witness to violence and peacebuilding. As Ann Kaplan observes in *Trauma Culture*, the same documentary about rape in Rwanda can inspire sharply contrasting responses from viewers, ranging from agonised empathy towards victims' suffering, to indignation towards the filmmaker who has invaded the privacy of powerless victims. The difficulty is that either set of distanced emotions is founded upon 'vicarious trauma', which can lead to 'empty empathy'.[33] Such 'empty empathy' is 'elicited by images of suffering provided without any context or background knowledge'.[34]

A few of the films examined in chapters 4 and 5 did attempt to provide a historical context to their narratives. As well as attempting to reveal aspects of the 'awful truth', they put a spotlight onto, and thereby celebrate, effective peacebuilding practice. It is much more, however, than simply a film's content that achieves this. The ways in which films are produced, the settings in which they are shown and the audience interactions all contribute to how effective they are in portraying memories truthfully, and in such a way as to contribute to reconciliation. This can be seen in diverse genres of films from the documentaries *The Imam and the Pastor*, set in Nigeria and *An African Answer*, set in Kenya, through to feature films such as *Shooting Dogs*, set in Rwanda or *London River*, set in England's capital.

Feature film-making was traditionally a craft demanding considerable expenditure and equipment. While this remains the case with many productions, the advent of pocket film cameras, which are often embedded in mobile phones, has led to the democratisation of movie-making. With online sites such as YouTube, home-made films can be shot, edited, mixed, dubbed and distributed globally within minutes or even seconds of recording. These are often forms of isolated personal expression rather than sustained dialogue.[35] As we saw in chapter 6, digital technologies also allow for multiple images to be created, uploaded and made public. In contexts of national debate or local trauma, the images did sometimes become catalysts for brief digital discussion. I have demonstrated how images have been put to a wide range of rhetorical uses, before, during and after acts of terrorism and state oppression. These images can be used to promote violence, but they can also be used to protest non-violently against acts of terrorism or oppression.

The various engagements with new media discussed in chapter 6 emerges out of both the 'non-violent social change, the "revolutionary" camp', and the 'mediation, the "resolutionary" camp'.[36] As we saw, agents for social change, such as during the Arab Spring in 2011, and peaceful mediation, such as in some of the non-violent responses to the terrorist attacks in London, are increasingly employing new media. This is often spontaneous, immediate and untrained. These forms of expression can appear transient and seemingly ephemeral, but digital material is proving to be far from impermanent. Sites, traces and connections remain. Digital memorials can easily be excavated and put to different uses. Drawing on the experience and remains of these digitised outbursts, there is the need for education and training to see how these forms of communication can be employed for peaceable, as opposed to violent, ends. The ways that different media can contribute both to educator-led 'prescriptive' and 'elicitive' grassroots forms of training merits careful analysis. Both old media and new media can shed light on and contribute to the five activities associated with a more participatory or 'elicitive' approach to training, described by Lederach as discovery, description, evaluation, adaptation and actual practice.[37] New media are already inextricably involved in each of these processes.

What can the ease and immediacy of digital connection contribute to the area of training for conflict transformation and peacebuilding? How effectively do digital protest, memorial and mediation promote more peaceful forms of communicative interaction? What kinds of lasting peace have been or are being achieved through online communities? These questions are worthy of further research. Nonetheless, the discussions in chapter 6 highlighted the potential for transformative, playful and creative engagement through embracing new media. 'We must explore', claims Lederach, 'the creative process itself, not as a tangential inquiry, but as the wellspring that feeds the building of peace'.[38] Digital media may facilitate forms of communicative and creative peacebuilding, but they are not alone in providing resources for facing the past with courage and envisaging a more peaceful future.

Offline forms of artistic expression have a role to play in creating an opportunity for individuals and communities to remember wisely, to question critically and to hope realistically. Media arts that can actually be walked around or touched can also challenge the assumptions that fear, rooted in histories of violence, will necessarily lead to despair or further conflict. Two examples will suffice. The first illustrates how a piece of physical art can raise questions about why violence begins and escalates. British artist Paul Hobbs created an exhibit of a machete placed behind protective glass (figure 7.2).

Figure 7.2 Fear Action. Courtesy of Paul Hobbs. See: www.arthobbs.com.

Like a fire alarm, it has printed on the glass 'In emergency break glass'. Beside it are instructions, entitled 'Fear Action', where viewers are 'encouraged' to call the 'fear brigade' at the first sign of fear or suspicion. This is visually reminiscent of the edition of *Kangura* that displayed a machete (see chapter 3), though Hobbs had very different intentions. Created soon after the Rwandan genocide, this piece provoked strong responses when exhibited in the central London church St Martin in the Fields. One former British soldier was incandescent, furious because of the memories of violence that it stirred. He only calmed down after a long conversation with the artist, who was able to help him understand the cause of his anger and the aim of the exhibit, which was to evoke wonderings about the place of fear in leading people to kill 'the other'.[39] This illustrates the importance of dialogue around the expressive arts and how a piece of art can raise questions about what it is that can provoke acts of violence.

A second example illustrates how forms of artistic expression that are commonly connected with sectarian division can be transformed to convey more peaceful messages. In Northern Ireland, for instance, during the first sixty years of the Northern Irish state, Protestant Loyalists (Unionists) would paint murals on the sides of buildings in Belfast and beyond, many celebrating the victory of King William of Orange (King Billy) in 1690 at the Battle of the Boyne. There were also several commemorative pictures of Irish troops fighting at the Battle of the Somme in 1916. It was not until the hunger strikes of 1981 that the opposing Catholic Nationalist (Republican) communities became involved in painting wall murals. These commonly juxtaposed religious imagery with statements or images of protest against British rule. From the early 1980s, both sides began to use these murals as a way of promoting their own cause, their own martyrs and the 'rightness' of resorting to the gun. Art itself became a 'weapon', an expression of anger, protest and grief, reinforced by religious iconography and language.[40] For example, one Republican portrayal, on Beechmount Drive from 1981, has Jesus with an open 'sacred heart' overlooking an incarcerated and emaciated blanket-man, marking the dirty protest and the hunger strikes in the Maze Prison.[41]

With the Good Friday agreement (10 April 1998) and the ongoing peace process in Ireland, Belfast's murals are gradually being transformed.[42] It is even possible to go online and paint one's own digital mural under the title of 'Give my head peace'.[43] Some of the more extreme images, inciting violence, have been whitewashed away and replaced with pictorial memorials of individuals, historical scenes or even mythological images. Many still remain as visual reminders of Ireland's violent past. It is now possible online to take a virtual walk down Newtownards Road in Belfast, for instance, and see murals commemorating 'Ulster's Past Defenders', which include paramilitary organisations such as the UDA and the UDF. Memories are not easily wiped away. A masked gunman still points his gun out towards the viewer. Nearby, another mural shows crosses and the names of locations of bomb attacks. This process of visual memorialisation has not entirely ceased. In spring 2011, in the Newtownards Road area, a mural of several football players was painted over and replaced with a picture of two men wearing balaclavas and holding guns. While many condemned this action as an 'unfortunate return to a violent past', some locals saw it as a justified visual response to the recent painting of a mural of Bobby Sands' funeral, which portrayed masked men firing into the air over his coffin.[44] Like the murals in Iran (Chapter 2), these murals stand among a diversity of images, for example, a mural commemorating the building of the *Titanic* (which took place in Belfast) and a more recent poster advertising the next generation of mobile phones. These murals are part of the everyday visual landscape of Belfast.

Some artists from the opposing Loyalist and Republican traditions are now working together. Increasing numbers of murals are more neutral, celebrating

Belfast as a city of industry, or sport or supported by public services. Some even have peacebuilding as their central theme. On Limestone Street a mural encourages viewers to say 'no' to dealers, drugs, hate, violence and riots, and 'yes' to sport, music, culture, education, diversity and peace.[45] Under the guidance of professional artists, teenagers are encouraged to paint their hopes for Northern Ireland. For example, on 31 May 2010 on Lower Newtownards Road in Belfast, a new peace mural (by artist John Stewart) was unveiled, bringing together individuals from many different local communities.[46] The mural brings together memories of past wars with hopes for future peace. At the top it states, 'Remember the fallen from War'. Beneath this text, black, grey and white depictions of a damaged building and a crumpling human form are surrounded by red poppies and other colourful patterns, along with the words 'Peace cannot be kept by force it can only be achieved by understanding'. A local Catholic church and Methodist church are named and depicted in close proximity. This process, of creating murals, is gradually turning a form of communication commonly connected with divisiveness and conflict into a form that is emerging out of local communities and attempting to promote unity and peace. It is one striking way, resonating with the metallic *Throne* and *Tree of Life* from Mozambique, in which part of a community with a long and painful history of violence is drawing upon local art forms to imagine and to express hope for a more peaceful future.

Transforming 'swords into ploughshares'

Some peacebuilding practitioners or scholars believe that the phrase from the book of Isaiah, 'swords into ploughshares', is somewhat 'hackneyed'.[47] They would hesitate before employing this ancient text, perceiving it as an overused metaphor that has lost its original force.[48] The phrase has been absorbed into popular culture and is to be found in several well-known settings. Over 50 million people have now seen the longest-running musical in the world, based on Victor Hugo's 1862 novel *Les Misérables*, where in the rousing finale the chorus sing, 'They will live again in freedom, in the garden of the Lord. They will walk behind the ploughshare, they will put away the sword'.[49] This is a reprise of an angrier earlier version of the song, which is a call to resistance. The sword, at the end of the musical, is put away rather than transformed, but the community who had fought behind the barricades would now till the soil. In his song 'Heal the World' (1991) Michael Jackson sings: 'Create a world with no fear, together we'll cry happy tears, see the nations turn their swords into ploughshares'.[50] The accompanying music video, one of the few in his repertoire that does not show the singer himself, depicts children giving flowers to soldiers who then drop their guns and throw down their weapons. This is a shocking image for those soldiers who are trained to cherish, care for and never let go of their rifle. In the anti-war song 'The Vine and the Fig Tree', the ordering of the phrase is changed, but the hopeful sentiments remain the same: 'Everyone neath their vine and fig tree shall live unafraid. Nations shall learn war no more. And into ploughshares beat their swords'.[51] These musical visions celebrate liberty, the end of fear and violence emerging from the establishment of peace are full of hopeful sentiments, but how realistic are they?

In 2005, a group of academics met in Florence to discuss Isaiah's vision of 'Swords into Ploughshares'. It was a rare event because it brought together both Biblical and International Relations' scholars. They discussed in detail the meaning of the phrase in its original context. An edited book emerged out of their cross-disciplinary conversations entitled *Isaiah's Vision of Peace in Biblical and Modern International Relations: Swords into Plowshares*. In it one of the leading Hebrew Bible scholars present, Hugh Williamson, persuasively argues that the 'voluntary disarmament by the nation in Isaiah 2:4 (Micah 4:3) is an innovative move by its author'. For Williamson this 'is a development from, not just a reiteration of, a traditional motif, and moreover it envisages a reversal of what was the standard and familiar procedure of equipping the conscript army for war'.[52] Rather than farmers using their tools to kill, they would transform them into implements to cultivate the land. This interdisciplinary gathering also considered the pertinence of Isaiah's vision for today's fractured world. In the conclusion the editors opine: 'Isaiah's vision is not a practical manual for bringing peace to a strife-ridden planet. It is an idealized model, the end of the rainbow, to be sought but never attained'.[53] From this perspective, to attempt to turn this irenic vision into reality is like ploughing the sand, an 'endless or impossible task'.[54] A further concern relating to this text is that by concentrating upon a yet to be realised future, the phrase, as commonly expressed, fails to capture the concrete demands and messy business of building peace in the here and now.

Moreover, even if the phrase 'swords into ploughshares' from Isaiah (and Micah) is well known, the less commonly cited words from Joel 3.10, 'Beat your ploughshares into swords, and your pruning hooks into spears', appear to reflect more accurately the violence described in the first part of this book. In Rwanda, neighbours wielded farming tools, such as hoes and machetes, to kill their own neighbours. In Iran and Iraq, resources were taken away from agricultural production and instead invested in weapon manufacture during the 1980–8 war. In Flanders, agricultural production was largely halted when trenches full of mud and broken bodies carved their way across swathes of farming land during the First World War. In other contexts, such as the USA, scythes were turned into swords in an eighteenth-century slave uprising,[55] farmers became soldiers during the nineteenth-century Civil War,[56] and following the Second World War in the twentieth century a 'military industrial complex' became a dominant force within the USA.[57] Even classical authors, such as Virgil in his *Georgics*, observed: 'Respect for the plough has gone. Our lands, robbed of the tillers, lie waste and curved pruning hooks are forged into straight blades'.[58] There is a diverse and long history of turning 'ploughshares into swords'. This is also recognised within popular culture, where the Scottish band Runrig's 1987 song 'Protect and

Survive' includes: 'You took your sacrifice to the gods of war, traded your children's lives for a mess of gold, and beat your ploughshares into swords'.[59] There is an implicit question about the wisdom of turning farming tools into weapons underlying this song, which is made explicit by the American folk-rock group Hoots and Hellmouth in their *Holy Open Secret* album when they sing: 'What good are plowshares, if we use them like swords? Don't spoil the harvest, we ain't got much more'.[60]

Nevertheless, in spite of these lyrical questions, popular adaptations and violent histories, the more irenic phrase 'swords into ploughshares' has inspired creative responses aiming to promote peace in different parts of the world. As we have seen in Mozambique it was the inspiration for a scheme that has led to the decommissioning of thousands of weapons and the creation of many pieces of new art. They are intended to be 'memorials that redeem the past' and not 'monuments that continue to glorify a triumphant nation or keep alive ethnic hatred'.[61] There is even a stop-motion animation film, *Little Fiel*, currently in production that brings some of the decommissioned weapons to life as 'a little Mozambican boy, Fiel, growing up during the Civil War'.[62] He is gradually awakening to the devastation going on around him. In the earliest rushes of these films it is possibly to see a short sequence where a bullet disappears into the ground and bursts back through the earth as a flower. This film can be seen as a further separate development from the original project of 'Transforming Arms into Tools'. The founder of the project, Bishop Sengulane, told 'people we are not disarming you. We are transforming your guns into ploughshares, so you can cultivate your land and get your daily bread'.[63] This project does appear to have had some positive impacts upon local economies.[64]

There is a sense, however, in which the *Throne of Weapons* has been tamed now it is safely within a large display case in the British Museum. When it was exhibited around the United Kingdom, it evoked a range of interpretations. Among the 100,000 people who saw this object, some saw it as an over 'aggressive' advocate for peace, simply because the gun parts that make it up continue to act as a reminder of the violent deaths of some 1 million people who were killed during the Mozambican civil war. By contrast, others saw this as powerful physical reminder of how weapons of destruction can become transformed into symbols that embody peace. For example, one inmate in Pentonville Prison in London responded by saying: 'The most powerful thing you can do is pick up a book not a gun'.[65] In Mozambique this was brought to life when 'a young university student received a copy of the *Oxford English Dictionary* in exchange for his weapon'.[66]

The Mozambican project has also inspired or, at least, has been influential in the establishment of other projects devoted to transforming arms into art. Compared to the mimetic violence discussed in the first part of the book, these are more peaceful forms of imitation. In October 2003, the British artist Sasha Constable, with the assistance of the government in Phnom Penh, helped to establish and coordinate the Peace Art Project Cambodia (PAPC). It was directly influenced by the project in Mozambique. In early December 2003, some '876 destroyed weapons from a Khmer Rouge weapons cache in the Cardamom Mountains were transported and then used in the PAPC workshop', which was also supported by the local Fine Arts University.[67] One reason for the success of this project was that Sasha Constable worked closely with an officer for the European Union's Assistance on Curbing Small Arms and Light Weapons in the Kingdom of Cambodia (EU ACSA), who 'donated the decommissioned weapons' to the arts project 'after they were destroyed through local Flames of Peace ceremonies'.[68] In this way many weapons were transformed into sculptured animals as well as ornate furniture. While the end result in most cases was to create something less than functionally useful or particularly comfortable, the project trained young people in metalwork, while also creating something aesthetically thought-provoking.

In other contexts, the process has led to the creation of actual farm implements. For example, following an eleven-year civil war in Sierra Leone (1991–2002), which claimed over 50,000 lives, two NGOs developed a project that turned decommissioned weapons into tools for farming.[69] In this setting 'AK47 assault rifles, rocket launchers and even tanks are dismantled and then forged into shovels, sickles or possibly even ploughshares, providing an income for the blacksmith, good, cheap tools for the farmers and putting the weapons forever beyond use'.[70] In Guatemala, a nation that endured three decades of civil war, a scheme was established where guns were to be exchanged for bicycles.[71]

On a different continent, the 'Weapons into Water' project emerged in a conflict zone between Georgian and Ossetian villages, near to the Russian border. Over '1,300 units of arms and ammunition and 210 kg of pure explosives' were 'handed over to the Joint Peace Keeping Forces (JPKF)' in exchange repair work was carried out on 'a 40-kilometre irrigation channel' that 'ran between the villages'.[72] Nearby, computers were given to the parents at a school in the Tskhinvali, in the disputed region of South Ossetia, when they handed over thirty-six rockets. This form of exchange is reminiscent of another scheme, based in the UK, known as 'Guns into Goods'.[73] This was a joint project between the University of Salford and the Manchester Police. Weapons were handed in, melted down and made into peace medals, other works of arts and useful items. In Iraq an arts association has been established where sculptures, including fish and candles, have been made out of decommissioned Iraqi weapons.[74]

In several cities and counties in the USA, particularly where gun crime is a blight on the local community, weapons have been turned into monuments or works of art. For instance, in 1998 John Ricker, who lost several friends to gun crime when he was a young man, established Guns into Art in San Francisco. His team, Peaceful Streets, have attempted to curb gun violence through research, creating works of art, and public education. They have taught thousands of 8- to 12-year-olds about the perils of not only playing with guns, but seeing weapons 'as problem-solving tools' that one turns to in the first instance when confronted with a problem. They have also coordinated 'public events called Gun Bakes, during which banned assault weapons are melted down and transformed into art by professional blacksmiths and their teenage apprentices'. These events commonly take place with schools and local community groups, and are often situated close to 'the site of a gun-related death' as a way of helping a community try to 'reclaim' a park or a school after a shooting incident. From these melted assault weapons, Peaceful Streets and its team of blacksmiths create memorial park benches and bicycle racks for parks or schools, as well as smaller art pieces such as candleholders and jewellery. Consider Precita Park memorial bench in San Francisco. This striking piece of public furniture was made with 130 melted-down guns as a memorial to a young couple who were murdered by an unstable relative. They believe that: 'creating permanent art fixtures in honor [sic] of gun victims is a way of transforming the negative power of violence into a positive, lasting memory'.[75]

These local artist expressions are less monumental than the bronze sculpture standing within the United Nations' garden of a muscular man beating a sword into the ploughshare. Created by Evgeniy Vuchetich, it was given to the United Nations in 1959 by the Soviet Union in the midst of the Cold War. This was a war that was played out in developing nations such as Mozambique. It speaks of peace achieved through might. Here is a heroic individual who is fighting for peace. Etched in capitals onto the marble plinth is the statement '*We Shall Beat Our Swords Into Plowshares*'. It was reproduced in many different contexts, from large sculptures in New York and Moscow to crafted replicas to be given as gifts to friends of the Soviet government. It was used on stamps in the Soviet Union during the 1970s (figure 7.3). The image stands in sharp contrast with *Tree of Life* or *Throne of Weapons*.

In other settings this Cold War symbol of peacemaking through force was subverted. In East Germany, this image was replicated on thousands of cloth badges and bookmarks in 1981.[76] The phrase *Schwerter zu Pflugscharen* (German for 'Swords into Ploughshares') was the slogan of 'the German church's second annual *Dekade,* or ten day gathering, in November 1981'.[77] Over 100,000 badges were produced and they became a symbol of resistance, in particular against the increasing emphasis upon semi-military training in schools, where 14- to 16-year-olds had to take military studies. In response to the militarization of the state and education system, and the persecution by the state, the image, the badge and the phrase, cited as from Micah 4, were all put to use by the churches, who established an 'education for peace' initiative, with the slogan 'Peace Education, not Defense Education'. Alongside the picture of the UN's sculpture it also became 'the symbol of the East German independent peace movement'.[78] Members of a rapidly growing independent youth peace movement, called 'swords to ploughshares', also took this image as their symbol. There were severe consequences for those who dared to adopt this simple symbol. 'Wearers of this badge who refused to take it off were expelled from schools and higher education or were refused apprenticeships and forbidden to enter their work place.

Figure 7.3 Soviet stamp, *We Shall Beat Our Swords Into Plowshares*, 1970. Commemorating 25 years of the United Nations. Courtesy of rook76 / Shutterstock.com.

Badges were forcefully cut out of clothes by teachers and policemen or the whole garment confiscated'.[79]

It is somewhat ironic that this image, which outside the United Nations building implicitly spoke of Soviet power to bring peace through force, became one of the symbols of a movement that would contribute to its downfall. Eight years later the same movement were supporting weekly prayers in the *Nikolai-kirche*, Leipzig and in other parts of Germany. For many historians this was a significant moment in the collapse of the East German regime. (This was one of a number of governments who had exported weapons to Mozambique for use in the Civil War.) Here is an example of a popular movement that predates the Mozambican project, but also finds inspiration from the irenic vision of Isaiah (reiterated in Micah). The image, and phrase, continued to be used even after the fall of the Berlin Wall in 1989 (figure 7.4).

Not every artist or peace activist attempting to turn armaments into art cites Isaiah as their source. Several examples stand out. One North American artist, Jillian Maslow, created a dress made out of bullets, bullet shells and dog-tags as a form of peaceful protest against the 2003 invasion of Iraq. It weighed 48 pounds. She called the project *TARGET: Peace!* and claimed to have been inspired by the Greek play, *Lysistrata* (c.411 BCE), Aristophanes' comedy where the women refused to have sex with their male partners unless they stopped fighting and ended the Peloponnesian war.[80] In Colombia, César López, a local peace activist and musician, observed how a policeman, attending the scene of the 2003 *El Nogal* club bombing in Bogota, held his gun just like a musician would hold his guitar. Seeing this was an inspiration for him to purchase several guns, including a number of AK-47s, and turn them into musical instruments, known as *Escopetarra*.[81] He has created them as musical symbols of peace. A third, slightly different, example illustrates how artists can use their craft to envisage a time when weapons will be decommissioned. The cartoonist Jonathan Shapiro used not a biblical text but his craft, at a time when South Africa was on the edge of a precipice of violence, to illustrate how weapons can be 'put out ... of action' (figure 7.5).

Nevertheless, the passage from Isaiah continues to have an impact and to be used all over the world. In Jersey City, New Jersey, over 900 guns were handed in, then shredded and are being turned into a peace angel. The local police have also donated weapons to the project and hope that the works of art will encourage further donations of weapons. 'The Art of Peace Charitable Trust is making the statue. The winged angel will stand nearly 5 feet tall and consist of confiscated and repurposed street weapons and non-radioactive nuclear missile casings'. This is part of a larger project, established by the artist Lin Evola. The website cites the artist as using 'the "swords to ploughshares" paradigm for empowering change'. She aims to create various angels of peace, made out of weapons, and bring them to different cities in North America. One was originally exhibited in Manhattan beside Ground Zero.[82] In another county in the USA, a *Guns for Gift Cards* scheme was established.[83]

Figure 7.4 Schwerter zu Pflugscharen, a German *Swords into Ploughshares* placard used by a protestor in Berlin, 1990. Courtesy of Bundesarchiv, Bild 183-1990-0518-028/ photographer: Bernd Settnik.

Figure 7.5 AK47 Out of Action (published in *Sowetan* on 18 October 1994).   Zapiro
Cartoons © 2011 Zapiro (All rights reserved) Printed with permission from
www.zapiro.com.

A more organic project in Richmond, Virginia, explicitly underlines the productive and prophetic side of the phrase from Isaiah. The artists Noah Scalin
and Christopher Humes, directly inspired by the text itself, developed a scheme
entitled Plant the Piece (figure 7.6) to highlight the high murder rate, mostly by
gunshot, in Richmond, Virginia. They adapted the 'traditional art of seed ball
making', where a seed is embedded in a ball of clay or dirt. They fashioned
instead a 9mm 910 pistol out of red clay powder and organic compost 'for each
person murdered in the city' (figure 7.7). For nine months they exhibited these
clay guns around the city in many different locations, though the number of
exhibits grew each month as more people were murdered. The displays became
both a protest at the waste of life and a catalyst for communal discussions as to
how gun crime could be reduced. The artists believe that the Plant the Piece
series is 'an inversion of the destructive use of firearms, creating life rather than
taking it away'.[84] Rather than shots, each of the clay guns began to sprout new
shoots of green life. Online this organic memorial project is subtitled 'Swords
into Plowshares'. These examples illustrate how this text, which emerged in the
Iron Age, continues to ripple across history.

Each of these sprouting guns also resonate with the *Tree of Life* sculpture. A
documentary, *The Tree of Guns,* produced for the BBC, and running on a loop in
a shortened version at the British Museum, tells the story of the four artists who

Figure 7.6 Plant the Piece *Logo*, Courtesy of Noah Scalin, with thanks to Christopher Humes.

Figure 7.7 Plant the Piece *Clay Gun,* Courtesy of Noah Scalin.

created the tree (figure 0.2 and front cover). This object is redolent with meaning in a country where trees took on great significance during the civil war. With so many schools, hospitals and homes destroyed by the long-running conflict, trees became meeting places, temporary hospitals and schools. They were places of shelter and even hope, until troops came close. As in so many conflicts, both the wildlife and trees in particular, suffered because of the war. Thousands of animals and hundreds of hectares of trees and farming land were destroyed, contributing to further environmental degradation. And yet, during the Mozambique floods in 2000, thousands of people were rescued from trees, rooftops and other isolated locations. One woman even gave birth to her baby, Rosita, in a tree.[85] The symbolic power of the *Tree of Life* should not be understated, as it points to an ancient phrase that underlines the relation of humans not only to each other but also to the earth.

The central argument of this book is encapsulated in these three challenging and unsettling words: 'swords into ploughshares'.[86] While chapters 1–3 were devoted to exploring how violence is incited, the aim of this analysis was neither to celebrate the sword, nor to demonise those who wield weapons; rather, the intention was to shed light on the recurring practice of incitement to fight. By understanding more accurately how violence is incited, peacebuilders will be able to see more clearly how future incitements can be reduced or even halted. Chapters 4–6 were devoted to exploring the ways in which different media can be used to bear witness to the reality and effects of violence, to try to search for truth and reconciliation, and to attempt to counter the downward spirals of revenge. Such concrete portrayals can enable audiences to imagine how swords might be transformed into ploughshares and how both the people and the land, who so often suffer through violence, might be liberated from histories of violence. Media audiences, creative artists and religious activists commonly have the skills and resources to highlight how weapons of destruction can be transformed into productive tools of peace. They can help turn the 'big words' of truth, reconciliation and peace into concrete stories and actions that can be imagined and imitated around the globe. For those intent on building peace, one challenge is to show in vivid, memorable and playful fashion how the escalation of violence can be halted, how future conflicts can be prevented and how different media can be used to promote peace.

Notes

Introduction

1 This is contra Walter Benjamin's claim in his essay on 'The Work of Art in the Age of Mechanical Reproduction', in G. Mast, M. Cohen and L. Braudy (eds), *Film Theory and Criticism*, 4th edn, Oxford: Oxford University Press, 1992, pp. 665–81. For a more detailed critique of Benjamin's thesis, see D. Morgan, *Protestants and Pictures: Religion, Visual Culture and the Age of American Mass Production*, Oxford: Oxford University Press, 1999, especially the conclusion on 'The Return of Aura', pp. 339–48.

2 See, for example, how 'young people from New Horizon Youth Centre' debate issues raised by the use of transformed guns in art. The British Museum, *Talking Objects: Throne of Weapons*, Online. HTTP: : <http://www.britishmuseum.org/the_museum/museum_in_london/community_work/talking_objects/the_great_wave_talking_object.aspx> (accessed 30 April 2011).

3 N. MacGregor, 'Director's Foreword', in J. Holden et al. (eds), *Throne of Weapons: A British Museum Tour*, London: British Museum, 2006, p. 5. Online PDF. HTTP: <www.britishmuseum.org/explore/highlights/highlight_objects/aoa/t/throne_of_weapons.aspx> (accessed 18 April 2011).

4 C. Canhavato (Kester) quoted in 'Throne of Weapons', *BBC A History of the World*. Online. HTTP: <www.bbc.co.uk/ahistoryoftheworld/objects/97OnxVXaQkehlbliKKDB6A> (accessed 18 April 2011).

5 N. MacGregor, *A History of the World in 100 Objects*, London: Allen Lane, an imprint of Penguin Books, 2010, p. 645.

6 C. Spring, 'Tree of Life', unpublished draft 2005, adapted for use in British Museum Publication.

7 N. MacGregor, 'Throne of Weapons', *BBC A History of the World*, episode 98.

8 The British Museum, *Throne of Weapons and Tree of Life*, Global Citizenship classroom resource: Key stage 3–4. Online PDF. HTTP: <www.britishmuseum.org/pdf/Citizenshp_ThroneTree_Presnotes_KS3&4.pdf> (accessed 18 April 2011).

9 The *Tree of Life* was created by four Mozambican artists, Adelino Serafim Maté, Hilario Nhatugueja, Fiel dos Santos, and the creator of the *Throne of Weapons*, Cristóvão Canhavato (Kester). See 'Tree of Life', *British Museum*. Online. HTTP: <www.britishmuseum.org/explore/highlights/highlight_objects/aoa/t/tree_of_life.aspx> (accessed 18 April 2011).

10 'Tree of Life', *British Museum*. Online. HTTP: <www.britishmuseum.org/explore/highlights/highlight_objects/aoa/t/tree_of_life.aspx> (accessed 18 April 2011).

11 Cited in several locations including Amy Schwartzott's article, 'Transforming Arms into Ploughshares: Weapons that Destroy and Heal in Mozambican Urban Art', in

L. Bisschoff and S. Van de Peer (eds), *Art and Trauma in Africa: Representations of Reconciliation in Film, Art, Music and Literature*, London: I.B. Tauris, forthcoming 2012.

12 N. MacGregor, *A History of the World in 100 Objects*, London: Penguin, 2010, p. 644.

13 For more on material culture and religion, see D. Morgan (ed.), *Religion and Material Culture: The Matter of Belief*, London: Routledge, 2010.

14 See R.S. Appleby, *The Ambivalence of the Sacred: Religion, Violence, and Reconciliation*, Lanham, MD: Rowman & Littlefield, 2000. See also Appleby's essay 'What Can Peacebuilders Learn from Fundamentalists?', in S. Hoover and N. Kaneva (eds), *Fundamentalisms and the Media*, New York and London: Continuum, 2009.

15 For other useful examples, see C.J. Hamelink, *Media and Conflict: Escalating Evil*, Boulder, CO: Paradigm Publishers, 2011. See especially his discussions of 'Media and the Spiral of Escalation' and 'Taming the Spiral of Escalation', pp. 31–68.

16 See J. Mitchell, 'Media', in W.A. Dyrness and Veli-Matti Kärkkäinen (eds), *Global Dictionary of Theology*, Downers Grove, IL: IVP, 2008, pp. 524–8; and J. Mitchell, *Media Violence and Christian Ethics*, Cambridge: Cambridge University Press, pp. 5–7.

17 Cited from personal email from David Morgan, 27 April, 2011.

18 H. Jenkins, *Convergence Culture: Where Old and New Media Collide*, New York and London: New York University Press, 2006, p. 3.

19 See, for example, the evolving field of media, religion and culture and books such as: G. Lynch, J. Mitchell and A. Strhan (eds), *Religion, Media and Culture: A Reader*, London and New York: Routledge, 2012; D. Morgan (ed.), *Key Words in Religion, Media and Culture*, London: Routledge, 2008; G. Lynch (ed.), *Between Sacred and Profane: Researching Religion and Popular Culture*, London: I.B. Tauris, 2007; P. Horsfield, M.E. Hess and A.M. Medrano (eds), *Belief in Media: Cultural Perspectives on Media and Christianity*, Aldershot: Ashgate, 2004; J. Mitchell and S. Marriage (eds), *Mediating Religion: Conversations in Media, Religion and Culture*, London and New York: T&T Clark/Continuum, 2003; S.M. Hoover and L. Schofield Clark (eds), *Practicing Religion in the Age of the Media: Explorations in Media, Religion, and Culture*, New York: Columbia University Press, 2002; and S. Hoover and K. Lundby (eds), *Rethinking Media, Religion and Culture*, Thousand Oaks, CA: Sage, 1997.

20 See, for example, S. Allan and B. Zelizer (eds), *Reporting War: Journalism in Wartime*, London: Routledge, 2004; D.C. Hallin, *The 'Uncensored War'*, Berkeley, Los Angeles and London: University of California Press, 1986; and P. Knightley, *The First Casualty*, 3rd edn, Baltimore, MD: Johns Hopkins University Press, 2004.

21 For exceptions, see G. Wolfsfeld, *Media and the Pathway to Peace*, Cambridge: Cambridge University Press, 2004. See also L. Reychiler and T. Paffenholz (eds), *Peacebuilding: A Field Guide*, Boulder, CO: Lynne Rienner Publishers, 2001, pp. 301–21. See note 22 for texts on peace journalism.

22 See J. Lynch and A. McGoldrick, *Peace Journalism*, Stroud: Hawthorn Press, 2005; D. Shinar and W. Kempf (eds), *Peace Journalism: The State of the Art*, Berlin: Regener, 2007; R.L. Keeble, J. Tulloch and F. Zollmann (eds), *Peace Journalism, War and Conflict Resolution*, New York: Peter Lang, 2010; J. Lynch and J. Galtung, *Reporting Conflict: New Directions in Peace Journalism*, St Lucia, Queensland: University of Queensland Press, 2010.

23 See James Page's discussion of 'Aesthetic Ethics and Peace Education', in J. Page, *Peace Education: Exploring Ethical and Philosophical Foundations*, Charlotte: Information Age Publishing, 2008, pp. 119–58.

24 Some discussions within 'peace journalism' texts provide an exception to this observation, offering analysis of the role of media and religion (commonly Islam). See, for example, J. Lynch, *Debates in Peace Journalism*, Sydney: Sydney University Press, 2008, especially chapter 8 on 'The "Islam Problem" in News Journalism and Scope for Media Activism', pp. 163–82.

25 See J.P. Lederach, *The Moral Imagination: The Art and Soul of Building Peace*, Oxford and New York: Oxford University Press, 2005. See also Lederach's *The Little Book of*

Conflict Transformation, Intercourse, PA: Good Books, 2003; *The Journey toward Reconciliation*, Pennsylvania: Herald Press, 1999; *Building Peace: Sustainable Reconciliation in Divided Societies*, US Institute of Peace Press, 1997; and his *Preparing for Peace: Conflict Transformation across Cultures*, New York: Syracuse University Press, 1995.

26 Lederach, *The Moral Imagination*, p. 5.

27 Ibid.

28 See, for example, C. Deacy and G. Ortiz, *Theology and Film: Challenging the Sacred/Secular Divide*, Oxford: Blackwell, 2008; J. Mitchell, *Media Violence and Christian Ethics*, Cambridge: Cambridge University Press, 2007; J. Lyden, *Film as Religion: Myths, Morals and Rituals*, New York and London: New York University Press, 2003.

29 See H. Campbell, *When Religion Meets New Media*, Abingdon, Oxon: Routledge, 2010.

30 'Positive peace' is much more than simply absence of violence (which is often described as 'negative peace'). Positive peace is commonly seen as the eradication of structural violence and the establishment of just societies. See D. Cortright, *Peace: A History of Movements and Ideas*, Cambridge: Cambridge University Press, 2008, pp. 6–7.

31 For more on 'structural' and 'hidden violence', see P. Farmer, *Pathologies of Power: Health, Human Rights and the New War on the Poor*, Berkeley and Los Angeles: University of California Press, 2003.

1 Visualising holy war

1 This poster portrays a group of six diversely uniformed men and women involved in different kinds of war work with a field gun in the background, a woman factory worker making bullets in the middle and a double-edged question in the foreground: 'Are YOU in this?' A seventh figure, in civilian dress with a bow tie, has hands in his pockets. He is doing nothing, except for looking on uncomfortably. See J. Aulich and J. Hewitt, *Seduction or Instruction? First World War Posters in Britain and Europe*, Manchester: Manchester University Press, 2007, p. 42.

2 See C.P. Allix, Swaffham Prior Parish Church, 'Description of War Memorial Windows Designed by C.P. Allix – 1920', Cambridgeshire Archives, no. P150/6/19.

3 This phrase has its origin in a speech at Wolverhampton by David Lloyd George (Earl Lloyd-George of Dwyfor) 1863–1945. 'What is Our Task? To Make Britain a Fit Country for Heroes to Live in' (23 November 1918), quoted in *The Times*, 25 November 1918. See also T. Augarde (ed.), *The Oxford Dictionary of Modern Quotations*, Oxford: Oxford University Press, 1991.

4 See T. Hyman, *Sienese Painting: The Art of a City Republic (1278–1477)*, London: Thames and Hudson, 2003, pp. 94–121.

5 'Alfred Leete's Lord Kitchener design started life as a cover of the 5 September 1914 number of the weekly magazine *London Opinion* and went through many different versions. J. Darracott and B. Loftus, *First World War Posters*, London: Imperial War Museum, 1981 (1972), pp. 37, 63. The image was widely imitated around the world, see p. 64.

6 For a full list of names and further details, see A. Thompson and P. Gariepy, 'Cambridgeshire Swaffham Prior St Mary – Roll of Honour', 2000. Online. HTTP: <www.roll-of-honour.com/Cambridgeshire/SwaffhamPriorStMary.html> (accessed 4 March 2011).

7 J. Winter, *Sites of Memory, Sites of Mourning: The Great War in European Cultural History*, Cambridge: Cambridge University Press, 1995, p. 177. For more on Otto Dix, see pp. 159–64.

8 See the Imperial War Museum's 'United Kingdom National Inventory of War Memorials' (IWM's UKNIWM) currently lists over 40,000 (40,329) First World War memorials. Online. HTTP: <www.ukniw.org.uk> (accessed 14 July 2011).

9 On 21 November 2011, the IWM's UKNIWM listed 2,080 First World War window memorials.

10 G. Hill, *Triumph of Love*, New York: Mariner Books, 2000 (1998), p. 40.
11 See, for example, P.M. Taylor and M.L. Sanders, *British Propaganda During the First World War*, London: Macmillan, 1982; G.S. Messinger, *British Propaganda and the State in the First World War*, Manchester: Manchester University Press, 1992. See also J. Winter, *Sites of Memory, Sites of Mourning*.
12 See A. King, *Memorials of the Great War in Britain: The Symbolism and Politics of Remembrance*, Oxford: Berg, 1998.
13 See, for example, G. Sheffield, *Forgotten Victory: The First World War: Myths and Realities*, London: Headline Book Publishing, 2001; D. Todman, *The Great War: Myth and Reality*, London: Hambledon Continuum, 2007.
14 These articles are also to be found in Swaffham Prior Parish Church, 'Swaffham Prior Church, St. Mary's Restoration Book', Cambridgeshire Archives, 1805–1932, P150/3/13, p. 186.
15 S. Jenkins, *England's Thousand Best Churches*, London: Penguin Books, 2000 (1999), p. 53.
16 J. Winter, *Sites of Memory, Sites of Mourning*, pp. 91–2.
17 S. Goebel, *The Great War and Medieval Memory: War, Remembrance and Medievalism in Britain and Germany, 1914–1940*, Cambridge: Cambridge University Press, 2007, p. 212.
18 'St Mary, Swaffham Prior'. Online. HTTP: <www.flickr.com/photos/therevsteve/sets/72157603952261523/with/2464314321/> (accessed 9 March 2011). At the time of writing, Steve Day was an Anglican Team Vicar in the Papworth Team Ministry in Cambridgeshire, UK.
19 T. Morgan, 'A Glass Memorial', 1997. Online. HTTP: <www.fylde.demon.co.uk/church.htm> (accessed 9 March 2011).
20 N. Trevithick (prod.) *Through a Glass Darkly*, BBC Radio 4, 14 September 1995.
21 Interviewed on Trevithick (prod.), *Through a Glass Darkly*, 14 September 1995.
22 See also E. Everitt and R. Tricker, *Swaffham-Two-Churches*, Mildenhall, Suffolk: E.G.M. Mann, 1996, p. 43.
23 In a church window of remembrance in Pieffefitte-Nestalas (Hautes Pyrénées) the Virgin appears holding baby Jesus above the trench while a chaplain speaks to the soldiers, one guard looks on, but there is no fighting – the guns are not raised in anger. A. Becker, *War and Faith: The Religious Imagination in France, 1914–1930*, trans. H. McPhail, Oxford: Berg, 1998, fig. 15, p. 156.
24 For an exception, see the memorial window in St Luke's, Bath, where beneath a set of angelic and chivalric figures two roundels include a biplane and warship. See J. Taylor, 'Lest We Forget, Stained Glass Memorial Windows of the Great War', Online. HTTP: <buildingconservation.com/articles/lestweforget/lestweforget.htm>
25 N.J. Saunders (ed.), *Matters of Conflict: Material Culture, Memory and the First World War*, Abingdon: Routledge, 2004, pp. 5–6.
26 See N. Ferguson, *The Pity of War: Explaining World War I*, London: Allen Lane/The Penguin Press, 1999 (1998), pp. 293–6.
27 Winter, *Sites of Memory, Sites of Mourning*, p. 224.
28 D. Lloyd, *Battlefield Tourism: Pilgrimage and the Commemoration of the Great War in Britain, Australia and Canada, 1919–1939*, Oxford: Berg, 1998, p. 217.
29 See Imperial War Museum, *Searchlight*, 'War Graves and Cemeteries', for a photograph of one of 'the largest collections' of wooden crosses that were brought back to Britain, 'comprising 22 crosses', which 'is held in St Mary's Church, Byfleet'. NIWM 23510–23531. Online. HTTP: <http://www.iwm.org.uk/searchlight/server.php?show=nav.24352> (accessed 29 April 2011). See also Salisbury Cathedral, where several wooden crosses are displayed in the cloisters.
30 Lloyd, *Battlefield Tourism*, p. 144.
31 See King, *Memorials of the Great War in Britain*, p. 55.

32 See Imperial War Museum, *Searchlight*, 'Rolls of Honour', HU 58985. Online. HTTP: <http://www.iwm.org.uk/searchlight/server.php?show=nav.24446> (accessed 29 April 2011).

33 For full list of names and further details, see Online. HTTP: <http://www.roll-of-honour.com/Cambridgeshire/SwaffhamPriorStMary.html> and <http://www.roll-of-honour.com/Cambridgeshire/SwaffhamPriorZion.html> (accessed 29 April 2011).

34 See Imperial War Museum, *Searchlight*, 'Rolls of Honour', MGH 2619. Online. HTTP: <http://www.iwm.org.uk/searchlight/server.php?show=nav.24446> (accessed 29 April 2011).

35 Allix died aged 79 in June 1921. He was educated at Harrow and Trinity College, Cambridge, and was a former member of the Regiment of the Mounted Horse, which became the Suffolk Yeomanry.

36 C.W.R.D. Mosely, *Reach: A Brief History*, 2nd edn (2001), < http://www.reach-vil-lage.co.uk/brief_history.html > (accessed 11 November 2011).

37 Charles Allix Lavington Yate (1872–1914) was a distant cousin, who received a Victoria Cross for his courage in an action which ultimately cost him his life in 1914.

38 According to the 1911 census Swafham Prior had a population of 934, which had dropped in 1921 to 892 residents.

39 See *Scrapbook of C.P. Allix, 1908–18*, Cambridgeshire Archives: R85/7, no page numbers.

40 J. Bartlett and K. M. Ellis, 'Remembering the Dead in Northop: First World War Memorials in a Welsh Parish', *Journal of Contemporary History*, April 1999, vol. 34, no. 2, p. 242.

41 V. Brittain, *Testament of Youth: An Autobiographical Study of the Years 1900–1925*, Harmondsworth: Penguin, 1994 (1933), p. 496. See also p. 275 for how Roland's death vividly revisited her.

42 Ibid., p. 371.

43 For parish accounts see Swaffham Prior Parish Church, 'Scrapbook of Newspaper Cuttings, Forms, Pamphlets etc'., 1914–1918 compiled by L. Fisher, Cambridgeshire Archives, P150/28/7. The cross cost £46 and the brass £10, which along with the window (£40), making a total of £96, which would be worth well over £3,000 today, or nearly US $5,000. The entire monument therefore cost about £176 (well over £5,000).

44 Brittain, *Testament of Youth: An Autobiographical Study of the Years 1900–1925*, p. 416.

45 Swaffham Prior Parish Church, 'Description of War Memorial Windows Designed by C.P. Allix – 1920', p. 4.

46 Ibid., p. 7.

47 Personal email to author, 23 April 2009. Allix also financed the oak rood screen.

48 St Mary's is one of two churches in the same churchyard, which both probably date back to Norman times and around 1100. Like its neighbour, St Cyriac and St Julietta, St Mary's has had a turbulent history, being partly destroyed by a lightning strike in 1779 and enduring decades of neglect during the nineteenth century. Allix's father bought it and turned it into a family mausoleum. In 1900–1 Allix financed the renova-tion of St Mary's, despite opposition from the previous low-church incumbent. Allix was determined that his preferred high-church Anglicanism would be celebrated in the renovated St Mary's, and ensured this through the Anglo-Catholic Lawrence Fisher.

49 Also cited in Trevithick (prod.), *Through a Glass Darkly*, 14 September 1995. This description highlights how Allix was the driving force behind their design. G. Maile and Son, a stained-glass firm, which was 'active in the nineteenth and twentieth centuries', appear to have been employed to act as 'designer' (probably the manu-facturer) of the windows and Mr Thomas F. Curtis to be the 'artist'. Their precise role in the creation of the windows is not clear from the 'National Inventory of War

Memorials', which cites their names in these roles. Online. HTTP: <www.ukniw.
org.uk> (accessed 14 July 2011).

50 King, *Memorials of the Great War in Britain*, p. 246. For more on the rivalry between
different communities who were creating their own memorials, see pp. 246–51.

51 Copy in *Scrapbook of C.P. Allix, 1918–21*, Cambridgeshire Archives: R.

52 See C.P. Allix's address at the dedication of Reach memorial, 13 June 1920: 'The
names of the Dead, good soldiers and brave, from this little Fenside village that gave
their lives for their country are engraved on the sides of this monolith'. *Scrapbook of
C.P. Allix, 1918–21*, R85/7.

53 D. Boorman, *At the Going Down of the Sun: British First World War Memorials*, York:
Ebor Press, 1988, p. 49.

54 See W.T. McSkimming, *West Kilbride Memorial Book*, unpublished, available via West
Kilbride Museum, 'The ex-servicemen protested vigorously but their wishes were
ignored', p. 6.

55 It is not clear from the records if his daughter assisted him, though Allix's written
notes suggests that she will.

56 Also cited in Trevithick (prod.), *Through a Glass Darkly*, 14 September 1995.

57 G.L. Mosse, *Fallen Soldiers: Reshaping the Memory of the World Wars*, New York: Oxford
University Press, 1991, p. 7.

58 Interviewee in Trevithick (prod.), *Through a Glass Darkly*, 14 September 1995.

59 Ibid.

60 Brittain, *Testament of Youth: An Autobiographical Study of the Years 1900–1925*, p. 127.

61 P. Fussell, *The Great War and Modern Memory*, New York: Oxford University Press,
1975. Some recent accounts have criticised the limited scope of Fussell's work. See,
for example, G. Sheffield, *Forgotten Victory: The First World War: Myths and Realities*,
London: Headline Book Publishing, 2001, pp.18–19.

62 'On the Opening of the War Memorial in St Mary's Church Swaffham Prior', p. 1.
From *Scrapbook of C.P. Allix, 1918–21*, Cambridgeshire Archives: R.

63 'On the Opening of the War Memorial in St Mary's Church Swaffham Prior', p. 3.

64 Also cited in Trevithick (prod.), *Through a Glass Darkly*, 14 September 1995.

65 See G.K. Chesterton, *The Autobiography of G.K. Chesterton*, San Francisco: Ignatius
Press, 2006 (1936), pp.228–38, within chapter 11, 'The Shadow of the Sword'.

66 E. Short, *I Knew My Place*, London: Macdonald and Co, 1983, pp. 34–6.

67 King, *Memorials of the Great War in Britain*, p. 89.

68 See K. S. Inglis, 'The Homecoming: The War Memorial Movement in Cambridge,
England', *Journal of Contemporary History*, October 1992, vol. 27, no. 4, pp. 583–605.
Inglis describes in detail the discussions and fund-raising leading up to the creation
of this smaller than originally planned statue of a victorious returning home
soldier (*Homecoming*), the list of the dead in Ely Cathedral and an extension for
Addenbrooke's Hospital. The colleges concentrated upon creating their own
memorials, so overall the University contributed very little to the city and county's
memorials.

69 C.P. Allix, compiler, *Scrapbook of C.P. Allix, 1908–1918*, Cambridgeshire Archives,
R 85/7.

70 See A. Wilkinson, *The Church of England and the First World War*, London: SCM, 1996
(1978), p. 204.

71 C.P. Allix, address 'On the Opening of the War Memorial in St Mary's Swaffham-
Prior', p. 3 of address. Dated incorrectly as 'December 21, 1920', it should be the
same day, but 1919 not 1920. From *Scrapbook of C.P. Allix, 1918–21*, Cambridgeshire
Archives: R85/7.

72 John 15.13: 'Greater love has no man than this, that a man lay down his life for his
friends'. This was a popular text on memorials. See also 1 John 3.16.

73 A. Gregory, *The Silence of Memory: Armistice Day – 1919–1946*, Oxford: Berg, 1994, pp. 34–41, 226.

74 Ibid., p. 173–93.

75 S. Hynes, *A War Imagined: The First World War and English Culture*, London: Bodley Head, 1991. Hynes echoes Robert Graves' poem 'Big Words' from E.B. Osborn (ed.), *The Muse in Arms,* London: John Murray, 1917, p.25.

76 Fussell, *The Great War and Modern Memory*, p.175.

77 See B. Bushaway, 'Name Upon Name: The Great War and Remembrance', in R. Porter (ed.), *Myths of the English*, Cambridge: Polity Press, 1992; and B. Bushaway, 'The Obligation of Remembrance or the Remembrance of Obligation: Society and the Memory of World War', in J. Bourne, P. Liddle and I. Whitehead (eds), *The First World War 1914–45*, vol. 2, London: Harper Collins, 2001, pp. 491–507.

78 See, for example, the poet Siegfried Sassoon's *A Soldier's Declaration*, published on the front page of *The Times* (July 1917), which he wrote in order: 'to destroy the callous complacency with which the majority of those at home regard the contrivance of agonies which they do not share, and which they have not sufficient imagination to realize'.

79 M. Arthur (ed.), *We Will Remember Them: Voices from the Aftermath of the Great War,* London: Orion Group, 2009, audio CD 4, track 9.

80 S.J. Brown, '"A Solemn Purification by Fire": Responses to the Great War in the Scottish Presbyterian Churches, 1914–19'. *Journal of Ecclesiastical History*, January 1994, vol. 45, no. 1 pp. 82–104.

81 These are also recurring themes in Allix's public addresses. See, for example, his address at the dedication of the Swaffham Bulbeck Memorial, 16 June 1921, which is discussed in the main text. *Scrapbook of C.P. Allix, 1918–1921*, Cambridgeshire Archives R.

82 Ida Clark was born in Swaffham Prior and was daughter of the landlord of the Red Lion. This interview comes from a 1983 local radio programme *On Your Doorstep,* which was made about the village of Swaffham Prior. It is cited in the *Swaffham Crier,* April 2006, vol. 30, no. 4.

83 A. Freedman, 'Zeppelin Fictions and the British Home Front', *Journal of Modern Literature*, 2004, vol. 27, no. 3, pp. 47–62 (50).

84 G. B. Shaw, *Heartbreak House*, Harmondsworth: Penguin, 1964 (1919), p. 160.

85 G. De Syon, *Zeppelin!: Germany and the Airship, 1900–1939*, Baltimore, MD: Johns Hopkins University Press, 2002.

86 Swaffham Prior Parish Church, 'Description of war memorial windows designed by C.P. Allix – 1920', pp. 2–3, from *Scrapbook of C.P. Allix, 1918–21*, Cambridgeshire Archives: R85/7.

87 C. Stephenson, *Zeppelins: German Airships 1900–40*, Oxford: Osprey Publishing, 2004, p. 13. For eye witness accounts of another larger raid see: T. Morgan, 'The Great Zeppelin Raid: 31 January 1916', *World War I Document Archive*, 1996. Online. HTTP: <net.lib.byu.edu/~rdh7/wwi/memoir/zeppelin.html> (accessed 9 March 2011).

88 Swaffham Prior Parish Church, 'Swaffham Prior Church, St. Mary's Restoration Book', p. 182–3.

89 De Syon, *Zeppelin!*, pp. 72–5. See also B. C. Lavelle, *Zeppelinitis*, Honolulu, HI: University Press of the Pacific, 2005.

90 From *Scrapbook of C.P. Allix, 1908–1918*, Cambridgeshire Archives, R. Cutting from *The Daily Graphic*, 6 February 1909, which reproduced an early print from 1807.

91 De Syon, *Zeppelin!*, p. 72.

92 Ibid., p. 88.

93 Ibid., p. 97. Some suggest even lower numbers of casualties (557) and raids (51). See D. H. Robinson, *The Zeppelin in Combat: 1912–1918*, London: G.T. Foulis & Co, 1962, pp. 345–6.

94 Shaw, 'Preface', *Heartbreak House*, p. 19. The play was largely written during the war, soon after the catastrophes of Verdun and the Somme offensive and within the earshot of the guns in France.

95 Ibid., p. 88.

96 P. Stanley, *What Did You Do in the War Daddy? A Visual History of Propaganda Posters*, Melbourne: Oxford University Press, 1983, p. 23. Stanley suggests that 'the War stimulated the evolution of the propaganda poster … and was probably the most extensive mobilization of printed pictorial propaganda for political purposes in history. Millions of copies of thousands of designs were produced'. p. 7.

97 See S. Sillars, *Art and Survival in First World War Britain*, New York: Macmillan Press, 1987, p. 108.

98 Ibid., p. 91.

99 Ibid.

100 Freedman, 'Zeppelin Fictions and the British Home Front', p. 48.

101 Ibid., pp. 50–1.

102 C.P. Allix (comp.), *Scrapbook of C.P. Allix, 1908–1918*, Cambridgeshire Archives, R 85/7.

103 Allix, *Scrapbook*, R 85/7.

104 Freedman, 'Zeppelin Fictions and the British Home Front', pp. 56–8.

105 There are a couple of notable exceptions where parishioners have preserved some of the debris of Zeppelins that were shot down nearby. First, at St Mary the Virgin and All Saints, in the All Souls Chapel, at Potters Bar, North London, there is an altar-cross made from the metal taken from the wreck of L-31. Second, a small part of the frame of L-48 can be seen at St Peter's Church, Therberton, Suffolk.

106 Allix's windows, p. 2.

107 Ibid., p. 6.

108 'This poster was published in June 1915 by the Boston Committee of Public Safety'. Darracott and Loftus, *First World War Posters*, p. 53. For other examples of propaganda posters, see also Aulich and Hewitt: *Seduction or Instruction?*

109 Allix, *Scrapbook*, R 85/7.

110 Allix, *Scrapbook*, R 85/7, from *Daily Graphic*, 22 October 1915. For more on how Cavell's execution was put to propaganda use, see also C.M. Kingsbury, *For Home and Country: World War 1 Propaganda on the Home Front*, Lincoln, NE: University of Nebraska, 2010, pp. 106–13, 219–47.

111 Shaw, 'Preface', *Heartbreak House*, p. 26.

112 See M. Snape, 'Church of England Army Chaplains in the First World War: Goodbye to "Goodbye to All That"', *Journal of Ecclesiastical History*, vol. 62, no. 2, April 2011, pp. 318–45.

113 M. and S. Harries, *The War Artists: British Official War Art of the Twentieth Century*, London: Michael Joseph with the Imperial War Museum and the Tate Gallery, 1983. 'One prime example' of an empty battlefield 'is Bone's *Panorama from Scherpenberg*, in which the British bombardment of Wytschaete and Messines appears no doubt exactly as he saw it – as a few puffs of smoke on the horizon', p. 76.

114 C.P. Allix address at the dedication of the Swaffham Bulbeck Memorial, 16 June 1921, Allix, *Scrapbook*, no page numbers.

115 C.P. Allix, Reach Memorial Address, 13 June 1920, from Allix, *Scrapbook*, no page numbers.

116 J. Horne and A. Kramer, *German Atrocities, 1914: A History of Denial*, New Haven: Yale University Press, 2001. In a detailed study they provide persuasive evidence that the Germans did execute around 6,500 innocent civilians partly motivated by the mistaken fear that they were confronting *franc-tireurs*, similar to those who had provided strong resistance during the Franco-Prussian war of 1870–1.

117 N.D. Hillis, *Murder Most Foul,* date and publisher unknown, also available at *The First World War Poetry Digital Archive.* Online. HTTP: <www.oucs.ox.ac.uk/ww1lit/collections/document/5112/4123> (accessed 17 March 2011), p.5.

118 Ibid., p. 6.

119 Ibid., pp. 14, 16.

120 For more on Hillis, see M. Sproule, *Propaganda and Democracy: The American Experience of Media and Mass Persuasion,* Cambridge: Cambridge University Press, 1997, pp. 1, 10–11, 15.

121 See J. Simpson's discussion of the bellicose role of *The Times* and *Daily Mail* before and during the War, *Unreliable Sources: How the 20th Century was Reported,* London: Macmillan, 2010.

122 A. Marrin, *The Last Crusade: The Church of England in the First World War,* Durham, NC: Duke University Press, 1974, p. 103 (where he cites Winnington-Ingram admitting that he is drawing from the *Daily Mail*), p. 175 cites the infamous sermon by entitled 'A World of Cheer'.

123 A.F. Winnington-Ingram, *The Potter and the Clay,* London: W.G. Darton, 1917, p. 42.

124 A.F. Winnington-Ingram, *The Church in Time of War,* London: Wells Gardner, Darton and Co, 1916, p. 275.

125 Like many other atrocity stories this appeared in various forms, with a nurse from Dumfries purportedly suffering a similar fate. As with so many other stories, the veracity of this tale was questioned by A. Ponsonby, *Falsehood in War-Time: Propaganda Lies of the First World War,* London: George Allen and Unwin, 1928, see chapter 6, 'The Mutilated Nurse'. Online. HTTP: <www.vlib.us/wwi/resources/archives/texts/t050824i/ponsonby.html> (accessed 17 March 2011).

126 Ibid., p. 55. This story from 12 September 1914 was also quoted on a propaganda poster 'Remember Belgium', Aulich and Hewitt: *Seduction or Instruction?,* p. 74.

127 One Irish recruiting poster depicts 'a man at a plough addressed by the spirit of St Patrick dominating the ruins of Rheims Cathedral in an image that would resonate with the Catholic farming communities of Ireland'. Ibid., p. 51, and plate 7.

128 See Goebel, *The Great War and Medieval Memory,* p. 83–98.

129 C.L. Warr, *The Glimmering Landscape,* London: Hodder and Stoughton, 1960, pp. 118–19. Also cited by S.J. Brown, 'A Solemn Purification by Fire', p. 101.

130 S.J. Brown, 'A Solemn Purification by Fire', p. 82–104.

131 A. Kramer, *Dynamic of Destruction: Culture and Mass Killing in the First World War,* Oxford: Oxford University Press, 2007, pp. 175–80.

132 Brittain, *Testament of Youth,* p. 395.

133 See King, *Memorials of the Great War in Britain.* King suggests that, while bereavement was a determinative factor, memorials were not only put to conservative uses but also to more radical causes.

134 N. Ferguson, *The Pity of War: Explaining World War I,* New York: Basic Books, 1999, pp. 204–8. For Ferguson the 'sense that the world had arrived at the Biblical Armageddon was the most powerful of all the "ideas of 1914". And how like Armageddon it proved'.

135 Kramer, *Dynamic of Destruction,* p. 244, citing Fussell, *The Great War and Modern Memory.*

136 This is a recurring theme in Ingram's sermons. See, for example, Winnington-Ingram's 1916 collection of sermons, *The Church in Time of War.*

137 Allix notes how the statue was created by the Italian Bartholdi and given by the French to the American nation. This representation, like the inclusion of an Italian bugler and French hospital on other windows, was intended to provide 'a permanent record' of transatlantic and other wartime alliances whose objective was to fight for 'liberty'. Swaffham Prior Parish Church, 'Description of War Memorial Windows Designed by C.P. Allix – 1920', p. 6.

138 Arthur (ed.), *We Will Remember Them: Voices from the Aftermath of the Great War*, audio CD 4, track 8.

139 J. Vance, *Death so Noble: Memory, Meaning, and the First World War*, Vancouver, BC: University of British Columbia, 1997, p. 41. See also the window at the back of St Thomas' Church, Belfast.

140 P. Breen, 'The Art of Sacrifice', *UKIWM*. Online. HTTP: <ukniwm.wordpress.com/2010/03/31/the-art-of-sacrifice/> (accessed 17 November 2011).

141 Lance Corporal William Sharpe, in Arthur (ed.), *We Will Remember Them: Voices from the Aftermath of the Great War*, audio CD 4, track 10.

142 J. Winter, *Remembering War: The Great War Between Memory and History in the Twentieth Century*, New Haven: Yale University Press, 2006, pp. 163–4, 208. See also Winter, *Sites of Memory, Sites of Mourning*, p. 6, where he suggests that war not only brutalised but also evoked 'compassion', which helped to bring about recovery from the war.

143 Impaled babies and defiled women commonly recurred in 'hate propaganda'. For another example, see R. Douglas, *The Great War: 1914–1918: The Cartoonists' Vision*, London: Routledge, 1995, p. 43. He reproduces a picture of a cruel-looking soldier holding an impaled baby aloft, ironically titled as 'The Gentle German', from E. J. Sullivan, *The Kaiser's Garden*, London: William Heinemann, 1915.

144 Cited in Messinger, *British Propaganda and the State in the First World War*, p. 247. Montague, like other post-war writers such as Rupert Graves, were also highly critical of Anglican chaplains, especially when embracing 'soldiering' and the 'brutal business of war'. See Snape, 'Church of England Army Chaplains … ', p. 327.

145 Fussell, *The Great War and Modern Memory*, p. 316.

146 Winter, *Sites of Memory, Sites of Mourning*, p. 6.

147 M. Yorke, *Eric Gill: Man of Flesh and Spirit*, London: I.B. Tauris, 2000 (1981), pp. 220–5.

148 See many publications reiterating suspicion or worse after the war, such as *Punch*, 14 May 1919. In this example a cartoon depicts a German man in uniform drawing a sharp sword out of a scabbard, while next to him perches a single sheet of paper entitled 'Allied Peace Terms' with the tag line: 'GERMANY DRAWS THE PEN. "It's not exactly a sabre but I daresay I can keep it rattling for a bit"', p. 383.

149 Harries, *The War Artists*, p. 76.

2 Celebrating martyrdom

1 See A. Badrkhani, 'Put a Stop to it', *Iranian*, 8 October 2003. Online. HTTP: <www.iranian.com/AssalBadrkhani/2003/October/Peace/index.html> (accessed 11 March 2011).

2 See C. Gruber, Online. HTTP: <aschcenter.smugmug.com/Other/Christiane-Gruber-Visualizing/16162622_4K9Lv#1213624476_kXbhX> (accessed 1 June 2011).

3 See, for example, S. Paivandi, *Discrimination and Intolerance in Iran's Textbooks*, New York: Freedom House Press, 2008, pp. 4, 16. See citation of *Reading Literature Textbook, Grade 3*, Tehran: Government, Publisher not known, 1990, p. 48.

4 R. Baer, 'The Making of a Suicide Bomber', *Sunday Times*, 3 September 2006.

5 See C. Gruber, Online. HTTP: <aschcenter.smugmug.com/Other/Christiane-Gruber-Visualizing/16162622_4K9Lv#1213624476_kXbhX> (accessed 1 June 2011)

6 See R. Varzi, *Warring Souls: Youth, Media and Martyrdom in Post-Revolution Iran*, Durham, NC: Duke University Press, 2006.

7 Her fiancé Caspan Makan told BBC Persian TV: 'She was near the area (of the demonstration), a few streets away, from where the main protests were taking place, near the Amir-Abad area. She was with her music teacher, sitting in a car and stuck in traffic. She was feeling very tired and very hot. She got out of the car for just for a few minutes. And that's when it all happened'. 'Death Video Woman "Targeted by

Militia"', *BBC News*, 22 June 2009. Online. HTTP: <news.bbc.co.uk/1/hi/world/middle_east/8113552.stm> (accessed 11 March 2011).

8 T. Norman, 'Neda: The Face of a New Iranian Revolution', *Pittsburgh Post-Gazette*, 23 June 2009. Online. HTTP: <www.post-gazette.com/pg/09174/979208-153.stm> (accessed 11 March 2011).

9 'Neda: The Face of a New Iranian Revolution', *IBTimes*, 22 June 2009. Online. HTTP: <www.ibtimes.co.uk/articles/20090624/neda-death-iran-iranian-protests.htm> (accessed 11 March 2011).

10 First broadcast in August 2005, <www.channel4.com/news/microsites/C/cult_suicide_bomber/index.html> (accessed 17 September 2006, no longer available at this link, but available as DVD set).

11 B. Kates, 'Ahmadinejad Calls Iranian Martyr Neda's Death "Suspicious"', *New York Daily News*, 29 June 2009. Online. HTTP: <www.nydailynews.com/news/us_world/2009/06/29/2009-06-29_ahmadinejad_calls_iranian_martyr_nedas_death_suspicious.html> (accessed 11 March 2011).

12 C. Reuter, *My Life is a Weapon: A Modern History of Suicide Bombing*, trans. H. Ragg-Kirby, Princeton: Princeton University Press, 2004.

13 Varzi, *Warring Souls*, p. 47.

14 F. Rajaee (ed.), *The Iran–Iraq War: The Politics of Aggression*, Gainesville: University Press of Florida, 1993, p. 206.

15 Varzi, *Warring Souls*, p. 56.

16 P. Chelkowski, 'The Art of Revolution and War: The Role of Graphic Arts in Iran', in S. Balaghi and L. Gumpel (eds), *Picturing Iran: Art, Society and Revolution*, London: I.B. Tauris, 2003, p. 128.

17 See C. Gruber, 'Media/ting Conflict: Iranian Posters of the Iran–Iraq War (1980–88)', in J. Anderson (ed.), *Crossing Cultures: Conflict, Migration, Convergence*, Melbourne: Melbourne University, 2009, pp. 710–15. See also 'The Graphics of Revolution and War: Iranian Poster Arts', Online: HTTP: <www.lib.uchicago.edu/e/webexhibits/iranianposters/revolution.html> (accessed 21 November 2011).

18 See, for example, 'War between Iran and Iraq', a collection of 45 CD-ROMs and other materials available at the International Institute of Social History, Amsterdam, with more details online at HTTP: <www.iisg.nl/archives/en/files/w/10930603full.php> (accessed 11 March 2011).

19 The Martyrs' Foundation recognised 218,000 martyrs, created a hierarchy of martyrs and only started painting murals in 1991. See E. Blankevoort, 'The Image of War: Visual Propaganda in the Islamic Republic of Iran', unpublished master's thesis, University of Amsterdam, 2005. See her interview with Amir Hosseini, manager of the 'memories and ceremonies' department of the Martyrs' Foundation (*Bonyad-e Shahid*), pp. 161–2.

20 P. Chelkowski and H. Dabashi, *Staging a Revolution: The Art of Persuasion in the Islamic Republic of Iran*, New York: New York University Press, 1999, p. 74.

21 See, for example, Kazem Chalipa's pictures entitled *Zoljinah* and *Rooted in Love* (c.1984–8).

22 See 'The new Karbala' at 'The Graphics of Revolution and War: Iranian Poster Arts'. Online. HTTP: <www.lib.uchicago.edu/e/webexhibits/iranianposters/new-karbala.html> (accessed 11 October 2011).

23 F. Christia, '"Walls of Martyrdom": Tehran's Propaganda Murals', *Centerpiece*, 2007, vol. 21, no. 1. Online. HTTP: <www.wcfia.harvard.edu/misc/publications/centerpiece/win07_vol21_no1/feature_christia.html> (accessed 11 March 2011).

24 M. Ruthven, *Islam: A Very Short Introduction*, Oxford: Oxford University Press, 1997, p. 55.

25 V.J. Schubel, *Religious Performance in Contemporary Islam: Shi'i Devotional Rituals in South Asia*, Columbia, South Carolina: University of South Carolina Press, 1993, p. 95.

26 Chelowski and Dabashi, *Staging a Revolution*, p. 46.

27 Chelowski, 'The Art of Revolution and War', in Balaghi and Gumpel (eds), *Picturing Iran*, p. 135.

28 See P. Chelkowski (ed.), *Eternal Performance: Ta'ziyeh and Other Shiite Rituals*, London: Seagull Books, 2010; Jamshid Malekpour, *The Islamic Drama*, London: Frank Cass Publishers, 2004; Jalal Asghar, *A Historical Study of the Origins of Persian Passion Plays*, Michigan: Ann Arbor Publishing, 1963.

29 Ibid., p. 77.

30 Ibid., p. 55.

31 I have not yet discovered a mural that includes a spade, though several depict unburied bodies.

32 A. Amanat, *Apocalyptic Islam and Iranian Shi'ism*, London and New York: I.B. Tauris, 2009, pp. vii–viii.

33 For a more detailed discussion of this image, see C.J. Gruber, 'The Message is on the Wall: Mural Arts in Post-Revolutionary Iran', *Persica*, 2008, vol. 22, pp. 15–46, especially pp. 28–30. Gruber points out how this mural 'recalls' an earlier painting, which also appeared in the Martyrs' foundation magazine, *Shadid*.

34 M. Hegland, 'Two Images of Husain: Accommodation and Revolution in an Iranian Village', in N.R. Keddie (ed.), *Religion and Politics in Iran: Shi'ism from Quietism to Revolution*, New Haven: Yale University Press, 1983, pp. 218–36.

35 W. Madelung, *Succession to Muhammed: A Study of the Early Caliphate*, Cambridge: Cambridge University Press, 1997, p. 308. The attack took place on 17 Ramadan January 661.

36 S. Gieling, *Religion and War in Revolutionary Iran*, London and New York: I.B. Tauris, 1999, p. 179.

37 Ibid., p. 176.

38 Ibid., p. 55.

39 K.S. Aghaie, *The Martyrs of Karbala: Shi'i Symbols and Rituals in Modern Iran*, Seattle: University of Washington Press, 2004, p. 134.

40 Ibid., p. 58.

41 E. Blankevoort, 'The Image of war: Visual Propaganda in the Islamic Republic of Iran', unpublished master's thesis, University of Amsterdam, 2005, pp. 41–2.

42 S. Chubin and C. Tripp, *Iran and Iraq at War*, London: I.B. Tauris, 1988, p. 10. See also C. Tripp, *A History of Iraq*, Cambridge: Cambridge University Press, 2002.

43 See E. Karsh, *The Iran-Iraq War: 1980–88*, Oxford: Osprey, 2002, pp. 36–61.

44 Reuter, *My Life is a Weapon*, pp. 44–5. This description is reminscent of the classroom scenes in the film *All Quiet on the Western Front* (Lewis Milestone, 1930), where German teenagers are exhorted to join the army and volunteer to fight.

45 Ibid., p. 47.

46 J.A. Bill, 'Morale vs. Technology: The Power of Iran in the Persian Gulf War', in F. Rajaee (ed.), *The Iran–Iraq War*, p. 204.

47 See M. Ruthven, *Islam in the World*, 3rd edn, Oxford: Oxford University Press, 2006, p. 415.

48 Reuter, *My Life is a Weapon*, p. 44.

49 Cited by Reuter, *My Life is a Weapon*, p. 44.

50 M. Satrapi, *Persepolis*, London: Vintage Books, 2008 (2000), p. 99.

51 See Blankevoort, 'The Image of War', pp.100–101.

52 See Chelkowski and Dabashi, *Staging a Revolution*, p. 162, figure 9.32; and C.J. Gruber, 'The Message is on the Wall', pp. 15–46 (p. 43, n. 94). Gruber contrasts this 1980 'mater dolorosa' with a more hopeful 'mother and child' mural produced in 1997.

53 M. Moezzi, 'Iran's Red Tulip Revolution', 29 July 2009. Online. HTTP: <www. huffingtonpost.com/melody-moezzi/irans-red-tulip-revolutio_b_246949.html> (accessed 11 March 2011).

54 S. Balaghi, 'Iranian Visual Arts in the Century of Machinery', in S. Balaghi and L. Gumpel (eds), *Picturing Iran*, p. 32.

55 Blankevoort cites and translates *Ithar*, in 'The Image of War', p. 119, while *Yaqin* is used at: Online. HTTP: <http://www.lib.uchicago.edu/e/webexhibits/iranianposters/newkarbala.html> (accessed 17 November 2011), p. 118.

56 Translation by Miriam Shatanawi, curator at KIT (Koninklijk Instituut voor de Tropen), cited in Blankevoort, 'The image of war', p. 118.

57 See J. Davis, *Martyrs: Innocence, Vengeance, and Despair in the Middle East*, New York: Palgrave Macmillan, 2003, p. 49.

58 Compare the standing Father figure in Masaccio's *Trinity* (Santa Maria Novella, Florence, Fresco, 1425–8), with seated grieving Mary holding the body of Jesus in Michelangelo's *Pietà* (St Peter's Basilica, The Vatican, 1489–99).

59 Schubel, *Religious Performance in Contemporary Islam*, p. 13.

60 P.J. Chelkowski, 'Iconography of the Women of Karbala', in K. S. Aghaie (ed.), *The Women of Karbala: Ritual Performance and Symbolic Discourses in Modern Shi'i Islam*, Austin: University of Texas Press, 2005, pp. 134–5.

61 See U. Marzolph, 'The Martyr's Way to Paradise: Shiite Mural Art in the Urban Context', in R. and J. Bendix (eds), *Sleepers, Moles and Martyrs*, Copenhagen: Museum Tusculanum Press, 2004, p. 95.

62 Blankevoort, 'The Image of War', p. 119.

63 The implication here is that, as Jay Winter suggested, the 'experience of mass bereavement' was at the 'heart of the experience' of the First World War 'for millions', so heartbreak and bereavement was to be found during and after the Iran–Iraq war, though it was often expressed in different ways. See J. Winter, *Sites of Memory, Sites of Mourning: The Great War in European Cultural History*, Cambridge: Cambridge University Press, 1995, p. 224.

64 Cited in Reuter, *My Life is a Weapon*, p. 49.

65 See M. Halbwachs, *The Collective Memory*, trans. F. J. Ditter and V. Y. Ditter, New York: Harper Colophon, 1950 (1980).

66 Gruber, 'The Message is on the Wall', pp. 15–46 (p. 33, n. 66).

67 Ibid., p. 45.

68 P. Karimi, 'Imagining Warfare, Imaging Welfare: Tehran's post Iran–Iraq Murals and their Legacy', *Persica*, 2008, vol. 22, pp. 47–63 (61).

69 Ibid., p. 53.

70 H.E. Chehabi and F. Christia, 'The Art of State Persuasion: Iran's Post-Revolutionary Murals', *Persica*, 2008, vol. 22, pp. 1–13.

71 C. de Bellaigue, *In the Rose Garden of Martyrs: A Memoir of Iran*, New York: Harper Perennial, 2005. Over 23,000 men from the entire Isfahan province lost their lives during the conflict. Figure cited in R. Varzi's documentary (writer and producer), *Plastic Flowers Never Die*, Watertown, MA: Hapu Productions, 2008.

72 This part of the discussion develops and expands upon material first published in J. Mitchell, 'Contesting Martyrdom', in C. Deacy and E. Arweck (eds), *Exploring Religion and the Sacred in a Media Age*, Farnham, Surrey: Ashgate, 2009, pp. 73–7.

73 M. Ignatieff, 'Iranian Lessons', *New York Times Magazine*, 17 July 2005.

74 See K. Sites, 'All my Fathers, All My Sons', *Yahoo News*, 16 January 2006. Online. HTTP: <hotzone.yahoo.com/b/hotzone/blogs2234> (accessed 12 February 2009, not available now).

75 H. Barlow, *Dead for Good: Martyrdom and the Rise of the Suicide Bomber*, Boulder, CO: Paradigm Publishers, 2006.

76 'Martyr's Cemetery (Tehran, Iran)'. Online. HTTP: <www.dooyoo.co.uk/destinations-international/martyrs-cemetery-tehran-iran/1044805/> (accessed 14 March 2011). This review appears at another travel review site but with a different headline: 'A Peaceful Reminder of a Turbulent Past', a review by Koshka on Martyrs' Cemetery, Tehran, 18 January 2007. Online. HTTP: <travel.ciao.co.uk/Martyrs_Cemetery_Tehran – 6610012> (accessed 14 March 2011).

77 R. Fisk, 'Voices from the Martyrs' Cemetery', *Independent*, 27 February 2000.

78 R. Fisk, 'Traitors, Martyrs or Just Brave Men', *Independent*, 15 April 2006. Online. HTTP: <www.informationclearinghouse.info/article12756.htm> (accessed 14 March 2011).

79 F. Montaigne, 'Iran: Testing the Waters of Reform', *National Geographic*, July 1999.

80 Aghaie, *The Martyrs of Karbala*, p. 154.

81 See, for example, Varzi, *Warring Souls*, especially chapter 3. See, also, N. Pak-Shiraz, *Shi'i Islam in Iranian Cinema: Religion and Spirituality in Film*, London: I.B.Tauris, 2011, especially chapter 5.

82 Mitchell, 'Contesting martyrdom', in Deacy and Arweck (eds), *Exploring Religion and the Sacred in a Media Age*, pp. 73–7.

83 J. Riley-Smith, *The First Crusade and the Idea of Crusading*, Philadelphia: University of Philadelphia Press, 1986, p. 152. See also L. Baldwin Smith, *Fools, Martyrs, Traitors: The Story of Martyrdom in the Western World*, New York: Knopf, 1997.

84 E.B. Osborne (ed.), *The Muse in Arms*, London: Murray, 1917. This is one of nine poems from the 'In Memoriam' section. Online. HTTP: <www.firstworldwar.com/poetsandprose/mia_lastsalute.htm> (accessed 14 March 2011).

3 Cultivating violence

1 See, for example, African Rights, *Rwanda: Death Despair and Defiance*, 2nd edn, London: African Rights, 1995.

2 Estimates range from half a million to one million victims. See G. Prunier, 'How Many Were Killed?', in *The Rwanda Crisis: History of a Genocide*, London: Hurst and Company, 1997, pp. 259–65. Prunier makes a strong case for there being about 850,000 victims.

3 See R. Carver, 'Introduction', in L. Kirschke, *Broadcasting Genocide: Censorship, Propaganda & State-Sponsored Violence in Rwanda 1990–1994*, London: Article 19, 1996, p. 3.

4 See S. Cohen, *States of Denial: Knowing About Atrocities and Suffering*, Cambridge: Polity, 2001, p. 284; and P. Gourevitch, *We Wish to Inform You that Tomorrow We Will be Killed with Our Families: Stories from Rwanda*, New York: Farrar, Straus, Giroux, 1998.

5 R. Carver, 'Broadcasting & Political Transition', in R. Fardon and G. Furniss (eds), *African Broadcast Cultures: Radio in Transition*, Oxford: James Currey, 2000, p. 189. Carver cites Ed Broadbent a journalist writing in the *Gazette* (Montreal), 3 May 1994.

6 C. Kellow and H. Leslie Steeves, 'The Role of Radio in the Rwandan Genocide', *Journal of Communication*, 1998, vol. 48, no. 3, pp. 107–28 (124).

7 D. Li, 'Echoes of Violence', in N. Mills and K. Brunner (eds), *The New Killing Fields: Massacre and the Politics of Intervention*, New York: Basic Books, 2002, pp. 117–28 (118).

8 Ibid., p.128. Li's account is more nuanced in a later essay, D. Li, 'Echoes of Violence: Considerations on Radio and Genocide in Rwanda', *Journal of Genocide Research*, March 2004, vol. 6, no. 1, pp. 9–27. Reprinted in A. Thompson (ed.), *The Media and the Rwandan Genocide*, London: Pluto Press, 2007, pp. 90–109.

9 D. Yanagizawa, 'Propaganda and Conflict: Theory and Evidence from the Rwandan Genocide', IIES, Stockholm University, 2009. Online. HTTP: <people.su.se/~daya0852/Rwanda_jmp.pdf> (accessed 27 November 2011).

10 Carver, 'Broadcasting & Political Transition', in Fardon and Furniss (eds), *African Broadcast Cultures*, pp. 190–1.

11 S. Strauss, *The Order of Genocide: Race, Power, And War in Rwanda*, New York: Cornell University Press, 2006, p. 148.

12 See A. Sennitt (ed.), *Media Network Dossier, Hate Radio*, Hilversum: Radio Netherlands, 2004. For an analysis of hate media in the USA, especially radio, see R.L. Hilliard and M.C. Keith, *Waves of Rancor: Tuning in the Radical Right*, Armonk, NY: M.E. Sharp, 1999.

13 There are several different figures for non-literacy in Rwanda during the twentieth century. I have based mine upon the UN Human Development Reports that show how in 1990 the adult (15 years and above) literacy rate was 53.3 per cent and in 2001 had risen to 68 per cent of the population.

14 T. Gatwa, 'The Churches and Ethnic Ideology in the Rwandan Crisis (1900–1994)', unpublished thesis, University of Edinburgh, 1998, p. 167. See also a more recent book of the same title, T. Gatwa, *The Churches and Ethnic Ideology in the Rwandan Crisis (1900–1994)*, Milton Keynes: Regnum Books International, 2005.

15 MRND (Mouvement Révolutionnaire National pour le Développement (National Revolutionary Movement for Development)).

16 D. Temple-Raston, 'Journalism and Genocide', *Columbia Journalism Review*, September/October 2002, p. 18.

17 Alison Des Forges, historian and expert witness, cited in *The Prosecutor* v. *Ferdinand Nahimana, Jean-Bosco Barayagwiza, Hassan Ngeze (Judgement and Sentence)*, ICTR-99-52-T, International Criminal Tribunal for Rwanda (ICTR), 3 December 2003, p. 117, paragraph 342. Online. HTTP: <www.unhcr.org/refworld/docid/404468bc2. html> (accessed 20 March 2011).

18 François Xavier Nsanzuwera, who was Prosecutor in Kigali in 1994 and expert witness at ICTR, cited in *The Prosecutor* v. *Ferdinand Nahimana* et al., p. 117, paragraph 343.

19 See, for example, E. Broadbent, 'Media, Even in the West, is Partly to Blame for the Rwandan Massacres', *Gazette* (Montreal), 3 May 1995. Also cited by R. Carver in Kirschke, *Broadcasting Genocide*, p. 2.

20 Cited by R. Carver in Kirschke, *Broadcasting Genocide*, p. 5.

21 See, for example, M. McLuhan, *Understanding Media: The Extensions of Man*, London: Ark, 1987, pp. 297–307.

22 This resonates with the Hamitic hypothesis, which emphasised the idea that Tutsis came through Ethiopia on their way to Rwanda. For more details on the Hamitic hypothesis, see M. Mamdani, *When Victims Become Killers: Colonialism, Nativism and Genocide in Rwanda*, Princeton: Princeton University Press, 2002, pp. 34–5, 79–87, and P. Gourevitch, *We Wish to Inform You that Tomorrow We Will be Killed with Our Families*, New York: Farrar, Straus and Giroux, 1998, p. 50.

23 Kirschke, *Broadcasting Genocide*, pp. 38–40. Mugesera also employed this reference to the river Nyabarongo in a RTLM broadcast in Kinyarwanda between the period of September 1993–March 1994. Also cited in African Rights, *Rwanda: Death, Despair and Defiance*, p. 79.

24 Léon Mugesera, from a speech delivered on 22 November 1992, extracts of which were repeated on RTLM and Radio Rwanda.

25 A.L. Des Forges, *Leave None to Tell the Story: Genocide in Rwanda*, New York: Human Rights Watch, 1999, pp. 83–6.

26 Ibid., p. 72.

27 For 'The Hutu Ten Commandments' in full, see African Rights, *Rwanda: Death, Despair and Defiance*, pp. 42–3. See also a brief discussion in Kirschke, *Broadcasting Genocide*, p. 68.

28 For a clear discussion of the Ten Commandments, see *The Prosecutor* v. *Ferdinand Nahimana* et al., pp. 45–53, paragraphs 138–59.

29 Ibid., p. 148, paragraph 438.

30 Ibid., p. 47, paragraph 140.

31 Ibid., p. 47, paragraph 141.

32 Ibid., p. 48, paragraph 142.

33 *Kangura*, no. 3, January 1992.

34 See Des Forges, *Leave None to Tell the Story*, p. 245–6.

35 RTLM, 2 July 1994. Given the timing, the context and the speaker, it is not entirely unreasonable to interpret *Inkotayni* as being used synonymously here with the Tutsi people as a whole. For a slightly different interpretation see: *The Prosecutor* v. *Ferdinand Nahimana* et al., p. 137, paragraphs 403–4.

36 Prosecution Witness GO, a civil servant in the Ministry of Information whose job it was to monitor RTLM before 6 April 1994, cited in: *The Prosecutor* v. *Ferdinand Nahimana* et al., p. 117, paragraph 435.

37 J.M.V. Higiro, 'Distorsions et omissions dans l'ouvrage Rwanda, les médias du génocide', *Dialogue*, 190, 1996, p. 171, cited in Des Forges, *Leave None to Tell the Story*, p. 70.

38 See L. Hilsum, 'The Radio Station Whose Call Sign is Mass Murder', *Observer*, 15 May 1994, p. 19. She continues: 'Over the past five weeks it [RTML] has played a key part in inciting the massacres … '

39 F. Chalk, 'Radio Broadcasting in the Incitement of Interdiction of Gross Violations of Human Rights, Including Genocide', in R. Smith (ed.), *Genocide: Essays Toward Understanding, Early-Warning, and Prevention*, Williamsburg, VA: Association of Genocide Scholars, 1999, pp. 185–203. See also F. Chalk, 'Hate Radio in Rwanda', in H. Adelman and A. Suhrke (eds), *The Path of a Genocide: The Rwanda Crisis from Uganda to Zaire*, New Brunswick, NJ: Transaction Publishers, 1999, pp. 99–107.

40 Kinyarwanda is the universal Bantu language spoken by all groups in the population. The language is also known as Ikinyarwanda, Orunyarwanda, Urunyaruanda, Ruanda and Rwanda. There are a number of different dialects spoken.

41 Prosecution Witness BI, cited in *The Prosecutor* v. *Ferdinand Nahimana* et al., p. 117, paragraph 342.

42 The *Interahamwe* were linked with the MRND, while the *Impuzamugambi* were closely linked with the CDR.

43 Kirschke, *Broadcasting Genocide*, p. 84.

44 D. Li, 'Echoes of Violence', in A. Thompson (ed.), *The Media and the Rwanda Genocide*, London: Pluto Press, 2007, pp. 98–9.

45 Ibid., p. 124, paragraphs 364–5.

46 See P. Nzacahayo, 'Shared Life as God's People: An Exploration of Exclusion and Koinonia in Social Relations in Rwanda', unpublished thesis, University of Edinburgh, 2000.

47 For further details on the content of *Kangura* propaganda, see Des Forges, *Leave None to Tell the Story*, pp. 70–82; and African Rights, *Rwanda: Death, Despair and Defiance*, pp. 70–5. For details on the period which began with the disturbances or *muyaga* (strong but unpredictable wind) of 1959 to the day Rwanda became formally independent on 1 July 1962, see Prunier, *The Rwanda Crisis*, pp. 41–54.

48 Sebahinzi is a proper name which literally means the 'Father of the Cultivators'.

49 Des Forges, *Leave None to Tell the Story*, p. 77.

50 *The Prosecutor* v. *Simon Bikindi (Judgment)*, ICTR 2001-01-72-T, International Criminal Tribunal for Rwanda (ICTR), 2 December 2008, p. 3, paragraph 37. Online. HTTP: <www.unhcr.org/refworld/docid/493524762.html> (accessed 21 March 2011).

51 From a recording of RTLM broadcasts, 17–31 October 1993; and also cited in a slightly different form in Des Forges, *Leave None to Tell the Story*, p. 83.

52 Witness BI and Nsanzuwera, cited in *The Prosecutor* v. *Ferdinand Nahimana* et al., p. 117, paragraph 342–3, and p. 148, paragraph 440.

53 Witness BI cited in *The Prosecutor* v. *Ferdinand Nahimana* et al., p. 117, paragraph 342, and p. 150, paragraph 443. 'those who have the same goal'

54 This phrase was coined by François-Xavier Nsanzuwera, the former Prosecutor of Kigali, who asserted that to be named by *Kangura* could lead at the very least to losing your job or your freedom. *The Prosecutor* v. *Ferdinand Nahimana* et al., p. 77, paragraph 237.

55 For a discussion of this Kangura front cover, see ibid., pp. 53–8, paragraphs 160–73.

56 See F. Grünfeld and A. Huijboom, *The Failure to Prevent Genocide in Rwanda: The Role of Bystanders*, Leiden: Brill, 2007, pp.21–6. Note their identification (p. 24) of the figure on the *Kangura* (no. 26) front cover as a Hutu under-chief is incorrect, as the same image is identified as Kayibanda in a special edition of *Kangura* and also in *The Prosecutor* v. *Ferdinand Nahimana* et al., pp. 53–8.

57 Ibid., p. 56, paragraph 168.

58 See M. Mamdani, *When Victims Become Killers: Colonialism, Nativism, and the Genocide in Rwanda*, Princeton: Princeton University Press, 2001, p. 192; and L. Melvern, *Conspiracy to Murder: The Rwandan Genocide*. London: Verso, 2004, p. 27.

59 *The Prosecutor* v. *Ferdinand Nahimana* et al., p. 8, paragraph 187.

60 See C. Hamelink, *Media and Conflict: Escalating Evil*, Boulder, CO: Paradigm Publishers, 2011, pp. 54–5.

61 'A Cockroach Cannot Give Birth to a Butterfly', *Kangura*, February 1993, no. 40.

62 *The Prosecutor* v. *Ferdinand Nahimana* et al., pp. 59–60, paragraph 179.

63 Broadcast on 3 June and cited by Kirschke, *Broadcasting Genocide*, p. 113. See also, Prunier, *The Rwanda Crisis*, p. 402.

64 *The Prosecutor* v. *Ferdinand Nahimana* et al., p. 76, paragraph 235.

65 Ibid., pp. 39–40, paragraph 122.

66 Carver, 'Broadcasting & Political Transition', in Fardon and Furniss (eds), *African Broadcast Cultures*, p. 192.

67 *The Prosecutor* v. *Ferdinand Nahimana* et al., p. 316, paragraph 943.

68 Account from witness GO, who monitored RTLM almost every day from day of its creation to the end of the genocide. See *The Prosecutor* v. *Ferdinand Nahimana* et al., p. 147, paragraph 437.

69 Ibid., p. 150, paragraph 444.

70 Ibid.

71 Prunier, *The Rwanda Crisis*, p. 189.

72 For more detail on this and other aspects of the role of radio, and other media, in Rwanda, see A.Thompson (ed.), *The Media and the Rwanda Genocide*, London: Pluto Press, 2007, pp. 41–142.

73 Carver, 'Broadcasting & Political Transition', in Fardon and Furniss (eds), *African Broadcast Cultures*, p. 190.

74 S. Monasebain, 'The Pre-Genocide Case against RTLM', in Thompson (ed.), *The Media and the Rwanda Genocide*, p. 320.

75 Kirschke, *Broadcasting Genocide*, p. 115.

76 Ibid., p. 116, 118–19.

77 African Rights, *Rwanda: Death, Despair and Defiance*, p. 1003.

78 Ibid., p. 80.

79 H.L. Gulseth, 'The Use of Propaganda in the Rwandan Genocide: A Study of Radio-Télévision Libre des Mille Collines (RTLM)', unpublished thesis, University of Oslo, 2004, p. 98.

80 Witness GO, cited in *The Prosecutor* v. *Ferdinand Nahimana* et al., p. 147, paragraph 437.
81 C. Mironko, 'The Effect of RTLM's Rhetoric of Ethnic Hatred in Rural Rwanda', in A. Thompson (ed.), *The Media and the Rwanda Genocide*, London: Pluto, 2007, pp. 125–35 (133).
82 See *Panorama, Valentina's Story*, 10 February 1997. Online. HTTP: <news.bbc.co.uk/hi/english/static/audio_video/programmes/panorama/transcripts/transcript_10_02_97.txt> See also Chapter 4.
83 Kirschke, *Broadcasting Genocide*, p. 121.
84 Ibid., p. 127.
85 *The Prosecutor* v. *Ferdinand Nahimana* et al., p. 152, paragraph 449.
86 *The Prosecutor* v. *Ferdinand Nahimana* et al., p. 139, paragraph 410.
87 Physicians for Human Rights, *Rwanda 1994: A Report of the Genocide*, Dundee, Scotland: The Royal Infirmary, 1994, p. 22.
88 Kirschke, *Broadcasting Genocide*, pp. 130–1. For the role of RTLM on the attack of the Islamic Cultural Centre, see *The Prosecutor* v. *Ferdinand Nahimana* et al., p. 152, paragraph 450.
89 African Rights, *Rwanda: Death, Despair and Defiance*, pp. 250–2. See also 'Hopeless, Helpless, Horror beyond Belief ... There is Nothing the West Can Do, Says Annabel Heseltine, after Witnessing the Rwanda bloodbath', *Sunday Times*, 8 May 1994; also cites J. Mulaa, 'Decades of Hatred and Bloodletting', *Sunday Nation* (Kenya), 10 April 1994.
90 See, for example, the leading articles in the *Independent*, 11 April 1994, and the *New York Times*, 12 April 1994. Both are also briefly cited in African Rights, *Rwanda: Death, Despair and Defiance*, p. 253.
91 African Rights, *Rwanda: Death, Despair and Defiance*, p. 252.
92 *Le Monde*, 27 May 1994; also cited in Prunier, *The Rwanda Crisis*, p. 277.
93 See J. Eldridge (ed.), *Getting the Message: News, Truth and Power*, London: Routledge, 1993.
94 Radio Rwanda, 25 April 1994, cited in *The Prosecutor* v. *Ferdinand Nahimana* et al., p. 184, paragraph 539, and discussed on p. 321, paragraph 966.
95 *The Prosecutor* v. *Ferdinand Nahimana* et al., p. 164, paragraph 482.
96 J.F. Metzl, 'Rwandan Genocide and the International Law of Radio Jamming', *American Journal of International Law*, 1997, vol. 91, pp. 628–51.
97 Kirschke, *Broadcasting Genocide*, p. 166.
98 See E. Staub, *The Roots of Evil: The Origins of Genocide and Other Group Violence*, Cambridge: Cambridge University Press, 1989, p. 18. Through the book Staub identifies a number of common roots to the Holocaust, the Armenian and Cambodian genocides and the disappearances in Argentina.
99 Carver, 'Broadcasting & Political Transition', in Fardon and Furniss (eds), *African Broadcast Cultures*, p. 192.
100 African Rights, *Rwanda: Death, Despair and Defiance*, p. 85.
101 Des Forges, *Leave None to Tell the Story*, p. 770.
102 S.A. Lowery and M.L. DeFleur, *Milestones in Mass Communication Research: Media Effects*, 3rd edn, White Plains, NY: Longman, 1995, pp. 45–67.
103 C.L. Kellow and H.L. Steeves, 'The Role of Radio in the Rwandan Genocide', *Journal of Communication*, 1998, vol. 48, no. 3, pp. 107–28.
104 See H. Cantril, *The Invasion from Mars: A Study in the Psychology of Panic*, Princeton: Princeton University Press, 1940.
105 *The Prosecutor* v. *Ferdinand Nahimana* et al., p. 164, paragraph 482. For summaries and transcripts of RTLM broadcasts (in Kinyarwanda, French and English), see both the ICTR site and 'Rwanda Genocide'. Online. HTTP: <surplusknowledge.com/index.php?option=com_content&view=article&id=53&Itemid=60> (accessed 1 December 2011).

106 Ibid., p. 359, paragraph 1099.
107 Ibid., p. 351, paragraph 1073.
108 In 2007 the appeals chamber of the ICTR upheld and reversed some of Ngeze's convictions. His sentence was changed to thirty-five years.
109 See R.L. Bytwerk, *Julius Streicher*, 2nd edn, New York: Cooper Square, 2001. See also *The Prosecutor* v. *Ferdinand Nahimana* et al., p. 335, paragraph 1007; pp. 351–2, paragraphs 1073 and 1075.
110 M. Alexis and I. Mpambara, *IMS Assessment Mission Report: The Rwanda Media Experience from the Genocide*, Copenhagen: International Media Support, 2003.
111 *The Prosecutor v. Ferdinand Nahimana* et al., p. 194, paragraph 569.
112 Ibid., pp. 194–210, paragraphs 571–619.
113 See Kigali Memorial Centre. Online. HTTP: <www.kigalimemorialcentre.org/old/centre/gardens/worldmap.html> (accessed 27 November 2011).
114 See also A. Thompson (ed.), *The Media and the Rwanda Genocide*, London: Pluto, 2007, pp.137–237.
115 Aegis Trust, *Jenoside*, Kigali: Kigali Memorial Centre, 2004, p. 24.

Part I Conclusions

1 See the conclusion of this book for a broader discussion of this phrase from Joel 3.10 and its antithesis from Isaiah 2.4.
2 See R. Girard, *Violence and the Sacred*, trans. Patrick Gregory, Baltimore: Johns Hopkins University Press, 1977, pp. 14–15. See also J. Mitchell, *Media Violence and Christian Ethics*, Cambridge: Cambridge University Press, 2007, especially chapter 5.
3 See M. Volf, *The End of Memory: Remembering Rightly in a Violent World*, Grand Rapids: Wm. B. Eerdmans, 2006.
4 See Walter Wink. *Engaging the Powers: Discernment and Resistance in a World of Domination*, Minneapolis: Fortress Press, 1992, and *The Powers that Be: Theology for a New Millennium*, New York: Doubleday, 1998.
5 Ibid. Wink claims that the 'myth of redemptive violence' can contribute to the 'maintenance of international conflict', p. 25.

4 Bearing witness through film

1 It has since been renamed as the *École Technique de Kicukiro*.
2 See, *Left to Die at ETO and Nyanza: The Stories of Rwandese Civilians Abandoned by UN Troops on 11 April* (1994), African Rights, 2001. For extracts, see *Pambazuka News*. Online. HTTP: <www.pambazuka.org/en/category/conflict/7119> (accessed 7 December 2011).
3 A. Richards and J. Mitchell, 'Journalists as Witnesses to Violence and Suffering', in R. Fortner and M. Silk (eds), *Global Communication Ethics*, vol 2, *Practices and Case Studies*, Oxford: Blackwell, 2011, pp. 752–73. See also the discussion of 'Witness' in J. Mitchell, *Media Violence and Christian Ethics*, Cambridge: Cambridge University Press, 2007, pp. 282–90.
4 J. Peters, 'Witnessing', in *Media, Culture and Society*, 2001, vol. 23, no. 6, pp. 707–24 (708–9, 717).
5 J. Mitchell, 'Searching for Peace in Films about Genocide', in G. Watkins (ed.), *Teaching Film and Religion*, Oxford: Oxford University Press, 2008, pp. 283–94. Parts of my discussion of *Shooting Dogs* are drawn and adapted from this earlier analysis.
6 For exceptions, see R. Bromley, 'After such knowledge, what forgiveness?: cultural representations of reconciliation in Rwanda', *French Cultural Studies*, 2009, vol. 20, pp. 181–97.

7 See, for example, A. Insdorf, *Indelible Shadows: Film and the Holocaust*, 3rd edn, Cambridge: Cambridge University Press, 2003.

8 B. Zelizer, *Remembering to Forget: Holocaust Memory through the Camera's Eye*, Chicago: University of Chicago, 1997, p. 227.

9 T.W. Adorno, *Can One Live after Auschwitz? A Philosophical Reader*, ed. R. Tiedemann, Stanford: Stanford University Press, 2003, p. 34. See, for example, M. Cooke, 'The Ethics of Post-Holocaust Art: Reflections on Redemption and Representation', *German Life and Letters*, April 2006, vol. 59, no. 2, pp. 266–79.

10 T.W. Adorno, *Negative Dialectics*, New York: Continuum, 1973, p. 362.

11 A. Huyssen, 'Of mice and mimesis: reading Spiegelman with Adorno', *New German Critique*, Autumn 2000, no. 81, pp. 65–82 (65).

12 T. Cole, *Selling the Holocaust: From Auschwitz to Schindler, How History is Bought, Packaged and Sold*, New York: Routledge, 1999, p. 3.

13 Ibid., p. 18.

14 M. Janovich, 'Shadows and Bogeyman: Horror, Stylization and the Critical Reception of Orson Welles during the 1940s', *Participations: Journal of Audience and Reception Studies*, May 2009, vol. 6, no. 1, pp. 25–51 (37). Cites Crowther's *New York Times* review below.

15 B. Crowther, 'The Screen: *The Stranger*, with Edward G. Robinson, Loretta Young and Orson Welles, of Palace', *New York Times*, 11 July 1946, p. 18.

16 See S. Felman, 'Film as Witness: Claude Lanzmann's *Shoah*', in G. Hartman (ed.), *Holocaust Remembrance: The Shapes of Memory*, Oxford: Blackwell, 1994. See also C. Lanzmann, *Shoah: The Complete Text of the Acclaimed Holocaust Film by Claude Lanzmann*, New York: De Capo Press, 1995.

17 Insdorf, *Indelible Shadows*, p. 238.

18 Ibid., p. 240.

19 Ibid., p. 245.

20 See Y. Loshitzky, 'Holocaust Others: Spielberg's *Schindler's List* versus Lanzman's *Shoah*', in Y. Loshitzky (ed.), *Spielberg's Holocaust: Critical Perspectives on* Schindler's List, Bloomington: Indiana University Press, 1997.

21 J. McBride, *Steven Spielberg*, London: Faber and Faber, 1997, pp. 414–16.

22 L.D. Friedman and B. Notbohm (eds) *Stephen Spielberg: Interviews*, Jackson: University Press of Mississippi, 2000, p. 158.

23 Cole, *Selling the Holocaust*, p. 80.

24 Insdorf, *Indelible Shadows*, p. 259.

25 S. Schiff, 'Seriously Spielberg', in L.D. Friedman and B. Notbohm (eds) *Stephen Spielberg: Interviews*, Jackson: University Press of Mississippi, 2000, p. 176.

26 For an extensive annotated list of films and documentaries, see the videography prepared by William Schulman et al. at the website *A Teacher's Guide to the Holocaust*. Online. HTTP: <fcit.usf.edu/holocaust/resource/films.htm> (accessed 26 March 2011).

27 See 'Cambodian Genocide Program', *Yale University, Genocide Studies Program*, 2010. Online. HTTP: <www.yale.edu/cgp/> (accessed 26 March 2011).

28 Socheata Poeuv has now established *Khmer Legacies*, 'a project in which children interview their parents about surviving the Cambodian genocide and which she hopes will result in 10,000 videotaped testimonials'. Online. HTTP: <www.khmer-legacies.org/> (accessed 26 March 2011). See also her profile at 'Faces of Entrepreneurship', *New York Times*. Online. HTTP: <www.nytimes.com/slideshow/2008/03/09/magazine/0309-FACES_5.html> (accessed 26 March 2011).

29 S. Holden, '"Enemies of the People": One Man's Quest for Truth about Cambodia's "Killing Fields"', *New York Times*, 20 January 2011.

30 See L. Torchin, 'Since We Forgot: Remembrance and Recognition of the Armenian Genocide in Virtual Archives', in R. Hallas and F. Guerin (eds), *The Image and the*

Witness: Trauma, Memory and Visual Culture, London: Wallflower Press, 2007, pp. 82–97. See also G. Lewy, *The Armenian Massacres in Ottoman Turkey: A Disputed Genocide*, Salt Lake City: University of Utah Press, 2005; and D. Bloxham, *The Great Game of Genocide: Imperialism, Nationalism, and the Destruction of the Ottoman Armenians*, Oxford: Oxford University Press, 2005.

31 A. Slide (ed.) *Ravished Armenia and the Story of Aurora Mardiganian*, Lanham, MD and London: Scarecrow Press, 1997.

32 See L. Torchin, 'Ravished Armenia: Visual Media, Humanitarian Advocacy, and the Formation of Witnessing Publics', *American Anthropologist*, March 2006, no. 108, pp. 214–20.

33 See F. and M.A. Brussat, '*Ararat*: Film Review', *Spirituality and Practice: Resources for Spiritual Journeys*. Online. HTTP: <www.spiritualityandpractice.com/films/films.php?id=5342> (accessed 26 March 2011).

34 See, for example, G. Convents, *Images et Paix. Les Rwandais et les Burundais face au cinéma et à l'audiovisuel. Une Histoire politico–culturelle du Rwanda–Burundi allemand et belge et des Républiques du Rwanda et du Burundi (1896–2008)*, Leuven: Signis, 2008.

35 M. Hron, '*Kumaramaza*? Representing the Rwandan Killer', paper presented at the 6th Global Conference on 'Probing the Boundaries', 3 May 2007. Online. HTTP: <www.inter-disciplinary.net/ptb/hhv/vcce/vcce1/hron%20paper.pdf> (accessed 1 March 2011). See also M. Hron, 'Interview with Film Producer Eric Kabera', from 'Symposium: Post-Genocide Rwanda', in the special edition of *Peace Review: A Journal of Social Justice*, 2009, vol. 21, no. 3, pp. 359–62.

36 E. Wiesel, *Night*, New York: Hill & Wang, 1960 [1958], p. 32.

37 Geoff Andrew, '*Shooting Dogs* review', *Time Out London*, no. 1858, 2006, 29 March–5 April.

38 This statement resonates with the German theologian Jurgen Moltmann's approach in *The Crucified God*, London: SCM, 1974 (1972). Moltmann goes further, however, than the script of *Shooting Dogs* with the claim that God is 'hanging there on the gallows' with a youth in Auschwitz, pp. 273–4.

39 See, for example, P.A. Cieplak, 'The Rwandan Genocide and the Bestiality of Representation in *100 Days* (2001) and *Shooting Dogs* (2005)', *Journal of African Cinemas*, July 2010, vol. 2, no. 1, pp. 49–63.

40 K. Honeycutt, '*Beyond the Gates:* Bottom Line: Saga of the Genocide in Rwanda takes the Tired Point of View of White Westerners'. Originally Online. HTTP: <http://www.hollywoodreporter.com/hr/film/reviews/article_display.jsp?&rid=8883> (No longer available).

41 See Online. HTTP: <http://uk.rottentomatoes.com/m/beyond_the_gates/> (Accessed 1 August 2011).

42 C. Petrie, 'The Failure to Confront Evil – A Collective Responsibility', in Carol Rittner, J.K. Roth and W. Whitworth (eds), *Genocide in Rwanda: Complicity of the Churches?* St Paul, MN: Paragon House, 2004, pp. 87–8.

43 Ritnner et al. *Genocide in Rwanda*.

44 I have found this through using this film over the last five years in undergraduate classes on *Film, Religion and Ethics* and graduate classes on *Film and Religion*.

45 Mitchell, 'Searching for peace in films about genocide', in G. Watkins (ed.) *Teaching Film and Religion*, pp. 283–94.

46 Alice O'Keefe, 'Anger at BBC Genocide Film', *Observer*, 19 March 2006. See also Linda Melvern, 'History? This Film is Fiction', *Observer*, 19 March 2006.

47 See *MSN Movie News*, 'Hurt says Genocide Film a Wake-Up'. Online. HTTP: <http://movies.msn.com/movies/article.aspx?news=219603> (no longer available).

48 See B. Nichols, *Representing Reality: Issues and Concepts in Documentary*, Bloomington: Indiana University Press, 1991; and his more recent *Introduction to Documentary*,

Bloomington: Indiana University Press, 2001. He describes six modes: Poetic, Expository, Observational, Interactive, Reflexive, and Performative. For a critical account of his approach, see S. Bruzzi, *New Documentary: A Critical Introduction*, London: Routledge, 2000.

49 See, *Panorama*, Rwanda Programmes, *BBC News*, 2 April 2004. Online. HTTP: <news.bbc.co.uk/1/hi/programmes/panorama/3585473.stm> (accessed 26 March 2011).

50 F. Keane, *Season of Blood: A Rwandan Journey*, London: Penguin, 1996 (1995), pp. 73–93.

51 J. Pottier, *Re-imagining Rwanda: Conflict, Survival and Disinformation in the late Twentieth Century*, Cambridge: Cambridge University Press, 2002, pp. 64–6.

52 See, for example, Robert Genoud's film *La France au Rwanda: une neutralité coupable*, Etat d'Urgence Production, Les Films du Village, Télévision Création Citoyenne, 1999.

53 S. Davies, 'Fergal Keane: Trying to Change the World, One TV Screen at a Time', *Telegraph*, 19 June 2009. Online. HTTP: <www.telegraph.co.uk/culture/tvandradio/5575881/Fergal-Keane-Trying-to-change-the-world-one-TV-screen-at-a-time.html> (accessed 26 March 2011).

54 For full transcript of the programme, see *BBC Panorama*. Online. HTTP: <news.bbc.co.uk/hi/english/static/audio_video/programmes/panorama/transcripts/transcript_10_02_97.txt> (accessed 26 March 2011).

55 F. Keane, 'The Rwandan Girl who Refused to Die', *Sunday Times*, 1997, reprinted at *Frontline*. Online. HTTP: <www.pbs.org/wgbh/pages/frontline/shows/rwanda/reports/refuse.html> (26 March 2011).

56 M. MacDonald, 'Rethinking Personalisation in Current Affairs Journalism', in C. Sparks and J. Tulloch (eds), *Tabloid Tales: Global Debates over Media Standards*, Lanham, MD: Rowman and Littlefield, 2000, p. 262.

57 Cited in L. Beattie, E. Miller, D. Miller and G. Philo, 'The Media and Africa: Images of Disaster and Rebellion', in G. Philo (ed.), *Message Received*, London: Longman, 1999.

58 Ibid., p. 262.

59 See *Panorama*, Rwanda Programmes, *BBC News*, 2 April 2004. Online. HTTP: <news.bbc.co.uk/1/hi/programmes/panorama/3585473.stm> (accessed 26 March 2011).

60 See also *Kigali: images contre massacre* (Jean-Christophe Klotz, France, 2005); *Rwanda Rwanda, une justice prise en otage* (Pierre Hazan and Gonzalo Arijon, France/Switzerland, 2003); *Rwanda, un cri d'un silence inouï* (Anne Laine, France, 2003); *Rwanda, let mots des âmes* (Andrea Canetta, Switzerland, 2001); and *Soleil dans la nuit* (Marc Renaud, Canada, 1995).

61 See *Rwanda: In Search of Hope*. Online: HTTP: <www.whitepinepictures.com/sales/shop/dvd-rwanda-in-search-of-hope/> (accessed 26 March 2011).

62 See C. Rittner, J.K. Roth and W. Whitworth (eds), *Genocide in Rwanda: Complicity of the Churches?* St Paul, MN: Paragon House, 2004.

63 'Rwanda/Genocide – Kibuye Town Remembers its Dead', *Hirondelle News Agency, Foundation Hirondelle*, 20 April 2005. Online. HTTP: <www.hirondellenews.com/content/view/2354/26/> (accessed 26 March 2011).

64 C. McGreal, 'Rwanda – 10 Years on: "It's so Difficult to Live with What We Know"', *Guardian*, 29 March 2004. Online. HTTP: <www.guardian.co.uk/world/2004/mar/29/rwanda.chrismcgreal> (accessed 26 March 2011).

65 'Rwanda: History of a Genocide', *Filmmakers Library*. Online. HTTP: <www.filmakers.com/index.php?a=filmDetail& filmID = 768> (accessed 26 March 2011).

66 'Transcript: "Ghosts of Rwanda"', *Frontline*, 9 April 2004. Online. HTTP: <www.pbs.org/wgbh/pages/frontline/shows/ghosts/etc/script.html> (accessed 26 March 2011). Note how the transcript conflates two lines of this prayer.

67 Ibid.

68 *Panorama: Killers*, text of manuscript is reproduced Online. HTTP: <news.bbc.co.uk/ nol/shared/spl/hi/programmes/panorama/transcripts/killers.txt> (accessed 26 March 2011).

69 *Panorama: Killers*, ibid.

70 Cited in Toronto film festival description, '*The Last Just Man*', *Human Rights Watch*, 30 April 2002. Online. HTTP: <www.hrw.org/legacy/iff/2002/ny/last-review. html> (accessed 26 March 2011).

71 R. Dallaire and B.Beardsley, *Shake Hands with the Devil: The Failure of Humanity in Rwanda*, New York: Carroll and Graf, 2005 (2003), p. xxv.

72 'Rwanda: Genocide on Trial – Arusha Video Project'. Online. HTTP: <www.gppac. net/documents/Media_book_nieuw/p2_11_rwanda.htm> (accessed 26 March 2011).

73 Hirondelle News Agency, 'ICTR/Documentary – *From Arusha to Arusha*, First Documentary on the ICTR', 17 December 2009. Online. HTTP: <www.hirondellenews. com/content/view/13089/1188/>(accessed 1 August 2011).

74 'Rwanda Gacaca: A Question of Justice', *Amnesty International*, 17 December 2002. Online. HTTP: <www.amnesty.org/en/library/info/AFR47/007/2002> (accessed 26 March 2011).

75 See P. Clark, *The Gacaca Courts, Post-Genocide Justice and Reconciliation in Rwanda: Justice without Lawyers*, Cambridge: Cambridge University Press, 2010.

76 Aghion interviewed at S. Macaulay, 'Cannes: My Neighbor, My Killers Anne Aghion', *Filmmaker*, 17 May 2009. Online. HTTP: <www.filmmakermagazine.com/ news/2009/05/cannes-my-neighbor-my-killers-anne-aghion/> (accessed 26 March 2011).

77 J. Catsoulis, 'Movie Review: My Neighbor, My Killer (2009), Side by Side, With the Guilty, After Courts Send Them Home', *New York Times*, 12 January 2010. Online. HTTP: <movies.nytimes.com/2010/01/12/movies/12neighbor.html> (accessed 26 March 2011).

78 J. Merin, '*My Neighbor My Killer* – Movie Review – 2009, Rwanda Moves Towards Reconciliation', *About.com Guide*. Online. HTTP: <documentaries.about.com//od/ revie2/fr/myneighbormykil.htm> (accessed 26 March 2011).

79 D. Levit, 'Love Thy Neighbour', *Reel Talk Movie Reviews*. Online. HTTP: <www. reeltalkreviews.com/browse/viewitem.asp?type=review&id=3028> (accessed 26 March 2011).

80 E. Stover and H.M. Weinstein (eds), *My Neighbour, My Enemy: Justice and Community in the Aftermath of Mass Atrocity*, Cambridge: Cambridge University Press, 2004, p. 82, and especially chapters 2 and 3.

81 Ibid., p. 81.

82 *In the Tall Grass*. Online. HTTP: <www.inthetallgrass.com> (accessed 26 March 2011).

83 See S.M. Thomson, *Resisting Reconciliation: State Power and Everyday Life in Post-Genocide Rwanda*. Dalhouise University, Unpublished PhD thesis, 2009.

84 See *In the Tall Grass*. Online. HTTP: < www.torgovnik.com/projects/intended-con sequences> (accessed 26 March 2011).

85 See D. Fisher and J. Mitchell, 'Portraying Forgiveness through Documentary Film', *Studies in World Christianity*, (2012, forthcoming).

86 Thomas Sommer, producer, *Rwanda: Living Forgiveness*, personal email to author, 24 March 2011.

87 See, for example, P.A. Cantrell, 'The Anglican Church of Rwanda: Domestic Agendas and International Linkages', *Journal of Modern African Studies*, 2007, vol. 45, pp. 333–54. See also Pottier, *Re-imagining Rwanda*.

88 Thomas Sommer, *Rwanda: Living Forgiveness*, personal email, 24 March 2011.

89 See 'Customer Reviews' for *Rwanda: Living Forgiveness* on Amazon.com. Online. HTTP: <www.amazon.com/Rwanda-Living-Forgiveness/dp/B000CR5EES> (accessed 26 March 2011).

90 A.C. Wu, '*As We Forgive*: An Interview with Laura Waters Hinson', *Cardus*, 28 March 2008. Online. HTTP: <www.cardus.ca/comment/article/26/> (accessed 26 March 2011).

91 *As We Forgive*. Online. HTTP: <www.asweforgivemovie.com/> (accessed 26 March 2011).

92 '*Flowers of Rwanda: Making Peace with Genocide*', *Films on Demand*. Online. HTTP: <films.com/PreviewClip.aspx?id=16569> (accessed 26 March 2011).

93 Piotr A. Cieplak, 'Image and Memory: An Interview with Eric Kabera', *French Cultural Studies*, May 2009, vol. 20, no. 2, pp. 199–208 (202).

94 See, for example, *Rwanda Again* (2009), directed by Lawrence Blankenbyl for Swiss television, which attemps to tell a series of stories about 'survival and remembrance as a means for healing the wounds of Genocide'. Online. HTTP: <fabrica.it/project/rwanda-again-trailer> (accessed 21 November 2011).

95 Cieplak, 'Image and Memory, p. 202.

96 Ibid., p. 205.

97 Ibid., p. 201.

98 Bromley, 'After Such Knowledge, What Forgiveness? Cultural Representations of Reconciliation in Rwanda', p. 190; and cites H. Härting, 'Global Humanitarianism, Race, and the Spectacle of the African Corpse in Current Western Representations of the Rwandan Genocide', *Comparative Studies of South Asia, Africa and the Middle East*, 2008, vol. 28, no. 1, pp. 61–77 (61).

99 E. Kabera (dir.), *Keepers of Memory: Survivors' Accounts of the Rwandan Genocide* (2005).

100 E. Kabera, *Keepers of Memory* (2005).

101 A. d'Arcy Hughes, 'Rwandans Flock to "Hillywood" films', *BBC News*, 5 April 2007. Online. HTTP: <news.bbc.co.uk/1/hi/world/africa/6530227.stm> (accessed 26 March 2011); A. Dauge-Roth, 'The Pertinence of Impertinent Storytelling in Gilbert Ndahayo's Documentary *Rwanda: Beyond the Deadly Pit*', *Contemporary French and Francophone Studies*, 2010, vol. 14, no. 4, pp. 455–60; M. Broderick, 'Mediating Genocide: Producing Digital Survivor Testimony in Rwanda', in B. Sarkar and J. Walker (eds), *Documentary Testimonies: Global Archives of Suffering*, New York: Routledge, 2010, pp. 215–44.

102 'Gilbert Nadahyo on Rwandan Genocide', *YouTube*, 22 April 2009. Online. HTTP: <www.youtube.com/watch?v=viJhHpQjIhg> (accessed 26 March 2011).

103 'From Hillywood to Hollywood: One Rwandan Makes his Major Motion Picture Dreams Come True', *Sunday Times* (Rwanda), reprinted on *Zimbio*, 20 February 2008. Online. HTTP: <www.zimbio.com/member/sandalchild/articles/963482/ HILLYWOOD+HOLLYWOOD+One+Rwandan+Makes+Major> (accessed 26 March 2011).

104 *Africa is a Country*. Online. HTTP: <africasacountry.com/2009/12/31/film-daddy-ruhorahoza/> (accessed 26 March 2011).

105 Cieplak, 'The Rwandan Genocide and the Bestiality of Representation in *100 Days* (2001) and *Shooting Dogs* (2005)', pp. 49–63.

106 This image is also to be found on the additional materials of the DVD of M. Caton-Jones (dir.), *Shooting Dogs*, BBC Films, 2005.

107 For a detailed filmography, see Convents, *Images et Paix* and the filmography below.

108 C. Weingarten (dir.), *Film: Raindrops over Rwanda*. Online. HTTP: <explore.org/videos/player/raindrops-over-rwanda> (accessed 1 August 2011).

109 J. Rabasa, *Without History: Subaltern Studies The Zapatista Insurgency, and the Specter of History*, Pittsburgh: University of Pittsburgh Press, 2010, pp. 234, 237.

110 M. Menossi, 'Le Papillon face à la flamme: interview de Jean-Christophe Klotz', *Evene.fr*, November 2006. Online. HTTP: <www.evene.fr/cinema/actualite/inter-view-klotz-rwanda-kigali-images-massacre-kouchner-559.php> (accessed 26 March 2011).

111 D. Scranton, *Earth Made of Glass*. Online. HTTP: <www.hbo.com/documentaries/earth-made-of-glass/synopsis.html> (accessed 1 August 2011).

112 E. King, 'Memory Controversies in Post-Genocide Rwanda: Implications for Peacebuilding', *Genocide Studies and Prevention* – vol. 5, no. 3, winter 2010, pp. 293–309. King argues that the Rwandan RPF government, through official memorials and education, highlights some aspects of history and suppresses others to the detriment of building peace.

113 See within annotated bibliographies at United States Holocaust Memorial Museum. Online. HTTP: <www.ushmm.org/research/library/bibliography/?lang=en&content=rwanda> (accessed 1 August 2011).

114 See E. Staub, *The Roots of Evil: The Origins of Genocide and Other Group Violence*, Cambridge: Cambridge University Press, 1989; and his more recent work on healing and reconciliation in Rwanda: E. Staub, L.A. Pearlman, A. Gubin and A. Hagengimana, 'Healing, Reconciliation, Forgiving and the Prevention of Violence after Genocide or Mass Killing: An Intervention and its Experimental Evaluation in Rwanda', *Journal of Social and Clinical Psychology*, 2005, vol. 24, no. 3, pp. 297–334.

115 'Exploring Rwanda and Darfur', *NewsHour with Jim Lehrer*, PBS, 12 April 2006. Online. HTTP: <www.pbs.org/newshour/bb/africa/jan-june06/darfur_4–12.html> (accessed 26 March 2011).

5 Searching for truth and reconciliation

1 The 1953 Bantu Education Act aimed to separate races at all stages of the education process, ensuring that the non-white or black youth had minimal education which would result in them labouring in unskilled jobs. During the 1970s white children had ten times more money spent on them by the government than those of other races.

2 The 1974 Afrikaans Medium Decree aimed to ensure that all black children would be taught in school in Afrikaans and English on an equal basis. It was deeply unpopular to use Afrikaans, the 'language of the oppressor' (Tutu), in schools.

3 Modise Pheknonyane, filmed and recorded live by the author on Robben Island, 8 October 2008.

4 Recorded live by J. Mitchell, Robben Island, 8 October 2008.

5 M. Pheknonyane, *My Freedom, My Passion*, Eagan, MN: Kairos Publishing, 2004.

6 See, for example, C.M. Rothstein, 'Overcoming Apartheid Policies Yesterday and Today: An Interview with a Former Bantu Education Student and Present-Day Activist', *Global Perspectives on Human Language: The South African Context, Leland Stanford Junior University*, 19 September 2004. Online. HTTP: <www.stanford.edu/~jbaugh/saw/Chloe_Bantu_Education.html> (accessed 11 April 2011). This was also seen: Online. HTTP: <voice.unimelb.edu.au/news/6031/> (accessed 24 May 2010) (no longer available).

7 'Keys to Mandela's Cell', *South Africa Trip*, 6 February 2007. Online. HTTP: <blogs.messiah.edu/southafrica/> (accessed 11 April 2011).

8 N. Mandela, *Long Walk to Freedom: The Autobiography of Nelson Mandela*, New York: Back Bay Books, 1995 (1994), p. 387.

9 See, for example, J. Maingard, *South African National Cinema*, Abingdon, Oxon: Routledge, 2007; L. Saks, *Cinema in a Democratic South Africa*, Bloomington: Indiana University Press, 2010; and K. Tomaselli, *Encountering Modernity: Twentieth Century South African Cinemas*, Amsterdam: Rozenberg Publishers, 2006.

10 See, for example, P. Louw, *The Rise, Fall and Legacy of Apartheid*, Westport, CT: Praeger, 2004; and N. Clark and W. Worger, *South Africa: the Rise and Fall of Apartheid*, Harlow, UK: Pearson, 2004.

11 See, for example, W. Beinart, *Twentieth-Century South Africa*, 2nd edn, Oxford: Oxford University Press, 2001 (1994), p.128.

12 M. Botha, '110 Years of South African Cinema (Part 1)', *Kinema*, Fall 2006. Online. HTTP: <www.kinema.uwaterloo.ca/article.php?id=46&feature> (accessed 11 April 2011).

13 A. Paton, *Cry, the Beloved Country*, London: Vintage, 2002, p. 155.

14 Ibid., p. 156.

15 S. Holden, 'Movie review: *Cry the Beloved Country* (1995)', *New York Times*, 15 December 1995. Online. HTTP: <movies.nytimes.com/movie/review?res=9806E0DD17 39F936A25751C1A963958260& scp = 1& sq = stephen%20holden%20cry%20the %20beloved%20country& st = cse> (accessed 11 April 2011).

16 V. Canby, 'Movie Review: *Lost in the Stars*', *New York Times*, 7 May 1974. Online. HTTP: <movies.nytimes.com/movie/100217/Lost-in-the-Stars/> (accessed 11 April 2011).

17 See Paton, *Cry, the Beloved Country*, p. 67.

18 Ibid., pp. 71–2.

19 Ibid., p.129.

20 Ibid., p.235.

21 This is direct quote from Paton's *Cry, The Beloved Country*, p.57. Paton is himself quoting from Psalm 23 verse 4, the Kings James Version of the Bible.

22 From Paton's *Cry, The Beloved Country*, p.236.

23 R. Ebert, 'Movie Review: *Cry, The Beloved Country*', *rogerebert.com*, 20 December 1995. Online. HTTP: <rogerebert.suntimes.com/apps/pbcs.dll/article?AID=/19951220/ REVIEWS/512200301/1023> (accessed 11 April 2011).

24 Maingard, *South African National Cinema*, pp. 108, 115.

25 K. Thomas, 'Movie Review: *Cry, the Beloved Country*', *Los Angeles Times*, 15 December 1995. Online. HTTP: <www.calendarlive.com/cl-movie960406–17,0,4119878.story> (accessed 11 April 2011).

26 P. French, '*Cry, the Beloved Country*: Classic DVD Review', *Observer Review*, 7 February 2010, p. 16.

27 N. Mandela, 'World Premier Speech', recorded on DVD, 1995.

28 Maingard, *South African National Cinema*, p. 148. See also L. Dovey, *African Violence and Literature: Adapting Violence to the Screen*, New York: Columbia University Press, 2009.

29 P. Freire, *The Politics of Education: Culture, Power and Liberation*, trans. D. Macdeo, Westport, CN: Bergin and Garvey, 1985, p. 72.

30 P. Freire, 'The Process of Political Literacy', cited in P. Roberts, *Education, Literacy and Humanization: Exploring the Work of Paulo Freire*, Westport, CN: Bergin and Garvey, 2000, pp. 138, 145.

31 Ibid., p. 107.

32 See Nixon, *Homelands, Harlem and Hollywood*, p. 272, n.1.

33 J. Gulger, *African Film: Reimagining a Continent*, Bloomington: Indiana University Press, 2004, p. 80.

34 'Movie review: *Cry Freedom* (1987)', *Time Out Film Guide*. Online. HTTP: <www. timeout.com/film/reviews/69923/cry_freedom.html> (accessed 11 April 2011).

35 V. Carchidi, 'South Africa from Text to Film: *Cry Freedom* and *A Dry White Season*', in J.D. Simons (ed.), *Literature and Film in the Historical Dimension*, Gainesville, FL: University Press of Florida, 1994, pp. 47–61.

36 J. Maslin, 'Movie Review: *Cry Freedom* (1987)', *New York Times*, 6 November 1987. Online. HTTP: <movies.nytimes.com/movie/review?res=9B0DE6D61239F935 A35752C1A961948260> (accessed 11 April 2011).

37 Cited in Carchidi, 'South Africa from Text to Film', p. 58, originally from M. Gevisser, 'Movie review: *Cry Freedom*', *Nation*, January 1988, vol. 9, p. 31.

38 R. Nixon, *Homelands, Harlem and Hollywood: South African Culture and the World Beyond*, Abingdon: Routledge, 1994, p. 82. Others were critical that Denzel Washington, an American actor, and not a South African, was selected to play Biko.

39 R. Ebert, 'Movie Review: *Cry Freedom*', *rogerebert.com*, 6 November 1987. Online. HTTP: <rogerebert.suntimes.com/apps/pbcs.dll/article?AID=/19871106/REVIEWS/711060301> (accessed 11 April 2011).

40 Richard Attenborough, interview by C. Vieler-Porter, *UNESCO Courier*, August 1989, p. 4.

41 '*Cry Freedom*: Charting the Struggle', *BBC News*, 20 August 2001. Online. HTTP: <news.bbc.co.uk/1/hi/entertainment/1500240.stm> (accessed 11 April 2011).

42 See also J. Peffer, *Art and the End of Apartheid*, Minneapolis: University of Minnesota, 2009, pp. 53, 56; and S. Marschall, 'Pointing to the Dead: Victims, Martyrs and Public Memory in South Africa', *South African Historical Journal*, March 2008, no. 1, pp. 103–23.

43 R. Barthes, *Camera Lucida*, London: Fontana, 1984.

44 R. Ebert, '*A World Apart*', *Roger Ebert's Four Star Reviews: 1967–2007*, Kansas City, Missouri: Andrews McMeel Publishing, 2007, pp. 869–70.

45 Ibid.

46 Nixon, *Homelands, Harlem and Hollywood*, p. 87.

47 V. Canby, 'Movie Review: *A World Apart*', *New York Times*, 17 June 1988. Online. HTTP: <movies.nytimes.com/movie/review?res=940DE0D7123AF934A25755C0A96E948260> (accessed 11 April 2011).

48 '*A Dry White Season*', *Film 4*. Online. HTTP: <www.film4.com/reviews/1989/dry-white-season-a> (accessed 11 April 2011).

49 Nixon, *Homelands, Harlem and Hollywood*, p. 88.

50 Cited in Nixon, *Homelands, Harlem and Hollywood*, p. 272, n.1.

51 Tomaselli, *Encountering Modernity*, p. 35.

52 R. Ebert, '*A Dry White Season*', *Robert Ebert's Four Star Reviews, 1967–2007*, 22 September 1989, pp. 216–17.

53 L. Dovey, 'South African Film in Exile', *Journal of Postcolonial Writing*, November 2005, vol. 41, no. 2, pp.189–99.

54 Carchidi, 'South Africa from Text to Film', pp. 58–9, 48.

55 See, for example, Marlize du Plooy and Joy Wilson's twenty-seven-minute documentary, *This is South Africa*, 1990.

56 Tomaselli, *Encountering Modernity*, p. 101.

57 See, for example, the Peace Center in San Antonio, Texas, and their *Popcorn Peacemaking* site, Online. HTTP: <salsa.net/peace/popcorn/cryfree.html> (accessed 15 August 2011)

58 Tomaselli, *Encountering Modernity*, pp. 30–1. See F. Solanas and O. Getino, 'Towards a Third Cinema', in Bill Nichols (ed.), *Movies and Methods. An Anthology*, Berkeley: University of California Press, 1976, pp. 44–64.

59 K. Tomaselli, *The Cinema of Apartheid: Race and Class in South African Film*, New York: Smyrna, 1988, p. 226. He pinpoints 1986–7 as the pivotal moment for South African film.

60 See, for example, M. Krouse and J. Nathan, *Mapantsula: Screenplay and an Interview*, Johannesburg: COSAW, 1991. See also K. Tomaselli, 'Popular Communication in South Africa: Mapantsula and its Context of Struggle', *South African Theatre Journal*, 1991, vol. 5, no. 1, pp. 46–60.

61 Maingard, *South African National Cinema*, p. 149.

62 J. Maslin, 'Movie Review: *Mapantsula* (1989)', *New York Times*, 24 September 1988. Online. HTTP: <movies.nytimes.com/movie/review?res=940DE1D81331F937A15 75AC0A96E948260> (accessed 11 April 2011).

63 Maingard, *South African National Cinema*, pp. 150–1.

64 J. Maingard, 'New South African Cinema: *Mapantsula* and *Sarafina*', *Screen*, 1994, vol. 35, no. 3, pp. 235–43.

65 M. Botha, 'The South African Film Industry: Fragmentation, Identity Crisis and Unification', *Kinema*, spring 1995. Online. HTTP: <www.kinema.uwaterloo.ca/article. php?id=355&feature> (accessed 11 April 2011).

66 L. Modisane, 'Movie-ng the Public Sphere: The Public Life of a South African Film', *Comparative Studies of South Asia, Africa and the Middle East*, 2010, vol. 30, no. 1, pp. 133–46.

67 Modisane, 'Movie-ng the Public Sphere', pp. 133–46.

68 Maingard, *South African National Cinema*, p. 141.

69 Patrick O'Meara, '*Black Man Alive. Last Grave at Dimbaza. Land of Promise:* Films on South Africa', from *Jump Cut: A Review of Contemporary Media*, August 1978, vol. 18, pp.7–8.

70 M. Botha, 'Short Filmmaking in South Africa after Apartheid', *Kinema*, spring 2009. Online. HTTP: <www.kinema.uwaterloo.ca/article.php?id=451&feature> (accessed 11 April 2011).

71 IDAF was originally founded in the 1950s by Canon John Collins of St Paul's Cathedral, London.

72 S.I. Sopher (dir.) *Witness to Apartheid*, 1986 (fifty-eight minutes, nominated for a Best Documentary Oscar).

73 J. Gregory with B. Graham, *Goodbye Bafana: Nelson Mandela, My Prisoner, My Friend*, London: Headline Books, 1995.

74 See A. Sampson, *Mandela: The Authorised Biography*, London: Harper Collins, 1999, pp. 124, 217. For a less critical account of Gregory's role, see T. Lodge, *Mandela: A Critical Life*, Oxford: Oxford University Press, 2006, pp. 119, 142.

75 S. Papamichael, 'Movie review: *Goodbye Bafana*', *BBC Movies*, 10 May 2007. Online. HTTP: <www.bbc.co.uk/films/2007/05/07/goodbye_bafana_2007_review.shtml> (accessed 11 April 2011).

76 'Movie review: *Goodbye Bafana* (2007)' *Film4*, 2007. Online. HTTP: <www.film4. com/reviews/2007/goodbye-bafana> (accessed 11 April 2011).

77 A. Coombes, *History After Apartheid: Visual Culture and Public Memory*, Durham and London: Duke University Press, 2003, p. 101. Coombes cites Indres Naidoo's 'aptly named chapter "Chaos"' from his autobiography *Island in Chains: Prisoner 885/63: Ten Years on Robben Island*, Harmondsworth, Middlesex: Penguin Books, 1982.

78 See also E. Boehmer, *Nelson Mandela: A Very Short Introduction*, Oxford: Oxford University Press, 2008, pp.51–9.

79 F.L. Buntman, *Robben Island and Prisoner Resistance to Apartheid*, Cambridge: Cambridge University Press, 2003, pp. 196–7, n. 13. Buntman supports the view that the government deliberately aimed through 'dull and hard work, no news, poor food and constant impediments to study' to maintain or to cause low prisoner morale. Political prisoners were treated worse than other prisoners, especially during the 1960s and 1970s, which heightened the perception of 'intentional malice', p. 201.

80 M. Mojapelo, *Beyond Memory: Recording the History, Moments and Memories of South African Music*, Somerset Minds, South Africa: African Minds, 2008, p. 311. See also B. Hutton, *Robben Island: Symbol of Resistance*, Johannesburg: Sached Books, 1994, p.7.

81 R. Ebert, 'Movie Review: *Sarafina*', *rogerebert.com*, 25 September 1992. Online. HTTP: <rogerebert.suntimes.com/apps/pbcs.dll/article?AID=/19920925/REVIEWS/20925 0303/1023> (accessed 11 April 2011).

82 Mandela, *Long Walk to Freedom*, p. 460.
83 For more on the legal background, see 'Legal Background to the TRC', Truth and Reconciliation Commission, 2009. Online. HTTP: <www.justice.gov.za/trc/legal/index.htm> (accessed 11 April 2011).
84 M. Meredith, *Coming to Terms: South Africa's Search for Truth*, New York: Public Affairs, 1999, pp. 17–18.
85 *Truth and Reconciliation Commission Report*, Cape Town, 1998 (2001), vol. 1, chap. 48 and 49 (hereafter referred to as *TRC Report*).
86 'Background and Introduction', *Traces of Truth: Documents relating to the South African Truth and Reconciliation Commission*. Online. HTTP: <truth.wwl.wits.ac.za/about.php> (accessed 11 April 2011).
87 *TRC Report*, vol. 1, chap. 4, p. 54.
88 A. Krog, *Country of My Skull*, London: Vintage, 1999, p.viii.
89 *TRC Report*, vol. 1, chap. 4, p. 110.
90 M. Shore, *Religion and Conflict Resolution: Christianity and South Africa's Truth and Reconciliation Commission*, Farnham, Surrey: Ashgate, 2009, pp. 77–106.
91 *TRC Report*, vol. 1, chap. 4, p. 112.
92 A.R. Chapman and H. van der Merwe (eds), *Truth and Reconciliation in South Africa: Did the TRC Deliver?* Philadelphia: University of Pennsylvania Press, 2008.
93 'TRC Category – 4. Reparations', *Traces of Truth: Documents Relating to the South African Truth and Reconciliation Commission*. Online. HTTP: <truth.wwl.wits.ac.za/cat_descr.php?cat=4> (accessed 11 April 2011).
94 M. Mamdani, 'A Diminished Truth', in W. James and L.V. Vijer (eds), *After the TRC*, Athens: Ohio University Press, 2001, p. 58.
95 W.J. Danaher, 'Music That Will Bring Back the Dead? Resurrection, Reconciliation, and Restorative Justice in Post-Apartheid South Africa', *Journal of Religious Ethics*, January 2010, vol. 38, no. 1, pp. 115–41 (122).
96 *TRC Report*, vol. 1, chap. 5, p. 106–9.
97 Shore, *Religion and Conflict Resolution*, pp. 120–1.
98 Danaher, 'Music that will bring back the dead?', p. 115.
99 See Laura Miti, 'Reflections on Mandela: We Have a Lot to Live up to', and 'A Fever That is Killing Democracy', *Daily Dispatch*, 16 July 2008.
100 There are a number of definitions for this term, but one of the most widely cited is the single sentence: 'a person is a person through other persons'. See M. Battle, *Reconciliation: The Ubuntu Theology of Desmond Tutu*, Cleveland, OH: The Pilgrim Press, 1997.
101 K. Thomas, 'Movie review: *In My Country*', *Los Angeles Times*, 11 March 2005. Online. HTTP: <http://www.calendarlive.com/cl-et-country11mar11,0,3466087.story> (accessed 11 April 2011).
102 M. Sanders, 'Truth, telling, questioning: the Truth and Reconciliation Commission, Antjie Krog's *Country of My Skull*, and literature after apartheid', *Transformation*, 2000, vol. 42, pp. 73–91.
103 S. Holden, 'Movie Review: *In My Country*', *New York Times*, 11 March 2005. Online. HTTP: <movies.nytimes.com/2005/03/11/movies/11coun.html?_r=1&ref=john_boorman> (accessed 11 April 2011).
104 Thomas, 'Movie Review: *In My Country*'.
105 R. Ebert, *Roger Ebert's Movie Yearbook 2009*, Kansas City, MO: Andrews McMeel Publishing, 2009, p. 321.
106 Saks, *Cinema in a Democratic South Africa*, p. 110.
107 Ibid., p. 111.
108 S. Hall, 'Movie Review: Red Dust' *Sydney Morning Herald*, 16 November 2005. Online. HTTP: <www.smh.com.au/news/film-reviews/red-dust/2005/11/16/1132016861205.html> (accessed 11 April 2011).

109 Saks, *Cinema in a Democratic South Africa*, p. 112.
110 Botha, 'Short Filmmaking in South Africa after Apartheid', *Kinema*, spring 2009. I am indebted to Cara Moyer-Duncan for drawing my attention to *Ubuntu's Wounds*. See her essay on: 'Truth, Reconciliation and Cinema: Reflections on South Africa's Recent Past in *Ubuntu's Wounds* and *Homecoming*', in L. Bisschoff and S. Van de Peer (eds), *Art and Trauma in Africa: Representations of Reconciliation in Music, Visual Arts, Literature and Film*, London: I.B. Tauris, forthcoming.
111 Sechaba Morojele interviewed by S. Jacobs, 'Ubuntu's Wounds', *Chimurenga*. Online. HTTP: <www.chimurenga.co.za/page-41.html> (accessed 11 April 2011).
112 C. Moyer-Duncan, 'Truth, Reconciliation and Cinema: Reflections on South Africa's Recent Past in *Ubuntu's Wounds* and *Homecoming*', unpublished paper from *Africa in Motion: Edinburgh African Film Festival Symposium*, 24 October 2009, p. 9. See note 110.
113 Ibid., p. 10.
114 Botha, '110 Years of South African Cinema (Part 1)'.
115 J. Maingard, 'Love, Loss, Memory and Truth', in B. Peterson and R. Suleman, *Zulu Love Letter: A Screenplay*, Johannesburg: Wits University Press, 2009, pp. 5–17.
116 B. Peterson, 'Trauma, Art and Healing', in Peterson and Suleman, *Zulu Love Letter*, pp. 18–24.
117 Maingard, 'Love, Loss, Memory and Truth', in Peterson and Suleman, *Zulu Love Letter*, p. 16.
118 Ibid., p. 8.
119 R. Suleman, 'Director's Statement', in Peterson and Suleman, *Zulu Love Letter*, pp. 26–32 (30).
120 A. Ferrillo, 'A Space of (Im)Possibility: Ian Gabriel's *Forgiveness*', in P. Gobodo-Madikizela and C.N. Van der Merwe (eds), *Memory, Narrative and Forgiveness: Perspectives on the Unfinished Journeys of the Past*, Newcastle: Cambridge Scholars Publishing, 2009, pp. 237–57.
121 See M. Evans, 'Amnesty and Amnesia', in M. Botha (ed.), Marginal Lives and Painful Pasts: South African Cinema After Apartheid, Parklands: Genugtig!, 2007, pp. 255–81.
122 A. van der Hoven and J. Arnott, 'The Anxiety of Affect: Melodrama and South African Film Studies', *Social Dynamics*, 2009, vol. 35, no. 1, pp. 162–76.
123 D. Philips, 'Looking the Beast in the (Fictional) Eye: the Truth and Reconciliation Commission on Film', in V. Bickford-Smith and R. Mendelsohn (eds), *Black and White in Colour: Africa's History on Screen,* Oxford: James Currey and Athens: Ohio University Press, 2007, pp. 300–22.
124 J. Chesselet, 'South Africa: This Crazy Thing Called Grace', 1 April 1997. Online. HTTP: <www.journeyman.tv/?lid=9059& tmpl=transcript> (accessed 11 April 2011).
125 D. Tutu, *No Future Without Forgiveness*, New York: Image, Doubleday, 1999.
126 T. Brudholm, *Resentment's Virtue: Jean Améry and the Refusal to Forgive*, Philadelphia: Temple University Press, 2008.
127 Ibid., p. 36.
128 Ibid.
129 Saks, *Cinema in a Democratic South Africa*, pp. 90–2.
130 Oral communication at Africa in Motion: Edinburgh African Film Festival, 25 October 2010.
131 A. Dawson, 'Documenting the Trauma of Apartheid: *Long Night's Journey into Day* and South Africa's Truth and Reconciliation Commission', *Screen*, 2005, vol. 46, no. 4, pp. 473–86 (485).
132 J. Murphy, 'Foreword', in T. Brudholm, *Resentment's Virtue: Jean Améry and the Refusal to Forgive*, p. x.

133 Dawson, 'Documenting the Trauma of Apartheid', pp. 485–6.
134 Mandela, *Long Walk to Freedom*, Boston: Little Brown, 1994, p. 495.
135 Ibid., p. 544. Cited in T. Govier, *Forgiveness and Revenge*, New York and Abingdon: Routledge, 2002, pp. 70–1.
136 L. Thompson, *The History of South Africa*, 3rd edn, New Haven: Yale Nota Bene Books, 2001, pp. 274–7.
137 I am drawing here on J. Liechty, 'Putting Forgiveness in its Place: the Dynamics of Reconciliation', in D. Tombs and J. Liechty (eds), *Explorations in Reconciliation: New Directions in Theology*, Aldershot: Ashgate Publishing, 2006, p. 59.
138 The Kairos Theologians, *The Kairos Document: Challenge to the Church: a Theological Comment on the Political Crisis in South Africa*, 2nd edn, Johannesburg: Skotaville, 1986 (1985).
139 J.W. De Gruchy, *Reconciliation: Restoring Justice*, Minneapolis: Fortress Press, 2002, pp.1–2.
140 Athol Fugard (b. 1932) is best known for his anti-apartheid plays and for *Tsotsi*, which won an Oscar for the Best Foreign Language Film in 2005. Several of his other novels and plays have been adapted into films (e.g. *Master Harold … and the Boys*, 1985, and *The Road to Mecca*, 1991).

6 Promoting peace on screen

1 '*London River* (2009)', *Rotten Tomatoes*. Online. HTTP: <www.rottentomatoes.com/m/london_river/> (accessed 12 April 2011). Sixteen reviews are provided, with fourteen (88%) described as fresh. Contrast this with *Wikipedia*, which offers only four reviews, three of which are positive, though it claims that the 'critical reception to the film was mixed'. '*London River*', *Wikipedia*. Online. HTTP: <en.wikipedia.org/wiki/London_River> (accessed 12 April 2011).
2 See J.D. Bolter and R. Grusin, *Remediation: Understanding New Media*, Cambridge, MA: MIT Press, 2000.
3 D. Roberts (ed.), *Reading the Riots: Investigating England's Summer of Disorder*. London: The Guardian, 2011.
4 See 'Man Jailed for Facebook Incitement to Riot to Appeal', Online. HTTP: <www.bbc.co.uk/news/uk-england-14557772> (accessed 17 August 2011).
5 See, for example, G. Weimann, *Terror on the Internet: The New Arena, the New Challenges*, Washington, DC: United States Institute of Peace Press, 2006, pp. 111–45.
6 'July 7 Bomber's Goodbye Message to His Daughter', *Telegraph*, 16 February 2011. Online. HTTP: <www.telegraph.co.uk/news/uknews/terrorism-in-the-uk/8328195/July-7-bombers-goodbye-message-to-his-daughter.html> (accessed 12 April 2011).
7 'Keven Sites: Fallujah Mosque Shooting', *YouTube*, 21 April 2008. Online. HTTP: <www.youtube.com/watch?v=o4j50ghDeKA> (accessed 12 April 2011).
8 'Tunisia: We are not Afraid, We are not Afraid', *Kasama: Newsflash from the Malabar Front*, 18 January 2011. Online. HTTP: <kasamaproject.org/2011/01/18/awtw-on-tunisia-we-are-not-afraid-we-are-not-afraid/> (accessed 12 April 2011).
9 Earlier versions of this chapter appeared as J. Mitchell, 'Posting Images on the Web: The Creative Viewer and Non-Violent Resistance against Terrorism', *Material Religion*, July 2006, vol. 2, no. 2, pp. 146–73, and in E. Christianson and C. Partridge (eds), *Holy Terror: Understanding Religion and Violence in Popular Culture*, London: Equinox, 2010, pp.10–24.
10 C. Helland, 'Popular Religion and the World Wide Web: A Match Made in [Cyber] Heaven', in D.E. Cowan and L.L. Dawson (eds), *Religion Online: Finding Faith on the Internet*, New York: Routledge, 2004, pp. 21–33 (33); and C. Helland, 'Surfing for Salvation', *Religion*, October 2002, vol. 32, no. 4, pp. 293–302 (297).
11 G.R. Bunt, *Islam in the Digital Age: E-jihad, Online Fatwas, and Cyber Islamic Environments*, London: Pluto Press, 2003, pp. 67–123.

12 For a useful annotated bibliography, see H. Campbell, 'New Media and Religion', in J. Mitchell and S. Marriage (eds), *Mediating Religion: Conversations in Media, Religion and Culture*, London and New York: T&t Clark, Continuum, 2003, pp. 363–8 and H. Campbell, *When Religion Meets New Media*, Abingdon: Routledge, 2010.

13 See, for example, G.R. Bunt, 'Rip. Burn. Pray: Islamic Expression Online', in Cowan and Dawson, *Religion Online*; and B. Basher, *Give Me That Old Time Religion*, San Francisco, CA: Jossey Bass, 2001.

14 See S. Turkle, *Life on the Screen: Identity in the Age of the Internet*, New York: Simon and Schuster, 1995. Turkle's work has been both developed and criticised. See, for example, D.E. Cowan and L.L. Dawson (eds) *Religion Online*; and S.M. Hoover, L. Schofield Clark and D.F. Alters, *Media, Home, and Family*, New York: Routledge, 2004.

15 See, for example, H. Campbell, *Exploring Religious Community Online: We are One in the Network*, New York: Peter Lang Publishing, 2005; H. Rheingold, *The Virtual Community: Homesteading on the Electronic Frontier*, New York: Addison-Wesley, 2000 (1993); and B. Wellman, *Networks in the Global Village*, Boulder, CO: Westview Press, 1999.

16 L.L. Dawson, 'Religion and the Quest for Virtual Community', in Cowan and Dawson, *Religion Online*, p. 77.

17 See also Cowan's discussion on 'Online Community: Illusion or the Illusion of Reality?' in D.E. Cowan, *Cyberhenge: Modern Pagans on the Internet*, New York: Routledge, 2005, pp. 54–8.

18 B. Wellman and B. Hogan, 'The Immanent Internet', in J.R. McKay, *Netting Citizens*, Edinburgh: St. Andrew's Press, 2004, pp. 54–80 (72–75).

19 E. Durkheim, *The Elementary Forms of the Religious Life*, Oxford: Oxford University Press, 2001 (1912), p.18.

20 See, for example, P. Bourdieu, *Outline of a Theory of Practice*, Cambridge: Cambridge University Press, 1997 (1972), pp. 159–70. See also P. Bourdieu, *The Field of Cultural Production: Essays on Art and Literature*, ed. Randal Johnson. Cambridge: Polity Press, 1993.

21 I am grateful to Alfie Dennan for his time and assistance, including an extended interview in Camden Town, London, 25 October 2005.

22 J. Mitchell, interview with Dennan, Camden Town, London, 25 October 2005.

23 'About *We're not Afraid*', *We're not afraid.com*. Online. HTTP: <werenotafraid.com/about.html> (accessed 12 April 2011).

24 M. McLuhan, *Understanding Media: The Extensions of Man*, New York: McGraw-Hill Book Company, 1964.

25 See, for example, E. Levinas, *Totality and Infinity*, The Hague: M. Nijhoff, Kluwer Academic Publishers, 1979 (1961), pp. 79–81, 187–203 and his conversation with Philippe Nemo on the 'face' in *Ethics and Infinity*, Pittsburgh: Duquesne University Press, 1985 (982), pp. 85–92.

26 See R.N. Bellah, *Beyond Belief: Essays on Religion in a Post-Traditional World*, New York: Harper & Row, 1970, especially pp. 172–86. For a critical analysis of the term 'civil religion', see J. Demerath, 'Civil society and civil religion as mutually dependent', *Handbook of the Sociology of Religion*, Cambridge: Cambridge University Press, 2003, pp. 348–58.

27 I have fused Edward Bailey's definitions found in E. Bailey, *Implicit Religion: An Introduction*, London: Middlesex University Press, 1998, pp. 22–5.

28 J. Mitchell, interview with Dennan, Camden Town, London, 25 October 2005.

29 *Notinthenameofpeace.com* is now no longer available on the web. Online. HTTP: <www.notinthenameofpeace.com/?p=55>.

30 See *We're not afraid.com*.

31 Ibid.

32 Ibid.

33 '7/7 'We are still not afraid!', *Facebook*. Online. HTTP: <www.facebook.com/pages/77-we-are-still-not-afraid/140410359303656> (accessed 12 April 2011).

34 'We are not afraid', *Facebook*. Online. HTTP: <www.facebook.com/group.php?gid=114844558553693> (accessed 12 April 2011).
35 'Egyptian Uprising – We're Not Afraid', *YouTube*, 26 January 2011. Online. HTTP: <www.youtube.com/watch?v=U0U3cfvRFG4> (accessed 12 April 2011).
36 S. Gagin and P. Dray, *We Are Not Afraid: The Story of Goodman, Schwerner and Chaney and the Civil Rights Campaign for Mississippi*, rev. edn, New York: Nation Books, 2006.
37 See 'Tribute for Tunisian Who Sparked Protests', *YouTube*, 21 January 2011. Online. HTTP: <www.youtube.com/watch?v=qqCa7lQoPs8> (accessed 12 April 2011).
38 C. Ulrich, 'Tunisia: "We Are Not Afraid Anymore!"', *Global Citizen*, 2 January 2011. Online. HTTP: <globalcitizenblog.com/?p=2952> (accessed 12 April 2011).
39 'Guardian Reporter Jack Shenker on Egypt Protests: "Fear barrier seems to have been broken"', *Democracy Now!: The War and Peace Report*, 27 January 2011. Online. HTTP: <www.democracynow.org/2011/1/27/guardian_reporter_in_egypt_fear_barrier> (accessed 12 April 2011).
40 Wellman and Hogan, 'The Immanent Internet', in McKay, *Netting Citizens*, pp. 72–5.
41 See J. Hands, *@ is for Activism: Dissent, Resistance and Rebellion in a Digital Culture*, London and New York: Pluto Press, 2011, pp. 1–2.
42 See 'Lev Manovich', 'Against Search', 21 July 2011. Online: HTTP. <manovich.net> (accessed 18 August 2011). See also L. Manovich, *The Language of New Media*, Cambridge, MA: MIT Press, 2002 (2001).
43 Z. Bauman, *Liquid Fear*, Cambridge: Polity, 2006, p. 2.
44 See, for example, Levinas, *Totality and Infinity*, and his conversation with Philippe Nemo on the 'face' in *Ethics and Infinity*.

7 Conclusion: 'Swords into ploughshares'

1 See C. Spring, 'Tree of Life', *British Museum Magazine-1*, no. 51, spring 2005; see also C. Spring, *African Art in Detail*, London/Cambridge, MA: British Museum Press and Harvard University Press, 2009; C. Spring, *Angaza Afrika: African Art Now*, London: Laurence King, 2008.
2 C. Nordstrom, *A Different Kind of War Story: The Ethnography of Political Violence*, Philadelphia: University of Pennsylvania Press, 1997, p. 220.
3 Ibid., p. 220.
4 J.P. Lederach, *The Moral Imagination: The Art and Soul of Building Peace*, Oxford and New York: Oxford University Press, 2005, p. 5.
5 Ibid., p. 5.
6 See Spring, *African Art in Detail*; and Spring, *Angaza Afrika: African Art Now*.
7 Maya Angelou, *The Complete Collected Poems of Maya Angelou*, New York: Random House, 1994, p. 272. The precise quote about facing history is from *On the Pulse of Morning*, which she read at Bill Clinton's presidential inauguration on 20 January 1993. It is also quoted in the documentary film *Long Night's Journey into Day* (1995, Deborah Hoffmann and Frances Reid), discussed in chapter 5.
8 By contrast, the population of Iraq appears to have been galvanised more through incitements to support the leadership cult of Saddam Hussein. This became more effective when Iraq's own territories came under threat. See E. Karsh, *The Iran-Iraq War*, New York, NY: Rosen Publishing, 2009, p. 65.
9 These were primarily RTLM, Radio Rwanda and the RPF's Radio Muhabura.
10 T. Gatwa, *The Churches and Ethnic Ideology in the Rwandan Crises 1900–1994*, Milton Keynes: Regnum Books, 2005, p. 156.
11 See J. Riley-Smith (ed.), *The Oxford Illustrated History of the Crusades*, Oxford: Oxford University Press, 2001. See also Christoph Maier's discussion of model sermons in

Preaching and the Crusades: Mendicant Friars and the Cross in the Thirteenth Century, Cambridge Studies in Medieval Life and Thought, Cambridge: Cambridge University Press, 1998 (1994); and C. Maier, *Crusade Propaganda and Ideology: Model Sermons for Preaching the Cross*, Cambridge: Cambridge University Press, 2000.

12 See, for example, Ridley Scott's film *Kingdom of Heaven* (2005), which depicts the fall of Jerusalem to Saladin (1187).

13 See M. Radovic, 'Representation of Religion in *Pretty Village, Pretty Flame*', in C. Deacy and E. Arweck (eds) *Exploring Religion and the Sacred in a Media Age*, Farnham, Surrey: Ashgate, 2009, pp. 190–1.

14 See A. Rajagopal, *Politics after Television: Hindu Nationalism and the Reshaping of the Public in India*, Cambridge: Cambridge University Press, 2001.

15 See J. Mitchell, *Media Violence and Christian Ethics*, Cambridge: Cambridge University Press, 2007, especially chapter 1 on 'Remembering Violence'. On handling memories wisely see M. Volf, *The End of Memory: Remembering Rightly in a Violent World*, Grand Rapids: Eerdmans, 2006.

16 See J.W. De Gruchy, *Christianity, Art and Transformation: Theological Aesthetics in the Struggle for Justice*, Cambridge: Cambridge University Press, 2001, p. 211.

17 E. Gardner, 'The role of the media in conflicts', in L. Reychiler and T. Paffenholz (eds) *Peacebuilding: A Field Guide*, Boulder, Colorado: Lynne Rienner Publishers, 2001, pp. 301–11.

18 See J. Galtung, 'Three Approaches to Peace: Peacekeeping, Peacemaking and Peacebuilding', in *Peace, War and Defence – Essays in Peace Research*, vol. 2, Copenhagen: Christian Ejlers, 1975, pp. 282–304.

19 See J.P. Lederach, *Building Peace: Sustainable Reconciliation in Divided Societies*, Washington: United States Institute of Peace, 1997, pp.76–7. Lederach outlines the time dimension in peacebuilding, which he describes as moving from crisis intervention (2–6 months), to preparation and training (1–2 years), to design of social change (5–10 years), and to a desired future (20+ years).

20 P. Dahinden, 'Information in Crisis Areas as a Tool for Peace: The Hirondelle Experience', in A. Thompson (ed.), *The Media and the Rwanda Genocide*, London: Pluto Press, 2007, pp. 381–8.

21 Gardner, 'The Role of the Media in Conflicts', in Reychiler and Paffenholz (eds), *Peacebuilding: A Field Guide*, p. 308.

22 D. Lindley, *Promoting Peace with Information: Transparency as a Tool of Security Regimes*, Princeton: Princeton University Press, 2007, p. 208. See also M. Kimani, 'Broadcasting Peace: Radio a Tool for Recovery', *Africa Renewal*, 2007, vol. 23, no. 3, p. 3. Online. HTTP: <www.un.org/ecosocdev/geninfo/afrec/vol21no3/213-radio.html> (accessed 21 March 2011).

23 See J.P. Lederach and A.J. Lederach, *When Blood and Bones Cry out: Journeys Through the Soundscape of Healing and Reconciliation*, Brisbane: University of Queensland Press, 2010.

24 O. Chow, 'Alfredo Jaar and the Post-Traumatic Gaze', *Tate Papers*, Spring 2008. Online. HTTP: <www.tate.org.uk/research/tateresearch/tatepapers/08spring/chow.shtm> (accessed 31 August 2011).

25 A. Jaar, *The Eyes of Gutete Emerita*. Online. HTTP: <www.alfredojaar.net/gutete/gutete.html> (accessed 31 August 2011).

26 A. Braembussche, 'Presenting the Unpresentable. On Trauma and Visual Art', *Intercultural Aesthetics*, 2009, vol. 9, pp. 119–136.

27 Recorded Interview by Jolyon Mitchell with Ashafa and Wuye in Edinburgh, 28 November 2008.

28 See *Africa in Motion: Edinburgh African Film Festival, 22nd October–1st November*, 2009, Edinburgh: Filmhouse Catalogue, 2009, p. 4.

29 See 'A Cinema of Healing: Two Rwandan Films', Online: HTTP: <http://blogs.warwick.ac.uk/zanzibar/entry/a_cinema_of/> (accessed 19 August 2011).

30 J.C. Bass (dir.), *The Tunnel*, Online: HTTP: <http://vimeo.com/12566896> (accessed 22 August 2011, password required from production company Fox Fire Films), 2010.

31 De Gruchy, *Christianity, Art, and Transformation*, p. 206. See also S. Williamson, *Resistance Art in South Africa*, revised edn, Cape Town: David Philip, 2004 (1989); and G. Younge, *Art of the South African Townships*, London: Thames and Hudson, 1988.

32 D. Tutu, *No Future Without Forgiveness: A Personal Overview of South Africa's Truth and Reconciliation Commission*, London: Rider, imprint of Random House, 1999, p. 218.

33 E.A. Kaplan, *Trauma Culture: The Politics of Terror and Loss in Media and Literature*, New Brunswick, NJ: Rutgers University Press, 2005, pp. 87–100.

34 Ibid., p. 93.

35 See L. van Zoonen, F. Vis and S. Mihelj, 'YouTube Interactions between Agonism, Antagonism and Dialogue: Video Responses to the Anti-Islam Film *Fitna*', *New Media and Society*, June 2011, pp. 1–18. On the basis of cybermetric network analysis they found that the video responses posted were 'mostly isolated reactions to the film', concluding that '*YouTube* enabled a multiplication of views rather than an exchange or dialogue between them'.

36 J.P. Lederach, *Preparing for Peace: Conflict Transformation Across Cultures*, Syracuse, NY: Syracuse University Press, 1995, p. 11.

37 Ibid., pp. 47–70.

38 Lederach, *The Moral Imagination*, p. 5.

39 Personal conversation with the artist Paul Hobbs near Gloucester, July 2011.

40 M. Gerry, 'West Belfast, Northern Ireland: The Peace Walls and the Murals', *Associated Content*, 6 April 2006. Online. HTTP: <www.associatedcontent.com/article/25134/west_belfast_northern_ireland_the_peace_pg3.html?cat=37> (accessed 21 March 2011).

41 B. Rolston, *Politics and Painting: Murals and Conflict in Northern Ireland*, London and Toronto: Associate University Presses, 1991, p. 82. See picture from Beechmount Drive, 1981.

42 N. Carnduff, 'Belfast Lines Redrawn: The Changing Face of Belfast's City's Murals', *Irish Times*, 15 May 2009. Online. HTTP: <ourfuturetogether.posterous.com/2009/05/belfasts-lines-redrawn-irish-times.html> (accessed 21 March 2011).

43 'Give my Head Peace'. *BBC*. Online. HTTP: <www.bbc.co.uk/northernireland/gmhp/murals.shtml> (accessed 21 March 2011).

44 'New UVF Murals Painted in East Belfast', UTV, 10 May 2011. Online. HTTP: <http://www.u.tv/news/New-UVF-murals-painted-in-east-Belfast/cbd77d79-ac55–46a3–889f-f67ef5886be7> (accessed 30 October 2011).

45 H. Merron, 'Belfast – Neural Mural on Limestone Road "no to"', *D-Space at Cambridge*, CRIC images collection, 27 July 2009. Online. HTTP: <www.dspace.cam.ac.uk/handle/1810/218746> (accessed 21 March 2011).

46 'Mural Launch and Panel Discussion', *Charter for Northern Ireland: Making a Positive Difference*. Online. HTTP: <www.charterni.com/projects/crossing-the-bridges/mural-launch-and-panel-discussion/> (accessed 21 March 2011).

47 I am indebted to Scott Appleby, the director of the Kroc Institute for International Peace Studies, University of Notre Dame, for this insight, provided in Cambridge, UK, August 2011.

48 Ibid.

49 *Les Misérables,* musical by Claude-Michel Schönberg, French lyrics by Alain Boublil, English version by Herbert Kretzmer. The original French production was in Paris, September 1980, with the adapted version in English opening in October 1985,

which was produced by Cameron Mackintosh and directed by Trevor Nunn and John Caird.

50 *Heal the World* is from Michael Jackson's album *Dangerous*, 1991.

51 See 'The Vine and the Fig Tree', *Greenham Common Women's Peace Camp Songbook, The Danish Peace Academy*, Online. HTTP: <www.fredsakademiet.dk/abase/sange/greenham/song9.htm> (accessed 30 August 2011).

52 H. Williamson, 'Swords into Plowshares: The Development and Implementation of a Vision', in R. Cohen and R. Westbrook (eds), *Isaiah's Vision of Peace in Biblical and Modern International Relations: Swords into Plowshares*, New York, NY: Palgrave Macmillan, 2008, pp.139–49, p. 147.

53 R. Cohen and R. Westbrook (eds), 'Conclusion', in *Isaiah's Vision of Peace in Biblical and Modern International Relations*, pp. 238–9.

54 J. Ayto (rev.), *Brewer's Dictionary of Phrase and Fable*, 17th edn, London: Weidenfeld and Nicolson, 2005, p.1079.

55 See J. Sidbury, *Ploughshares into Swords: Race, Rebellion and Identity in Gabriel's Virginia, 1730–1810*, Cambridge: Cambridge University Press, 1997, p. 69.

56 See P. Koistinen, *Beating Plowshares into Swords: the Political Economy of American Warfare, 1606–1865*, Lawrence: University Press of Kansas, 1996.

57 See President Eisenhower's *Farewell Address to the Nation*, 17 January 1961. For Eisenhower the 'Military Industrial Complex' was the 'conjunction of an immense military establishment and a large arms industry', which was 'new in the American experience'. He warned that 'we must guard against the acquisition of unwarranted influence, whether sought or unsought, by the military-industrial complex'. He too celebrated Isaiah's vision of 'swords into ploughshares'. See also J. Kurth, 'Military-Industrial Complex', in J. Chambers II (ed.), *The Oxford Companion to American Military History*, Oxford: Oxford University Press, 1999, pp. 440–2.

58 Cited, along with texts from Ovid (*Fasti*, I, 697–700) and Martial (*Epigr*, XIV, 34) in Williamson, 'Swords into Plowshares', pp.143–144.

59 The title of this somewhat apocalyptic song is taken from the British government's late 1970s pamphlet, *Protect and Survive*, which was intended to inform the civilian population what they should do in the event of nuclear attack. It appeared on *The Cutter and the Clan* 1987 album.

60 Hoots and Hellmouth (music album), *The Holy Open Secret*, Online. HTTP: <www.hootsandhellmouth.com/music.php> (accessed 5 September 2011).

61 De Gruchy, *Christianity, Art and Transformation*, p. 211.

62 I. Patkanian (dir.), *Little Fiel*, clips from film in production and Online. HTTP: <www.littlefiel.com> (accessed 5 September 2011).

63 D. Howitt (dir. and prod.), *Mozambique: Tree of Guns*, BBC and Christian Aid, 2005.

64 For instance, one 'young man whose home was destroyed by the [2000] floods was able to begin the process of home reconstruction with the help of the cement he received in exchange for an AK-47 he kept in his home'. A. Forguilha, '*Transforming Arms into Ploughshares*'. Online. HTTP: <www.peoplebuildingpeace.org/thestories/print.php?id=147& typ=theme> (accessed 8 September 2011).

65 This is now displayed on the throne's case in the British Museum.

66 A. Forguilha, '*Transforming Arms into Ploughshares*'. Cites a wide range of other 'success stories'.

67 'Peace Art Project Cambodia'. Online. HTTP. <sashaconstable.co.uk/projects/peace-art> (accessed 26 August 2011).

68 S. Constable, 'Personal Email to Author', 27 August 2011.

69 'Sierra Leone: NGO Turns to Farm Tools', MAPCO, Online. HTTP. <allafrica.com/stories/200108030106.html> (accessed 29 August 2011).

70 Dominick Tyler Photography, APT Enterprises is second NGO behind this project, 'Guns to Tools', Online. HTTP. <www.dominicktyler.com/editorial/guns-to-tools/#> (accessed 29 August 2011).

71 'Guatemala Swaps Guns for Bicycles', BBC News, 10 July 2004. Online. HTTP: <news.bbc.co.uk/1/hi/world/americas/3883023.stm> (accessed 1 August 2011).

72 'Weapons into Water', Organisation for Security and Co-Operation in Europe, Online. HTTP: <www.osce.org/georgia-closed/54530> (accessed 21 August 2011).

73 'Guns into Goods', 2008, Online. HTTP: <www.youtube.com/watch?v=y3JLLVK3d9Q>, and 'Guns into Goods Events', March 2011, Online. HTTP: <www.facebook.com/note.php?note_id=157174320989277> (accessed 21 August 2011).

74 M. Churlov, 'The Sculptures Made out of Iraqi Weapons', Sunday 29 August 2010, *Guardian* website. Online. HTTP: <www.guardian.co.uk/world/2010/aug/29/iraq-artist-sculptures> (accessed 12 May 2011).

75 See *Art of Peace Charitable Trust*, Online. HTTP: <www.aopct.org/> 'The mission of the Art of Peace Charitable Trust (AOPCT) is to prevent and eradicate the proliferation of small firearms and weapons of destruction through innovative and durable approaches to arms reduction'.

76 J. Swoboda, *The Revolution of the Candles: Christians in the Revolution of the German Democratic Republic*, ed. R. Pierard, Macon, GA: Mercia University Press, 1996, pp. 20, 96.

77 W.C. Bartee, *A Time to Speak Out: The Leipzig Citizen Protests and the Fall of East Germany*, Westport, CT: Praeger, 2000. See also *The Sword and the Ploughshare: Autonomous Peace Initiatives in East Germany*, London: Merlin Press, 1983. Note also how the Micah version of the 'Swords into Ploughshares' text is employed.

78 P. Burke, 'Peace Movements in Eastern Europe', in N. Young (ed.), *The Oxford International Encyclopedia of Peace*, Oxford: Oxford University Press, 2010, pp. 9–16, (11).

79 Online. HTTP: <www.bbc.co.uk/ahistoryoftheworld/objects/CXrfizyzQP2YFgx-BniBBw> (accessed 5 September 2011).

80 *Lysistrata* was 'performed on March 3, 2003 by 1,100 theatre troupes, in 59 different countries, and multiple languages SIMULTANEOUSLY as a form of humanitarian protest to the potential onset of the US-Iraq war'. 'Target Peace', HTTP: <vimeo.com/17775286> (accessed 31 August 2011).

81 Online. HTTP: <www.youtube.com/watch?v=p9N6rLfZM7E> (accessed 5 September 2011).

82 BBC News, 'Mozambique Floods 2000, Full Coverage', Online. HTTP: <news.bbc.co.uk/1/hi/world/africa/655510.stm> (accessed 31 August 2011)

83 'More Than 200 Guns Taken Off Salinas', Online. HTTP: <www.Streetshttp://www.youtube.com/watch?v=snZJRQYMtO0&NR=1> (accessed 21 August 2011).

84 'Guns into Art', Online. HTTP: <www.meltguns.com/> (accessed 11 August 2011).

85 *BBC News*, 'Born above the Floodwaters', 2 March 2000, Online. HTTP: <news.bbc.co.uk/1/hi/world/africa/662472.stm > See also F. Christie and J. Hanlon, *Mozambique and the Great Flood of 2000*, Oxford: International African Institute in association with James Currey, 2001.

86 A. Hyde-Price, ' "Praise the Lord and Pass the Ammunition" A Realist Response to Isaiah's Irenic Vision', in Cohen and Westbrook (eds), *Isaiah's Vision of Peace in Biblical and Modern International Relations*, pp. 211–28.

Bibliography

Adorno, T.W., *Can One Live After Auschwitz? A Philosophical Reader*, ed. R. Tiedemann, Stanford: Stanford University Press, 2003.

Adorno, T.W., *Negative Dialectics*, New York: Continuum, 1973.

Aegis Trust, *Jenoside*, Kigali: Kigali Memorial Centre, 2004.

African Rights, *Rwanda: Death Despair and Defiance*, 2nd edn, London: African Rights, 1995.

Aghaie, K.S., *The Martyrs of Karbala: Shi'i Symbols and Rituals in Modern Iran*, Seattle: University of Washington Press, 2004.

Alexis, M. and I. Mpambara, *IMS Assessment Mission Report: The Rwanda Media Experience from the Genocide*, Copenhagen: International Media Support, 2003.

Allan, S. and B. Zelizer (eds), *Reporting War: Journalism in Wartime*, London: Routledge, 2004.

Amanat, A., *Apocalyptic Islam and Iranian Shi'ism*, London and New York: I.B.Tauris, 2009.

Andrew, G., 'Shooting Dogs', review in *Time Out London*, 1858, 29 March–5 April, 2006.

Angelou, M., *The Complete Collected Poems of Maya Angelou*, New York: Random House, 1994.

Appleby, R.S., *The Ambivalence of the Sacred: Religion, Violence, and Reconciliation*, Lanham, MD: Rowman & Littlefield Publishers, 2000.

——, 'What Can Peacebuilders Learn from Fundamentalists?', in S. Hoover and N. Kaneva (eds), *Fundamentalisms and the Media*, New York and London: Continuum, 2009.

Arthur, M. (ed.), *We Will Remember Them: Voices from the Aftermath of the Great War*, London: Orion Group, 2009.

Augarde, T. (ed.), *The Oxford Dictionary of Modern Quotations*, Oxford: Oxford University Press, 1991.

Aulich, J. and J. Hewitt, *Seduction or Instruction? First World War Posters in Britain and Europe*, Manchester: Manchester University Press, 2007.

Baer, R., 'The Making of a Suicide Bomber', *Sunday Times*, 3 September 2006.

Bailey, E., *Implicit Religion: An Introduction*, London: Middlesex University Press, 1998.

Balaghi, S., 'Iranian Visual Arts in the Century of Machinery', in S. Balaghi and L. Gumpel (eds), *Picturing Iran: Art, Society and Revolution*, London: I.B. Tauris, 2003.

Baldwin Smith, L, *Fools, Martyrs, Traitors: The Story of Martyrdom in the Western World*, New York: Knopf, 1997.

Barlow, H., *Dead for Good: Martyrdom and the Rise of the Suicide Bomber*, Boulder, CO: Paradigm Publishers, 2006.

Bartee, W.C., *A Time to Speak Out: The Leipzig Citizen Protests and the Fall of East Germany*, Westport, CT: Praeger, 2000.

Barthes, R., *Camera Lucida*, London: Fontana, 1984.

Bartlett, J. and K.M. Ellis, 'Remembering the Dead in Northop: First World War Memorials in a Welsh Parish', *Journal of Contemporary History*, April 1999, vol. 34, no. 2, pp. 231–42.

Basher, B., *Give Me that Old Time Religion*, San Francisco, CA: Jossey Bass, 2001.

Battle, M., *Reconciliation: the Ubuntu Theology of Desmond Tutu*, Cleveland, OH: The Pilgrim Press, 1997.

Bauman, Z., *Liquid Fear*, Cambridge: Polity, 2006.

Beattie, L., E. Miller, D. Miller and G. Philo, 'The Media and Africa: Images of Disaster and Rebellion', in G. Philo (ed.), *Message Received*, London: Longman, 1999.

Becker, A., *War and Faith: The Religious Imagination in France, 1914–1930*, trans. H. McPhail, Oxford: Berg, 1998.

Beinart, W., *Twentieth-Century South Africa*, 2nd edn, Oxford: Oxford University Press, 2001.

Bellah, R.N., *Beyond Belief: Essays on Religion in a Post-Traditional World*, New York: Harper & Row, 1970, especially pp. 172–86.

Benjamin, W., 'The Work of Art in the Age of Mechanical Reproduction', in G. Mast, M. Cohen and L. Braudy (eds), *Film Theory and Criticism*, 4th edn, Oxford: Oxford University Press, 1992, pp. 665–81.

Bill, J.A., 'Morale vs Technology: The Power of Iran in the Persian Gulf War', in F. Rajaee (ed.), *The Iran–Iraq War: The Politics of Aggression*, Gainesville: University Press of Florida, 1993.

Blankevoort, E., 'The Image of War: Visual Propaganda in the Islamic Republic of Iran', unpublished Master's thesis, University of Amsterdam, 2005.

Bloxham, D., *The Great Game of Genocide: Imperialism, Nationalism, and the Destruction of the Ottoman Armenians*, Oxford: Oxford University Press, 2005.

Boehmer, E., *Nelson Mandela: A Very Short Introduction*, Oxford: Oxford University Press, 2008.

Bolter, J.D. and R. Grusin, *Remediation: Understanding New Media*, Cambridge, MA: MIT Press, 2000.

Boorman, D., *At the Going Down of the Sun: British First World War Memorials*, York: Ebor Press, 1988.

Botha, M., 'Short Filmmaking in South Africa After Apartheid', *Kinema*, spring 2009.

Bourdieu, P., *The Field of Cultural Production: Essays on Art and Literature*, ed. R. Johnson, Cambridge: Polity Press, 1993.

——, *Outline of a Theory of Practice*, Cambridge: Cambridge University Press, 1997 (1972).

Brittain, V., *Testament of Youth: An Autobiographical Study of the Years 1900–1925*, Harmondsworth: Penguin, 1994 (1933).

Broadbent, E., 'Media, Even in the West, is Partly to Blame for the Rwandan Massacres', *Gazette* (Montreal), 3 May 1995.

Broderick, M., 'Mediating Genocide: Producing Digital Survivor Testimony in Rwanda', in B. Sarkar and J. Walker (eds), *Documentary Testimonies: Global Archives of Suffering*, New York: Routledge, 2010, pp. 215–44.

Bromley, R., 'After Such Knowledge, What Forgiveness?: Cultural Representations of Reconciliation in Rwanda', *French Cultural Studies*, 2009, vol. 20, pp. 181–97.

Brudholm, T., *Resentment's Virtue: Jean Améry and the Refusal to Forgive*, Philadelphia: Temple University Press, 2008.

Bruzzi, S., *New Documentary: A Critical Introduction*, London: Routledge, 2000.

Bunt, G.R., *Islam in the Digital Age: E-jihad, Online Fatwas, and Cyber Islamic Environments*, London: Pluto Press, 2003.

——, 'Rip. Burn. Pray: Islamic Expression Online', in D.E. Cowan and L.L. Dawson (eds), *Religion Online: Finding Faith on the Internet*, New York: Routledge, 2004.

Buntman, F.L., *Robben Island and Prisoner Resistance to Apartheid*, Cambridge: Cambridge University Press, 2003.

Bushaway, B., 'Name Upon Name: The Great War and Remembrance', in R. Porter (ed.), *Myths of the English*, Cambridge: Polity Press, 1992.

——, 'The Obligation of Remembrance or the Remembrance of Obligation: Society and the Memory of World War', in J. Bourne, P. Liddle and I. Whitehead (eds), *The Great World War 1914–45*, vol. 2, London: HarperCollins, 2001, pp. 491–507.

Bytwerk, R.L., *Julius Streicher*, 2nd edn, New York: Cooper Square, 2001.

Campbell, H., *Exploring Religious Community Online: We are One in the Network*, New York: Peter Lang Publishing, 2005.

——, 'New Media and Religion' in J. Mitchell and S. Marriage (eds), *Mediating Religion: Conversations in Media, Religion and Culture*, London and New York: T&T Clark, Continuum, 2003, pp. 363–8.

——, *When Religion Meets New Media*, Abingdon, Oxon: Routledge, 2010.

Cantrell, P.A., 'The Anglican Church of Rwanda: Domestic Agendas and International Linkages', *Journal of Modern African Studies*, 2007, vol. 45, pp. 333–54.

Cantril, H., *The Invasion from Mars: A Study in the Psychology of Panic*, Princeton: Princeton University Press, 1940.

Carchidi, V., 'South Africa from Text to Film: *Cry Freedom* and *A Dry White Season*', in J.D. Simons (ed.), *Literature and Film in the Historical Dimension*, Gainesville: University Press of Florida, 1994, pp. 47–61.

Carlin, J., *Playing the Enemy: Nelson Mandela and the Game that Made a Nation*, London: Atlantic Books, 2008.

Carver, R., 'Broadcasting & Political Transition', in R. Fardon and G. Furniss (eds), *African Broadcast Cultures: Radio in Transition*, Oxford: James Currey, 2000.

——,'Introduction', in L. Kirschke, *Broadcasting Genocide: Censorship, Propaganda & State-Sponsored Violence in Rwanda 1990–1994*, London: Article 19, 1996.

Chalk, F., 'Hate Radio in Rwanda', in H. Adelman and A. Suhkre (eds), *The Path of a Genocide: The Rwanda Crisis from Uganda to Zaire*, New Brunswick, NJ: Transaction Publishers, 1999, pp. 99–107.

——, 'Radio Broadcasting in the Incitement of Interdiction of Gross Violations of Human Rights, Including Genocide', in R. Smith (ed.), *Genocide: Essays Toward Understanding, Early-Warning, and Prevention*, Williamsburg, VA: Association of Genocide Scholars, 1999, pp. 185–203.

Chapman, A.R. and H. van der Merwe (eds), *Truth and Reconciliation in South Africa: Did the TRC Deliver?* Philadelphia: University of Pennsylvania Press, 2008.

Chehabi, H.E. and F. Christia, 'The Art of State Persuasion: Iran's Post-Revolutionary Murals', *Persica*, 2008, vol. 22, pp. 1–13.

Chelkowski, P., 'The Art of Revolution and War: The Role of Graphic Arts in Iran', in S. Balaghi and L. Gumpel (eds), *Picturing Iran: Art, Society and Revolution*, London: I.B. Tauris, 2003.

——, 'Iconography of the Women of Karbala', in K.S. Aghaie (ed.), *The Women of Karbala: Ritual Performance and Symbolic Discourses in Modern Shi'i Islam*, Austin: University of Texas Press, 2005.

Chelkowski, P. and H. Dabashi, *Staging a Revolution: The Art of Persuasion in the Islamic Republic of Iran*, New York: New York University Press, 1999.

Chesterton, G.K., *The Autobiography of G.K. Chesterton*, San Francisco: Ignatius Press, 2006 (1936).

Christianson, E. and C. Partridge (eds), *Holy Terror: Understanding Religion and Violence in Popular Culture*, London: Equinox, 2010.

Christie F. and Hanlon J., *Mozambique and the Great Flood of 2000*, Oxford: International African Institute in association with James Currey, 2001.

Chubin, S. and C. Tripp, *Iran and Iraq at War*, London: I.B. Tauris, 1988.

Cieplak, P.A., 'The Rwandan Genocide and the Bestiality of Representation in *100 Days* (2001) and *Shooting Dogs* (2005)', *Journal of African Cinemas*, July 2010, vol. 2, no. 1, pp. 49–63.

——, 'Image and Memory: An Interview with Eric Kabera', *French Cultural Studies* May 2009 vol. 20, no. 2, pp. 199–208.

Clark N. and W. Worger, *South Africa: the Rise and Fall of Apartheid*, Harlow, UK: Pearson, 2004.

Clark P., *The Gacaca Courts, Post-Genocide Justice and Reconciliation in Rwanda: Justice without Lawyers*, Cambridge: Cambridge University Press, 2010.

Cohen, S., *States of Denial: Knowing About Atrocities and Suffering*, Cambridge: Polity, 2001.

Cole, T., *Selling the Holocaust: From Auschwitz to Schindler, How History is Bought, Packaged and Sold*, New York: Routledge, 1999.

Convents, G., *Images et paix. Les Rwandais et les Burundais face au cinéma et à l'audiovisuel. Une histoire politico-culturelle du Rwanda-Burundi allemand et belge et des Républiques du Rwanda et du Burundi (1896–2008)*, Leuven: Signis, 2008.

Cooke, M., 'The Ethics of Post-Holocaust Art: Reflections on Redemption and Representation', *German Life and Letters*, April 2006, vol. 59, no. 2, pp. 266–79.

Coombes, A., *History After Apartheid: Visual Culture and Public Memory*, Durham and London: Duke University Press, 2003.

Cortright, D., *Peace: A History of Movements and Ideas*, Cambridge: Cambridge University Press, 2008.

Cowan, D.E., *Cyberhenge: Modern Pagans on the Internet*, New York: Routledge, 2005.

Cowan, D.E. and L.L. Dawson (eds), *Religion Online: Finding Faith on the Internet*, New York: Routledge, 2004.

Crowther, 'The Screen: *The Stranger*, with Edward G. Robinson, Loretta Young and Orson Welles, of Palace', *New York Times*, 11 July 1946.

Dahinden, P., 'Information in Crisis Areas as a Tool for Peace: The Hirondelle Experience', in A. Thompson (ed.), *The Media and the Rwanda Genocide*, London: Pluto Press, 2007, pp. 381–8.

Dallaire, R. and B. Beardsley, *Shake Hands with the Devil: The Failure of Humanity in Rwanda*, New York: Carroll and Graf, 2005 (2003).

Danaher, W.J., 'Music that Will Bring Back the Dead? Resurrection, Reconciliation, and Restorative Justice in Post-Apartheid South Africa', *Journal of Religious Ethics*, January 2010, vol. 38, no. 1, pp. 115–41.

Darracott, J. and B. Loftus, *First World War Posters*, London: Imperial War Museum, 1981 (1972).

Dauge-Roth, A., 'The Pertinence of Impertinent Storytelling in Gilbert Ndahayo's Documentary *Rwanda: Beyond the Deadly Pit*', *Contemporary French and Francophone Studies*, 2010, vol. 14, no. 4, pp. 455–60.

Davis, J., *Martyrs: Innocence, Vengeance, and Despair in the Middle East*, New York: Palgrave Macmillan, 2003.

Dawson, A., 'Documenting the Trauma of Apartheid: *Long Night's Journey into Day* and South Africa's Truth and Reconciliation Commission', *Screen*, 2005, vol. 46, no. 4, pp. 473–86.

——'Religion and the Quest for Virtual Community', in D.E. Cowan and L.L. Dawson (eds), *Religion Online: Finding Faith on the Internet*, New York: Routledge, 2004.

Deacy, C. and G. Ortiz, *Theology and Film: Challenging the Sacred/Secular Divide*, Oxford: Blackwell, 2008.

de Bellaigue, C., *In the Rose Garden of Martyrs: A Memoir of Iran*, New York: Harper Perennial, 2005.

De Gruchy, J., *Christianity, Art, and Transformation: Theological Aesthetics in the Struggle for Justice*, Cambridge: Cambridge University Press, 2001.

——, *Reconciliation: Restoring Justice*, Minneapolis: Fortress Press, 2002, pp. 1–2.

De Syon, G., *Zeppelin!: Germany and the Airship, 1900–1939*, Baltimore, MD: Johns Hopkins University Press, 2002.

Demerath, J., 'Civil Society and Civil Religion as Mutually Dependent', *Handbook of the Sociology of Religion*, Cambridge: Cambridge University Press, 2003, pp. 348–58.

Des Forges, A.L., *Leave None to Tell the Story: Genocide in Rwanda*, New York: Human Rights Watch, 1999.

Douglas, R., *The Great War: 1914–1918: The Cartoonists' Vision*, London: Routledge, 1995.

Dovey, L., *African Violence and Literature: Adapting Violence to the Screen*, New York: Columbia University Press, 2009.

——, 'South African Film in Exile', *Journal of Postcolonial Writing*, November 2005, vol. 41, no. 2, pp. 189–99.

Durkheim, E., *The Elementary Forms of the Religious Life*, trans. Carol Cosman, Oxford: Oxford University Press, 2001 (1912).

Ebert, R., '*A Dry White Season*', *Robert Ebert's Four Star Reviews, 1967–2007*, 22 September 1989, pp. 216–17.

——, '*A World Apart*', *Roger Ebert's Four Star Reviews: 1967–2007*, Kansas City, MO: Andrews McMeel Publishing, 2007, pp. 869–70.

——, *Roger Ebert's Movie Yearbook 2009*, Kansas City, MO: Andrews McMeel Publishing, 2009.

Eldridge, J. (ed.) *Getting the Message: News, Truth and Power*, London: Routledge, 1993.

Evans, M., 'Amnesty and Amnesia', in M. Botha (ed.), Marginal Lives and Painful Pasts: South African Cinema After Apartheid, Parklands: Genugtig!, 2007, pp. 255–81.

Everitt, E. and R. Tricker, *Swaffham-Two-Churches*, Mildenhall, Suffolk: E.G.M. Mann, 1996.

Farmer, P., *Pathologies of Power: Health, Human Rights and the New War on the Poor*, Berkeley and Los Angeles: University of California Press, 2003.

Felman, S., 'Film as Witness: Claude Lanzmann's *Shoah*', in G. Hartman (ed.), *Holocaust Remembrance: The Shapes of Memory*, Oxford: Blackwell, 1994.

Ferguson, N., *The Pity of War: Explaining World War I*, London: Allen Lane, The Penguin Press, 2006 (1999).

Ferrillo, A., 'A Space of (Im)Possibility: Ian Gabriel's *Forgiveness*', in P. Gobodo-Madikizela and C.N. Van der Merwe (eds), *Memory, Narrative and Forgiveness: Perspectives on the Unfinished Journeys of the Past*, Newcastle: Cambridge Scholars Publishing, 2009, pp. 237–57.

Fisher, D. and J. Mitchell, 'Portraying Forgiveness Through Documentary Film', in R. Woods (ed.) *Evangelicals and Popular Culture*, Boulder, CO: Praeger, forthcoming 2012.

Fisk, R., 'Voices from the Martyrs' Cemetery', *Independent*, 27 February 2000.

Freedman, A., 'Zeppelin Fictions and the British Home Front', *Journal of Modern Literature*, 2004, vol. 27, no. 3, pp. 47–62.

Freire, P., *The Politics of Education: Culture, Power and Liberation*, trans. D. Macdeo, Westport, CN: Bergin and Garvey, 1985.

French, P., '*Cry, the Beloved Country*: Classic DVD Review', *Observer Review*, 7 February 2010.

Friedman, L.D. and B. Notbohm (eds), *Stephen Spielberg: Interviews*, Jackson: University Press of Mississippi, 2000.

Fussell, P., *The Great War and Modern Memory*, New York: Oxford University Press, 1975.

Gagin, S. and P. Dray, *We are Not Afraid: The Story of Goodman, Schwerner and Chaney and the Civil Rights Campaign for Mississippi*, rev. edn, New York: Nation Books, 2006.

Galtung, J., 'Three Approaches to Peace: Peacekeeping, Peacemaking and Peacebuilding', in *Peace, War and Defence – Essays in Peace Research*, vol. 2, Copenhagen: Christian Ejlers, 1975, pp. 282–304.

Gardner, E., 'The Role of the Media in Conflicts', in L. Reychiler and T. Paffenholz (eds), *Peacebuilding: A Field Guide*, Boulder, CO: Lynne Rienner Publishers, 2001, pp. 301–11.

Gatwa, T., 'The Churches and Ethnic Ideology in the Rwandan Crisis (1900–1994)', unpublished thesis, University of Edinburgh, 1998.

——, *The Churches and Ethnic Ideology in the Rwandan Crisis (1900–1994)*, Milton Keynes: Regnum Books International, 2005.

Gevisser, M., 'Movie Review: *Cry Freedom*', *Nation*, January 1988, vol. 9, p. 31.

Gieling, S., *Religion and War in Revolutionary Iran*, London and New York: I.B. Tauris, 1999.

Goebel, S., *The Great War and Medieval Memory: War, Remembrance and Medievalism in Britain and Germany, 1914–1940*, Cambridge: Cambridge University Press, 2007.

Gourevitch, P., *We Wish to Inform You that Tomorrow We Will be Killed with Our Families: Stories from Rwanda*, New York: Farrar, Straus, Giroux, 1998.

Govier, T., *Forgiveness and Revenge*, New York and Abingdon: Routledge, 2002.

Gregory, A., *The Silence of Memory: Armistice Day – 1919–1946*, Oxford: Berg, 1994.

Gregory, J. with B. Graham, *Goodbye Bafana: Nelson Mandela, My Prisoner, My Friend*, London: Headline Books, 1995.

Gruber, C.J., 'The Message is on the Wall: Mural Arts in Post-Revolutionary Iran', *Persica*, 2008, vol. 22, pp. 15–46.

——, 'Media/ting Conflict: Iranian Posters of the Iran–Iraq War (1980–88)', in J. Anderson (ed.), *Crossing Cultures: Conflict, Migration, Con-vergence*, Melbourne: Melbourne University, 2009, pp. 710–15.

Gulger, J., *African Film: Reimagining a Continent*, Bloomington: Indiana University Press, 2004.

Gulseth, H.L., 'The Use of Propaganda in the Rwandan Genocide: A Study of Radio-Télévision Libre des Mille Collines (RTLM)', unpublished thesis, University of Oslo, 2004.

Halbwachs, M., *The Collective Memory*, trans. F.J. Ditter and V.Y. Ditter, New York: Harper Colophon, 1950 (1980).

Hallin, D.C., *The 'Uncensored War'*, Berkeley, Los Angeles and London: University of California Press, 1986.

Hamelink, C.J., *Media and Conflict: Escalating Evil*, Boulder, CO: Paradigm Publishers, 2011.

Hands, J., *@ is for Activism: Dissent, Resistance and Rebellion in a Digital Culture*, London and New York: Pluto Press, 2011.

Harries, M., *The War Artists: British Official War Art of the Twentieth Century*, London: Michael Joseph with the Imperial War Museum and the Tate Gallery, 1983.

Härting, H., 'Global Humanitarianism, Race, and the Spectacle of the African Corpse in Current Western Representations of the Rwandan Genocide', *Comparative Studies of South Asia, Africa and the Middle East*, 2008, vol. 28, no. 1, pp. 61–77.

Hegland, M., 'Two Images of Husain: Accommodation and Revolution in an Iranian Village', in N.R. Keddie (ed.), *Religion and Politics in Iran: Shi'ism from Quietism to Revolution*, New Haven: Yale University Press, 1983.

Helland, C., 'Popular Religion and the World Wide Web: A Match Made in [Cyber] Heaven', in D.E. Cowan and L.L. Dawson (eds), *Religion Online: Finding Faith on the Internet*, New York: Routledge, 2004, pp. 21–33.

——, 'Surfing for Salvation', *Religion*, October 2002, vol. 32, no. 4, pp. 293–302.

Higiro, J.M.V., 'Distorsions et omissions dans l'ouvrage Rwanda, les médias du génocide', *Dialogue*, 190, 1996.

Hill, G., *Triumph of Love*, New York: Mariner Books, 2000 (1998).

Hilliard, R.L. and M.C. Keith, *Waves of Rancor: Tuning in the Radical Right*, Armonk, NY: M.E. Sharp, 1999.

Hilsum, L., 'The Radio Station Whose Call Sign is Mass Murder', *Observer*, 15 May 1994.

Højsgaard, M. and M. Warburg (eds), *Religion and Cyberspace*, New York and Abingdon: Routledge, 2005.

Holden, S., '"Enemies of the People": One Man's Quest for Truth About Cambodia's "Killing Fields"', *New York Times*, 20 January 2011.

Hoover, S., *Religion in the Media Age*, Hove: Psychology Press, 2006.

Hoover, S. and K. Lundby (eds), *Rethinking Media, Religion and Culture*, Thousand Oaks, CA: Sage, 1997.

Hoover, S.M. and L. Schofield Clark (eds), *Practicing Religion in the Age of the Media: Explorations in Media, Religion, and Culture*, New York: Columbia University Press, 2002.

Hoover, S.M., L. Schofield Clark and D.F. Alters, *Media, Home, and Family*, New York: Routledge, 2004.

Horne, J. and A. Kramer, *German Atrocities, 1914: A History of Denial*, New Haven: Yale University Press, 2001.

Horsfield, P., M.E. Hess and A.M. Medrano (eds), *Belief in Media: Cultural Perspectives on Media and Christianity*, Aldershot: Ashgate, 2004.

Hron, M., 'Interview with Film Producer Eric Kabera', from 'Symposium: Post-Genocide Rwanda', *Peace Review: A Journal of Social Justice*, 2009, vol. 21, no. 3, pp. 359–62.

Hron, M. '*Kumaramaza*? Representing the Rwandan Killer', paper presented at the 6th Global Conference on 'Probing the Boundaries', 3 May 2007. Online. HTTP: <www.interdisciplinary.net/ptb/hhv/vcce/vcce1/hron%20paper.pdf> (accessed 1 March 2011).

Huda, Q. (ed.), *Crescent and Dove: Peace and Conflict Resolution in Islam*, Washington: United States Institute of Peace Press, 2010.

Huyssen, A., 'Of Mice and Mimesis: Reading Spiegelman with Adorno', *New German Critique*, autumn 2000, no. 81, pp. 65–82.

Hyde-Price A., ' "Praise the Lord and Pass the Ammunition" A Realist Response to Isaiah's Irenic Vision', in Cohen and Westbrook (eds), *Isaiah's Vision of Peace in Biblical and Modern International Relations*, pp. 211–28, 2008.

Hyman, T., *Sienese Painting: The Art of a City Republic (1278–1477)*, London: Thames and Hudson, 2003.

Hynes, S., *A War Imagined: The First World War and English Culture*, London: Bodley Head, 1991.

Ignatieff, M., 'Iranian Lessons', *New York Times Magazine*, 17 July 2005.

Inglis, K.S., 'The Homecoming: The War Memorial Movement in Cambridge, England', *Journal of Contemporary History*, October 1992, vol. 27, no. 4, pp. 583–605.

Insdorf, A., *Indelible Shadows: Film and the Holocaust*, 3rd edn, Cambridge: Cambridge University Press, 2003.

Janovich, M., 'Shadows and Bogeyman: Horror, Stylization and the Critical Reception of Orson Welles during the 1940s', *Participations: Journal of Audience and Reception Studies*, May 2009, vol. 6, no. 1, pp. 25–51.

Jenkins, H., *Convergence Culture: Where Old and New Media Collide*, New York and London: New York University Press, 2006.

Jenkins, S., *England's Thousand Best Churches*, London: Penguin Books, 2000 (1999).

The Kairos Theologians, *The Kairos Document: Challenge to the Church: A Theological Comment on the Political Crisis in South Africa*, 2nd edn, Johannesburg: Skotaville, 1986 (1985).

Kangura, 'A Cockroach Cannot Give Birth to a Butterfly', February 1993, no. 40.

Kaplan, E.A., *Trauma Culture: The Politics of Terror and Loss in Media and Literature*, New Brunswick, NJ: Rutgers University Press, 2005.

Karimi, P., 'Imagining Warfare, Imaging Welfare: Tehran's Post Iran–Iraq Murals and Their Legacy', *Persica*, 2008, vol. 22, pp. 47–63.

Karsh, E., *The Iran–Iraq War: 1980–88*, Oxford: Osprey, 2002 and New York: Rosen Publishing, 2009.

Keane, F., *Season of Blood: A Rwandan Journey*, London: Penguin, 1996 (1995).

Keeble, R.L., J. Tulloch and F. Zollmann (eds), *Peace Journalism, War and Conflict Resolution*, New York: Peter Lang, 2010.

Kellow, C. and H. Leslie Steeves, 'The Role of Radio in the Rwandan Genocide', *Journal of Communication*, 1998, vol. 48, no. 3, pp. 107–28.

Khosronejad, P., (ed.), *Unburied Memories: The Politics of Bodies of Sacred Defense Martyrs in Iran*, London and New York: Routledge, 2012.

King, A., *Memorials of the Great War in Britain: The Symbolism and Politics of Remembrance*, Oxford: Berg, 1998.

King, E., 'Memory Controversies in Post-Genocide Rwanda: Implications for Peacebuilding', *Genocide Studies and Prevention*, winter 2010, vol. 5, no. 3, pp. 293–309.

Kingsbury, C.M., *For Home and Country: World War 1 Propaganda on the Home Front*, Lincoln: University of Nebraska Press, 2010.

Knightley, P., *The First Casualty*, 3rd edn, Baltimore, MD: Johns Hopkins University Press, 2004.

Koistinen, P., *Beating Plowshares into Swords: The Political Economy of American Warfare, 1606–1865*, Lawrence: University Press of Kansas, 1996.

Kramer, A., *Dynamic of Destruction: Culture and Mass Killing in the First World War*, Oxford: Oxford University Press, 2007.

Krog, A., *Country of My Skull*, London: Vintage, 1999.

Krouse M. and J. Nathan, *Mapantsula: Screenplay and an Interview*, Johannesburg: COSAW, 1991.

Kurth, J., 'Military-Industrial Complex', in J. Chambers II (ed.), *The Oxford Companion to American Military History*, Oxford: Oxford University Press, 1999, pp. 440–2.

Lanzmann, C., *Shoah: The Complete Text of the Acclaimed Holocaust Film by Claude Lanzmann*, New York: De Capo Press, 1995.

Lavelle, B.C., *Zeppelinitis*, Honolulu, HI: University Press of the Pacific, 2005.

Lederach, J.P., *The Moral Imagination: The Art and Soul of Building Peace*, Oxford and New York: Oxford University Press, 2005.

——, *The Little Book of Conflict Transformation*, Intercourse, PA: Good Books, 2003.

——, *The Journey toward Reconciliation*, Pennsylvania: Herald Press, 1999.

——, *Building Peace: Sustainable Reconciliation in Divided Societies*, Washington, DC: US Institute of Peace Press, 1997.

——, *Preparing for Peace: Conflict Transformation Across Cultures*, Syracuse, New York: Syracuse University Press, 1995.

Lederach, J.P. and A.J. Lederach, *When Blood and Bones Cry Out: Journeys Through the Soundscape of Healing and Reconciliation*, Brisbane: University of Queensland Press, 2010.

Levinas, E., *Totality and Infinity*, The Hague: M. Nijhoff, Kluwer Academic Publishers, 1979 (1961).

Lewy, G., *The Armenian Massacres in Ottoman Turkey: A Disputed Genocide*, Salt Lake City: University of Utah Press, 2005.

Li, D., 'Echoes of Violence', in A. Thompson (ed.) *The Media and the Rwandan Genocide*, London: Pluto Press, 2007, pp. 90–109.

——, 'Echoes of Violence', in N. Mills and K. Brunner (eds) *The New Killing Fields: Massacre and the Politics of Intervention*, New York: Basic Books, 2002, pp. 117–28.

——, 'Echoes of Violence: Considerations on Radio and Genocide in Rwanda', *Journal of Genocide Research*, March 2004, vol. 6, no. 1, pp. 9–27.

Liechty, J., 'Putting Forgiveness in its Place: The Dynamics of Reconciliation', in D. Tombs and J. Liechty (eds), *Explorations in Reconciliation: New Directions in Theology*, Aldershot: Ashgate Publishing, 2006, p. 59.

Lindley, D., *Promoting Peace with Information: Transparency as a Tool of Security Regimes*, Princeton: Princeton University Press, 2007.

Lloyd, D., *Battlefield Tourism: Pilgrimage and the Commemoration of the Great War in Britain, Australia and Canada, 1919–1939*, Oxford: Berg, 1998.

Lodge, T., *Mandela: A Critical Life*, Oxford: Oxford University Press, 2006.

Longman, T., *Christianity and Genocide in Rwanda*, Cambridge: Cambridge University Press, 2009.

Loshitzky, Y., 'Holocaust Others: Spielberg's *Schindler's List* versus Lanzman's *Shoah*', in Y. Loshitzky (ed.), *Spielberg's Holocaust: Critical Perspectives on Schindler's List*, Bloomington: Indiana University Press, 1997.

Louw, P., *The Rise, Fall and Legacy of Apartheid*, Westport, CT: Praeger, 2004.

Lowery, S.A. and M.L. DeFleur, *Milestones in Mass Communication Research: Media Effects*, 3rd edn, White Plains, NY: Longman, 1995.

Lyden, J., *Film as Religion: Myths, Morals and Rituals*, New York and London: New York University Press, 2003.

Lynch, G. (ed.), *Between Sacred and Profane: Researching Religion and Popular Culture*, London: I.B. Tauris, 2007.

Lynch, G., J. Mitchell and A. Strhan (eds), *Religion, Media and Culture: A Reader*, London and New York: Routledge, 2011.

Lynch, J., and A. McGoldrick, *Peace Journalism*, Stroud: Hawthorn Press, 2005.

Lynch, J., *Debates in Peace Journalism*, Sydney: Sydney University Press, 2008.

Lynch, J. and J. Galtung, *Reporting Conflict: New Directions in Peace Journalism*, St Lucia: University of Queensland Press, 2010.

McBride, J., *Steven Spielberg*, London: Faber and Faber, 1997.

MacDonald, M., 'Rethinking Personalisation in Current Affairs Journalism', in C. Sparks and J. Tulloch (eds), *Tabloid Tales: Global Debates Over Media Standards*, Lanham, MD: Rowman and Littlefield, 2000.

MacGregor, N., *A History of the World in 100 Objects*, London: Penguin, Allen Lane, 2010.

McLuhan, M., *Understanding Media: The Extensions of Man*, New York: McGraw-Hill Book Company, 1964 and London: Ark, 1987.

Madelung, W., *Succession to Muhammed: A Study of the Early Caliphate*, Cambridge: Cambridge University Press, 1997.

Maier, C., *Crusade Propaganda and Ideology: Model Sermons for Preaching the Cross*, Cambridge: Cambridge University Press, 2000.

——, *Preaching and the Crusades: Mendicant Friars and the Cross in the Thirteenth Century*, Cambridge Studies in Medieval Life and Thought, Cambridge: Cambridge University Press, 1998 (1994).

Maingard, J., 'Love, loss, memory and truth', in B. Peterson and R. Suleman, *Zulu Love Letter: A Screenplay*, Johannesburg: Wits University Press, 2009, pp. 5–17.

——, 'New South African Cinema: *Mapantsula* and *Sarafina*', *Screen*, 1994, vol. 35, no. 3, pp. 235–43.

——, *South African National Cinema*, Abingdon, Oxon: Routledge, 2007.

Mamdani, M., 'A Diminished Truth', in W. James and L.V. Vijer (eds), *After the TRC*, Athens: Ohio University Press, 2001.

——, *When Victims Become Killers: Colonialism, Nativism and Genocide in Rwanda*, Princeton: Princeton University Press, 2002.

Mandela, N., *Long Walk to Freedom: The Autobiography of Nelson Mandela*, New York: Back Bay Books, 1995 (1994).

Manovich, L., *The Language of New Media*, Cambridge, MA: MIT Press, 2002 (2001).

Marrin, A., *The Last Crusade: The Church of England in the First World War*, Durham, NC: Duke University Press, 1974.

Marschall, S., 'Pointing to the Dead: Victims, Martyrs and Public Memory in South Africa', *South African Historical Journal*, March 2008, no. 1, pp. 103–23.

Marsden, L. and H. Savigny (eds), *Media, Religion and Conflict*, Farnham, Surrey: Ashgate, 2009.

Marzolph, U., 'The Martyr's Way to Paradise: Shiite Mural Art in the Urban Context', in R. and J. Bendix (eds), *Sleepers, Moles and Martyrs*, Copenhagen: Museum Tusculanum Press, 2004.

Melvern, L., 'History? This Film is Fiction', *Observer*, 19 March, 2006.

——, *Conspiracy to Murder: the Rwandan Genocide*. London: Verso, 2004.

Meredith, M., *Coming to Terms: South Africa's Search for Truth*, New York: Public Affairs, 1999, pp. 17–18.

Messinger, G.S., *British Propaganda and the State in the First World War*, Manchester: Manchester University Press, 1992.

Metzl, J.F., 'Rwandan Genocide and the International Law of Radio Jamming', *American Journal of International Law*, 1997, vol. 91, pp. 628–51.

Meyer, B., and A. Moors (eds) *Religion, Media and the Public Sphere*, Bloomington: Indiana University Press, 2006.

Meyer, B. (ed.), *Aesthetic Formations: Media, Religion and the Senses*, New York: Palgrave Macmillan, 2010.

Mironko, C., 'The Effect of RTLM's Rhetoric of Ethnic Hatred in Rural Rwanda', in A. Thompson (ed.), *The Media and the Rwanda Genocide,* London: Pluto, 2007, pp. 125–35.

Mitchell, J., 'Contesting Martyrdom', in C. Deacy and E. Arweck (eds), *Exploring Religion and the Sacred in a Media Age,* Farnham, Surrey: Ashgate, 2009.

——, 'Searching for Peace in Films About Genocide', in G. Watkins (ed.), *Teaching Film and Religion,* Oxford: Oxford University Press, 2008, pp. 283–94.

——, *Media Violence and Christian Ethics,* Cambridge: Cambridge University Press, 2007.

——, 'Posting Images on the Web: The Creative Viewer and Non-Violent Resistance Against Terrorism', *Material Religion,* July 2006, vol. 2, no. 2, pp. 146–73.

Mitchell, J. and S. Marriage (eds), *Mediating Religion: Conversations in Media, Religion and Culture,* London and New York: T&T Clark/Continuum, 2003.

Modisane, L., 'Movie-ng the Public Sphere: The Public Life of a South African Film', *Comparative Studies of South Asia, Africa and the Middle East,* 2010, vol. 30, no. 1, pp. 133–46.

Mojapelo, M., *Beyond Memory: Recording the History, Moments and Memories of South African Music,* Somerset Minds, South Africa: African Minds, 2008.

Moltmann, J., *The Crucified God,* London: SCM, 1974 (1972).

Montaigne, F., 'Iran: Testing the Waters of Reform', *National Geographic,* July 1999.

Morgan, D. (ed.), *Religion and Material Culture: The Matter of Belief,* London: Routledge, 2010.

——, *Key Words in Religion, Media and Culture,* London: Routledge, 2008.

——, *The Lure of Images,* London: Routledge, 2007.

——, *Protestants and Pictures: Religion, Visual Culture and the Age of American Mass Production,* Oxford: Oxford University Press, 1999.

Morozov, E., *The Net Delusion: How Not to Liberate the World,* London: Allen Lane, 2011.

Mosse, G.L., *Fallen Soldiers: Reshaping the Memory of the World Wars,* New York: Oxford University Press, 1991.

Moyer-Duncan, C., 'Truth, Reconciliation and Cinema: Reflections on South Africa's Recent Past in *Ubuntu's Wounds* and *Homecoming'*, in L. Bisschoff and S. Van de Peer (eds), *Art and Trauma in Africa: Representations of Reconciliation in Music, Visual Arts, Literature and Film,* London: I.B. Tauris, forthcoming.

Mulaa, J., 'Decades of hatred and bloodletting', *Sunday Nation* (Kenya), 10 April 1994.

Murphy, A. (ed.) *The Blackwell Companion to Religion and Violence,* Malden, MA: Wiley-Blackwell, 2010.

Murphy, J., 'Foreword', in T. Brudholm, *Resentment's Journey: Jean Améry and the Refusal to Forgive,* Philadelphia: Temple University Press, 2008.

Naidoo, I., *Island in Chains: Prisoner 885/63: Ten Years on Robben Island,* Harmondsworth, Middlesex: Penguin Books, 1982.

Nichols, B., *Introduction to Documentary,* Bloomington: Indiana University Press, 2001.

——, *Representing Reality: Issues and Concepts in Documentary,* Bloomington: Indiana University Press, 1991.

Nixon, R., *Homelands, Harlem and Hollywood: South African Culture and the World Beyond,* Abingdon: Routledge, 1994.

Nordstrom, C., *A Different Kind of War Story: the Ethnography of Political Violence,* Philadelphia: University of Pennsylvania Press, 1997.

Nzacahayo, P., 'Shared Life as God's People: An Exploration of Exclusion and Koinonia in Social Relations in Rwanda', unpublished thesis, University of Edinburgh, 2000.

O'Keefe, A., 'Anger at BBC Genocide Film', *Observer*, 19 March, 2006.

O'Meara, P., 'Films on South Africa *Black Man Alive. Last Grave at Dimbaza. Land of Promise*', *Jump Cut: A Review of Contemporary Media*, August 1978, vol. 18, pp. 7–8.

Page, J., *Peace Education: Exploring Ethical and Philosophical Foundations*, Charlotte: Information Age Publishing, 2008.

Paton, A., *Cry, the Beloved Country*, London: Vintage, 2002 (1948).

Paivandi, S., *Discrimination and Intolerance in Iran's Textbooks*, New York: Freedom House Publication, 2008.

Peffer, J., *Art and the End of Apartheid*, Minneapolis: University of Minnesota, 2009.

Peters, J., 'Witnessing', *Media, Culture and Society*, 2001, vol. 23, no. 6, pp. 707–24.

Peterson, B., 'Trauma, Art and Healing', in B. Peterson and R. Suleman, *Zulu Love Letter*, pp. 18–24, 2009.

Petrie, C., 'The Failure to Confront Evil – A Collective Responsibility', in Carol Rittner et al. (eds), *Genocide in Rwanda: Complicity of the Churches?* St Paul, MN: Paragon House, 2004.

Pheknonyane, M., *My Freedom, My Passion*, Eagan, MN: Kairos Publishing, 2004.

Philips, D., 'Looking the Beast in the (Fictional) Eye: the Truth and Reconciliation Commission on Film', in V. Bickford-Smith and R. Mendelsohn (eds), *Black and White in Colour: Africa's History on Screen*, Oxford: James Currey/Athens: Ohio University Press, 2007, pp. 300–22.

Physicians for Human Rights, *Rwanda 1994: A Report of the Genocide*, Dundee, Scotland: The Royal Infirmary, 1994.

Pottier, J., *Re-imagining Rwanda: Conflict, Survival and Disinformation in the late Twentieth Century*, Cambridge: Cambridge University Press, 2002.

Prunier, G., 'How Many Were Killed?', in *The Rwanda Crisis: History of a Genocide*, London: Hurst and Company, 1997.

Rabasa, J., *Without History: Subaltern Studies The Zapatista Insurgency, and the Specter of History*, Pittsburgh: University of Pittsburgh Press, 2010.

Radovic, M., 'Representation of Religion in *Pretty Village, Pretty Flame*', in C. Deacy and E. Arweck (eds), *Exploring Religion and the Sacred in a Media Age*, Farnham, Surrey: Ashgate, 2009.

Rajaee, F. (ed.), *The Iran–Iraq War: The Politics of Aggression*, Gainesville: University Press of Florida, 1993.

Rajagopal, A., *Politics After Television: Hindu Nationalism and the Reshaping of the Public in India*, Cambridge: Cambridge University Press, 2001.

Reuter, C., *My Life is a Weapon: A Modern History of Suicide Bombing*, trans. H. Ragg-Kirby, Princeton: Princeton University Press, 2004.

Reychiler, L. and T. Paffenholz (eds), *Peacebuilding: A Field Guide*, Boulder, CO: Lynne Rienner Publishers, 2001.

Rheingold, H., *The Virtual Community: Homesteading on the Electronic Frontier*, New York: Addison-Wesley, 2000 (1993).

Richards A. and J. Mitchell, 'Journalists as Witnesses to Violence and Suffering', in R. Fortner and M. Silk (eds), *Global Communication Ethics*, Oxford: Blackwell, in press, forthcoming 2011.

Riley-Smith, J., *The First Crusade and the Idea of Crusading*, Philadelphia: University of Philadelphia Press, 1986.

Riley-Smith, J. (ed.), *The Oxford Illustrated History of the Crusades*, Oxford: Oxford University Press, 2001.

Rittner, C., J.K. Roth and W. Whitworth (eds), *Genocide in Rwanda: Complicity of the Churches?* St Paul, Minnesota: Paragon House, 2004.

Robinson, D.H., *The Zeppelin in Combat: 1912–1918*, London: G.T. Foulis & Co., 1962.

Rolston, B., *Politics and Painting: Murals and Conflict in Northern Ireland*, London and Toronto: Associate University Presses, 1991.

Ruthven, M., *Islam in the World*, 3rd edn, Oxford: Oxford University Press, 2006.

——, *Islam: A Very Short Introduction*, Oxford: Oxford University Press, 1997.

Saks, L., *Cinema in a Democratic South Africa*, Bloomington: Indiana University Press, 2010.

Sampson, A., *Mandela: The Authorised Biography*, London: HarperCollins, 1999.

Sanders, M., 'Truth, Telling, Questioning: The Truth and Reconciliation Commission, Antjie Krog's *Country of My Skull*, and Literature After Apartheid', *Transformation*, 2000, vol. 42, pp. 73–91.

Sandford, J., *The Sword and the Ploughshare: Autonomous Peace Initiatives in East Germany*, London: Merlin Press, 1983.

Satrapi, M., *Persepolis*, London: Vintage Books, 2008 (2000).

Saunders, N.J. (ed.), *Matters of Conflict: Material Culture, Memory and the First World War*, Abingdon: Routledge, 2004.

Schiff, S., 'Seriously Spielberg', in L.D. Friedman and B. Notbohm (eds) *Stephen Spielberg: Interviews*, Jackson: University Press of Mississippi, 2000.

Schubel, V.J., *Religious Performance in Contemporary Islam: Shi'i Devotional Rituals in South Asia*, Columbia, South Carolina: University of South Carolina Press, 1993.

Schwartzott, A., 'Transforming arms into ploughshares: weapons that destroy and heal in Mozambican urban art', in L. Bisschoff and S. Van de Peer (eds) *Art and Trauma in Africa: Representations of Reconciliation in Film, Art, Music and Literature*, London: I.B. Tauris, forthcoming 2012.

Sennitt, A. (ed.) *Media Network Dossier, Hate Radio*, Hilversum: Radio Netherlands, 2004.

Shaw, G.B., *Heartbreak House*, Harmondsworth: Penguin, 1964 (1919).

Shinar D. and W. Kempf (eds), *Peace Journalism: The State of the Art*, Berlin: Regener, 2007.

Shore, M., *Religion and Conflict Resolution: Christianity and South Africa's Truth and Reconciliation Commission*, Farnham, Surrey: Ashgate, 2009.

Short, E., *I Knew My Place*, London: Macdonald and Co, 1983.

Sidbury, J., *Ploughshares into Swords: Race, Rebellion and Identity in Gabriel's Virginia, 1730–1810*, Cambridge: Cambridge University Press, 1997.

Sillars, S., *Art and Survival in First World War Britain*, New York: Macmillan Press, 1987.

Slide, A. (ed.), *Ravished Armenia and the Story of Aurora Mardiganian*, Lanham, MD and London: Scarecrow Press, 1997.

Snape, M. 'Church of England Army Chaplains in the First World War: Goodbye to *Goodbye to All That*', *Journal of Ecclesiastical History*, vol. 62, no. 2, April 2011, pp. 318–45.

Solanas, F. and O. Getino, 'Towards a Third Cinema', in Bill Nichols (ed.), *Movies and Methods. An Anthology*, Berkeley: University of California Press, 1976.

Spring, C., *African Art in Detail*, London and Cambridge, MA: British Museum Press and Harvard University Press, 2009.

——, *Angaza Afrika: African Art Now*, London: Laurence King, 2008.

——, 'Tree of Life', *British Museum Magazine-1*, no. 51, spring 2005.

Sproule, M., *Propaganda and Democracy: The American Experience of Media and Mass Persuasion*, Cambridge: Cambridge University Press, 1997.

Stanley, P., *What Did You Do in the War Daddy? A Visual History of Propaganda Posters*, Melbourne: Oxford University Press, 1983.

Staub, E., *The Roots of Evil: The Origins of Genocide and Other Group Violence*, Cambridge: Cambridge University Press, 1989.

Staub, E., L.A. Pearlman, A. Gubin and A. Hagengimana, 'Healing, Reconciliation, Forgiving and the Prevention of Violence After Genocide or Mass killing: An Intervention and its Experimental Evaluation in Rwanda', *Journal of Social and Clinical Psychology*, 2005, vol. 24, no. 3, pp. 297–334.

Stephenson, C., *Zeppelins: German Airships 1900–40*, Oxford: Osprey Publishing, 2004.

Stover, E. and H.M. Weinstein (eds), *My Neighbour, My Enemy: Justice and Community in the Aftermath of Mass Atrocity*, Cambridge: Cambridge University Press, 2004.

Strauss, S., *The Order of Genocide: Race, Power, and War in Rwanda*, New York: Cornell University Press, 2006, p. 148.

Suleman, R., 'Director's Statement', in B. Peterson and R. Suleman, *Zulu Love Letter*, pp. 26–32, 2009.

Sullivan, E.J., *The Kaiser's Garden*, London: William Heinemann, 1915.

Sunday Times 'Hopeless, Helpless, Horror Beyond Belief … There is Nothing the West Can Do, Says Annabel Heseltine, After Witnessing the Rwanda bloodbath'. 8 May 1994.

Swaffham Prior Parish Church, 'Swaffham Prior Church, St Mary's Restoration Book', Cambridge County Council Archives, 1805–1932, no. P150/3/13.

Swoboda, J., *The Revolution of the Candles: Christians in the Revolution of the German Democratic Republic*, ed. R. Pierard, Macon, GA: Mercia University Press, 1996.

Taylor, P.M. and M. L. Sanders, *British Propaganda During the First World War*, London: Macmillan, 1982.

Temple-Raston, D., 'Journalism and Genocide', *Columbia Journalism Review*, September/ October 2002.

Tester, F.J., 'Art and Disarmament: Turning Arms into Ploughshares in Mozambique', *Development in Practice*, vol. 16, no. 2, April 2006, pp. 169–78.

Thompson, A. (ed.) *The Media and the Rwanda Genocide*, London: Pluto Press, 2007.

Thompson, L., *The History of South Africa*, 3rd edn, New Haven: Yale Nota Bene Books, 2001.

Tomaselli, K., *Encountering Modernity: Twentieth Century South African Cinemas*, Amsterdam: Rozenberg Publishers, 2006.

——, 'Popular communication in South Africa: *Mapantsula* and its context of struggle', *South African Theatre Journal*, 1991, vol. 5, no. 1, pp. 46–60.

——, *The Cinema of Apartheid: Race and Class in South African Film*, New York: Smyrna, 1988.

Torchin, L, 'Ravished Armenia: Visual Media, Humanitarian Advocacy, and the Formation of Witnessing Publics', *American Anthropologist*, March 2006, no. 108, pp. 214–20.

——, 'Since We Forgot: Remembrance and Recognition of the Armenian Genocide in Virtual Archives', in R. Hallas and F. Guerin (eds), *The Image and the Witness: Trauma, Memory and Visual Culture*, London: Wallflower Press, 2007, pp. 82–97.

Trevithick, N. (prod.) *Through a Glass Darkly*, BBC Radio 4, 14 September 1995.

Tripp, C., *A History of Iraq*, Cambridge: Cambridge University Press, 2002.

Turkle, S., *Life on the Screen: Identity in the Age of the Internet*, New York: Simon and Schuster, 1995.

Tutu, D., *No Future Without Forgiveness*, New York: Image, Doubleday, 1999.

van der Hoven, A. and J. Arnott, 'The Anxiety of Affect: Melodrama and South African Film Studies', *Social Dynamics*, 2009, vol. 35, no. 1, pp. 162–76.

van Zoonen, L., F. Vis and S. Mihelj, 'YouTube Interactions Between Agonism, Antagonism and Dialogue: Video Responses to the Anti-Islam Film *Fitna*'. *New Media and Society*, June 2011, pp. 1–18.

Vance, J., *Death so Noble: Memory, Meaning, and the First World War*, Vancouver, BC: University of British Columbia, 1997.

Varzi, R., *Warring Souls: Youth, Media and Martyrdom in Post-Revolution Iran*, Durham, NC: Duke University Press, 2006.

Vaux, S., *The Ethical Vision of Clint Eastwood*, Grand Rapids, MI: Wm. B. Eerdmans, 2011.

Vieler-Porter, C., 'Richard Attenborough', *UNESCO Courier*, August 1989.

Volf, M., *The End of Memory: Remembering Rightly in a Violent World*, Grand Rapids, MI: Wm. B. Eerdmans, 2006.

Wagner, R., *Godwired: Religion, Ritual and Virtual Reality*, London and New York: Routledge, 2011.

Weimann, G., *Terror on the Internet: The New Arena, the New Challenges*, Washington, DC: United States Institute of Peace Press, 2006.

Wellman, B., *Networks in the Global Village*, Boulder, CO: Westview Press, 1999.

Wellman, B. and B. Hogan, 'The immanent internet', in J.R. McKay (ed.), *Netting Citizens*, Edinburgh: St. Andrew's Press, 2004, pp. 54–80.

Wiesel, E., *Night*, New York: Hill & Wang, 1960 (1958).

Wilkinson, A., *The Church of England and the First World War*, London: SCM, 1996 (1978).

Williamson, H., 'Swords into Plowshares: The Development and Implementation of a Vision', in R. Cohen and R. Westbrook (eds), *Isaiah's Vision of Peace in Biblical and Modern International Relations: Swords into Plowshares*, New York, NY: Palgrave Macmillan, 2008, pp. 139–49.

Williamson, S., *Resistance Art in South Africa*, rev. edn, Cape Town: David Philip, 2004 (1989).

Winnington-Ingram, A.F., *The Potter and the Clay*, London: W.G. Darton, 1917.

——, *The Church in Time of War*, London: Wells Gardner, Darton and Co, 1916.

Winter, J., *Remembering War: The Great War Between Memory and History in the Twentieth Century*, New Haven: Yale University Press, 2006.

——, *Sites of Memory, Sites of Mourning: The Great War in European Cultural History*, Cambridge: Cambridge University Press, 1995.

Wolfsfeld, G., *Media and the Pathway to Peace*, Cambridge: Cambridge University Press, 2004.

Yorke, M., *Eric Gill: Man of Flesh and Spirit*, London: I.B. Tauris, 2000 (1981).

Younge, G., *Art of the South African Townships*, London: Thames and Hudson, 1988.

Zelizer, B., *Remembering to Forget: Holocaust Memory Through the Camera's Eye*, Chicago: University of Chicago, 1997.

Filmography

100 Days (2001), N. Hughes, United Kingdom/Rwanda.
Africa United (2010), D. Gardner-Paterson, United Kingdom.
An African Answer (2008), A. Channer, United Kingdom.
Any Child is My Child (1988), B. Feinberg, South Africa.
Ararat (2002), A. Egoyan, Canada/France.
The Arusha Tapes (2000), M. Jacobson, Rwanda.
As We Forgive (2008), L. Waters Hinson, United States.
The Bang, Bang Club (2010), Steven Silver, Canada/South Africa.
Behind this Convent (2008), G. Ndahayo, Rwanda.
Between Joyce and Remembrance (2003), M. Kaplan, South Africa.
Beyond the Gates, United States, see *Shooting Dogs*.
The Bloody Tricolour (1995), BBC *Panorama*, United Kingdom.
Catch a Fire (2006), P. Noyce, France/United Kingdom/South Africa/United States.
Chronicle of a Genocide Foretold (1996), D. Lacourse and Y. Patry, Canada.
Come Back, Africa (1959), L. Rogosin, South Africa/United States.
Confession (2008), D. Ruhorahoza, Rwanda.
Cry Freedom (1987), R. Attenborough, United Kingdom.
A Cry from the Grave (1999), L. Woodhead, United Kingdom/United States/Netherlands.
Cry, the Beloved Country (1951), Z. Korda, United Kingdom.
Cry, the Beloved Country (1995), D. Roodt, South Africa/United States.
A Culture of Murder (1994), BBC *Panorama* with S. Bradshaw, United Kingdom.
The Diary of Immaculée (2006), P. LeDonne, United States.
Disgrace (2008), Steve Jacobs, Australia.
District 9 (2009), N. Blomkamp, United States/New Zealand/Canada/South Africa.
A Dry White Season (1989), E. Palcy, United States.
The Dumping Grounds (1973), N. Mahomo, United Kingdom.
Earth Made of Glass (2010), D. Scranton, United States.
Enemies of the People (2009), R. Lemkin and T. Sambath, Cambodia/United Kingdom.
Facing the Truth (1999), PBS with Bill Moyers, United States.
Flame (1996), I. Sinclair, Zimbabwe.
Flowers of Rwanda (Flores de Ruanda) (2008), D. Munoz, Spain.
Flower in the Gun Barrel (2009), G. Cowan, United States.
Forgiveness (2004), I. Gabriel, South Africa.
Forsaken Cries: The Story of Rwanda (1997), A. Torrice, United States.

La France au Rwanda: une neutralité coupable (1999), R. Genoud, France.

From Arusha to Arusha (2008), C. Gargot, France.

Gacaca, Living Together Again in Rwanda? (2002), A. Aghion, France/United States.

Generation After Genocide (2009), T. Kohara and J. Weiman, Canada.

Gerrie and Louise (1997), S. Gunnarsson, Canada.

Ghosts of Rwanda (2004), PBS Frontline, G. Baker and K. Darren, United States.

God Sleeps in Rwanda (2005), K. Acquaro and S. Sherman, United States.

Goodbye Bafana (2007), B. August, Germany/France/Belgium/South Africa/Italy/United Kingdom/Luxembourg.

Hotel Rwanda (2004), T. George, United States/United Kingdom/Italy/South Africa.

Icyizere: Hope (2009), Patrick Mureithi, Kenya/Rwanda.

The Imam and the Pastor (2006), A. Channer, United Kingdom.

In My Country (2004), J. Boorman, United Kingdom/Ireland/South Africa.

In Rwanda We Say ... The Family That Does Not Speak Dies (2004), A. Aghion, France/United States.

In the Tall Grass (2006), J. Coll Metcalfe, Rwanda/United States.

Intended Consequences (2009), J. Torgovnik, United States.

Invictus (2009), C. Eastwood, United States.

ISETA: The Road Block (2008), J. Reina, Kenya.

Itsembatsemba: Rwanda One Genocide Later (1996), A. Cordesse and E. Sivan, France.

Jaws (1975), S. Spielberg, United States.

Jerusalema (2008), R. Ziman, South Africa.

The Jesus Film (1979), P. Sykes, J. Krisch and J. Heyman, United States.

Journey into Darkness (1994), BBC *Panorama* with F. Keane, United Kingdom.

Keepers of Memory: Survivors' Accounts of the Rwandan Genocide (2005), *Gardiens de la mémoire*, E. Kabera, Rwanda.

Kigali, des images contre un massacre (2006), J.-C. Klotz, France.

Kigali: Images contre Massacre (2005), J.-C. Klotz, France.

Killers (2004), BBC *Panorama* with F. Keane, United Kingdom.

The Killing Fields (1984), R. Joffé, United Kingdom.

Kingdom of Heaven (2005), R. Scott, Unites States/United Kingdom/Spain/Germany/Morocco.

Kinyarwanda (2011), Alrick Brown, United States/Rwanda.

Land of Promise (1974), South African Information Service, South Africa.

Last Grave at Dimbaza (1974), N. Mahomo, United Kingdom.

The Last Just Man (2001), S. Silver, Canada.

Une Lettre d'amour à mon pays (*A Love Letter to My Country*, 2006), D. Thierry, Rwanda.

Life is Beautiful (*La Vita è Bella*, 1997), R. Benigni, Italy.

London River (2009), R. Bouchareb, United Kingdom/France/Algeria.

Long Night's Journey into Day (2000), D. Hoffman and F. Reid, United States.

Mapantsula (1988), O. Schmitz, South Africa.

Master Harold ... and the Boys (1985) M. Lindsay-Hogg, United States.

Master Harold ... and the Boys (2010) L. Price South Africa.

Matière Grise (*Grey Matter*) (2011), K. Ruhorahoza, Rwanda/Australia.

The Matrix (1999), A. and L. Wachowski, United States/Australia.

Mothers Courage: Thriving Survivors (2005), L. Kalinda, Canada.

Munyurangabo (2007), L.I. Chung, Rwanda.

My Neighbor, My Killer (2009), A. Aghion, United States/France.

Nda Mona (*I Have Seen*, 1999), R. Pakleppa, Namibia.

New Year Baby (2006), S. Poeuv, United States.

The Notebooks of Memory (2009), A. Aghion, France/United States.

Our Forbidden Places (*Nos Lieux interdits*, 2008), L. Kilani, France/Morocco.

Plastic Flowers Never Die (2008), R. Varzi, United States.

Radio Okapi, radio de la vie (2006), P. Guyot, France.

Raindrops over Rwanda (2010), C.A. Weingarten, United States.

Ravished Armenia (1919), O. Apfel, United States.

Red Dust (2004), T. Hooper, United Kingdom/South Africa.

A Republic Gone Mad: Rwanda 1894–1994 (1996), L. de Heusch and K. de Béthune, United States.

The Road to Mecca (1991) A. Fugard and P. Goldsmith, South Africa.

Rwanda: A Killer's Homecoming (2004), D. Völker, United Kingdom.

Rwanda Again (2009), L. Blankenbyl, Switzerland.

Rwanda: Beyond the Deadly Pit (2010), G. Ndahayo, Rwanda/United States.

Rwanda, How History Can Lead to Genocide (1995), R. Genoud, United States.

Rwanda: In Search of Hope (1999), P. Raymont, Canada.

Rwanda, les collines parlent (2005), B. Bellefroid, Belgium.

Rwanda, les mots des âmes (2001), A. Canetta, Switzerland.

Rwanda: Living Forgiveness (2005), R. Springhorn, United States.

Rwanda Rwanda, une justice prise en otage (2003), P. Hazan and G. Arijon, France/Switzerland.

Rwanda, un cri d'un silence inouï (2003), A. Laine, France.

S-21 (2003), R. Panh, Cambodia/France.

Sarafina! (1992), D. Roodt, France/South Africa/United Kingdom/United States.

Schindler's List (1993), S. Spielberg, United States.

Shake Hands with the Devil (2007), R. Spottiswoode, Canada.

Shake Hands with the Devil: The Journey of Roméo Dallaire (2004), P. Raymont, Canada.

Shoah (1985), C. Lanzmann, France.

Shooting Dogs (2005), M. Caton-Jones, United Kingdom/Germany.

Soleil dans la nuit (1995), M. Renaud, Canada.

Sometimes in April (2005), R. Peck, France/United States.

The Sound of Music (1965), R. Wise, United States.

Stories My Country Told Me: Tutu and the Rainbow Nation (2000), T. May, United Kingdom.

The Stranger (1946), O. Welles, United States.

A Sunday in Kigali (2006), R. Favreau, Canada.

This Crazy Thing Called Grace: Desmond Tutu and the Truth and Reconciliation Commission (1997), J. Chesselet, South Africa.

Through My Eyes: A Film About Rwandan Youth (2006), E. Kabera, Rwanda.

Triumph of Evil (1999), PBS Frontline, United States.

True Stories: Rwanda After Genocide (2011), D. Scranton, United States.

Tsotsi (2005), G. Hood, United Kingdom/South Africa.

Ubuntu's Wounds (2001), S. Morojele, South Africa.

Uganda: Ready to Forgive (2008), R. Springhorn, United States.

The Unfolding of Sky (1999), A. Krog and R. Loots, South Africa.

Valentina's Story (1997), BBC *Panorama* with M. Robinson and F. Keane, United Kingdom.

We Are All Rwandans (2008), D. Gardner-Paterson, Rwanda/United Kingdom.

We Never Give Up (2002), C. McLaughlin, South Africa.

When Good Men Do Nothing (1998), BBC *Panorama* with S. Bradshaw, United Kingdom.

Where Truth Lies (1999), M. Kaplan, United States.

Why Did They Kill Their Neighbours? (1998), K. Igarashi, Japan.
Witness to Apartheid (1986), S.I. Sopher, United States.
A World Apart (1988), C. Menges, United Kingdom/Zimbabwe.
Zulu Love Letter (2004), T. Suleman, France/South Africa/Germany.

Webography

'7/7 We Are Still Not Afraid!', *Facebook*. Online. HTTP: <www.facebook.com/pages/77-we-are-still-not-afraid/140410359303656> (accessed 12 April 2011).

'A Cinema of Healing: Two Rwandan Films', Online. HTTP: <http://blogs.warwick.ac.uk/zanzibar/entry/a_cinema_of/> (accessed 19 August 2011).

'*A Dry White Season*', *Film 4*. Online. HTTP: <www.film4.com/reviews/1989/dry-white-season-a> (accessed 11 April 2011).

'A Peaceful Reminder of a Turbulent Past', A review by koshka on Martyrs' Cemetery, Tehran, 18 January 2007. Online. HTTP: <travel.ciao.co.uk/Martyrs_Cemetery_Tehran – 6610012> (accessed 14 March 2011).

'About *We're not Afraid*', *We're not afraid.com*. Online. HTTP: <werenotafraid.com/about.html> (accessed 12 April 2011).

Africa is a Country. Online. HTTP: <africasacountry.com/2009/12/31/film-daddy-ruhorahoza/> (accessed 26 March 2011).

Aghion, A., *Gacaca, Living Together Again in Rwanda?*, *In Rwanda We Say … The Family That Does Not Speak Dies*, *The Notebooks of Memory*. Online. HTTP:

As We Forgive. Online. HTTP: (accessed 26 March 2011).

Annotated Bibliographies. United States Holocaust Memorial Museum. Online. HTTP: <www.ushmm.org/research/library/bibliography/?lang=en&content=rwanda> (accessed 1 August 2011).

'Background and Introduction', *Traces of Truth: Documents Relating to the South African Truth and Reconciliation Commission*. Online. HTTP: <truth.wwl.wits.ac.za/about.php> (accessed 11 April 2011).

Badrkhani, A., 'Put a Stop to it', *Iranian*, 8 October 2003. Online. HTTP: <www.iranian.com/AssalBadrkhani/2003/October/Peace/index.html> (accessed 11 March 2011).

Bass, J.C. (dir.), *The Tunnel*, Online. HTTP: <http://vimeo.com/12566896> (accessed 22 August 2011, password required from production company Fox Fire Films), 2010.

BBC News, 'Born above the Floodwaters', 2 March 2000, Online. HTTP: <news.bbc.co.uk/1/hi/world/africa/662472.stm > (accessed 30 August 2011).

BBC Online: Religion and Ethics. Online. HTTP: <www.bbc.co.uk/religion/> (accessed 22 April 2011).

BBC Panorama. Online. HTTP: <news.bbc.co.uk/hi/english/static/audio_video/programmes/panorama/transcripts/transcript_10_02_97.txt> (accessed 26 March 2011).

Botha, M., '110 Years of South African Cinema (Part 1)', *Kinema*, fall 2006. Online. HTTP: <www.kinema.uwaterloo.ca/article.php?id=46&feature> (accessed 11 April 2011).

——'Short Filmmaking in South Africa after Apartheid', *Kinema*, spring 2009. Online. HTTP: <www.kinema.uwaterloo.ca/article.php?id=451&feature> (accessed 11 April 2011).

——'The South African Film Industry: Fragmentation, Identity Crisis and Unification', *Kinema*, spring 1995. Online. HTTP: <www.kinema.uwaterloo.ca/article.php?id=355&feature> (accessed 11 April 2011).

Breen, P., 'The Art of Sacrifice', *UKIWM*. Online. HTTP: <ukniwm.wordpress.com/2010/03/31/the-art-of-sacrifice/> (accessed 17 November 2011).

British Museum, *Throne of Weapons and Tree of Life*, Global Citizenship classroom resource: Key Stage 3–4. Online PDF. HTTP: <www.britishmuseum.org/pdf/Citizenshp_ThroneTree_Presnotes_KS3&4.pdf> (accessed 18 April 2011).

Brussat, F. and M.A., 'Ararat: Film Review', *Spirituality and Practice: Resources for Spiritual Journeys*. Online. HTTP: <www.spiritualityandpractice.com/films/films.php?id=5342> (accessed 26 March 2011).

'Cambodian Genocide Program', *Yale University, Genocide Studies Program*, 2010. Online. HTTP: <www.yale.edu/cgp/> (accessed 26 March 2011).

Canby, V., 'Movie Review: *Lost in the Stars*', *New York Times*, 7 May 1974. Online. HTTP: <movies.nytimes.com/movie/100217/Lost-in-the-Stars/> (accessed 11 April 2011).

——'Movie Review: *A World Apart*', *New York Times*, 17 June 1988. Online. HTTP: <movies.nytimes.com/movie/review?res=940DE0D7123AF934A25755-C0A96E948260> (accessed 11 April 2011).

Carnduff, N., 'Belfast Lines Redrawn: The Changing Face of Belfast's City's Murals', *Irish Times*, 15 May 2009. Online. HTTP: <ourfuturetogether.posterous.com/2009/05/belfasts-lines-redrawn-irish-times.html> (accessed 21 March 2011).

Catsoulis, J. 'Movie Review: My Neighbor, My Killer (2009), Side by Side, with the Guilty, after Courts Send Them Home', *New York Times*, 12 January 2010. Online. HTTP: <movies.nytimes.com/2010/01/12/movies/12neighbor.html> (accessed 26 March 2011).

Center for Media Literacy. Online. HTTP: <www.medialit.org/> (accessed 22 April 2011).

Chesselet, J., 'South Africa: *This Crazy Thing Called Grace*', 1 April 1997. Online. HTTP: <www.journeyman.tv/?lid=9059& tmpl=transcript> (accessed 11 April 2011).

Chow, O., 'Alfredo Jaar and the Post-Traumatic Gaze', *Tate Papers*, spring 2008. Online. HTTP: <www.tate.org.uk/research/tateresearch/tatepapers/08spring/chow.shtm> (accessed 31 August 2011).

Christia, F., '"Walls of Martyrdom": Tehran's Propaganda Murals', *Centerpiece*, 2007, vol. 21, no. 1. Online. HTTP: <www.wcfia.harvard.edu/misc/publications/centerpiece/win07_vol21_no1/feature_christia.html> (accessed 11 March 2011).

'*Cry Freedom*: Charting the Struggle', *BBC News*, 20 August 2001. Online. HTTP: <news.bbc.co.uk/1/hi/entertainment/1500240.stm> (accessed 11 April 2011).

'Customer Reviews' for *Beyond The Gates (Shooting Dogs)* on *Rotten Tomatoes*. Online. HTTP: <http://uk.rottentomatoes.com/m/beyond_the_gates/> (accessed 1 August 2011).

'Customer Reviews' for *Rwanda: Living Forgiveness* on *Amazon.com*. Online. HTTP: <www.amazon.com/Rwanda-Living-Forgiveness/dp/B000CR5EES> (accessed 26 March 2011).

d'Arcy Hughes, A., 'Rwandans Flock to "Hillywood" Films', *BBC News*, 5 April 2007. Online. HTTP: <news.bbc.co.uk/1/hi/world/africa/6530227.stm> (accessed 26 March 2011).

Davies, S., 'Fergal Keane: Trying to Change the World, One TV Screen at a Time', *Telegraph*, 19 June 2009. Online. HTTP: <www.telegraph.co.uk/culture/tvandradio/

5575881/Fergal-Keane-Trying-to-change-the-world-one-TV-screen-at-a-time.html> (accessed 26 March 2011).

'Death Video Woman "Targeted by Militia"', *BBC News*, 22 June 2009. Online. HTTP: <news.bbc.co.uk/1/hi/world/middle_east/8113552.stm> (accessed 11 March 2011).

Dominick Tyler Photography, APT Enterprises, 'Guns to Tools', Online. HTTP: <www.dominicktyler.com/editorial/guns-to-tools/# > (accessed 29 August 2011).

Ebert, R., 'Movie Review: *Cry, the Beloved Country*', *rogerebert.com*, 20 December 1995. Online. HTTP: <rogerebert.suntimes.com/apps/pbcs.dll/article?AID=/19951220/REVIEWS/512200301/1023> (accessed 11 April 2011).

——'Movie Review: *Cry Freedom*', *rogerebert.com*, 6 November 1987. Online. HTTP: <rogerebert.suntimes.com/apps/pbcs.dll/article?AID=/19871106/REVIEWS/71106 0301> (accessed 11 April 2011).

——'Movie Review: *Sarafina!*', *rogerebert.com*, 25 September 1992. Online. HTTP: <rogerebert.suntimes.com/apps/pbcs.dll/article?AID=/19920925/REVIEWS/209250303/1023> (accessed 11 April 2011).

'Egyptian Uprising – We're Not Afraid', *YouTube*, 26 January 2011. Online. HTTP: <www.youtube.com/watch?v=U0U3cfvRFG4> (accessed 12 April 2011).

'Exploring Rwanda and Darfur', *NewsHour with Jim Lehrer*, PBS, 12 April 2006. Online. HTTP: <www.pbs.org/newshour/bb/africa/jan-june06/darfur_4–12.html> (accessed 26 March 2011).

'Faces of Entrepreneurship', *New York Times*. Online. HTTP: <www.nytimes.com/slideshow/2008/03/09/magazine/0309-FACES_5.html> (accessed 26 March 2011).

Fisk, R., 'Traitors, Martyrs or Just Brave Men', *Independent*, 15 April 2006. Online. HTTP: <www.informationclearinghouse.info/article12756.htm> (accessed 14 March 2011).

'*Flowers of Rwanda: Making Peace with Genocide*', *Films on Demand*. Online. HTTP: <films.com/PreviewClip.aspx?id=16569> (accessed 26 March 2011).

Forguilha, A., '*Transforming Arms into Ploughshares*'. Online. HTTP: <www.peoplebuildingpeace.org/thestories/print.php?id=147& typ=theme> (accessed 8 September 2011).

'From Hillywood to Hollywood: One Rwandan Makes His Major Motion Picture Dreams Come True', *Sunday Times* (Rwanda), reprinted on *Zimbio*, 20 February 2008. Online. HTTP: <www.zimbio.com/member/sandalchild/articles/963482/HILLY WOOD+HOLLYWOOD+One+Rwandan+Makes+Major> (accessed 26 March 2011).

Genocide Archive Rwanda. Online. HTTP: <http://genocidearchiverwanda.org.rw/index.php/Welcome_to_Genocide_Archive_Rwanda> (accessed 11 November 2011).

Gerry, M., 'West Belfast, Northern Ireland: The Peace Walls and the Murals', *Associated Content*, 6 April 2006. Online. HTTP: <www.associatedcontent.com/article/25134/west_belfast_northern_ireland_the_peace_pg3.html?cat=37> (accessed 21 March 2011).

'Gilbert Nadahyo on Rwandan Genocide', *YouTube*, 22 April 2009. Online. HTTP: <www.youtube.com/watch?v=viJhHpQjIhg> (accessed 26 March 2011).

'Give my Head Peace'. *BBC*. Online. HTTP: <www.bbc.co.uk/northernireland/gmhp/murals.shtml> (accessed 21 March 2011).

'Guardian Reporter Jack Shenker on Egypt Protests: "Fear Barrier Seems to Have Been Broken"', *Democracy Now!: The War and Peace Report*, 27 January 2011. Online. HTTP: <www.democracynow.org/2011/1/27/guardian_reporter_in_egypt_fear_barrier> (accessed 12 April 2011).

'Guatemala Swaps Guns for Bicycles', *BBC News*, 10 July 2004. Online. HTTP: <news.bbc.co.uk/1/hi/world/americas/3883023.stm > (accessed 1 August 2011).

'Guns into Art', Online. HTTP: <www.meltguns.com/> (accessed 11 August 2011).

'Guns into Goods', 2008, Online. HTTP: <www.youtube.com/watch? v=y3JLLVK3d9Q> (accessed 21 August 2011).

'Guns into Goods Events', March 2011, Online. HTTP: <www.facebook.com/note.php? note_id=157174320989277> (accessed 21 August 2011).

Gruber, Christiane, 'Visualizing Post-Revolutionary Iranian Culture Through the Mural Arts' at Solomon Asch Center for Ethnopolitical Conflict, Online. HTTP: <hhttp:// aschcenter.smugmug.com/Other/Christiane-Gruber-Visualizing/ 16162622_4K9Lv#1213622723_kz7TH> (accessed 11 August 2011).

Hall, S., 'Movie Review: *Red Dust*' *Sydney Morning Herald*, 16 November 2005. Online. HTTP: <www.smh.com.au/news/film-reviews/red-dust/2005/11/16/1132016861205. html> (accessed 11 April 2011).

Hillis, N.D., *Murder Most Foul*, date and publisher unknown, also available at *The First World War Poetry Digital Archive*. Online. HTTP: <www.oucs.ox.ac.uk/ww1lit/collections/ document/5112/4123> (accessed 17 March 2011).

Hirondelle News Agency, 'ICTR/Documentary – *From Arusha to Arusha*, First Documentary on the ICTR', 17 December 2009. Online. HTTP: <www.hirondellenews. com/content/view/13089/1188/>(accessed 1 August 2011).

Holden, S., 'Movie Review: *Cry the Beloved Country* (1995)', *New York Times*, 15 December 1995. Online. HTTP: <movies.nytimes.com/movie/review?res=9806E0DD1739-F936A25751C1A963958260& scp=1&sq=stephen%20holden%20cry%20the%20beloved %20country&st=cse> (accessed 11 April 2011).

——'Movie Review: *In My Country*', *New York Times*, 11 March 2005. Online. HTTP: <movies.nytimes.com/2005/03/11/movies/11coun.html?_r=1&ref=john_boorman> (accessed 11 April 2011).

Hoots and Hellmouth (music album), *The Holy Open Secret*, Online. HTTP: < www.hoot sandhellmouth.com/music.php > (accessed 5 September 2011).

Kirk Honeycutt, '*Beyond the Gates:* Bottom Line: Saga of the Genocide in Rwanda Takes the Tired Point of View of White Westerners'. Online. HTTP: <http://www.holly woodreporter.com/hr/film/reviews/article_display.jsp?&rid=8883> (expired)

In the Tall Grass. Online. HTTP: <www.inthetallgrass.com> (accessed 26 March 2011).

International Christian Media Commission. Online. HTTP: <www.icmc.org/> (accessed 22 April 2011).

Jaar, A., *The Eyes of Gutete Emerita*. Online. HTTP: <www.alfredojaar.net/gutete/gutete. html> (accessed 31 August 2011).

——*Real Pictures*. Online. HTTP: <www.mocp.org/collections/permanent/jaar_alfredo. php> (accessed 31 August 2011).

Jacobs, S., 'Ubuntu's Wounds', *Chimurenga*. Online. HTTP: <www.chimurenga.co.za/ page-41.html> (accessed 11 April 2011).

Journal of Religion and Film. Online. HTTP: <avalon.unomaha.edu/jrf/> (accessed 22 April 2011).

Journal of Religion and Popular Culture. Online. HTTP: <www.usask.ca/relst/jrpc/index. html> (accessed 22 April 2011).

'July 7 Bomber's Goodbye Message to His Daughter', *Telegraph*, 16 February 2011. Online. HTTP: <www.telegraph.co.uk/news/uknews/terrorism-in-the-uk/8328195/ July-7-bombers-goodbye-message-to-his-daughter.html> (accessed 12 April 2012).

Kates, B., 'Ahmadinejad Calls Iranian Martyr Neda's Death "Suspicious"', *New York Daily News*, 29 June 2009. Online. HTTP: <www.nydailynews.com/news/us_world/2009/

06/29/2009-06-29_ahmadinejad_calls_iranian_martyr_nedas_death_suspicious.html> (accessed 11 March 2011).

Keane, F., 'The Rwandan Girl who Refused to Die', *Sunday Times*, 1997, reprinted at *Frontline*. Online. HTTP: <www.pbs.org/wgbh/pages/frontline/shows/rwanda/reports/refuse.html> (26 March 2011).

'Keven Sites: Fallujah Mosque Shooting', *YouTube*, 21 April 2008. Online. HTTP: <www.youtube.com/watch?v=o4j50ghDeKA> (accessed 12 April 2011).

'Keys to Mandela's Cell', *South Africa Trip*, 6 February 2007. Online. HTTP: <blogs.messiah.edu/southafrica/> (accessed 11 April 2011).

Khmer Legacies. Online. HTTP: <www.khmerlegacies.org/> (accessed 26 March 2011).

Kimani, M., 'Broadcasting Peace: Radio a Tool for Recovery', *Africa Renewal*, 2007, vol. 23, no. 3, p. 3. Online. HTTP: <www.un.org/ecosocdev/geninfo/afrec/vol21no3/213-radio.html> (accessed 21 March 2011).

'*The Last Just Man*', *Human Rights Watch*, 30 April 2002. Online. HTTP: <www.hrw.org/legacy/iff/2002/ny/last-review.html> (accessed 26 March 2011).

'Legal Background to the TRC', *Truth and Reconciliation Commission*, 2009. Online. HTTP: <www.justice.gov.za/trc/legal/index.htm> (accessed 11 April 2011).

Levit, D., 'Love Thy Neighbour', *Reel Talk Movie Reviews*. Online. HTTP: <www.reeltalkreviews.com/browse/viewitem.asp?type=review& id=3028> (accessed 26 March 2011).

'*London River* (2009)', *Rotten Tomatoes*. Online. HTTP: <www.rottentomatoes.com/m/london_river/> (accessed 12 April 2011).

'*London River*', *Wikipedia*. Online. HTTP: <en.wikipedia.org/wiki/London_River> (accessed 12 April 2011).

Macaulay, S., 'Cannes: My Neighbor, my Killers Anne Aghion', *Filmmaker*, 17 May 2009. Online. HTTP: <www.filmmakermagazine.com/news/2009/05/cannes-my-neighbor-my-killers-anne-aghion/> (accessed 26 March 2011).

McGreal, C., 'Rwanda – 10 Years on: "It's so Difficult to Live with What We Know"', *Guardian*, 29 March 2004. Online. HTTP: <www.guardian.co.uk/world/2004/mar/29/rwanda.chrismcgreal> (accessed 26 March 2011).

MacGregor, N., 'Director's Foreword', in J. Holdone (ed.), *Throne of Weapons: A British Museum Tour*, London: British Museum, 2006. Online PDF. HTTP: <www.britishmuseum.org/explore/highlights/highlight_objects/aoa/t/throne_of_weapons.aspx> (accessed 18 April 2011).

'Man Jailed for Facebook Incitement to Riot to Appeal', Online. HTTP: <www.bbc.co.uk/news/uk-england-14557772> (accessed 17 August 2011).

Manovich, L., 'Against Search', 21 July 2011. Online: HTTP. <manovich.net> (accessed 18 August 2011).

'Martyr's Cemetery (Tehran, Iran)'. Online. HTTP: <www.dooyoo.co.uk/destinations-international/martyrs-cemetery-tehran-iran/1044805/> (accessed 14 March 2011).

Maslin, J., 'Movie Review: *Cry Freedom* (1987)', *New York Times*, 6 November 1987. Online. HTTP: <movies.nytimes.com/movie/review?res=9B0DE6D61239F935A35752C1A961948260> (accessed 11 April 2011).

——'Movie Review: *Mapantsula* (1989)', *New York Times*, 24 September 1988. Online. HTTP: <movies.nytimes.com/movie/review?res=940DE1D81331F937A1575AC0A96E948260> (accessed 11 April 2011).

Menossi, M., 'Le Papillon face à la flamme: interview de Jean-Christophe Klotz', *Evene.fr*, November 2006. Online. HTTP: <www.evene.fr/cinema/actualite/interview-klotz-rwanda-kigali-images-massacre-kouchner-559.php> (accessed 26 March 2011).

Merin, J., '*My Neighbor My Killer* – Movie Review – 2009, Rwanda Moves Towards Reconciliation', *About.com Guide*. Online. HTTP: <documentaries.about.com//od/revie2/fr/myneighbormykil.htm> (accessed 26 March 2011).

Merron, H., 'Belfast – Neural Mural on Limestone Road "no to:"', *D-Space at Cambridge*, CRIC images collection, 27 July 2009. Online. HTTP: <www.dspace.cam.ac.uk/handle/1810/218746> (accessed 21 March 2011).

Moezzi, M., 'Iran's Red Tulip Revolution', 29 July 2009. Online. HTTP: <www.huffingtonpost.com/melody-moezzi/irans-red-tulip-revolutio_b_246949.html> (accessed 11 March 2011).

Morgan, T., 'A Glass Memorial', 1997. Online. HTTP: <www.fylde.demon.co.uk/church.htm> (accessed 9 March 2011).

——'The Great Zeppelin Raid: 31 January 1916', *World War I Document Archive*, 1996. Online. HTTP: <net.lib.byu.edu/~rdh7/wwi/memoir/zeppelin.html> (accessed 9 March 2011).

'More Than 200 Guns Taken off Salinas', Online. HTTP: <www.Streetshttp://www.youtube.com/watch?v=snZJRQYMtO0&NR=1> (accessed 21 August 2011).

'Movie Review: *Cry Freedom* (1987)', *Time Out Film Guide*. Online. HTTP: <www.timeout.com/film/reviews/69923/cry_freedom.html> (accessed 11 April 2011).

'Movie Review: *Goodbye Bafana* (2007)' *Film4*, 2007. Online. HTTP: <www.film4.com/reviews/2007/goodbye-bafana> (accessed 11 April 2011).

'Mozambique Floods 2000, Full Coverage', Online. HTTP: <news.bbc.co.uk/1/hi/world/africa/655510.stm> (accessed 31 August 2011).

MSN Movie News, 'Hurt Says Genocide Film a Wake-Up'. Online. HTTP: <http://movies.msn.com/movies/article.aspx?news=219603> (expired).

'Mural Launch and Panel Discussion', *Charter for Northern Ireland: Making a Positive Difference*. Online. HTTP: <www.charterni.com/projects/crossing-the-bridges/mural-launch-and-panel-discussion/> (accessed 21 March 2011).

'Neda: The Face of a New Iranian Revolution', *IBTimes*, 22 June 2009. Online. HTTP: <www.ibtimes.co.uk/articles/20090624/neda-death-iran-iranian-protests.htm> (accessed 11 March 2011).

New Mexico Media Literacy Project. Online. HTTP: <www.nmmlp.org/> (accessed 22 April 2011).

'New UVF Murals Painted in East Belfast', UTV, 10 May 2011. Online. HTTP: <http://www.u.tv/news/New-UVF-murals-painted-in-east-Belfast/cbd77d79-ac55–46a3–889f-f67ef5886be7> (accessed 30 October 2011).

Norman, T., 'Neda: The Face of a New Iranian Revolution', *Pittsburgh Post-Gazette*, 23 June 2009. Online. HTTP: <www.post-gazette.com/pg/09174/979208–153.stm> (accessed 11 March 2011).

Osborne, E.B. (ed.), *The Muse in Arms*, London: Murray, 1917. Online. HTTP: <www.firstworldwar.com/poetsandprose/mia_lastsalute.htm> (accessed 14 March 2011).

Panorama: Killers, text of manuscript is reproduced Online. HTTP: <news.bbc.co.uk/nol/shared/spl/hi/programmes/panorama/transcripts/killers.txt> (accessed 26 March 2011).

'*Panorama*, Rwanda programmes', *BBC News*, 2 April 2004. Online. HTTP: <news.bbc.co.uk/1/hi/programmes/panorama/3585473.stm> (accessed 26 March 2011).

Papamichael, S., 'Movie Review: *Goodbye Bafana*', *BBC Movies*, 10 May 2007. Online. HTTP: <www.bbc.co.uk/films/2007/05/07/goodbye_bafana_2007_review.shtml> (accessed 11 April 2011).

'Peace Art Project Cambodia'. Online. HTTP. <sashaconstable.co.uk/projects/peace-art> (accessed 26 August 2011).

Ponsonby, A., *Falsehood in War-Time: Propaganda Lies of the First World War*, London: George Allen and Unwin, 1928. Online. HTTP: <www.vlib.us/wwi/resources/archives/texts/t050824i/ponsonby.html> (accessed 17 March 2011).

Popcorn Peacemaking, Online. HTTP: <salsa.net/peace/popcorn/cryfree.html>(accessed 15 August 2011).

The Prosecutor v. *Ferdinand Nahimana, Jean-Bosco Barayagwiza, Hassan Ngeze (Judgement and Sentence)*, ICTR-99-52-T, International Criminal Tribunal for Rwanda (ICTR), 3 December 2003. Online. HTTP: <www.unhcr.org/refworld/docid/404468bc2.html> (accessed 20 March 2011).

The Prosecutor v. *Simon Bikindi (Judgment)*, ICTR 2001–01-72-T, International Criminal Tribunal for Rwanda (ICTR), 2 December 2008. Online. HTTP: <www.unhcr.org/refworld/docid/493524762.html> (accessed 21 March 2011).

Religion Newswriters Association. Online. HTTP: <www.religionwriters.com/> (accessed 22 April 2011).

Resource Center for Media, Religion and Culture. Online. HTTP: <www.colorado.edu/Journalism/mcm/mrc/> (accessed 22 April 2011).

Revealer (New York University Center for Religion and Media Journal). Online. HTTP: <www.therevealer.org/> (accessed 22 April 2011).

Rothstein, C.M., 'Overcoming Apartheid Policies Yesterday and Today: An Interview with a Former Bantu Education Student and Present-Day Activist', *Global Perspectives on Human Language: The South African Context, Leland Stanford Junior University*, 19 September 2004. Online. HTTP: <www.stanford.edu/~jbaugh/saw/Chloe_Bantu_Education.html> (accessed 11 April 2011).

Ruah, E., 'The Graphics of Revolution and War: Iranian Poster Arts'. Online. HTTP: <http://www.lib.uchicago.edu/e/webexhibits/iranianposters/index.html> (accessed 27 November 2011).

'Rwanda Gacaca: A Question of Justice', *Amnesty International*, 17 December 2002. Online. HTTP: <www.amnesty.org/en/library/info/AFR47/007/2002> (accessed 26 March 2011).

'Rwanda/Genocide – Kibuye Town Remembers its Dead', *Hirondelle News Agency, Foundation Hirondelle*, 20 April 2005. Online. HTTP: <www.hirondellenews.com/content/view/2354/26/> (accessed 26 March 2011).

'Rwanda: Genocide on Trial – Arusha Video Project'. Online. HTTP: <www.gppac.net/documents/Media_book_nieuw/p2_11_rwanda.htm> (accessed 26 March 2011).

'Rwanda: History of a Genocide', *Filmakers Library*. Online. HTTP: <www.filmakers.com/index.php?a=filmDetail& filmID=768> (accessed 26 March 2011).

Rwanda: In Search of Hope. Online: HTTP: <www.whitepinepictures.com/sales/shop/dvd-rwanda-in-search-of-hope/> (accessed 26 March 2011).

Schulman, W., et al., *A Teacher's Guide to the Holocaust*. Online. HTTP: <fcit.usf.edu/holocaust/resource/films.htm> (accessed 26 March 2011).

Scranton, D., *Earth Made of Glass*. Online. HTTP: <www.hbo.com/documentaries/earth-made-of-glass/synopsis.html > (accessed 1 August 2011).

'St Mary, Swaffham Prior'. Online. HTTP: <www.flickr.com/photos/therevsteve/sets/72157603952261523/with/2464314321/> (accessed 9 March 2011).

'Sierra Leone: NGO Turns to Farm Tools', MAPCO, Online. HTTP. < allafrica.com/stories/200108030106.html > (accessed 29 August 2011).

'Target Peace', HTTP: <vimeo.com/17775286> (accessed 31 August 2011).

Thomas, K., 'Movie Review: *Cry, the Beloved Country*', *Los Angeles Times*, 15 December 1995. Online. HTTP: <www.calendarlive.com/cl-movie960406–17,0,4119878.story> (accessed 11 April 2011).

——'Movie Review: *In My Country*', *Los Angeles Times*, 11 March 2005. Online. HTTP: <http://www.calendarlive.com/cl-et-country11mar11,0,3466087.story> (accessed 11 April 2011).

Thompson, A. and P. Gariepy, 'Cambridgeshire Swaffham Prior St. Mary – Roll of Honour', 2000. Online. HTTP: <www.roll-of-honour.com/Cambridgeshire/Swaff hamPriorStMary.html> (accessed 4 March 2011).

'Throne of Weapons', *BBC A History of the World*. Online. HTTP: <www.bbc.co.uk/ahis toryoftheworld/objects/97OnxVXaQkehlbliKKDB6A> (accessed 18 April 2011).

'Transcript: "Ghosts of Rwanda"', *Frontline*, 9 April 2004. Online. HTTP: <www.pbs. org/wgbh/pages/frontline/shows/ghosts/etc/script.html> (accessed 26 March 2011).

'TRC Category – 4. Reparations', *Traces of Truth: Documents Relating to the South African Truth and Reconciliation Commission*. Online. HTTP: <truth.wwl.wits.ac.za/cat_descr.php? cat=4> (accessed 11 April 2011).

'Tree of Life', *British Museum*. Online. HTTP: <www.britishmuseum.org/explore/high lights/highlight_objects/aoa/t/tree_of_life.aspx> (accessed 18 April 2011).

'Tribute for Tunisian who Sparked Protests', *YouTube*, 21 January 2011. Online. HTTP: <www.youtube.com/watch?v=qqCa7lQoPs8> (accessed 12 April 2011).

'Tunisia: We are not Afraid, We are not Afraid', *Kasama: Newsflash from the Malabar Front*, 18 January 2011. Online. HTTP: <kasamaproject.org/2011/01/18/awtw-on-tunisia-we-are-not-afraid-we-are-not-afraid/> (accessed 12 April 2011).

Ulrich, C., 'Tunisia: "We Are Not Afraid Anymore!"', *Global Citizen*, 2 January 2011. Online. HTTP: <globalcitizenblog.com/?p=2952> (accessed 12 April 2011).

'United Kingdom National Inventory of War Memorials'. Online. HTTP: <www.ukniw. org.uk> (accessed 14 July 2011).

'War between Iran and Iraq', *International Institute of Social History*. Online. HTTP: <www. iisg.nl/archives/en/files/w/10930603full.php> (accessed 11 March 2011).

'We are not afraid', *Facebook*. Online. HTTP: <www.facebook.com/group.php? gid=114844558553693> (accessed 12 April 2011).

'Weapons into Water', *Organisation for Security and Co-operation in Europe*, Online. HTTP: <www.osce.org/georgia-closed/54530> (accessed 21 August 2011).

We're not afraid.com. Online. HTTP: <werenotafraid.com/> (accessed 12 April 2011).

Weingarten, C. (dir.) *Film: Raindrops over Rwanda*. Online. HTTP: <explore.org/videos/ player/raindrops-over-rwanda> (accessed 1 August 2011).

World Association for Christian Communication. Online. HTTP: <www.wacc.org.uk/> (accessed 22 April 2011).

Wu, A.C., '*As We Forgive*: An Interview with Laura Waters Hinson', *Cardus*, 28 March 2008. Online. HTTP: <www.cardus.ca/comment/article/26/> (accessed 26 March 2011).

Index